The Uniqueness of Jesus Christ in the Theocentric Model of the Christian Theology of World Religions

The Uniqueness of Jesus Christ in the Theocentric Model of the Christian Theology of World Religions:

An Elaboration and Evaluation of the Position of John Hick

Gregory H. Carruthers, S.J.
Lonergan Research Institute
Toronto

UNIVERSITY
PRESS OF
AMERICA

Lanham • New York • London

Copyright © 1990 by

University Press of America®, Inc.
4720 Boston Way
Lanham, Maryland 20706

3 Henrietta Street
London WC2E 8LU England

Library of Congress Cataloging-in-Publication Data

Carruthers, Gregory H., 1945-
The uniqueness of Jesus Christ in the theocentric model
of the Christian theology of world religions : an elaboration
and evaluation of the position of John Hick / Gregory H. Carruthers.
p.   cm.
Includes bibliographical references and index.
1. Jesus Christ—History of doctrines—20th century.
2. Hick, John—Contributions in Christology.
3. Christianity and other religions.   I. Title.
BT198.C335   1990   232'.092—dc20   90-38888 CIP

ISBN 0–8191–7889–6 (alk. paper)

 The paper used in this publication meets the minimum requirements of
American National Standard for Information Sciences—Permanence
of Paper for Printed Library Materials, ANSI Z39.48–1984.

To
Mom and Dad

This is an unlimited God and one who has revealed himself specifically. It is one who became man and rose from the dead. It is one who confounds the senses and the sensibilities, one known early on as a stumbling block. There is no way to gloss over this specification or to make it more acceptable to modern thought.

—Flannery O'Connor

Acknowledgements

I am especially grateful to Jacques Dupuis, S.J. for his direction of this work as an S.T.D. thesis. Also, I extend thanks to Professor John Hick who was always helpful and gracious, even though I disagree with his Christology.

A debt of gratitude is due to the Lonergan Research Institute for allowing me to take the time to work on the manuscript, and quote from the works of Bernard Lonergan, S.J. I wish to thank Robert Doran, S.J. and Gerald Tait, S.J., as well as Peter McGehee who prepared the final copy.

I alone, of course, am responsible for this work.

The author gratefully acknowledges permission to reproduce material from the following works:

From *God and the Universe of Faiths*, by John Hick, 1973. Used by permission of Macmillan, London and Basingstoke. From *God Has Many Names*, by John Hick. © John Hick 1980, 1982. Used by permission of Westminster/John Knox Press. From "Jesus and World Religions" by John Hick, in *The Myth of God Incarnate* edited by John Hick, 1977; and from *Christology in the Making*, by James D.G. Dunn, 1980. (There is now a 1989 edition.) Both used by permission of SCM Press. From *Christ in Christian Tradition* (Volume One) From the Apostolic Age to Chalcedon (451) Second Revised Edition, by Aloys Grillmeier, S.J. Translated by John Bowden. Published in Great Britain by A. R. Mowbray & Co. Limited and in the United States by John Knox Press. © A. R. Mowbray & Co. Limited. 1st edition, 1965, 2nd edition 1975. Used by permission of Westminster/John Knox Press. From *Jesus the Christ*, by Walter Kasper, 1976. Used by permission of Burns & Oates Ltd. From *The Open Secret*, by Lesslie Newbigin, 1978. Used by permission of Wm. B. Eerdmans, Ltd. From *The New Oxford Annotated Bible with Apocrypha*, Revised Standard Version Bible, copyright 1946, 1952, 1971 by the Division of Christian Education of the National Council of Churches of Christ in the USA and used by permission. From *The New Jerusalem Bible*, published and copyright 1985 by Darton, Longman and Todd Ltd. and Doubleday and Co. Ltd., and used by permission of the publishers. Excerpt from *Mystery and Manners*, by Flannery O'-Connor. Copyright © 1969 by the Estate of Mary Flannery O'Connor. Reprinted by permission of Harold Matson, Co., New York, and Farrar, Straus and Giroux, Inc.

Abbreviations

CAC   *Christianity at the Centre, 1968.*

COC   *The Centre of Christianity*, 1977.

GHMN   *God Has Many Names*, 1982.

GUF   *God and the Universe of Faiths*, 1973.

MGI   *The Myth of God Incarnate*, 1977.

Contents

Part One: Elaboration

CHAPTER ONE

Introduction

T he Church is always learning. Even when it teaches, it is teaching only what it has first learned[1]. One of the areas in which the Church is presently learning involves the relationship of Jesus with other religions.

How is the Christian to understand who Jesus Christ is in the context of world religions? Is He the unique mediator between God and humankind such that there is no other name in which any person of any religious faith can find salvation? If so, where does that leave other world faiths relative to God's universal salvific will? Or is He only one of the ways in which God offers salvation to His children? Is Jesus Saviour only for the Christian?

This complex of questions forms the general problematic within which this work is located. My aim is not to address all aspects of these questions, but to focus on the specific issue of the uniqueness of Jesus Christ.

John Hick, too, locates his Christological thought within this problematic. To the question, "How is the Christian to understand who Jesus Christ is in the context of world religions?", Hick offers us a solution: Jesus is not the unique and universal Saviour of humankind because He is not literally God become man. Only mythologically, claims Hick, can we speak of a Second Person of the Trinity becoming incarnate. The idea that Jesus of Nazareth is "God the Son" is simply the deification of the poetic title "Son of God." This deification process of passing from metaphor to metaphysics culminates with Nicea's *homoousios* and Chalcedon's two-natures Christology.

In fact, continues Hick, Jesus is simply one of those people who were especially open to God's presence in the world and in their lives. He is one among many people to whom God has chosen to reveal Himself. His uniqueness is only relative. That is, He is unique as the founder of Christianity. But Christianity is just one among equal paths to God. For Hick, God would never have chosen to reveal Himself completely in one person or through one religion since that would have given unfair access to salvation to those who happened to encounter that one person, or who happened by dint of where they were born, to share in that one faith. Such a way of proceeding on God's part would have violated His universal salvific will by giving exclusive preference to one religion over another.

While I agree that the Church needs to learn much in this area of Jesus and world religions, my own response to Professor Hick is that he would have us unlearn what in fact remains valid. That is, if the Church is to advance in learning as it explores this new field, it will not be able to do so by abandoning the truth that it has already learned correctly.

For that reason I find that John Hick's solution to the the issue of the uniqueness of Jesus Christ is not a helpful one for the Christian. His solution, as appealing as it may appear, neither represents a faithful explanation of the origins of how the Church came to learn of the uniqueness of Jesus, nor does it offer a faithful advance in the reinterpretation of that Christian affirmation.

It is true that many of Hick's arguments raise important, indeed, challenging questions. Nevertheless, as I hope to demonstrate, the interpretations he proposes are inattentive to all the relevant data, and so in the end they are inaccurate.

Because Hick's Christology is not at all simplistic, and because it is so challenging, I have dedicated a large portion of this work to a detailed elaboration of his position, so that it may be properly appreciated and understood.The major portion, however, is reserved for my evaluative critique.

My response organizes Hick's Christological claims into two groups: primary and secondary. Hick's primary claims include those relating to: (1) the consciousness of Jesus, (2) Scripture, and (3) Christian tradition. His secondary claims include: (1) theological positions (other than primary ones), (2) linguistic claims, (3) epistemology, (4) the call for a Copernican revolution in theology, (5) divine inhistorisation and *homoagape*, and (6) his critique of the resurrection of Jesus.

My concluding Chapter offers some thoughts on the implication of my own position relative to the original problematic which occasioned this work: How is the Christian to understand who Jesus is in the context of world religions?

Limits

Perhaps two words about the limits of this study are in order. I am doing theology, specifically Christology in the context of fundamental theology. The first word, then, can be stated in the form of what I am *not* doing. I am not doing philosophy. Therefore, I do not prescind from faith in my method. Faith, in fact, is what grounds my method and makes my point of view interesting. While some scholars may consider faith a limiting, distorting squint, I on the other hand consider it an ampler light illuminating a wider horizon.

Nor am I doing religious studies: that is, I am definitely not doing comparative religion, history of religions, nor a phenomenology, sociology or psychology of religion.

I am doing theology. Given Christianity's contemporary interaction with world faiths, I am trying more deeply to understand from within the standpoint of Christian faith some aspects of the mystery of who Jesus is. Specifically, I am examining the position of John Hick regarding the person of Jesus, and assessing its adequacy as a correct understanding for the Christian confronted with the complex issues involved in thinking about Jesus and the plurality of world religions.

Even within the field of fundamental Christology, one is confronted with many complex issues. This fact leads me to my second word about limits. Again, I begin by stating what I am *not* doing. I am not attempting to examine, let alone resolve, the issues involved in inter-religious dialogue, religious pluralism or theological method. I am not proposing a Christian theology of world religions. Nor am I examining in what sense either Jesus fulfills other religions or in what sense the rays of truth in non-Christian religions can be regarded as *preparatio evangelica*. I do not examine in what sense the Holy Spirit is active or the Word is present in non-Christian religions, nor how to discern that activity or presence. My concern is not with the presence or absence of revelation in the sacred writings or rituals of non-Christian religions. Nor do I try to resolve the issue of God's universal salvific will with the Judeo-Christian doctrine of election.

What am I concerned with? My focus is the very specific one of who Jesus is: is He or is He not as traditional Christian faith has literally affirmed, true God and true man—the Second Person of the Trinity, Incarnate? John Hick says "no;" I say "yes."

Although there have been many responses to Hick's writings[2], including his Christology, these responses limit themselves to a selection of claims from Hick's Christological position. None deals with his Christology in its totality. In several cases I did not find the responses to Hick especially persuasive. They did not, as it were, hit the nail on the head. My hope, then, is to provide a convincing response to all Hick's Christological claims. Equally, I wish to respond to Hick's contextual positions, e.g., his Copernican revolution in theology, etc., in as much as they bear on the Christological issue and determine its outcome.

Uniqueness

Since the focus of the following discussions revolves around the word "uniqueness", it would be helpful to say something about this term here.

Lesslie Newbigin writes that the issue of the uniqueness of Jesus Christ is "the life-and-death question for the missionary."[3] But the term "uniqueness" is not easy to define. For example, "uniqueness" can mean "one of a kind." But each of us can say: "There is only one of me. I am unique." That is true. In this sense, Jesus is unique in the same way that anyone who has ever existed is unique. There has been only one Jesus of Nazareth, and there will only ever be that one Jesus of Nazareth. It is clear, however, that this is not the sense of "unique" which concerns us here. No one, least of all Hick, is claiming that whereas everyone who has ever existed is unique in being themselves, that somehow Jesus of Nazareth is not unique in this particular way.

In what sense, then, am I using the term "unique"? The "uniqueness" of Jesus which interests us is the uniqueness found in Christian faith. One way of expressing this is Karl Rahner's account of one of

4

the tasks of Christology:

> Further, it [Christology] would have to demonstrate satisfactorily that *this Jesus* is the absolutely real presence of God in the world, that the work he has done as Man is really the redemption of the world ...[4]

In his work *Foundations of Christian Faith*, Rahner writes that

> ... the mystery which we call God, "is present" for our salvation, offering forgiveness and divine life, and is offered to us in such a way that God's offer in him [Jesus Christ] is final and ir-revocable.[5]

Another way of referring to the uniqueness of Jesus Christ which we intend can be found in the first volume of Richard P. McBrien's *Catholicism* where he writes:

> Jesus has this unique role in our salvation because he is at the same time divine and human. If he were not divine, by what power and authority does he redeem us from our sins? If he were not human, what does his redemptive work have to do with us or for us?[6]

And still a fourth expression of that uniqueness is given by Walter Kasper, who writes:

> Jesus Christ is not only the final self-definition of God, but the final definition of the world and man.[7]

It is this uniqueness of Jesus Christ which Hick wishes to rethink in the context of world religions. Hick writes:

> The older theological tradition of Christianity does not readily permit religious pluralism. For at its centre is the conviction that Jesus of Nazareth was God—the second Person of a divine Trinity living a human life. It follows from this that Christianity,

and Christianity alone, was founded by God in person on the only occasion on which he has ever become incarnate in this world, so that Christianity has a unique status as the way of salvation provided and appointed by God himself ... But in the light of our accumulated knowledge of the other great world faiths this conclusion has become unacceptable to all except a minority of dogmatic diehards. For it conflicts with our concept of God, which we have received from Jesus, as the loving heavenly Father of *all* mankind; could such a Being have restricted the possibility of salvation to those who happen to have been born in certain countries in certain periods of history [GHMN,26-7]?

From the above quotations I wish simply to indicate that the term "uniqueness" in the title of this work refers to the traditional identification of Jesus as God the Son, Second Person of the Trinity who became man, was crucified and rose from the dead, and this was all done for the salvation of the world.

Why, it might be asked, did I choose to refer to the Christian affirmation regarding Jesus Christ, specifically with the term "uniqueness?" Why did I not choose one of the frequently used alternatives, for example, "absoluteness" or "finality?" Both of these alternates appear in the above explanations.

I rejected "absoluteness" because it is too much a philosophical term. Nor did I wish to confuse my topic with Rahner's very specific notion of "absolute saviour."[8] In addition, the term "uniqueness" is closer to the scriptural *monogenes* ("only, unique").[9]

A more likely alternative to "uniqueness" is "finality." "Finality" has definite links with the notion of "eschatological prophet"—a notion which figures significantly in my response to Hick. Nevertheless, the term "finality" is usually employed more within a discussion of revelation. While not at all unrelated to our topic, the issues revolving around revelation are not immediately my concern. I concluded, therefore, that rather than "finality," the term "uniqueness" more accurately designated my specific interest in the person and identity of Jesus Christ.

On the issue of Jesus' uniqueness, Hick's approach begins by questioning the uniqueness of Christianity's claims about itself among world religions. He distinguishes what is *uniquely* Christian from what is *essentially* Christian, or most important to Christianity [GUF,108ff]. What is *essential*, or most important, to Christianity is the Christ-event. This constitutes Christianity as a way to salvation, and that is what is important. The Christ-event is the only part of Christianity that is "permanent and unchanging" [GUF,111]. What is *uniquely* Christian according to Hick, however, is the developed elements of Christian worship and belief. These latter do not constitute part of the Christ-event [GUF,114].

From this distinction, Hick is led to reconsider the Christian claims regarding the uniqueness of Jesus. As we shall see, Hick's version of theocentrism will allow him to say that Jesus has only a "relative uniqueness."

An Objection Answered

It might be objected that the issue of the uniqueness of Jesus Christ is already settled. The response to Hick is obvious, and the question is in no need of further examination. The Church has reflected on its faith in Jesus and stated clearly what that faith is, especially in the early Christological Councils. Neither that faith nor that doctrine has changed. There remains simply to find appropriate ways to proclaim, offer and teach that faith to others who do not yet know who Jesus is or what He did. Why raise this issue of Jesus' identity once again?

Until the latter half of the last century, the Christian theological understanding was that Jesus could be the only saviour of the world because He alone was both truly and fully human and truly and fully divine. In fact, this understanding still remains the position of the major Christian churches. But during the past century, the advances in scholarship, especially in Biblical criticism, and the development of modern historical consciousness, have all contributed, at the very least, to a serious nuancing of traditional understanding.

Even more to the point, during the past century the contact among world religions has increased. Genuine knowledge among and about world religions has replaced the half-truths, ignorance and prejudice that so long prevailed. Modern communications, travel, and mass movements of peoples have all brought adherents of different religions into immediate proximity to each other. There has been progression from contact, to knowledge, to dialogue. The fact of a religiously plural world is being experienced in new, immediate and challenging ways. Inevitably, new, immediate and challenging questions arise. New learning needs to take place. What has been believed and understood cannot help but be rethought in light of new experience and data. Hence, the question of who Jesus is in the context of the contemporary experience of world religions is undergoing new consideration. Consequently, we raise this issue because it is being raised anew in theological, as well as in pastoral, worlds.

Within this new global ecumenical experience, the Christian claim has remained its confessional faith in the uniqueness of Jesus, and therefore, in Christianity as representing the fullness of God's revelation. Other religions or faiths have seeds of the Word or rays of the Truth. The mission of the Church is to bring to these other faiths the knowledge of the unique salvation God has brought through Jesus, the Word-made-flesh.

This position has made the Christian appear superior, perhaps smug and arrogant, in the ecumenical dialogue. There seems to be no need for the Christian to search for religious truth, except in minor sorts of ways, because the fullness of God's self-revelation is already to be located in the founder of Christianity. Such a position is viewed by adherents of other faiths as obstructionist to ecumenical dialogue and divisive to the need for the world religions to co-operate in assisting mankind to solve its many problems. While this Christian attitude may have been tolerated up to now, it remains no longer helpful or constructive. Indeed, some theologians would say, given modern scholarship, that the traditional Christian position is no longer even intelligent. One such contemporary and controversial Christian theologian is the protestant John Hick. Thus, not only is it appropriate for us to raise the issue of the uniqueness of Jesus, it is also pertinent to focus on John Hick's position.

Theocentric Model

Another term perhaps needing some explanation is that of "theocentric model".

By model I mean "a way of thinking about something," or "a mental structure that organizes the key relationships among data." Although Hick does not define the term "model," he uses it [GHMN, 18-

19] to summarize his call for a shift from a "Ptolemaic" understanding of the universe of faiths, to a "Copernican" interpretation.

That is, Hick wants a "God-centered," or "theocentric," model of understanding the world's major religions. Hick's approach is to invite all world faiths to abandon their Ptolemaic self- or founder-centeredness, and to adopt a God-centered self-understanding.

Specifically, what is the function of this term "theocentric model" in this inquiry?

Christian theology of world religions can operate out of such models as an ecclesio-centered model, or a Christ-centered model, or a Spirit-centered model. These are only a few of the many possibilities. Hick opts for a theocentric model, indeed he champions it in his argument for a Copernican revolution in theology. If the Copernican revolution ushers in the theocentric model, then the theocentric model, in turn, ushers in the rethinking of the traditional Christological interpretation of the uniqueness of Jesus Christ. For as Hick writes, the theocentric model represents

...a paradigm shift from a Christianity-centred or Jesus-centred model to a God-centred model of the universe of faiths...This paradigm shift involves a reopening of the Christological question [GHMN,18-19].

My task then is the focused one of asking: Is Hick's Christology within the theocentric model an acceptable Christology?

World Religions

In the earlier section on the limits of this work, I stated that I am not in any way doing a study of world religions. World religions in this work, as for John Hick's Christology, provides the *context* in which questions arise regarding the uniqueness of Jesus Christ. By context, I mean that the difficulties posed by the pluralism of world religions, e.g., conflicting truth-claims, condition which Christological questions will be raised, how they will be posed, what arguments will be appropriate, what examples and analogies will be to the point, what solutions will appear unacceptable, and what new directions have to be considered.

Since world religions are a context and not a focus for this study,[10] I do not attempt to define what is or is not a religion or a world religion. I simply accept, only for the sake of argument, Hick's understanding of what constitutes world religions.[11]

Both terms "world" and "religions" are necessary for Hick, and therefore for us. The notion of "religions" indicates both an openness and cultural response to the Transcendent as the latter has impinged on human consciousness, especially during the axial period as defined by Karl Jaspers. "World" is meant to separate out those long-tested religions among large sectors of the world's populations, from smaller and more suspect religious expressions of the human spirit. For Hick, "religion" is where God has specifically revealed Himself; "world" is meant to distinguish "revelation-religions" from "pre-revelation" religions.

Elaboration and Evaluation

In one sense, the terms "elaboration" and "evaluation" are straightforward. But since they relate to the structure of this work, I wish to offer an explanation.

These two terms appertain to two functional specialties explained by Bernard Lonergan, S.J. In *Method in Theology* Lonergan differentiates eight functional specialties within the theological enterprise: research, interpretation, history, dialectic, foundations, doctrines, systematics and communications.[12] Briefly, functional specialties are methodical distinctions or tasks based on the immanent directives of the method of mind. This work is engaged primarily in the second and fourth functional specialties. That is, my inquiry methodologically involves interpretation (i.e., "elaboration") and dialectic (i.e., "evaluation").

Regarding "interpretation", Lonergan states that it "is just a particular case of knowing, namely, knowing what is meant" [MT, 154, 127]. It involves

> ... three basic exegetical operations: (1) understanding the text; (2) judging how correct one's understanding of the text is; and (3) stating what one judges to be the correct understanding of the text [MT, 155].

The written form of this work represents the third (which obviously contains the first two) of the above exegetical operations. In the method of mind as uncovered by Lonergan, the functional specialty "interpretation" operates on the second level of human consciousness, that is, the level of understanding, the level that poses questions for intelligence. Interpretation is part of the mediating phase of scientific method.

"Dialectic," according to Lonergan, operates on the fourth level of human consciousness, the level of value. As such, it is concerned with conflicts. These conflicts can occur in any of the eight functional specialties. For example, there can be conflicts in research, in interpretation, in history, in doctrines, etc. As such, dialectic is in full encounter with the past, or the tradition. Such an encounter is the purpose of the mediating phase of method. Dialectic is pivotal as well, for it is the passage from the mediating phase to the mediated phase of scientific method.

Not all conflicts are dialectical. Some conflicts can be resolved simply by uncovering fresh data. Other conflicts are perspectival. But dialectical conflicts go beyond these differences. They stem from explicit or implicit cognitional theories, ethical stances, or religious outlooks. Dialectical conflicts are, therefore, more fundamental than are perspectival conflicts. A dialectical conflict can be resolved only by a radical change in one's horizon, which change Lonergan calls "conversion": either intellectual, moral, or religious conversion, or some combination of all three.[13] Lonergan writes:

> The function of dialectic will be to bring such conflicts to light, and to provide a technique that objectifies subjective differences and promotes conversion [MT,235].

In its relation to interpretation, dialectic adds an evaluative hermeneutics. Thus, because of this foundational element, dialectic is involved with foundational horizons. When two foundational horizons conflict dialectically, they find themselves in genuine opposition. This is the case between Hick and myself. We are not opposed in the simpler sense of being merely complementary to each other, nor even opposed by some kind of genetic relationship of ideas. The only solution is to choose between the two fundamental horizons in which we operate. One cannot maintain that Jesus is both unique (our position) and not unique (Hick's position) as affirmed in the traditional Christian faith affirmation. A person must opt for, or be converted to, one or other position. They both cannot be maintained simultaneously. The reason is that in dialectical conflicts, what is intelligible, true, or good in one horizon, is unintelligible, false, or evil in another [MT, 236].

Usually decisions are made within established or received horizons. But sometimes we are challenged to change our horizon. This challenge is what Hick proposes in his Christology. But we must ask whether he is inviting us to a genuine conversion or to a counterfeit one. In answering that question we find ourselves engaged in a process of dialectic. We get to the root claims of Hick's positions, uncover the omissions in data, expose the misinterpretations, and finally reverse his judgments (i.e., conclusions).

Hence, after interpreting (elaborating) Hick's position on the uniqueness of Jesus Christ, I shall evaluate (engage in a dialectical response to) that position. The process of dialectic constitutes the second and major part of this work.

It should be stated that the eight functional specialties as accounted for by Lonergan are not isolated compartments. No more than the inner directives of the mind seeking to know, judge and decide are isolated compartments, are the subsequent methodical operations isolated actions. The inner directives are inter-related, and so also are the resultant functional specialties. Hence, while locating myself primarily in interpretation and dialectic, I am also involved in research, history, foundations, doctrines, systematics, and communications.

John Hick

This work elaborates and evaluates the uniqueness of Jesus Christ in the thought of John Hick. For those who may not yet be familiar him, it will be appropriate now to introduce this scholar.

Biography[14]

In our section immediately following this one, I treat the issue of whether Hick is a theologian or not. Later, in the first Chapter on John Hick (Chapter 2), I provide an account of his intellectual development. Here I wish simply to introduce the reader to some external details of his life.

John Harwood Hick is, at the time of this writing, Danforth Professor and Chair of the Department of Religion at Claremont University, California.

He was born on January 20, 1922, in Scarborough, England. His childhood religion was Anglican. He was educated at the University of Edinburgh, 1941-2, 1945-8, receiving an M.A., first class honours, in Philosophy. From 1948-50 he attended the University of Oxford, from where he received a D. Phil. (Ph.D. Cambridge, by incorporation). The title of his thesis was: "The Relation Between Belief and Faith." (This dissertation was to be the basis of his first book *Faith and Knowledge*).[15] He studied theology at Westminster Theological College, Cambridge, 1950-3. Further degrees which Hick has been awarded are: (1) D.Litt. (Edinburgh), 1974, (2) Hon. Teol. Dr. (Uppsala), 1977.

During the Second World War as a conscientious objector, Hick served in the Friends' Ambulance Unit, 1942-5. In 1953, the year of his marriage, he was also ordained in the Presbyterian Church of England. In the late fifties, 1956-9, he was Assistant Professor of Philosophy, Cornell University. From 1959-64 Hick was Stuart Professor of Christian Philosophy, Princeton Theological Seminary. Subsequently, for three years he was Lecturer in Divinity, Cambridge University. In 1967 he moved to Birmingham, and became H. G. Wood Professor of Theology, University of Birmingham. During this time, Hick was active in many of the local issues relating to inter-religious and racial problems. In 1972 he became Governor of Queens College, Birmingham. Then, in 1979 he became Danforth Professor at Claremont. In March, 1986, Hick along with Paul Knitter, organized a theological conference at Claremont to examine and evaluate the "theocentric" model in the study of world religions.[16] Later the same year, Hick gave Gifford Lectures in Edinburgh. An important work since then, and based on the Gifford Lectures, is his *An Interpretation of Religion* (London: Macmillan, 1988).

Hick as Theologian

Hick began his academic career, not as a theologian, but as a philosopher of religion. In addition, during the course of that career, he has never abandoned his interest in philosophical issues. So we might legitimately ask ourselves if, or in what sense, Hick may be considered a theologian.

In theological circles, Hick is best known for his editing of *The Myth of God Incarnate.*[17] This book examines and reinterprets from many angles, the traditional Christian affirmation of the uniqueness of Jesus Christ. In his own contribution to that work, "Jesus and the World Religions," Hick argues for a re-interpretation of the language of the doctrine of the Incarnation. [18]

But Hick's theological interests, indeed his Christological concerns, can be traced back to his 1958 article: "The Christology of D. M. Baillie."[19] But by 1973, with the publication of *God and the Universe of Faiths,*[20] Hick writes that because of the "immense" and "new" problem of pluralism, he can

> ... no longer find it possible to proceed as a *christian theologian* as though Christianity were the only religion in the world [GUF,viii; emphasis mine].

Hence, Chapters 8, 9 and 10 of that same work "seek to develop a *christian theology* of religions" [GUF,viii; emphasis mine]. In *Evil and the God of Love*[21] Hick also sees himself doing theology. Reflecting on that work he writes:

> I realized more fully in the course of writing this book that the kind of theology at which I was arriving has a long and respectable ancestry, going back through Schleiermacher ultimately to the earliest fathers of the church, particularly Irenaeus, after whom I have therefore named it [GHMN,17].

Yet, for Hick, the two fields of philosophy of religion and theology are never completely distinct. He can move from one to the other without feeling any frontier has been crossed. For example, *God and the Universe of Faiths* is subtitled "Essays in the Philosophy of Religion." Aware of the mutual overlapping of the two fields, Hick states in *God Has Many Names*[22] that his work is properly "philosophical theology." [23]

14

In specifying the kind of theology in which he engages, Hick distinguishes two kinds of theology: "dogmatics" and "problematics." He understands his own work to lie "more in the area of problematics than of dogmatics" [GHMN,13]. Dogmatic theology, according to Hick studies and preserves the inherited tradition. It need not be dogmatic in the sense of being assertive and unreasoning. Dogmatic theology accepts its fundamental structure as permanently valid, because divinely revealed. Problematic theology, however,

... takes place at the interface between the tradition and the world—both the secular world and the wider religious world—and is concerned to create new theology in the light of new situations [GHMN,13].

An important distinction between the two types of theology, continues Hick, is their attitude to their own conclusions. Dogmatic theology understands its basic positions to represent a final truth. Problematic theology, on the other hand,

... sees its conclusions as hypotheses, open to revision and always seeking greater adequacy, being comparable in this respect with the hypotheses of the sciences [GHMN,13].

Employing the image of faith as a ship, Hick visualizes dogmatic theology as the ballast, and problematic theology as the sails. He writes that both types of theology are necessary: "the one to keep the vessel upright and the other so that it may be carried onward before the winds of history" [GHMN,13].

Hick says that his theology reflects the "strain under which christian belief has come" [GUF,92]. This strain has led "many theologians today (including myself [Hick])" to hold as "untenable or open to serious doubt" many traditional Christian beliefs [GUF,92].[24]

Hick continues by stating that we should not be greatly disturbed by the "current repudiation" of these many traditional beliefs. The reason is that "theology is a creation of the human mind" and, therefore subject to change [GUF,93]. Hick elaborates. Theology is "the development of metaphysical systems to conceptualise the significance of

Jesus of Nazareth" and as such, it has been part of the history of the Christian West [GUF,93]. Most contemporary theologians now understand theology, explains Hick,

> ... as a human activity which seeks to state the meaning of revelatory events, and above all of the Christ-event. Theology begins with religious experience—the experience of encountering God in Christ and in one's own life—and then tries systematically and consistently to interpret this and to relate it to our other knowledge [GUF,93].

But the categories and the contexts of theological thinking are all part of the stream of human culture. Therefore, "theology necessarily changes through time. Accordingly, the christian theological tradition has always been a tradition of change" [GUF,93].[25] At some periods the change has been rapid, for example, the first four centuries A.D., as well as "our own time." Other periods, for example, the medieval period, were relatively stable [GUF,93-4].

For contemporary theology, past cultural categories and contexts are no longer determinative. Specifically, Hick mentions that the "metaphysical frameworks supplied by Greek philosophy" have been left behind [GUF,94]. Not only that, but with the rapid changing pace of all knowledge, the future of theological thinking is "open-ended." No limits, he writes, can be put on the change that theology and Christian faith might have to undergo. As long as there are individuals who respond in faith to Jesus, the ways these individual Christians "conceptualise their faith will be christian theologies" [GUF,94]. The Church, then, not only adjusts to the challenge of change, it also at times "reconstructs its Christ-affected picture of the universe."

Two contemporary factors which are transforming theology, says Hick, are (1) scientific and technological knowledge, and (2) the newly encountered fact of other world religions [GUF,94]. Our concern in this work is not with the former.[26] It is the latter that interests us, because it is this factor that eventually ushers in Hick's Copernican revolution in theology. As such, it reopens the Christological question on the identity of Christ. Later we will provide an account of these important issues in Hick's thought.[27] Here we intend simply to indicate how the pluralism of world religions helps to explain Hick's work as a theologian.

The recent, growing contact among world religions, says Hick, has provided a "new context" for theology.[28] The isolationism of the past is no longer an adequate horizon in which to do theology. Previously, Christian theology was carried out "in essential unawareness" of other world religions. Hick comments that it is no exaggeration "to say that traditional christian theology simply ignored the greater part of the human race!" [GUF,100]. Since the facts of our world no longer permit ignorance, Christian theology "is ready for further development and enlargement."

The starting point for theology, Hick says, must be God's universal love. The theologian cannot restrict this universal love. Hick writes:

> If God is the God of the whole world, we must presume that the whole religious life of mankind is part of a continuous and universal human relationship to him [GUF,101].

Religions, for Hick, are "distinguishable religio-cultural streams within man's history" [GUF,102]. It is no more appropriate, therefore, to speak of a religion as being true or false, any more than it is appropriate to speak of a civilization as being true or false. Drawing on Wilfred Cantwell Smith, Hick argues that there is a "questionable relation" between a resultant religion and its original founding event. For example, the Church as we know it, says Hick, "is widely different" from anything Jesus of Nazareth intended [GUF,92]. About religions in general, Hick writes:

> Religions as institutions, with the theological doctrines and the codes of behaviour which form their boundaries, did not come about so much because the religious reality required this as because human nature tends to surround truths and values with institutional walls which divide "us" from "them" [GUF,103].

But in the contemporary situation, with the world now a "communicational unity," theology must "transcend these cultural-historical boundaries" [GUF,103]. What does this mean specifically for the

Christian? We quote Hick at length:

> We, as Christians, owe our existence to that intersection of
> divine grace and human response in the life of Jesus of Nazareth
> in which we have seen the divine love made flesh. But it is far
> from self-evident that the activity of God's love in the life of
> Christ is incompatible with divine activity in other forms, in
> other times, in other places. On the contrary, if the religious life
> of mankind is a continuous field of relationship to the divine
> Reality, the theologian must try to include all forms of religious
> experience among his data, and all forms of religious ideas
> among the hypotheses to be considered. His theology should take
> account of all genuine human experience of the divine transcen-
> dent. For the varied but continuous field of the religious life of
> mankind demands unified theories of commensurate scope.
> These will not be christian theologies, or islamic theologies, or
> buddhist theologies, but human theologies, which are not sec-
> tional but global in their use of religious data [GUF,103].

The older view of theology, observes Hick, saw theology as a
"body of divinely revealed truths." The contemporary view understands theology "as a continuing process of human reflection and
theorizing aiming to clarify the meaning of man's religious experience" [GUF,104].[29]

The contemporary theological task is a new one. It would be "artificial," writes Hick, to continue to restrict theological data to "a single
culture" [GUF,104]. The new theological task, then, will involve two
operations: (1) the critical sifting of the various world religious traditions to uncover more clearly the forms of religious experience within
them, (2) "the construction of theologies (in the plural) based upon the
full range of man's religious awareness" [GUF,103].

This explanation of the contemporary theological task, describes
well Hick's own theological project. His concern is to work out a
global theology of religions. His Christological interests are to be understood within this wider context.

From the foregoing, it is clear that Hick considers himself a Christian theologian doing Christian theology. His type of theology is

"problematics," specifically "philosophical theology." He considers the contemporary task of theology to consist in transcending the cultural boundaries of the present, and certainly those of the past. Development and change, even radical development and change, may be required. Reflecting on his own personal growth in doing theology, Hick describes the experience as "one of continually expanding horizons as the investigation of one problem has brought upon another" [GHMN,16]. Notwithstanding, then, Hick's ongoing interests in the philosophy of religion, it is appropriate also to consider him a theologian.

Now that I have introduced and explained the topic, defined the terms, fixed the limits, and mapped out the task, we can advance to the body of our work.

Endnotes

1. For an original exploration into this idea, see Frederick E. Crowe, S.J., "The Church as Learner: Two Crises, One *Kairos*," in Michael Vertin, ed., *Appropriating the Lonergan Idea* (Washington, D.C.: The Catholic University of America Press, 1989): 370-84.

2. There are too many to enumerate here. Many will appear in footnotes throughout the text.

3. Lesslie Newbigin, *The Finality of Christ* (London: S.C.M., 1969), 8.

4. Karl Rahner and Herbert Vorgrimler, *Concise Theological Dictionary*, (London: Burns & Oates, 1965, 1976, 1981, 1983), 71.

5. Karl Rahner, *Foundations of Christian Faith: An Introduction to the Idea of Christianity* (New York: Crossroad, 1984), 205.

6. Richard P. McBrien, *Catholicism* (Minneapolis: Winston, 1980), 2 vols., 439.

7. Walter Kasper, *Jesus the Christ* (London: Burns & Oates, 1976), 185.

8. Rahner, *Foundations ...*, 193-5.

9. *A Concise Greek-English Dictionary of the New Testament.* Prepared by Barclay M. Newman, Jr., (London: United Bible Societies, 1971), 118. See also, *An Expository Dictionary of Biblical Words.* By W. E. Vine, Merrill F. Unger and William White, Jr., (Nashville: Thomas Nelson, 1984), 811-3. The New Testament

references of *monogenes* to Jesus Christ are: Jn 1:14, 18; 3:16, 18; Heb 11:17; 1 Jn 4:9. Also, "uniqueness," rather than "absoluteness" comes closer to the meaning of *prototokos* ("firstborn") especially in Col 1:15f. Michael Green, "Jesus in the New Testament," in Michael Green, ed., *The Truth of God Incarnate* (London: Hodder and Stoughton, 1977), 20, writes that "... 'firstborn', a fascinating word with a complex history, had long ceased to be used exclusively in its literal sense and had come to denote priority in rank as well as in time—cf. Psalm 89.27." See also, *An Expository Dictionary ...*, 434-5.

10. Our focus, as we have repeatedly said, is the issue of the unique identity of the person of Jesus Christ.

11. Later in Chapter 2 there is an elaboration of Hick's notion of world religions. Here I wish to note that nowhere does Hick give any complete list of world religions. However, from various references, we can assemble the following table: 1. Theistic forms of religion (The "Eternal One" as personal) [GHMN,24-5]: Judaism, Christianity, Islam, Hinduism (Vaishnavite, Shaivite, Bhakti), Sikhism, Buddhism (Amida), (Zoroastrianism), the "primal" religious life of Africa [GHMN,48]. 2. Non-theistic or transtheistic forms of religion (The "Eternal One" as non-personal) [GHMN,24-5,52]: Buddhism (Zen, Theravada, Mahayana), Hinduism (Advaita, the Vedanta), Jainism, Taoism, Confucianism. 3. Philosophy as an experience of the "Eternal One:" Greeks (Pythagoras, Socrates, Plato, Aristotle). 4. Non-religious world faiths: (Marxism, Maoism, Humanism).

A few comments on this table are in order. First, Hick's lists are exemplary, not exhaustive. Secondly, since Hick's notion of world religions is based on Karl Jaspers' account of the "axial period," Hick includes the Greek philosophers among world religions [cf. Karl Jaspers, *The Origin and Goal of History* (London: Routledge & Kegan Paul, 1953]. Thirdly, although Hick here refers to the African religions among world religions, when later distinguishing natural religions from world religions (based on revelatory moments), he excludes African religions from world religions [GHMN,43]. (Jaspers, for example, does not include them either. He says that Africa, including the Egyptian civilization, was completely by-passed by the axial period. Hick modifies Jaspers regarding Egyptian monotheism, by saying it was too brief to be counted a world religion [GHMN,47]). Fourthly,

Hick includes the "non-religious faiths" of Marxism, Maoism, and Humanism (which have nothing to do with the axial period) because they fit in with Hick's understanding of a global theology [GHMN, 21-2]. And yet, somewhat confusingly, Hick later writes that Marxism is not to be considered a world religion [GHMN,120]. Fourthly, the title, "the Eternal One," is Hick's preference over "God." The reason is that "God" weights the discussion in terms of those religions that experience God as personal, as opposed to those who experience God as non-personal. Nevertheless, Hick employs the term "God" frequently, since he contends there exists no neutral term [GHMN,91]. Sixthly, Zoroastrianism is in parentheses, because although it emerged during the axial period, it has, writes Hick, "since perished as an organized tradition, except for the relatively small Parsi community in India" [GHMN,46].

12. Bernard Lonergan, S.J., *Method in Theology* (New York: Herder and Herder, 1972). These eight functional specialties constitute all of Part II of *Method* .... However, they are introduced in Chapter V, "Functional Specialties," the last Chapter of Part I.

13. Robert M. Doran, S.J., grounded in Lonergan's thought, has argued also for a fourth conversion, "psychic conversion." See his: (1) *Subject and Psyche: Ricoeur, Jung, and the Search for Foundations* (Washington, D.C.: University Press of America, 1979), and (2) *Psychic Conversion and Theological Foundations: Toward a Reorientation of the Human Sciences* (Chico, CA: Scholars, 1981).

14. This section and the following derive their information from: (1) biographical references in various works of Hick, (2) Hick's *curriculum vitae*, and (3) *Who's Who 1986: An Annual Biographical Dictionary* (London: A & C Black, 1986), 806-807.

15. John Hick, *Faith and Knowledge: A Modern Introduction to the Problem of Religious Knowledge*. (Ithaca: Cornell University Press, 1957. 2nd ed., 1966).

16. The volume that resulted from that conference is: John Hick and Paul Knitter, eds., *The Myth of Christian Uniqueness: Towards a Pluralistic Theology of Religions* (New York: Maryknoll, 1987).

17. John Hick, ed., *The Myth of God Incarnate* (London: S.C.M., and Philadelphia: Westminster, 1977).

18. *Ibid.*, 167-85.

19. *Scottish Journal of Theology*, 11, 1 (March 1958): 1-12. This was written during the period of Hick's "credal orthodoxy." For a detailed account, see the unpublished doctoral dissertation by Noel K. Jason, "A Critical Examination of the Christology of John Hick, with Special Reference to the Continuing Significance of the *Definitio Fidei* of the Council of Chalcedon, A.D. 451," University of Sheffield, 1978, 20-65.

20. John Hick, *God and the Universe of Faiths: Essays in the Philosophy of Religion* (London: Macmillan, and New York: St. Martin's Press, 1973).

21. John Hick, *Evil and the God of Love* (London: Macmillan, New York: Harper & Row, and London: Collins-Fontana, 1966). 2nd ed., 1977.

22. John Hick, *God Has Many Names* (Philadelphia: Westminster, 1982).

23. *Ibid.*, 16.

24. Hick lists the beliefs that he and other theologians at least seriously doubt: the belief (1) that there are divinely revealed truths, e.g. the doctrine of the Trinity and the two natures in Christ; (2) that God created the world out of nothing; (3) that man was created finitely perfect, but rebelled, so that the human condition since then has been that of having fallen from grace; (4) that Christ came to rescue man from his fallenness, and redeemed "man's (or some men's) restoration to grace by his death on the cross;" (5) that Jesus was born of a virgin mother and with no human father; (6) that Jesus performed miracles involving the suspension of regularities in the natural order; (7) that his "dead body rose from the grave and returned to earthly life;" (8) that all men must respond to God through Jesus Christ in order to be saved; (9) that at death a person's relationship with God is irrevocably fixed; (10) that there are "two human destinies traditionally referred to under the symbols of heaven and hell" [GUF,92-3].

Hick's point, made here in Chapter 7, "The Reconstruction of Christian Belief," appeared earlier in the first part of Hick's two-part argument for the rationalization of Christian religious beliefs: "The Reconstruction of Christian Belief for Today and Tomorrow: 1," *Theology*, LXXIII, 602 (August 1970): 339-45, esp. 339.

25. Hick had made this point earlier in "The Reconstruction of

Christian Belief for Today and Tomorrow: 1," *Theology*, LXXIII, 602 (August 1970): 339-45, esp. 340.

26. For Hick's account of the relation between science and theology, see *God and The Universe of Faiths*, 94-99.

27. See our Chapter 2.

28. This point was made with striking clarity in Hick's significant—significant for his own intellectual development (see our Chapter 2)—argument for the rationalization of Christian beliefs: "The Reconstruction of Christian Belief for Today and Tomorrow: 2," *Theology*, LXXIII, 603 (September 1970): 399-405.

29. Later Hick writes: "...(T)heology is the human attempt to state the meaning of revelatory events experienced in faith ... (T)heology is part of the human, culturally conditioned response to the Christ-event" [GUF,117]. With this definition of theology, Hick says it is clear that there can be "many different christian theologies." For Hick, any theology of any Christian counts as a "christian theology." In his list [GUF,118-19] of examples of diverse Christian theologies, Hick mentions such theologies as: the Pope is the Antichrist, Trinitarian modalism, and the "death of God." Hick sees no need to discriminate among them. He writes: "What all these have in common, making it proper to call them christian, is a common origin in the Christ-event" [GUF,119].

CHAPTER TWO

The Context of Hick's Christology

Hick's Christology is not the central issue within his thought. His main project is to work out a global theology of religions. Also, as we have seen, Hick was initially more a philosopher of religion than a theologian. In addition, his re-examination of the Christological question of Christ's identity was required by his call for a Copernican revolution in theology. Therefore, in order to appreciate why Hick treats certain issues in Christology, and how he approaches these issues, I now provide an account of the context of Hick's Christology. We shall be focusing on four areas: (1) Hick's spiritual and intellectual development, (2) his notion of world religions, (3) his epistemology of religion, and (4) the Copernican revolution in theology. Each of these four areas constitute a section in this Chapter. Each section reveals why Hick believes it is necessary to reexamine the Christological question of Jesus' uniqueness. The purpose of this Chapter as *context* is to elaborate the reasons, from various approaches, why Hick believes Christianity must raise again the question of Jesus' identity. Hence, at the end of each section we specifically indicate how the issues raised in that section constitute a significant context for Hick's Christology.

Hick's Intellectual Development[1]

This first section provides an account of Hick's intellectual development. The first part describes his foundational religious experience and spiritual search. The second part elaborates on his intellectual quest with its ever-expanding horizons. It is important to record Hick's own foundational religious experience, as it will figure later in the foundations of his Christology. Also important is the fact that issues connected with world religions provide the wider context for his Christology, and not *vice versa*. Finally, Hick's theology is conditioned by conclusions from his philosophy of religion.

Spiritual Experience

Hick recalls that as a child, he experienced the Anglican services as an "infinite boredom" [GHMN,14]. Nevertheless, and according the Church no credit, he states that from his earliest years he

> ... had a rather strong sense of the reality of God as the personal and loving lord of the universe, and of life as having a meaning within God's purpose [GHMN,14].

When he was 18, Hick read a Western version of the Hindu Vedantic philosophy. He felt strongly attracted to "the first comprehensive and coherent interpretation of life" that he had encountered. However, he was not fully convinced of it. In the end he "consciously rejected it as being too tidy and impersonal." This was followed by a similar experience with Eastern Theosophy. All the while, Christianity "seemed utterly lifeless and uninteresting" [GHMN,14].

Around this time, Hick began the study of law at University College, Hull. It was there that he

> ... underwent a spiritual conversion in which the whole world of Christian belief and experience came vividly to life, and I became a Christian of a strongly evangelical and indeed fundamentalist kind [GHMN,14].

He began to read the New Testament and immediately found himself marvelling at the impact that Jesus had on His disciples. He was especially struck with "immense force" by the life of Jesus, in particular His sayings and parables, and by the impression of Jesus' personality as living Lord and Saviour. He writes:

26

I can remember well a period of several days of intense mental and emotional turmoil during which I was powerfully aware of a higher truth and greater reality pressing in upon my consciousness and claiming my recognition and response. At first this intrusion was highly unwelcome, a disturbing and challenging demand for nothing less than a revolution in personal identity. But presently the disturbing claim became a liberating invitation and I entered with great joy into the world of Christian faith [GHMN,14-5].

This "world of Christian faith" which Hick now embraced meant that he accepted "as a whole and without question" all the traditional Christian beliefs with their evangelical theology.

After his spiritual conversion, Hick formed the intention of entering Christian ministry. He joined the Presbyterian Church of England, "mainly because this was the church to which my Christian friends belonged" [GHMN,15]. He went to Edinburgh for a first year of a philosophy degree (1941-2). During the war he was a conscientious objector, and consequently joined the Friends' Ambulance Unit (1942-45). Throughout this time Hick was actively engaged in various evangelistic activities, e.g., Bible studies, prayer meetings, hospital ward services [GHMN,15].

Hick can recall during the initial years after his conversion, the resentment he felt at those who raised awkward questions that could upset the established orthodoxy. For this reason he says he can understand the similar resentment felt by many theologians and churchmen today [GHMN,16].

Intellectual Development

Hick greatly valued and benefitted from his evangelistic community, the Christian Union. But even at this early stage he began to feel its constraints as "a certain narrowness and a lack of sympathy with questioning thought" [GHMN,15]. For someone with a questioning intellect, Hick reflects, the conservative evangelical model will not be of service. Ultimately, such a person "will almost certainly be led by rational and moral considerations to modify or discard many of its elements" [GHMN,16].

Hence, after the war, when Hick returned to Edinburgh, he did not rejoin the Christian Union. He remained, however, "emphatically a Christian ... [and] in general, theologically rather conservative" [GHMN,15]. Nevertheless, his horizons began to expand. Writing much later in 1982, Hick observes that while he "can appreciate and respect the traditional orthodoxy," he "would not wish to return from the larger to a smaller vision" [GHMN,16]. The reason, he explains, is that while one's response to Jesus as Lord may remain the same,

> ... the body of theological theories associated with it in one's mind will usually change, and surely ought to change, in the light of further living, learning, and thinking [GHMN,16].

When Hick wrote his first book, *Faith and Knowledge*, 1957, he says he never expected to write another. He thought he had said all he had to say.[2] But no sooner had he finished that work than he found himself struggling with the theodicy issue: the question of whether suffering and wickedness are compatible with a loving God. The result was another book, *Evil and the God of Love*, 1966.[3] This work built upon the epistemology developed in *Faith and Knowledge*, particularly in the notion of "epistemic distance" and in the notion of faith as a fundamental expression of human freedom.[4]

No sooner was *Evil and the God of Love* completed, than he felt his horizons challenged once again to further expansion. In wrestling with the problem of evil, one of the conclusions Hick had reached was that any viable Christian theodicy must affirm the ultimate salvation of all God's creatures. It is not surprising, then, that the new challenge to Hick's horizon originated from the diversity of world religions. Each religion though different, claimed in some sense, says Hick, to be a revelation from God and the true way to salvation. How could the notion of there being one, and only one, true religion be reconciled with a belief in God's universal saving activity?

Hick could not accept the conclusion that, for example, Christianity was the true religion and the others were false. It would mean that the large majority of mankind, consisting of everyone except the adherents of one particular religion, would be walking in darkness.

There were other related and simultaneous developments in Hick's thought as well. According to Noel Jason, up until 1970 with the publication of Hick's two-part argument "The Reconstruction of Christian Belief for Today and Tomorrow," Hick was operating from within a framework of "credal orthodoxy," although with ever increasing tension.[5] Hick was already having serious questions about traditional Christian beliefs. In *Christianity at the Centre* he writes that as early as 1961-62 he was no longer affirming the doctrine of the virgin birth.[6] As early as 1959 he was claiming Jesus had only one nature and one will under the direction of a divine *Agape*.[7] As yet, these conclusions did not appear particularly heterodox to Hick.[8] Nor were they as yet foundationally grounded or systematized. That grounding and a subsequent limited system were soon to emerge.

It was at this time, in the late sixties, that Hick moved to Birmingham. Birmingham had large communities of worshippers who belonged to faiths other than Christianity. He mentions specifically the Muslim, Sikh, Hindu and Jewish communities. The challenge of different revelations, religions and faiths became "a live and immediate one."[9] With friends and colleagues in all these non-Christian religious communities, Hick occasionally would attend worship in a mosque or synagogue, a temple or gurdwara. His observation was that in these various places of worship, that essentially the same kind of thing was taking place as in a Christian church. Human beings were opening their minds to a higher divine Reality. Hick writes:

I could see that the Sikh faith, for instance, is to the devout Sikh what the Christian faith is to the sincere Christian; but that each faith is, naturally enough, perceived by its adherents as being unique and absolute [GHMN,18].

Hick's new awareness was deepened during a year's visit to India and Sri Lanka. His study of Hinduism and Buddhism revealed to Hick

... something of the immense spiritual depth and power of these two oriental religions. Without ever being tempted to become either a Hindu or a Buddhist I could see that within these ancient traditions men and women are savingly related to the eternal Reality from which we all live [GHMN,17-18].

Although Hick was growing in experience, as yet he had not found any intellectual breakthrough into his original question: how can there be many religions each claiming to be the true one?

Then, writes Hick, a "valuable clue" was given to him. It came from his reading of *The Meaning and End of Religion* by Wilfred Cantwell Smith.[10] He found convincing Cantwell Smith's critique of the concept of "a religion" and of the notion of religions as contraposed sociotheological communities. Hick's conclusion was that

> ... the religious life of mankind [is] a continuum within which the faith-life of individuals is conditioned by one or other of the different streams of cumulative tradition. From this point of view it is not appropriate to ask, Which is the true religion? For a true relationship to God may occur in the lives of people in each of the great religious traditions [GHMN,18].[11]

With this new insight Hick found he could dismantle the problem in its older and insoluble form. Now it was possible to develop the idea of a "Copernican revolution" in the theology of religions. This task Hick undertook in *God and the Universe of Faiths*. I will have more to say about this Copernican revolution later in this Chapter. In brief, it consisted in "a paradigm shift from a Christianity-centered or Jesus-centered model to a God-centered model of the universe of faiths" [GHMN,18]. From the vantage point of this theological revolution, it was now possible to see

> ... the great world religions as different human responses to the one divine Reality, embodying different perceptions which have been formed in different historical and cultural circumstances [GHMN,19].

This paradigm shift in theology necessarily involves, continues Hick, a reopening of the Christological question of Jesus' uniqueness. The reason why Christianity claimed a uniqueness for itself was because of the uniqueness of its founder. Hick explains:

For if Jesus was literally God incarnate, the second Person of the holy Trinity living a human life, so that the Christian religion was founded by God-on-earth in person, it is then very hard to escape from the traditional view that all mankind must be converted to the Christian faith [GHMN,19].

But if Christianity were not the one true religion (since there can be no one true religion), then perhaps Jesus was not unique in the way He has been traditionally understood. It is according to this route that Hick's reflections on world religions led to the Copernican revolution, which in turn brought him to completely reexamine Christology, provide it with a new foundation, and place it within a larger systematic understanding of a global theology of religions.

With the Copernican revolution in place, Hick could now seriously propose an alternative understanding of the identity of Jesus. This alternative view argues that the idea of divine incarnation is to be understood metaphorically rather than literally. The notion of divine incarnation is an essentially poetic expression of the Christian's devotion to his/her Lord. As such, so the argument continues, it should not be treated as a metaphysical truth from which to draw further conclusions. Specifically, one should not conclude from Jesus' "incarnation" that God's saving activity is confined to the single thread of human history documented in the Christian bible.

Hick found support for his new interpretation of Jesus' identity from modern scholarship. He singles out, and we shall treat them in detail later, contemporary investigations of Christian origins, New Testament criticism and patristic studies.[12]

Hick began discussing his new ideas about "divine incarnation" with colleagues. Soon a group of like-minded scholars were meeting for occasional discussions. The result was the controversial book, *The Myth of God Incarnate*, 1977. He writes that the intention of this book was

... to bring the idea of divine incarnation, which had long been something of a shibboleth in British church circles, back into the light of rational discussion [GHMN,19].[13]

Hick's horizons still continued to expand. We have seen that his interest in Christology stemmed from his concern with world religions, not *vice versa*. It is not surprising then, that subsequent to *The Myth of God Incarnate*, Hick should take up the project of developing the global theology of world religions which he had begun in *God and the Universe of Faiths*. A global theology of religions, writes Hick,

> ... would consist of theories or hypotheses designed to interpret the religious experience of mankind as it occurs not only within Christianity but also within the other great streams of religious life ... [GHMN,21].

Hick recognizes that such a project is vast. It requires the collaboration of many individual scholars and groups of experts over a period of several generations. Inter-religious dialogue will remain basic to such an undertaking. Out of it may come the needed comparative and constructive studies. Hick considers his own work, *Death and Eternal Life*, which came out in the same year as *The Myth of God Incarnate*, to be one such comparative study. That book is, he writes:

> ... intended as a Christian contribution to a global theology of death, exploring both the differences and the deeper convergences of insight on this subject between Christianity, Hinduism, and Buddhism [GHMN,22].

In his subsequent works Hick has continued to address the challenge posed by pluralism to a theology of world religions, and to refine and answer objections to his Christology. These smaller works, *God Has Many Names*, 1982 and *Problems of Religious Pluralism*, 1985 were preparatory for *An Interpretation of Religion*, 1989.[14]

Hicks' reflections then moved into the area of pluralism. One of the important issues to which he gave his attention was the effect that a pluralistic or global view of religions has upon one's—in particular the Christian's—understanding of and relationship to his/her own tradition. Hick poses the question from his own experience:

> However imperfectly (and in fact very imperfectly) this is reflected in my own life, I feel irrevocably challenged and

claimed by the impact of the life and teaching of Jesus; and to be thus decisively influenced by him is, I suppose, the basic definition of a Christian. How then is my Christian faith changed by acceptance of the salvific character of the other world religions [GHMN,26]?

For the Christian who has not undergone the Copernican revolution, such a question may seem heretical. For as Hick has noted, it questions the traditional faith about the identity of Jesus. For at the centre of Christianity

... is the conviction that Jesus of Nazareth was God—the second Person of a divine Trinity living a human life. It follows from this that Christianity, and Christianity alone, was founded by God in person on the only occasion on which he has ever become incarnate in this world, so that Christianity has a unique status as the way of salvation provided and appointed by God himself [GHMN,26].

The only solution for the Christian who cannot rethink the identity of Jesus, is not to accept real pluralism among all religions. That is, according to Hick, such Christians are bound to accept that adherents to faiths other than Christianity will not be saved. But, he argues,

... in the light of our accumulated knowledge of the other great world faiths this conclusion has become unacceptable to all except a minority of dogmatic diehards. For it conflicts with our concept of God, which we have received from Jesus, as the loving heavenly Father of *all* mankind; could such a Being have restricted the possibility of salvation to those who happen to have been born in certain countries in certain periods of history [GHMN,27]?

One is inevitably brought back, argues Hick, to the fundamental question of the identity of Jesus. This question is the important effect that the challenge of religious pluralism presents to the Christian's relationship to his/her own tradition. The traditional teaching that

Jesus is God the Son Incarnate must be reexamined. It is this reexamination which constitutes Hick's Christology and which is the topic of this work. Hick considers this reinterpretation of the doctrine of Jesus' Incarnation as vitally necessary, if the Christian wishes to participate in the religiously plural world as it moves into the twenty-first century.

Conclusion

In providing this account of Hick's intellectual development, I wish to indicate in what ways that development provides a context for his Christology. Three important observations can be made. First, Hick's Christology *results* from and is *not* the starting for his theology of world religions. Second, his theology was directly occasioned by his own religious experience as well as his social experience of meeting people of other faiths. Third, his theological reflections are shaped by conclusions he reached in his philosophy of religion.

The first observation means that Hick will submit his Christology to the conclusions of a phenomenology of worship in other religions. That is, given that all worshippers seem to be doing the same thing, any claim by any religion that it is doing something unique is simply a narrow view. Since Christianity's claim to uniqueness depends directly on its claims about the uniqueness of Christ, it follows that the need to reinterpret the identity of Jesus is vital.

The second observation reveals that Hick opts for individual experience over ecclesial experience.[15] The former (assuming sanity) is valid; the latter is highly suspect. There is no room for personal religious experience to be interpreted, validated or corrected by the wider ecclesial experience. Rather, the process is *vice versa*. Therefore, since traditional Christology depends on ecclesial experience, Christology will have to be corrected to meet the demands of personal and cultural experience.

The third observation indicates that when there is a conflict between his philosophy and traditional Christian theology, it is the latter that will have to be reexamined.

Having completed our presentation of Hick's intellectual development as a context for his Christology, we can now proceed to our next section. In it I will elaborate on Hick's notion of world religions and account for that notion as providing an important context for his Christology.

Hick's Notion of World Religions

In Chapter 1 there appeared a section on world religions. There it was stated which world religions were referred to in our title, and what role they played in our study. In this present Chapter we are exploring the context of Hick's Christology. To aid us in this task, we must now explicate Hick's understanding both of world religions and of the nature of religion itself. For Hick, Christianity is a valid expression of revealed religion, and as such it is subject to the same cultural forces in its origin and later development as are the other world religions. We begin our study first with Hick's analysis of the nature of religion itself. Then we present his account of what are world religions and how they came to be. Hick elaborates on his notions of religion and world religions in the third chapter, "God Has Many Names," in the book of the same title [GHMN,40-59]. We structure our presentation around that Chapter.

The Nature of Religion

The nature of religion and the nature of man are closely linked. Hick suggests that a reasonable definition of man is to stipulate

... that the evolving stream of hominid life had become man from the point—wherever this is to be located in the time sequence— at which a religious animal had emerged [GHMN,43].

Religion itself involves at least some "dim sense of the divine, expressed in religious practices" [GHMN,43].

It "involves an essential reference to the transcendent" [GHMN,120]. That is why Hick will speak of religion as "transcendent theism" [GUF,13]. In *God and the Universe of Faiths*, Hick gives the following working definition of religion:

[Religion is] an understanding of the universe, together with an appropriate way of living within it, which involves reference beyond the natural world to God or gods or to the Absolute or to

35

a transcendent order or process [GUF,134].[16]

In *God Has Many Names* Hick understands "a religion" to be a "complex totality" including such things as the religious community's foundational experience and image or images of God, its religious myths, symbols, theologies, art, ethics, life-styles, scriptures and particular traditions [GHMN,53].[17] All these elements interact with each other. Each religion is thus one of the varying human responses, within a culture, to the same infinite transcendent divine reality [GHMN, 53-54]. This transcendent reality Hick frequently refers to as the Eternal One.[18]

Religion and religions begin to emerge in recorded history, says Hick, between 3,000 B.C. and 2,000 B.C. Man's primitive religion was intimately linked with his social organization. He was aware of himself only as part of a social organism. A self-conscious individuality had not as yet emerged. The group mentality predominated, but that group mentality "was suffused by an awareness of the supernatural" [GHMN,43]. There was an immense variety of tribal gods and spirits. These gods and spirits in many cases personified the forces of nature. Alongside the gods, there were also "ancestors and legendary figures exalted to a divine or quasi-divine status" [GHMN,43]. In some cases primitive man expressed an awareness of a "High God, dwelling remotely in the skies" [GHMN,43]. Hick points out that these early forms of religious consciousness were "extremely dim and crude" [GHMN,43].

With their "crudities and cruelties" primitive religions are for Hick, expressions of "natural religion" [MGI,180]. The two main civilizations in which natural religion emerges are Mesopotamia in the Near East and the Indus valley of northern India [GUF,134]. Hick defines natural religion as "religion without revelation" [GHMN,44], or as a "prerevelational phase" [GHMN,45] in the religious history of mankind. Hence, in the Near East and India, these initial religious expressions represent the beginning and growth of religion "prior to any special intrusions of divine revelation or illumination" [GUF,134]. In natural religion the gods are to be feared and placated. Religious practices are designed to take advantage of the gods' good will or to avoid their anger. The moral demands of natural religion are simply those of the social organism of the tribe to ensure its survival or victory in warfare. In times of danger the gods can be propitiated with human sacrifice. Natural religion thus had its "terrible and savage aspects" in addition to celebrating the tribe's "cohesion and its security" [GHMN,44].

An important aspect of natural religion to which Hick draws our attention, is that "the Eternal One was reduced in human awareness to the dimensions of man's own image" [GHMN,44]. The gods simply reflected dimensions of the human beings who worshipped them, or dimensions of the tribe or nation, or of the cosmic forces of nature. The main geographic areas where natural religion was practiced, says Hick, were Africa, South America, Australasia and the South Sea Islands.

In summary, there is in man's nature a "natural religious tendency" [GHMN,44]—"the innate religiousness of the human mind" [GHMN,70]—that enables him to have a "dim and crude sense of the Eternal One" [GHMN,44]. Prior to revealed religion, this natural or innate tendency gave rise to what Hick calls "natural religion."

The Religious Interpretation of Religion

Before presenting Hick's account of the revealed religions, we must treat one other point about religion itself. Is or is not the object of religious worship and contemplation a creation of the human imagination?[19] It is not within the scope of our paper to present Hick's in-depth analysis of this issue. However, it is important for us to know where he finally situates himself.

Hick states that one can interpret the phenomenon of religion either naturalistically or religiously. The naturalistic interpretation holds that man has created the gods in his own image; they are projections of human hopes and fears. Hick mentions such alternative versions of this interpretation as those of Feuerbach, Marx and Freud.

Hick himself opts for the "religious interpretation" of religion [GHMN,42]. This interpretation of religion, while acknowledging the natural religious tendency of man, understands that tendency to be the "human response to a transcendent divine Reality which is other than us" [GHMN,42]. Religion, then, could be said to represent

... a range of responses to reality—even if variously inadequate responses—rather than being pure projection or illusion [GHMN,89].[20]

Nevertheless, Hick does not completely reject the naturalistic interpretation. He recognizes "an important element of truth in the projection theories" [GHMN,42]. But he subsumes this truth "within an account of our pluralistic human awareness of God."

Is natural religion, then, simply as Hick earlier defined it, "religion without revelation?" If it is, then it can be explained by the naturalistic interpretation. But Hick does not accept the naturalistic interpretation as the operative understanding of the nature of religion. Therefore, for natural religion to be validly interpreted by the religious interpretation, there must be at least some divine revelation even at this level. And so there is. But Hick says that it is a matter of proportion. In the primitive expressions of natural religion, there was much human projection and little divine disclosure [GHMN,44].

In the expressions of natural religion, then, there was "no startlingly challenging impact of the Eternal One upon the human spirit" [GHMN,45]. Revelation was a "minimum presence and pressure." Hick says it is true that the

... innumerable gods and spirits and demons were essentially projections, made possible by the innate religious character of the human mind [GHMN,45].

This is the part of the projection theories that Hick accepts. Yet all this primitive projection in turn constituted primitive man's response to the "dim sense of the Eternal One" which he experienced.

The Origin of World Religions

Religion, for Hick, as we have seen above, involves at least some sense of the divine. Natural religion, "religion without revelation," is mostly a form of projection grounded in man's natural religious instinct. But what are the world religions? Are they simply larger, more sophisticated versions of primitive natural religion?

While Hick does not use the term "supernatural religion," he does distinguish "natural religion" from "the great world faiths." He writes:

We must thus be willing to see God at work within the total religious life of mankind, challenging men in their state of 'natural religion', with all its crudities and cruelties, by the tremendous revelatory moments which lie at the basis of the great world faiths [MGI,180].[21]

What distinguishes natural religions from the great world religions are the "tremendous revelatory moments" which inaugurate the latter. Thus, when Hick speaks of "religions" or "world religions" or "world faiths," he is not referring to any of the manifestations of "natural religion." The world religions all have God's free revelation at their centre as the cause of their existence. Nevertheless, between natural religions and world religions there is a relationship. The former, "at best childish and at worst appallingly brutal and bloodthirsty" functioned as the "womb out which the higher religions were to be born" [GHMN,44]. They functioned as the womb for two reasons: (1) "in virtue of the natural religious tendency of their nature" [GHMN,44],[22] and (2) because the social organism of the tribe slowly evolved to the point where conditions "for the emergence of human individuality" were formed [GHMN,45].

Hick bases his own understanding of the emergence of world religions on Karl Jaspers' notion of the "axial period."[23] In his book *The Origin and Goal of History*, Jaspers has identified the centuries from about 800 BC to about 200 BC as the axial age or axial period.[24] During this time, writes Hick,

... outstanding individuals emerged and were able to be channels of new religious awareness and understanding—in traditional theological terms, of divine revelation. From their work there have flowed what we know today as the great world faiths [GHMN,47].[25]

These significant human individuals freely responded to the Eternal One, though adds Hick, "always within the existing setting of their own cultures" [GHMN,45]. By their response, these individuals immensely enlarged and developed man's awareness of the divine.[26]

39

The axial period, writes Hick, is "a uniquely significant band of time in man's religious history" [GHMN,46]. This is so because, with the obvious qualifications, all the major world religions have their roots here, and nothing comparable in the religious life of man has since occurred. Further, what distinguishes the axial period from other "concentrations of events," e.g., the Renaissance or the Industrial Revolution, is that the latter occurred within a culture, whereas the former was world wide and transcultural.

Why, we might ask, did the axial period occur at all? We have already indicated the answer. It has to do with "revelation." During the phase of natural religion man had not developed to the point where the Eternal One could make a significant self-revelation.[27] But once such development had been reached, man was ready

> ... to receive and respond to a new and much fuller vision of the divine reality and of the claim of that reality upon his life. Such a breakthrough is traditionally called revelation, ... [GHMN,48].

Revelation, for Hick, consists in the Eternal One pressing in on the human spirit [GUF,135], seeking to be known and responded to by the human person. The purpose of such "pressing in" is salvation. Hick writes that the

> ... great business of religion is salvation, the bringing of men and women to fullness of life or perfection of being in relation to the Eternal One [GHMN,57].

In this new revelation of the axial period, the Eternal One was able in a fuller way to attempt "to create the human animal into (in our Judeo-Christian language) a child of God, or toward a perfected humanity" [GHMN,48].

This axial revelation was in fact plural. It was not just *one* single revelation. The main reason that Hick gives for the plurality of revelation is that of communications. The cultures of India, China and the Near East at that time had at best tenuous and slow lines of communication between them. He writes:

A divine revelation intended for all mankind but occurring in China, or in India, or in Israel would have taken many centuries to spread to the other countries ... From this point of view it seems natural that the revelation should have been plural, occurring separately in the different centres of human culture [GHMN,48; cf.MGI,180; GUF,137].

According to Hick, then, two elements are involved in the constitution of a world religion: (1) the new revelation of the Eternal One during the axial period, (2) a free response, given usually by an individual, but which response subsequently by means of disciples blossoms into a major religion. Hence, because of (1), Hick will sometimes refer to the world religions as world "revelations" [GHMN,17].[28] Because of (2), he may refer to them as world "traditions" [GHMN,18; MGI,181], or world "faiths" [GUF,viii]. Because there has been no one single revelation according to Hick, he also will speak of world religions as "varying forms" of revelation or "various ways" in which God has affected human consciousness [MGI,180,181]. Both elements are found in the following description wherein Hick defines the great world religions as "different human responses to the one divine Reality, embodying different perceptions which have been formed in different historical and cultural circumstances" [GHMN,18-19].

Conclusion

In what way does the context of Hick's notion of world religions relate to our topic? For Hick, world religions are culturally-conditioned human responses to God's revelation.[29] Since there has not been a *singular* revelation, but a *plural* one, Hick contends that no one religion can claim to be the true religion. For a true relationship to God may occur in each of the great religious traditions. Consequently, argues Hick, the doctrine of Jesus' Incarnation should not be understood such that God's saving activity is confined to the single thread of human history known as Christianity. The Christian can no longer maintain that the Logos has acted in the life of only Jesus [MGI,181]. Hence, the Christological question of the identity of Christ must be reexamined, argues Hick. God's particular revelation in Jesus "saving-

41

ly concerns the Christian" [MGI,181]. But God's other particular revelations savingly concern those who adhere to the other world religions. All the major world religious traditions "are savingly related to the eternal Reality from which we all live" [GHMN,18]. Therefore, Hick concludes:

> I cannot then, as a Christian, solve the problem of religious pluralism by holding that my own religion is a response to the divine reality but that the others are merely human projections [GHMN,90].

If any one world faith declares itself to be the only true revelation of the way to salvation, it is in effect saying that the all-loving God who desires all His children be saved, has in fact declared, that only those who by some accident happen to have been born into "one particular thread of human history," (their own), are eligible for that salvation [MGI,180]. This view is no longer acceptable, argues Hick.

It is here that we come up against the phenomenon of each of the world religions claiming different, even conflicting things, about the God who savingly relates to them. Hick asks:

> Can the Eternal One be at once the Adonai of Judaism, the Father of Jesus Christ, the Allah of Islam, the Krishna and the Shiva of theistic Hinduism, the Brahman of advaitic Hinduism, the Dharmakaya or the Sunyata of Mahayana Buddhism, and the Nirvana of theravada Buddhism [GHMN,24]?

Keeping this question in mind, we leave this section of our discussion and move to the next.

Hick's Epistemology of Religion

From Hick's discussion of the nature of world religions, we saw that the plurality of world religions results from the varying cultural responses to the revelation of God or the Eternal One who invites His children to salvation. Given Hick's religious interpretation of religion, it is clear that this plurality of religions is not due to the fact that the faiths of the great religious traditions are mere projections of human hopes and fears. Faith results from a genuine, and not a supposed, divine initiative. This interpretation would be tidy, of course, if all the world religions agreed on what they said about the transcendent Reality and the nature of the salvation God offers.

But Hick is aware of the conspicuous difficulty of the very different and apparently conflicting reports about God and salvation issuing from the different religious traditions.

One solution to the different truth-claims would be the radical one of claiming that religious language does not and cannot say anything about what in fact is. It cannot reach truth. Hick rejects this solution. Instead, he opts for the "basic cognitive character of religious experience" [GHMN,24].[30] The "cognitive character" of religious experience is what Hick calls faith. He writes:

> What we call faith is the interpretive element in the religious way of experiencing the world and our lives within it. And faith is an act of cognitive freedom and responsibility [GHMN,50].[31]

In opting for the cognitive character of faith, or of religious experience, Hick is opting for the cognitive character of religious language. In particular, he opts for the cognitivist position regarding the distinctive use of religious language. He distinguishes three kinds of religious language. There are: (1) a core of distinctively or properly religious statements that make cognitive truth-claims about God, about the "metaphysical surplus," e.g., "God was at work in Jesus Christ," (2) various non-cognitive or mythological assertions that "revolve" around the core, e.g., "Jesus of Nazareth was God-become-man" and (3) historical, religious statements which represent "aspects of religious meaning" but which are not distinctively religious in character, e.g., "Christians believe that Jesus was divine."

Our concern here is with the first type, that is, with the distinctive or proper use of religious langauge. The problem is that there is no agreement on how to determine the truth-value of such statements. One could resolve the problem of the conflicting truth-claims about God which issue from the world religions, by claiming that this distinctive use of religious language is not cognitive. Hence, there would be no conflict at the level of truth. But if one accepts, as does Hick, that the distinctive use of religious language is cognitive, then how does one solve the problem of conflicting truth-claims? Is the only available option that of either (a) claiming one religion to be true and all the others equally, or in varying degrees, false, or (b) claiming that each religion is subjectively true for its own adherents, but none is probably true? The former option, says Hick, would imply "that God has revealed himself to mankind in a remarkably limited and ineffective way." The latter would amount to "religious suicide" [GUF,17]. Neither solution is acceptable to Hick.

Kant Grounds Hick's Solution

Hick says the solution to the problem of conflicting truth-claims among religions begins with a distinction. The important distinction to draw is that between "transcendent reality *an sich* and as it is experienced by human beings" [GHMN,83]. Hick explains that the distinction is between

> ... the Eternal One in itself, in its eternal self-existent being, beyond relationship to a creation, and the Eternal One in relation to mankind and as perceived from within our different human cultural situations [GHMN,52; cf.24,83].

The Eternal One in itself, *an sich*, is the "divine noumenon." The Eternal One as experienced by human beings in various cultures is "the range of divine phenomena witnessed to by the religious history of mankind," and which divine phenomena "take both theistic and nontheistic forms" [GHMN,83,110].[32]

It is not surprising that Hick states forcefully that his whole epistemology of religion "hinges upon the Kantian distinction between reality as it is in itself and that same reality as it is experienced by human beings" [GHMN,67].[33] Hick states that Kant is difficult to interpret because of the "several different strands of argument" he employs in the *Critique of Pure Reason*. Hick writes:

> The strand that I shall be using is the distinction between phenomenon and noumenon, but transposed from the problem of sense perception to that of the awareness of God [GHMN,104].

Hick accepts Kant's distinction between the noumenal world "which exists independently of and outside man's perception of it," and the phenomenal world which is the noumenal world as it appears to human consciousness [GHMN,105]. All that can be said about the noumenal world is that it is the "unknown reality whose informational input produces, in collaboration with the human mind, the phenomenal world of our experience" [GHMN,105].

Just as all our conscious experience of the environment is done by a selecting and integrating mind, so too suggests Hick, does this same pattern apply to our conscious experience of the divine. We are not directly aware of the divine reality as it is in itself. We experience it only from a distinctly human view. Inevitably, our awareness is partial, limited, finite, imperfect. Hick writes:

> We "see through a glass, darkly;" and the glass is constituted by the set of human concepts operating within our cultures. The result is the range of ways of conceiving and experiencing the divine to be found within the history of religions [GHMN,67].

Grounding himself in Kant, Hick summarizes his basic position on the existence of conflicting truth-claims among the world religions:

> ... we may distinguish between, on the one hand, the single divine noumenon, the Eternal One in itself, transcending the scope of human thought and language, and, on the other hand, the plurality of divine phenomena, the divine *personae* of the theistic religions and the concretizations of the concept of the Absolute in the nontheistic religions [GHMN,53].[34]

The world religions' truth-claims are cognitive because they say something true about the self-revealing Eternal One. They conflict because they say something true, not about the Eternal One in Himself, but about the Eternal One in relation to the world. Hence, we have the resultant plurality of *personae* and concretizations.

Because the *personae* are only images or pictures of God, the many *personae* do not indicate a plurality of gods or divine beings. Rather, the different *personae* are formed

> ... in the interaction of divine presence and human projection. The divine presence is the presence of the Eternal One to our finite human consciousness, and the human projections are the culturally conditioned images and symbols in terms of which we concretize the basic concepts of deity [GHMN,53].

Hence, to answer the question at the conclusion of the first section of this Chapter: Yes, Hick would say, the Eternal One can be at once the Yahweh of Israel, the Allah of Islam, the Brahman of advaitic Hinduism, etc. [GHMN,66-7].[35] In fact, the Eternal One is all of these because these are only *personae* or phenomenon of the inscrutable noumenon, which is Himself beyond any relationship with the world. Each of these phenomena are part of a wider complex, including religious myths, symbols, theologies, which constitute a religion. Hick believes that the theistic and the nontheistic forms of religious experience

> ... exhibit a common epistemological structure ... The broad differences between these [world religious] traditions, and between their different images of the eternal One, arise from the broad differences between human cultures ... [GHMN,86-87].

It may be helpful to provide a specific example at this point. Hick says that the Hebrews, in their religious experience of the Eternal One's relationship with them, formed the image or *persona* of Him as "Yahweh." Yahweh is a part of their history and they are a part of His. Hick continues: "But Yahweh is different from, say, Krishna, who is a distinctively Hindu *persona* of the Eternal One in relation to the Vaishnavite community of India" [GHMN,25].

The concrete concept or notion of God, is not of God in Himself, but of God in relation to a particular human community. Any concept of God is then "a specific divine *persona* or face or image or icon of the Eternal One" [GHMN,52]. Yahweh of Israel is one such *persona*. He exists in relationship with the people of Israel. He cannot be abstracted from this historical relationship, nor characterized except within that relationship. As such a divine *persona*, Yahweh

... represents a genuine, authentic, valid human perception of the Eternal One from within a particular human culture and strand of history [GHMN,53].

Both Yahweh and Krishna each are the Eternal One as experienced as concretely personal by and in relation to a different human community.[36] Hick's overall conclusion is, employing his "summarizing slogan," that "God Has Many Names." He writes:

... this pluralistic situation [of world religions] is rendered intelligible by the hypothesis of one infinite divine noumenon experienced in varying ways within different strands of human history, thereby giving rise to different divine personalities who are each formed in their interactions with a particular community or tradition [GHMN,109].[37]

Hick, as we have seen, wishes to distinguish between God and the images or *personae* or icons or concepts of God. Since the term "image" will recur in Hick's Christology, it may be helpful here to ask what Hick means by an "image" of God. He defines an image as that which "represents data molded into concrete forms by the imagination" [GHMN,96].

On the secular level, he says that partial analogies can be found for this kind of image in the work of historians. Different historians can give different impressions of the same individual who lived in the past. These impressions are what Hick calls "images." These images may vary not only among historians, but from one age to the next. There may exist oversimplified images, even caricatures, in the popular imagination. For example, among the historical people to whom all this applies would be Mary Queen of Scots, Stalin, Napoleon. Hick writes:

In such cases the distinction seems inevitable between the historical individual *an sich* and the images in terms of which he or she has become known to later consciousness [GHMN,96].

Wishing to move closer towards the notion of "image of God," Hick refers to images (that is to personalities and not to physical impressions) of saints, specifically Mary, within Catholic spirituality. "Mary, mother of Jesus" appears as "Our Lady of Lourdes," "Our Lady of Fatima," "Our Lady of Walsingham," etc. If, says Hick, we assume that Mary is a personal being in heaven yet still concerned with human affairs, then

> ... we are led to distinguish between Mary herself and a variety of partially different human images of her. It does not, however, necessarily follow from the fact of their plurality that these images are false. The alternative possibility is that they arise from genuine encounters with Mary in which, as she has met the varying needs of different individuals and communities, different images of her have legitimately been formed [GHMN,99].

Hick continues the supportive evidence for his analogy by referring to the different images within Christianity of Christ.
Hick writes:

> He [Christ] has, for example, been perceived, or imaged, or responded to as God incarnate; as a human teacher of the fatherhood of God and the brotherhood of man; as an apocalyptic preacher of the imminent end of history; as "gentle Jesus meek and mild"; as a social radical proclaiming that the lowly are to be exalted and the mighty brought down; as the "man for others," the embodiment of self-giving love; and of course as various mixtures of these. Different popular images of Jesus are expressed in the growing number of interpretations of him in films and rock operas [GHMN,98].

It is clear from all these different images of Jesus, says Hick, that the distinction must be maintained between Jesus "the historical individual" and "the plurality of images operating in the minds of different individuals and groups and communal traditions" [GHMN,98].[38]

48

Hick asks the important question: What role is played in religious awareness by the images of God? We have already touched on the reply. The images of God play essentially, but analogously, the same role as that

... played in sense perception by the concepts or recognitional capacities in terms of which we are conscious of the objects and situations constituting our physical environment [GHMN,103].

In short, the "images of God" in Hick's epistemology function as do the categories in Kant's account of human knowing. Hick says that the "religious person experiences the divine, not as a general idea, but under some specific and relatively concrete divine image" [GHMN,105]. Hick's categories or images of religious meaning function within a culture. They make possible and condition the religious phenomenal experience of the divine noumenon. It is this whole range of particular images of the divine, found in the variations of human culture, that

... inform man's actual religious experience, so that it is an experience specifically of the God of Israel, or of Allah, or of the Father of our Lord Jesus Christ, or of Vishnu or Shiva [GHMN,105-6].

Thus, with Kant, but transposed to the area of religious experience, Hick says the mind, by means of categories, makes its own contribution to the meaning experienced in its contact with the perceived environment.

We noted above that Hick says that not every image of God is valid. Only those tested over centuries in the great world religions are reliable. But there remains the question, whether among these images or *personae* or categories, there are some that are more adequate and valuable than others. This is the question of criteria. Do some images or categories mediate God to mankind better than others [GHMN,25-6,114-5]? What are the criteria for deciding; how are these criteria reached?

The objective grounds for making such a judgement, says Hick, will be two: moral grounds and spiritual grounds. As for the moral grounds, it is difficult to come to a decision. Each religion is so multi-form and complex, with periods of great moral teaching and practice, but also with incredible immorality, corruption and violence. Hick concludes when everything is put on the scales, it is "probably impossible" to reach an overall appraisal [GHMN, 55]. In addition, there is the likelihood that in applying moral criteria, one will operate out of the criteria which apply to his own religion. Hence, Hick concludes:

I really think, therefore, that the project of a comparative ethical assessment of the great religious totalities leads into an impossible morass from which nothing useful can emerge [GHMN,55].

What about spiritual grounds as criteria? Is the view that God is non-personal a superior spiritual view than the personalist view of God? Only "confessional assertion" can solve this dilemma, writes Hick. Again, there is no way of making proper judgement on these grounds.

Hick concludes that there are not any objective grounds on which to claim that one particular world religious tradition is superior to any other. Among the great world religions, the only objective criteria for one religion claiming to be the only true religion, would be "its own dogmatic assertion" [GHMN,90].[39]

Hick suggests that the notion of one religion being superior to another be abandoned. In place of "one and only one true religion" there should be adopted the notion of genuine "religious pluralism."[40] That is, instead of one religion being better than others, we ought to see them all as "several *different* forms of human awareness of and response to the Eternal One" [GHMN,56].

The difficulty which Hick sees in all this is that it is much harder for some religions to give up their exclusive claims than others. For example, with the Jewish people there is the notion of their being unique and exclusive because they are "God's Chosen People." Hick suggests that the Jews, without giving up their notion of being chosen, could see that other peoples have been chosen by God to fulfill religious vocations for the salvation of the world as well.

With the Christians it is the notion that their uniqueness is due to the uniqueness of Jesus, who alone is God-Incarnate. Hick's suggestion as to what the Christians have to do leads us into our conclusion.

Conclusion

Hick's epistemology of religion already conditions what will be acceptable to him in Christology. Since that epistemology does not allow for one true religion, then Christianity cannot make any objective claims to be such. Since the Christian theological basis for making such a claim lies with the traditional understanding of Jesus' identity, it follows that that identity must be reexamined. Along with Jews, therefore, Christians must give up any claims to exclusivity, about themselves, about their own particular phenomenal experience of the noumenal God.

The understanding of Jesus as literally God-Incarnate must be wrong, suggests Hick, and therefore, needs to be re-understood. It is wrong if only because it has been misunderstood. It has a truth-value, but it is the kind of truth that applies to mythological language. In this way, Hick believes he has maintained the cognitive truth-value of religious language, and solved the problem of the different truth-claims among world religions. (We shall see how all this specifically applies to his Christology in our next Chapter).

Since God cannot be known in Himself, but only as He relates to a particular historical community, Jesus represents just one of the ways God has so related to the world. Jesus becomes a *persona* of God. What is claimed about Jesus may be true, but it is true at the level of phenomenon, which is plural, and not of noumenon, which is singular. Hick has set up the limit that God could not have become man in the way Christians have traditionally understood Jesus. While what Christians thought about Jesus is appropriate, it is not literally true. (We shall speak of this, too, in greater detail in our next Chapter). Jesus is not unique in any objective manner. He is one of the phenomena of God.

This conclusion of Hick leads us directly to consider the final element in the context of his Christology, namely, the Copernican revolution in theology.

The Copernican Revolution in Theology

In Chapter 1 we encountered the term "theocentric model." There we saw that this term referred to a "God-centered" rather than a

51

"Christ-centered" or a "Church-centered" model for a theology of world religions. In our account of Hick's intellectual development we explained the importance of the "Copernican revolution" in his expanding horizons of thought. It was, in fact, the Copernican revolution that ushered in the theocentric model. At the end of our immediate section above on Hick's epistemology of religion, we saw that Christianity (like other religions) must give up its exclusivist claims to being *the* true religion. This means it must give up its claim to the uniqueness of Jesus Christ and move towards a God-centered theology. In short, argues Hick, Christianity must opt for the Copernican revolution. It is now time that we direct our attention to a presentation of what Hick means by a Copernican revolution for theology.[41]

Why a Copernican Revolution in Theology

In *God and the Universe of Faiths*, Hick presents us with "a fairly considerable process of rethinking" of the issue of the relationship among world religions [GUF,viii]. He takes "the decisive step" away from what he calls

> ... a Ptolemaic (i.e. one's-own-religion centered) to a Copernican (i.e. a God-centered) view of the religious life of mankind [GUF,viii-ix].

In astronomy, the Copernican revolution involved a transformation not only in how men and women understood the universe, but also how they understood their own location within it. The Copernican revolution consisted in a paradigm shift from the ancient, long-standing Ptolemaic dogma that the earth is the centre of the revolving universe to the realization that the sun is at the centre, with all the planets, including the earth, revolving around it.

The Ptolemaic understanding was feasible for a time, at least regarding the stars. However, it was not long before it was observed that the planets' revolutions did not fit such a theory. Remaining true to the traditional understanding, the ancient astronomers did not abandon the basic Ptolemaic scheme. Instead they "added a series of smaller supplementary circles, called epicycles revolving with their centres on the original circles" [GUF,125]. Hence, a planet was understood to move on one of these epicycles as it was revolving on the great circle around the earth. The resulting path of the planet, while more complex, was nearer to the truth of what was observed.

The advantage of the epicycles was that they rendered possible the maintenance of the basic dogma that the earth is the hub of the universe. Theoretically at least, it would be possible to maintain the earth as centre of the universe and to continue indefinitely to add epicycle to epicycle in order to reconcile the basic dogma with the facts. But such an option would become increasingly artificial and burdensome. In fact, it did so. The time came when the scientific mind was ready for the new Copernican conception that the sun, and not the earth, is at the centre. Once the old Ptolemaic view was discarded, it appeared in retrospect to be utterly antiquated and implausible.

Hick argues that what is needed in the theology of religions is a similar "Copernican revolution." Such a "Copernican revolution" will involve

> ... an equally radical transformation in our conception of the universe of faiths and the place of our own religion within it [GUF,131].

Just as there was a Ptolemaic astronomy prior to the Copernican revolution, so too there is a "Ptolemaic theology." The "fixed point" or "controlling assumption" of this Ptolemaic theology "is the principle that outside the church, or outside Christianity, there is no salvation" [GUF,125]. Such a Ptolemaic viewpoint may have been feasible when there was little contact among world faiths. But today with so much awareness, contact, communication and dialogue, the *facts* of the universe of faiths call for changes in the *theory*, i.e., in theology. Instead, like the ancient astronomers, argues Hick, the theologians have simply added one epicycle after another. Theoretically, such manoeuvres could continue indefinitely. Eventually, however, the "epicycle-option" reveals that the whole scheme is artificial, implausible and unconvincing. It then becomes time to reexamine the "controlling assumption." When this occurs, the theological mind is ready for the Copernican revolution. Hick writes that this needed Copernican revolution

... involves a shift from the dogma that Christianity is at the centre to the realization that it is *God* who is at the centre, and that all the religions of mankind, including our own, serve and revolve around him [GUF,131].[42]

Hick is fully aware that he is calling for "a radical displacement of thought" [GUF,131]. This radical displacement, he acknowledges, did not originate with himself. He states that the Copernican revolution was

... boldly advocated in the Conclusions of the Bombay Conference [1964] ... The Conference asked for a shift from an ecclesio-centric to a theocentric understanding of the religions [GUF,131].

Hick continues, however, that the conference failed to carry out the needed revolution "either in its own conclusions or in the published papers" [GUF,131]. Hence, the task still remains to be done. Hick sees his own work as "offering a contribution" to that challenge.

Because he is writing for Christian audiences, Hick speaks of "Ptolemaic Christianity" [GUF,132]. But an important point Hick wishes us to remember is that Ptolemaic theology is not confined to Christianity. As a way of doing theology, it can be operative not only in Christianity but also within Hinduism (Ptolemaic Hinduism), Buddhism, Islam, Jainism or Judaism and so on [GUF,132].

Hick acknowledges for any religion to opt for a Ptolemaic theology is "very natural." However, that is no argument against Ptolemaic theology's fundamental flaw. Hick points out in "a less theological way," that the basic fault in Ptolemaic theology no matter who practices it, is that it "normally depends upon where the believer happens to have been born" [GUF,132; cf.GHMN,37-38].

This latter point is significant for Hick. For how can the Ptolemaic believer remain so entirely confident that to have been born in one (his/her own) particular part of the world, carries with it the privilege of knowing the full religious truth? Hick asks, regarding Christianity, if this is not "some vestige of the imperialism of the Christian West" [GUF,132].[43] The fundamental flaw of any Ptolemaic theology is that it posits its "centre" on the basis of an accident of cultural geography. When this evident fact is not ignored but squarely faced, the Ptolemaic believer may begin to rethink his ancient conviction with all its epicycles.

It remains possible to retain the Ptolemaic point of view; but when we are conscious of its historical relativity we may feel the need for a more sophisticated, comprehensive and globally valid theory [GUF,132].

At this point, the theological mind is ripe for the "Copernican revolution."[44]

Christian Ptolemaic Theology

"Christian Ptolemaic Theology" is the theological view that Christianity is at the centre of the universe of faiths [GUF,125,131]. All the other religions revolve, to one degree or another, around it. In *God Has Many Names* Hick correctly notes that any claim that Christianity makes to being the true or a unique religion among religions, is due to the claimed uniqueness regarding Jesus Christ.[45] The key concept, he says, is that of "divine incarnation." He writes:

There is a direct line of logical entailment from the premise that Jesus was God, in the sense that he was God the Son, the second Person of a divine Trinity, living a human life, to the conclusion that Christianity, and Christianity alone, was founded by God in person; and from this to the further conclusion that God must want all his human children to be related to him through this religion which he has himself founded for us; and then to the final conclusion, drawn in the Roman Catholic dogma "Outside the church, no salvation" and its Protestant missionary equivalent "outside Christianity, no salvation" [GHMN,58].

Because Christianity "has seen itself from the beginning as a way of life and salvation" [GUF,120], the foundational principle in Christian Ptolemaic Theology is, says Hick, the last of the above conclusions: namely, that "outside the church, or outside Christianity

55

there is no salvation" [GUF,125]. Without making any particular reference, Hick notes that this "traditional and deeply entrenched dogma" was formed as early as the third century [GUF,123].[46]

To further support his view that such a principle is foundational in Christian Ptolemaic Theology, Hick refers to documents both from the Roman Catholic and Protestant traditions. From the Roman Catholic tradition he quotes from (1) the papal bull *Unam Sanctam* of Boniface VIII in 1302, and (2) the papal bull *Cantate Domino* of Eugene IV in 1441, in particular from the *Decretum pro Iacobitis* of the Council of Florence, 1438-45.

Within the Protestant tradition, Hick also finds support for Ptolemaic theology's foundational principle. He refers to (1) older missionary statements, and (2) recent statements from fundamental groups, e.g., (a) the Congress on World Mission at Chicago in 1960, (b) the Wheaton Declaration of 1966, and (c) the Frankfurt Declaration of 1970, [GUF,121].

Hick argues that given this foundational principle or "fixed point" in Christian Ptolemaic theology, the conclusion is that all men and women of whatever race or culture, must become Christians if they are to be saved [GUF,120]. However, this conclusion immediately ushers in a contradiction. The problem, as Hick sees it, is that such an understanding contradicts the Christian doctrine of God's universal salvific will.

Because of this inconsistency, modern Christian theologians have been driven, says Hick, to explore new ways of understanding the human religious situation [GUF,123]. But these "new ways," whether Catholic or Protestant, have turned out only to be epicycles added to the ancient Ptolemaic view.

Hick elaborates on five Roman Catholic epicycles and one Protestant epicycle. These epicycles can be listed as follows:

(A) The Roman Catholic epicycles of (1) "invincible ignorance" of Pius IX, 1854; (2) "implicit desire" of the Holy Office, 1949; (3) Vatican II, 1962-5; (4) "anonymous Christianity" of Karl Rahner, 1961; (5) "extraordinary/ordinary ways of salvation" of Hans Kung, 1964. (B) The Protestant epicycle of "post-mortem encounter" or "second chance after death." It is not necessary that we present Hick's critique of each epicycle.[47]

In the end, all the epicycles fail to rescue Christian Ptolemaic theology from the inherent inadequacy of its theory. It is true, says Hick, that these epicycles have served the useful purpose of both acknowledging the traditional dogma of "outside the church or Christianity, there is no salvation," while simultaneously accepting the fact that outside the Church there *is* salvation [GHMN 33-34]. However, these epicycles like those in Ptolemaic astronomy, can only operate as an interim measure. Hick explains:

Although to the ordinary nonecclesiastical mind this [use of theological epicycles] borders on doubletalk, in intention it is a charitable extension of the sphere of grace to people who had formerly been regarded as beyond the pale. As such it can function as a psychological bridge between the no-longer-acceptable older view and the new view which is emerging. But sooner or later we have to get off the bridge on to the other side. We have to make what might be called a Copernican revolution in our theology of religions [GHMN,69].

Hick claims that the epicycles both do not go far enough, and go too far. They do not go far enough because they do not extend to nontheistic faiths such as Buddhism and an important part of Hinduism. (Presumably only theists can have a sincere desire to do God's will). On the other hand, the epicycles go too far. If these "supplementary theories" can come to mean that salvation is a right relationship to the Eternal One as He is as variously understood in the different religious traditions, instead of meaning that everyone must necessarily become Christian, then, writes Hick "it would be time frankly to abandon the original dogma" [GUF,124]. Regardless of the fact that the original use of epicycles in theology was "thoroughly well-intentioned," in the end "they are an anachronistic clinging to the husk of the old doctrine after its substance has crumbled" [MGI,180].

When the last epicycle has been tried, and found wanting, that original dogma, that "controlling assumption" of Christian Ptolemaic theology, is seen to have been "stretched beyond recognition and is due to be replaced" [GUF,130]. It is to be replaced by a Copernican revolution which ushers in a theocentric, as opposed to an Ecclesiocentric or a Christo-centric, model of the theology of world religions [GUF,130-31].

Conclusion

How does Hick's call for a Copernican revolution in theology relate to our topic of the uniqueness of Jesus Christ? A Copernican revolution in theology is central to our study because it necessarily reopens "the Christological question" [GHMN,19]. Hick writes:

> As Christians we have to do justice to our distinctive faith in the uniqueness of Christ as God the Son incarnate. Here we have to ask what sort of language this is. Does the mystery of the incarnation represent a literal or a mythological use of language? If the latter, what is the relation of the idea of incarnation to other religious mythologies [GHMN,38-9]?

We have seen in our presentation of Hick's intellectual development, that the Copernican revolution requires a readjustment in the Christian's appropriation of his own tradition. Specifically, it forces one to reconsider the Christological doctrine regarding the identity of Christ. This is, Hick writes, "the most difficult of all issues for a christian theology of religions." Hick continues:

> But before adopting the new picture [God-centred model] a Christian must be satisfied that his devotion to Jesus as his personal Lord and Saviour is not thereby brought into question or its validity denied [GUF,148].

The "fixed point" in Christian Ptolemaic theology, that "Outside the Church or Christianity there is no salvation" is becoming unacceptable to increasing numbers of Christians. This is so because it is seen to be "untrue to the evident religious facts" [GHMN,58; cf GUF,148]. But this Ptolemaic position rests ultimately on the first principle that Jesus is God Incarnate. Therefore, argues Hick, we have to question that original premise.

At this point we complete our treatment of the significant issues that form the context of Hick's Christology. We are now able in our next Chapter to present his arguments for reinterpreting the uniqueness of Jesus Christ in the theocentric model of the Christian theology of world religions.

Endnotes

1. The basis of this presentation of Hick's intellectual development is his own account given in *God Has Many Names*, "A Spiritual Journey," 13-28. There Hick provides us with a "religious autobiography" [GHMN,14]. His purpose is to enable the reader to appreciate the kind of problematic theology he is engaged in. We also draw on other autobiographical material recorded in his works.

I mention here as well three short books, written by Hick, which trace in summary fashion his intellectual development. These books are aimed at the popular level. The first, *Christianity at the Centre*, 1968, is "a statement of a central position for those who like myself [Hick], are not satisfied either by reactionary conservatism or by the new radical interpretations" [Preface]. In this book there is a section titled "Jesus of Nazareth as God's Love Incarnate," 31-40. In it Hick argues for the replacement of *homoousios* with *homoagape*. The second book, *The Centre of Christianity*, 1977, is a revised edition of the first. The change of the title reflects the development in Hick's thought, from an ecclesio-centrism to a Christo-centrism involving a wide gulf between Jesus and the Church. Hick replaces the above-mentioned section with one titled "Was Jesus unique?," 26-33. Hick argues, on the basis of his reexamination of the language of Jesus' Incarnation, that Jesus is not unique in the way traditional theology has understood Him. The third and revised edition is again retitled, *The Second Christianity*, 1983. The Christological sections remain, and a section in the second edition on Christianity and world religions is now expanded to chapter status, titled "Christianity and Other Religions," 76-92. The "second" Christianity, in distinction from the "first," is "not the tribal religion of one section of humanity over against the rest, but rather one way amongst others of living out our common humanity in relation to a divine Presence which grasps us all" [Preface]. Here it is clear Hick is now fully theocentric.

2. It is not our intention to pursue the tangent of Hick's philosophy of religion. In a later section in this Chapter, which treats of Hick's

epistemology of religion, we present a brief understanding of his philosophical framework in as much as it has direct bearing on the outcome of his Christological thinking.

3. For summaries of some of Hick's points, see also: (1) "God, Evil and Mystery." *Religious Studies*, 3, 2 (April 1968): 539-546; (2) "The Problem of Evil in the First and Last Things." *Journal of Theological Studies*, N.S. XIX, Part 2 (October 1968): 591-602; (3) "Freedom and the Irenaean Theodicy Again," *Journal of Theological Studies*, XXI, Part 2 (October 1970): 419-22; (4) "Coherence and the Love of God Again," *Journal of Theological Studies*, N.S. XXIV, Part 2 (October 1973): 522-8; (5) "An Irenaean Theodicy, " in Stephen T. Davis, ed., *Encountering Evil: live options in theodicy* (Atlanta: John Knox Press, 1981): 39-68 (including critiques and response).

4. Hick also articulates his argument of "epistemic distance" in the two articles: (1) "Faith and Coercion," *Philosophy*, XLII, 161 (July 1967): 272-23; (2) "Faith, Evidence, Coercion Again," *Australasian Journal of Philosophy*, 49, 1 (May 1971): 78-81.

5. Jason provides a careful and insightful account of Hick's intellectual development in the realm of Christology during these years, (Jason, "A Critical Examination ...," 20-65). Beginning with Hick's "The Christology of D. M. Baillie," *Scottish Journal of Theology*, 11, 1 (March 1958): 1-12, Jason records Hick's critique of Baillie's adoptionist Christology.

Hick's "A Non-Substance Christology?," *The Colgate-Rochester Divinity School Bulletin* (May 1959): 41-54, later titled "Christology at the Cross Roads," in F. G. Healey, ed., *Prospect for Theology* (London: James Nisbet, 1966): 137-66, argues against a degree Christology. This article appears in part as Chapter 11, "Christ and Incarnation," in John Hick *God and the Universe of Faiths: Essays in the Philosophy of Religion* (New York: St. Martin's, 1973): 148-64.

In 1969, Jason says that Hick reached a watershed in his thought with the H. G. Wood inaugural lecture he gave on October 31, 1967, "Theology's Central Problem," in which Hick argues that Christian religious belief needs to be rationalized. This article appears as Chapter 1 in *God and the Universe of Faiths*, 1-17.

It was the following year that Hick broke with credal orthodoxy with his two-part argument intended to initiate the rationalizing process he had earlier called for: "The Reconstruction of Christian Belief for Today and Tomorrow: 1" and "...:2," *Theology*, LXXIII, 602 (August 1970): 339-45, and 603 (September 1970): 399-405. In these articles Hick comes out against the traditional understanding of the uniqueness of Jesus Christ. These articles appear as Chapter 7 in *God and the Universe of Faiths*, 92-107.

6. John Hick, *Christianity at the Centre*. (London: S.C.M., 1968), 10. It would appear as well that Hick is writing about himself, "Theological Table-Talk," *Theology Today*, XIX, 3 (October 1962): 402-11, in his account of a dispute within the Presbyterian Church about a minister not affirming the doctrine of the virgin birth..

7. Hick claimed his position was a faithful alternate interpretation of *homoousios*, "Christology at the Cross Roads," in F. G. Healey, ed., *Prospect ...*, 137-66. This article originally appeared under the title "A Non-Substance Christology?" *op. cit.*, 41-54.

8. Indeed, Hick would consider even his present position "an expansion rather than a reversal" [GUF, ix] of his earlier thinking within credal orthodoxy.

9. See also Hick: (1) "Practical Reflections of a Theologian," *The Expository Times*, in series "Living in a Multi-cultural Society: XI," LXXXIX, 4 (1978): 100-4; (2) "Pluralism and the Reality of the Transcendent," *The Christian Century*, in series "How My Mind Has Changed," XCVIII, 2 (January 21 1981): 45-8. This latter article forms part of Chapter 1 of Hick, *God Has Many Names*.

10. Wilfred Cantwell Smith, *The Meaning and End of Religion: A New Approach to the Religious Traditions of Mankind* (New York: Macmillan, 1963; reissued, San Francisco: Harper & Row, 1978).

11. This point was originally made by Hick shortly after reading Cantwell Smith, in part two of his significant two-part argument for the rationalization of Christian belief: "The Reconstruction of Christian Belief for Today and Tomorrow: 2," *Theology*, LXIII, 603 (September 1970): 399-405, esp. 400-401.

12. See our Chapter 3.

13. The book sparked a continuing debate. We would get too far afield if we attempted to elaborate here the arguments of the many participants in the controversy. Our own critique of Hick's Christology, however, will incorporate relevant arguments from that debate. It

would also be too lengthy to provide a list of every Christological work since *The Myth of God Incarnate* that treats of the issues. However, the following bibliography represents some works that are considered central to the debate. Those opposed to Hick's book: Michael Green, ed., *The Truth of God Incarnate*. London: Hodder and Stoughton, 1977. James D. G. Dunn, *Christology in the Making: An Inquiry into the Origins of the Doctrine of the Incarnation*. London: S.C.M. Press, 1980. Lesslie Newbigin, *The Open Secret: Sketches for a Missionary Theology*. Grand Rapids: William B. Eerdmans, 1978. A. E. Harvey, ed., *God Incarnate: Story and Belief*. London: SPCK, 1981. Thomas V. Morris, *The Logic of God Incarnate*. Ithaca: Cornell University Press, 1986. A work written to answer the main criticisms of Hick's book: Michael Goulder, ed., *Incarnation and Myth: The Debate Continued*. London: S.C.M., 1979.

14. This information was communicated to me in two letters from Professor Hick, one dated June 3, 1986, and the second, September 1, 1989. *An Interpretation of Religion* (London: Macmillan) is based on his Gifford Lectures, published by Yale University Press, 1989.

15. Hick's ecclesiology is particularly impoverished. In understanding the Church as solely a human institution, and exaggerating the distinction between Jesus the Head of the Church from the Church itself, Hick has little use for the role of the Church in religious experience. Doubtless, this reflects the lack of positive contribution of the Church to his own religious experience. We could quote many references on this exaggerated distinction, but the following is sufficient: "Everything that is of value in Christianity stems ultimately from him [Jesus]; and everything that is valueless or of positive disvalue is ecclesiastical or other excrescence, not essentially related to this key figure" [CAC,32].

16. Hick says that his definition is meant to include theistic, semi-theistic and non-theistic faiths. It does not include, he says, "the purely naturalistic systems of belief, such as communism and humanism, immensely important though these are today as alternatives to religious faith" [GUF,134].

17. See also: GUF,7; GHMN,113.

18. GHMN,22, 90-91.

19. In Chapter 5, "Sketch for a Global Theory of Religious

Knowledge," of *God Has Many Names*, Hick puts the question this way: "The basic issue in the philosophy of religion is thus whether religious experience is simply a modification of man's consciousness, generated from within the human mind, or arises from contact with supermundane reality and constitutes cognition, however incomplete and/or distorted, of our more ultimate environment" [GHMN,79-80].

20. In adopting what Hick calls "the basic religious conviction," namely that religion is not totally an illusion or self-deception, he does not wish to imply that "all religious experience is straightforwardly veridical or that all religious belief is straightforwardly true" [GHMN,89]. Given the fact that human response is involved in religious belief, the religious experience will be conditioned, maybe even distorted, by the cultural interpretative framework.

21. Hick gives accounts of the rise of world religions in *God Has Many Names*, as well as in Chapter 10, "The New Map of the Universe of Faiths," in *God and the Universe of Faiths*, 133-47.

22. Hick says that man's "innate capacity to experience life religiously" operates in primitive man as a "determining cause," and in civilized man only as an "inclining cause" [GUF,96].

23. Hick gives brief summaries of the axial period in Chapters 3, pp. 45-5, and 4, pp. 71-2. of *God Has Many Names*.

24. Karl Jaspers, *The Origin and Goal of History* (London: Routledge & Kegan Paul, 1953). Translated from the German by Michael Bullock.

25. Writing of the axial period and the emergence of world faiths, Hick says: "Theologically, such [revelatory] moments are intersections of divine grace, divine initiative, divine truth, with human faith, human response, human enlightenment" [GUF,102].

26. Hick refers specifically to Confucius and the writers of *Tao Te Ching* in China, Gautama the Buddha, Mahavira, the writers of the Upanishads and the *Bhagavad-Gita* in India, Zoroaster in Persia, the Hebrew prophets in Israel and the Greek philosophers. Jesus and Mohammed technically lie outside the axial period, but they are considered by Hick to be "new developments within the stream of Semitic monotheism" [GHMN,46].

27. For Hick, the revelation of the Eternal One is a "self-revelation." For example, Hick defines faith as "both God's self-revealing

activity and the answering human response" [GUF,111]. Revelatory events need faith for the person to see them precisely as that, revelatory. Otherwise, these events are not interpreted *as* God's activity, but solely in naturalistic ways. Christian faith sees God acting self-revealingly in Jesus; other world faiths see God acting self-revealingly through other revelatory moments [cf. "The Essence of Christianity," *God and the Universe of Faiths*, 108-19].

28. Later in the same work Hick writes: "This [fact that God is the centre of the universe of faiths] must mean that the different world religions have each served as God's means of revelation to a different stream of human life" [GHMN,71].

29. GHMN,72; GUF, 102.

30. For Hick's argumentation and the specific way he understands the cognitive character of religious experience, see "Theology's Central Problem" and "Religion as Fact-asserting" in *God and the Universe of Faiths*, 1-17, and 18-36, Chapters 1 and 2 respectively. The first Chapter was originally given on October 31, 1967 as Hick's inaugural H. G. Wood Lecture at the University of Birmingham. It appeared in an abridged form under the same title in *The Expository Times*, LXXX, 8 (May 1969): 228-32. The second Chapter appeared earlier as two articles. The first half of the Chapter, titled "Religion as Fact-asserting," was an editorial in *Theology Today* (April 1961); the second half appeared in *Theology* (March 1968). It is in "Theology's Central Problem," that Hick takes issue with the reduction of religious language to a Wittgensteinian language-game. This latter point he argues forcefully as well in "The Justification of Religious Belief," *Theology*, LXXI, 573 (March 1968): 100-7. See also: Hick, "Religious Pluralism and Absolute Claims," in *Religious Pluralism*, Leroy S. Rouner, ed., (Notre Dame: University of Notre Dame Press, 1984): 193-213; this article appears as Chapter 4 in Hick, *Problems of Religious Pluralism* (London: Macmillan, 1985): 46-66.

In the light of how Hick later will treat specifically Christian religious language as metaphoric, it is interesting to record here Hick's conclusion about those who hold that religious language is non-cognitivist: "The non-cognitivist is not offering an objective analysis of the language of faith as living speech but is instead recommending a quite new use for it. For the non-cognitivist theories are not descriptive but radically revisionary" [GUF,8]. And later:"There is therefore something deeply irrational ... to use the traditional language of religion, and to participate in the form of life of which it is the linguistic expression, after consciously rejecting the premiss upon which these depend for their appropriateness" [GUF,11].

31. In *God and the Universe of Faiths*, Hick writes: "For religious faith, in its most basic sense, is the cognitive choice whereby we experience events and situations as mediating divine activity" [GUF,112]. This particular Chapter, "The Essence of Christianity," was first delivered as a public lecture in Carrs Lane Church Centre, Birmingham, 1972.

32. Hick explains that no type of religious experience is experience of God in His noumenal self. Whether it be the religious experience of God as personal presence and will, or the religious experience of the cosmos as manifestation of the divine reality, or the religious unitive experience of being temporarily absorbed into the divine—none of these versions of religious experience are experiences with God in His Infinite Self. They are experiences of the phenomenal God. Hence, these various types of religious experiences are not competitive with each other. They are "different phenomenal experiences of the one divine noumenon, or, in another language, as different experiential transformations of the same transcendent informational output" [GHMN,94].

33. Hick also finds support for this distinction in: (1) Thomas Aquinas' dictum, "The thing known is in the knower according to the mode of the knower" [GHMN,24; *Summa Theologica*, II-II,q.1,a.2]; (2) the mystical and spiritual traditions of the religions themselves [GHMN,86,91-92]; and (3) contemporary sources [GHMN,92]. See also Hick's "Mystical Experience as Cognition," in *Mystics and Scholars*, Harold Coward and Terence Penelhum, eds., (Waterloo: Wilfred Laurier University, 1977): 41-56.

34. While Hick uses the Kantian philosophical framework, he does emphatically make one corrective. Hick notes that his own proviso is that the phenomenal world *is* the noumenal world as experienced by humans. He concludes:"the result is the distinctly non-Kantian thesis that the divine is experienced (rather than postulated, as Kant believed), but is experienced within the limitations of our human cog-

nitive apparatus in ways analogous to that in which he argued that we experience our physical environment" [GHMN,83,cf.103].

35. Hick does not say that every image or *persona* or idea of God is valid. Only those that emerge from the great religions can be trusted. He writes: "every conception of the divine which has come out of a great revelatory religious experience and has been tested through a long tradition of worship, and has sustained human faith over centuries of time and in millions of lives, is likely to represent a genuine encounter with the divine reality" [GUF,141].This variety of genuine images of God, says Hick, "provides a better foundation for theology than do the mere limited images from within any one religious tradition. For example, we learn that God is both personal and non-personal" [GHMN,110-11].

36. We have not the space to elaborate further on this notion of *personae*. We simply state briefly, that for Hick, the two main categories of religious experience are those which structure the phenomenon of the Eternal One as either personal or non-personal [GHMN,24-25]. (Hick contends that both forms of religious awareness appear within each of the world religions, though in different proportions). But Hick more importantly claims that it is *not* these two basic categories which form the actual religious experience of individuals or communities. What occurs is that these two categories take on more concrete and particular forms. These more particular forms are in fact the images, the *personae*, or the "pictures" of God peculiar to each world religion. What significantly conditions religious experience, according to Hick, is the more concrete images or *personae* of God that are derived from a religious tradition's prayer life, liturgy, philosophy, etc. In both theistic and non-theistic religions, Hick contends that it seems clear that "The thing known is in the knower according to the mode of the knower." See also, Hick: "Is God Personal," in *God: The Contemporary Discussion*, Frederick Sontag and M. Darrol Bryant, eds., (New York: The Rose of Sharon Press, 1982): 169-79.

37. Hick asks why God should be known in such a *variety* of ways. He attributes this variety to "finite freedom" and the ways this freedom has been exercised. Human freedom is preserved in relation to God by being aware of God only in terms of "limited and limiting concepts and images" [GHMN,111]. Hick calls this the "epistemic

distance," that is, the condition of cognitive freedom in which God created man, in order that man could genuinely exist as a "finite person over against God" [GUF,96,97].

38. In yet further support for his distinction of the thing in itself from its image, Hick draws on an analogy of mediumship from the field of parapsychology [GHMN,99-100]. To the same purpose, Hick also employs as analogy the parable of the blind men and the elephant [GUF,140]. These, of course, are only analogies. For an account of Hick's understanding of religious meaning and mediumship based on contemporary cybernetics, see GHMN,100-3. For a critique of Hick's use of the elephant analogy, see Gavin D'Costa, "Elephants, Ropes and a Christian Theology of Religions." *Theology*, LXXXVIII, 724 (July 1985): 259-68; see also Lesslie Newbigin, *The Open Secret* (Grand Rapids: Eerdmans, 1978), 184, as well as an earlier critique of this analogy by Newbigin in his *The Finality of Christ* (London: S.C.M., 1969), 16-7.

39. Strangely, Hick also writes that in addition to objective grounds, there is a subjective point to be taken into consideration:"Subjectively, however, each tradition is unique and superior for those who have been spiritually formed by it ... And, in short, we are so formed by the tradition into which we were born and in which we were raised that it is for us unique and absolute and final" [GHMN,56,57].

40. For a detailed account of Hick's view on religious pluralism, see also: (1) "Towards a Philosophy of Religious Pluralism," *Neue Zeitschrift für systematische Theologie und Religionsphilosophie*, 22, 2 (1980): 131-49; this article appears as Chapter 6, same title, in *God Has Many Names*, 88-115; (2) "Christology in an Age of Religious Pluralism," *Journal of Theology for Southern Africa*, 35 (June 1981): 4-9; (3) "On Grading Religions," *Religious Studies*, 17, 4 (December 1981): 451-67; this article appears as Chapter 5 in Hick, *Problems of Religious Pluralism* (London: Macmillan, 1985): 67-87; (4) "The Theology of Religious Pluralism," *Theology*, LXXXVI, 713 (September 1983): 335-40; this article appears retitled as "In Defence of Religious Pluralism," in Hick *Problems of Religious Pluralism*, 96-109; (5) "Religious Pluralism," in *The World's Religious Traditions: Current Perspectives in Religious Studies. Essays in honour of Wilfred Cantwell Smith*, Frank Whaling, ed., (Edinburgh: T. & T. Clark,

1984): 145-64; this article appears as Chapter 3, retitled "A Philosophy of Religious Pluralism," in Hick, *Problems of Religious Pluralism*, 28-45; (6) "The Philosophy of World Religions," *Scottish Journal of Theology*, 37, 2 (June 1984): 229-36.

41. Hick argues for a Copernican revolution in theology in Chapter 9, "The Copernican Revolution in Theology," *God and the Universe of Faiths*, 120-32. This chapter was delivered first as part of a public lecture series by Hick in Birmingham, England in February and March, 1972. Part of this chapter subsequently appeared in the *Expository Times*, November, 1972 in a series on "Learning from Other Faiths."

42. See also GHMN,71.

43. Hick describes the attitude of Christian religious imperialism in terms of traditional Christian mission: "And so we have in the past generally thought of the non-Christian world in negative terms, as the unfortunate not-yet-Christianized portion of humanity and as potential recipients of the divine grace which is coming through the missionaries whom we sent out to them" [GHMN,60]. However, several things have begun to shatter this attitude. Hick lists them: (1) modern media and travel have produced an awareness "of the sheer size and religious variety of mankind outside our Anglo-Saxon tribe" [GHMN,60], (2) the fact "evident to ordinary people (even though not always taken into account by theologians) that in the great majority of cases—say 98 or 99 percent—the religion in which a person believes and to which he adheres depends upon where he was born" [GHMN,61], (3) new, serious knowledge of world religions replaces ignorance, prejudice and caricature, and (4) immigration of Asians to the West.

The above references come from Chapter 4, "By Whatever Path...," of *God Has Many Names*, which Chapter first appeared as "Whatever Path Men Choose is Mine," *The Modern Churchman*, XVIII, 1/2 (Winter 1974): 8-17. See also, Hick: (1) "Is There Only One Way to God?," *Theology*, LXXXV, 703 (January 1982): 4-7; (2) "Only One Way to God?," *Theology*, LXXXVI, 710 (March 1983): 128-9.

44. See also Hick: (1) "The Christian View of Other Faiths," *The Expository Times*, in Series "Learning from Other Faiths: IX," LXXXIV, 2 (November 1972): 36-9; (2) "The Christian Church and People of Other Religions," *The Times*, October 4, 1975, 16.

45. Hick also refers to another claim Christianity makes for its uni-

queness: "Or again there is the claim that Christianity, properly under-stood, is not a religion but is a revelation which judges and supercedes all religions" [GHMN, 68].

46. Hick discerns three phases in the Christian attitude to other world religions: (1) the phase of "total rejection," (2) the phase of the "early epicycles" (up to Vatican II), (3) the phase of "later epicycles" [GHMN,29-36].

47. See: GUF, 123-127; GHMN, 67-68.

CHAPTER THREE

Hick's Christology (Part One)

The pluralism of world religions occasions for Hick the Copernican revolution in theology. This revolution subsequently gives rise to the theocentric model. In turn, the theocentric model now demands a reconsideration of the traditional teaching about the unique identity of Jesus. Hick recognizes that this question about "the person of our Lord" is of paramount importance to Christians. He poses the Christological question this way:

> What about the uniqueness of Christ, the belief that Jesus was God incarnate, the second Person of the holy Trinity become man, the eternal Logos made flesh [GHMN,72]?

It is Hick's multifaceted response to this question which constitutes the subject matter of this and the following Chapter. In this Chapter I present Hick's arguments against the traditional understanding of the uniqueness of Jesus. In the following Chapter I provide some further observations by Hick, his own alternative position, as well as the main advantages which he believes this alternative provides for the wider ecumenism among world religions.

In this introduction, in order to provide an initial understanding of Hick's basic response to the above question, I present below a few of Hick's conclusions about the identity and uniqueness of Jesus. These conclusions, presented in Hick's own words, help situate us before we launch into an elaboration of his supporting reasons.

Following these initial statements of Hick's fundamental Christological position, I present a brief outline of the general areas in which Hick locates his Christological arguments. The body of this Chapter will then present a detailed development of these arguments.

In our first reference to Hick's basic Christological position, we note that Hick focuses on three elements: the consciousness of Jesus, the divine *Agape* (as Hick will later call it), and the inadequacy of the "two-natures" Christology. He writes:

> Now we want to say of Jesus that he was so vividly conscious of God as the loving heavenly Father, and so startlingly open to God and so fully his servant and instrument, that the divine love was expressed, and in that sense incarnated, in his life. This was not a matter (as it is in official Christian doctrine) of Jesus having two complete natures, one human and the other divine. He was wholly human; but whenever self-giving love in response to the love of God is lived out in a human life, to that extent the divine love has become incarnate on earth [GHMN,58-9].

In our second reference, Hick focuses on the interpretation of the doctrine of the Incarnation (and by implication, the doctrine of the Trinity) and the issue of the meaning of metaphysical and mythological language. He writes:

> My own view is that the Christian mind will almost inevitably come to see the doctrine of the incarnation, and the doctrine of the Trinity which grew out of it, in a new way, no longer as precise metaphysical truths but as imaginative constructions giving expression—in the religious and philosophical language of the ancient world—to the Christian's devotion to Jesus as the one who has made the heavenly Father real to him. Or at any rate, I would suggest that this kind of development which the more intellectual part of the Christian mind (appropriately, in the human brain, the left hemisphere!) is likely to undergo, while its more emotional other half perhaps continues to use the traditional language of Christian mythology without raising troublesome

questions about its meaning [GHMN,125-6].

In our third reference, Hick provides us with a Christology which he considers to be "more intelligible than the oneness-of-substance formulation" [GUF,164]. Hick makes the following Christological statements:

(1) Jesus had "one nature, and this nature was wholly and unqualifiedly human; but the *agape* which directed it was God's,"

(2) Jesus had "one will, that of the man Jesus of Nazareth; but again, the *agape* that was the ruling motive of his life was God's *Agape* for mankind,"

(3) Jesus "was conscious of a special vocation from the time of his baptism by John ... This does not mean, however, that he was conscious of being God, or the Son of God, or the eternal Logos made flesh. He was consciously a human being distinct from God" [GUF,163].[1]

The arguments Hick will employ to support his basic Christological position can be outlined as follows:

(1) basing himself in the consciousness of the earthly Jesus, as reconstructed by some contemporary biblical scholarship, Hick maintains that Jesus was neither aware of nor did He teach in any sense that He was God;

(2) arguing from the religious impact of Jesus and from religious psychology, Hick contends that a crucial process at work in Christology was the deification of Jesus;

(3) finding support in contemporary studies of Christian historical and cultural origins, Hick claims that the idea of divine Incarnation is mythological, and that its language is just a metaphorical way of saying "something else;"

(4) after examining the Christian theological tradition about Jesus, Hick concludes that theology has not been able to give any intelligible content to the "two-natures" Christology;

(5) intending to make the traditional understanding of Jesus more credible to the contemporary mind, Hick proposes his own alternative of "divine inhistorisation." That is, the "something else" about Jesus which the mythological langauge is trying to articulate, is that Jesus was an Incarnation in history of the *Agape* of God. He was this Incarnation not by being true God and true man, but by being a human per-

son open to God's will and purpose in a spirit of selfless love;

(6) reasoning that all religions are culturally unique, Hick holds that any uniqueness of Jesus lies not in who he was, but in his impact and in the historical and cultural effect He has had by being, at least in His disciples' eyes, the founder of Christianity;

(7) hoping to construct a global theology of religions to encourage a more fruitful ecumenism between the world religions, Hick justifies his reinterpretation of Jesus' uniqueness on the grounds that it enables Christians to enter fully and maturely into the contemporary pluralistic context of world religions.

Since Christology by its nature is complex, it is not surprising that many of Hick's positions overlap and are interdependent. To treat one, for example, the process of deification, is already to intrude on another, the issue of the language of divine Sonship. Further, Hick has not yet developed a highly organized or systematized Christology.[2] This is not surprising since the Christological issue for him constitutes only a part of his more engaging concern, a global theology of religion and religions. Hence, my treatment of Hick, while organizing his arguments in a systematic and progressive manner, must at times respect the need to treat some of his arguments partially in one place and partially in another. Further, issues that arise under the above sections (5) and (7) are reserved for the following Chapter.

All the main components that go to construct Hick's Christology can be found in *God Has Many Names*, 1982. This work, however, is not primarily a Christological one. The book focuses on those issues specifically related to religious pluralism. One of these issues—and one that occurs in many different contexts—is of course, the Christological issue of Jesus' unique identity.

Hick's significant theocentric Christology was launched in *God and the Universe of Faiths*, 1973. It received further elaboration and enduring significance in the Chapter "Jesus and the World Religions," which he wrote for *The Myth of God Incarnate*, 1977. Our own presentation of Hick's Christology draws heavily on these three works, and uses as an operational framework the above-mentioned "Jesus and the World Religions."

I shall, then, present Hick's Christology in this Chapter according to the following order:

The first section shows that the foundation of Hick's Christology lies in the consciousness and the impact of Jesus.

The next section elaborates Hick's account of the many factors that contributed to what he calls "the process of the deification of Jesus."

The following section, and the most important in Hick's Christology, presents Hick's account of the language of divine Sonship, and its transposition in Scripture and theology.

The subsequent two sections analyze Hick's understanding of myth and present what he refers to as the "practical truth" of the doctrine of the Incarnation.

A final section presents some of Hick's remarks about the use in the Church of the mythological language of Jesus' divine Sonship. I then provide a summary.

I wish to point out as well that in this and the following Chapter I am simply presenting Hick's Christology. Apart from a few observations in some footnotes, we are not yet critiquing that Christology.

The Foundation of Hick's Christology

In this section I present the foundation of Hick's Christology. This foundation is twofold. First, the root and norm for Christology is the consciousness of the historical Jesus. Secondly, and inseparably linked to Jesus' consciousness, is His impact. Christology, for Hick, ultimately will be the articulation of the religious impact of Jesus on His disciples.

In *The Myth of God Incarnate*, Hick offers us his "own impression" of Jesus. He explains that in presenting us with this impression, he is simply doing what

... everyone else does who depicts the Jesus whom he calls Lord: one finds amidst the New Testament evidences indications of one who answers one's own spiritual needs [MGI,172].

In order to refer easily to parts of this impression in our presentation, it will be helpful here to quote a major section of this portrait. Hick writes of Jesus:

I see the Nazarene, then, as intensely and overwhelmingly conscious of the reality of God. He was a man of God, living in the

75

unseen presence of God, and addressing God as *abba*, father. His spirit was open to God and his life a continuous response to the divine love as both utterly gracious and utterly demanding. He was so powerfully God-conscious that his life vibrated, as it were, to the divine life; and as a result his hands could heal the sick, and the 'poor in spirit' were kindled to new life in his presence. If you or I had met him in first-century Palestine we would—we may have hoped—have felt deeply disturbed and challenged by his presence. We would have felt the absolute claim of God confronting us, summoning us to give ourselves wholly to him and to be born again as his children and as agents of his purposes on earth. To respond with our whole being might have involved danger, poverty, ridicule. And such is the interaction of body and mind that in deciding to give ourselves to God, in response to his claim mediated through Jesus, we might have found ourselves trembling or in tears or uttering the strange sounds that are called speaking with tongues [MGI,172].

In the above impression of Jesus, Hick presents us with a double-phenomenology. First, there is a phenomenology of the consciousness of Jesus. Secondly, there is a phenomenology of the impact of Jesus. First, let us consider the consciousness of Jesus.

What makes Jesus significant, for Hick, is His consciousness of God. Jesus was "intensely and overwhelmingly conscious of the reality of God ... He was so intensely God-conscious." It is this heightened consciousness of God that accounts for (1) Jesus' use of *abba*, (2) Jesus' openness of spirit and continuous response to God, (3) the power Jesus had to heal and bring new life, and (4) the impact He had on those who met Him.

Most important, however, from Hick's impression of Jesus, we learn that it is Jesus' consciousness of God which constitutes Him as mediator between God and man. Jesus experiences the "reality of God" as an "unseen presence." Because this presence is no ordinary presence, but God's presence, it has a "total" or "absolute" quality about it. It is "utterly gracious and utterly demanding." Because Jesus is so open and responsive to God's presence, He is able to mediate God's divine love and divine life to others. Jesus is mediator not simply by giving information about God. Rather, by being so conscious of and so permeated by the presence of God, Jesus' very life mediates God's presence. To come into Jesus' presence was in some sense to come into God's presence. For just as Jesus encountered the totality of God's claim, so too, those who encountered Jesus experienced "the absolute claim of God." Hick is explicit in clarifying in what sense one encountered God when one came into Jesus' presence. He writes:

> Thus in Jesus' presence, we should have felt that we are in the presence of God—not in the sense that the man Jesus literally *is* God, but in the sense that he was so totally conscious of God that we could catch something of that consciousness by spiritual contagion [MGI,172].[3]

This point of "spiritual contagion" leads us to our second consideration, the phenomenology of the impact of Jesus. Jesus' consciousness of God's presence constituted Him as a mediator of that presence. The result was a discernible impact on others, a religious experience. The person who met Jesus found himself/ herself "disturbed and challenged by his presence" and perhaps "kindled to new life in his presence". Such persons might find themselves "trembling," or "in tears," or "speaking in tongues." If the impact led to discipleship, the experience would be one of "dynamic joy." This joy resulted from

> ... a breakthrough into a new and better quality of existence, in harmony with the divine life and resting securely upon the divine reality [MGI,172].

Hick realizes, of course, that such a positive response to Jesus was not inevitable. There was always "the possibility of turning away from this challenging presence." By closing oneself to Jesus—and therefore to God's call coming through Him—one closes himself/ herself "at the same time to God." Therefore, to encounter Jesus could be the occasion of "a turning point in one's life, a crisis of salvation or judgment" [MGI,172].

The foundation, then, of Hick's Christology is the consciousness of the historical Jesus. What makes Jesus significant, what constitutes

Him as mediator, and what accounts for His impact, is His heightened consciousness of God's presence.

But this consciousness has an effect, that Hick frequently calls "the impact of Jesus." What draws one to surrender to Jesus is this impact one experiences. This religious experience can only be accounted for, says Hick, by Jesus' heightened consciousness of God.

Christology for Hick, as we shall see in greater detail as we progress, consists in the disciples' articulation of this impact. That is, Christology consists in the articulation of their own religious experience. The root and norm of such articulation must always be the consciousness of the historical Jesus. The error in traditional Christology, according to Hick, was to think that in expressing religious experience, Christological doctrines were really saying something literal about Jesus.

The Deification of Jesus

Because of His overwhelming and intimate consciousness of God's presence, "Jesus was a figure of tremendous spiritual power" [MGI,173]. Those who encountered Him and accepted the new life He offered, underwent a powerful religious experience. His disciples who were "born again" lived "consciously by God's presence" and served God's purposes on earth. Hick writes:

Once men and women had been transformed by their encounter with Jesus, he was for them the religious centre of their existence, the object of their devotion and loyalty, the Lord in following whom they were both giving their lives to God and receiving their lives renewed from God [MGI,174].

It is clear that the disciples' religious experience "was focused on Jesus" [MGI,174].

But how did this religious experience express itself? How were the disciples to articulate what had happened to them? They found themselves constrained to search for "an adequate language in which to speak about their master" [MGI,173]. They had to think of Him "in a way that was commensurate with the total discipleship which he evoked."

78

This search for an adequate and commensurate language involved a process. Hick describes this process as

... that which began with Jesus as the Messiah of the Jews and culminated in the Nicene definition of him as God the Son, Second Person of the Trinity, incarnate [MGI,174].

This process is central in Hick's Christological critique. It is no less than the process of the "deification" of Jesus. Hick writes:

This somewhat mysterious title [Messiah] developed in its significance within the mixed Jewish-Gentile church ultimately to the point of deification [MGI,173].

Our topic in this section is the process of the deification of Jesus: how Hick defines it, evidence for its presence in the New Testament, how and why it occurred historically.

The Process of Deification

Hick defines the process of "deification" as the coming "to worship a human being" [MGI,173]. In this case, the human being is Jesus. This process of deifying Jesus, argues Hick, can already be seen at work in the New Testament. Hick writes that "in the earliest Christian preaching," e.g., Acts 2:22, Jesus was first proclaimed as "a man attested to you by God" [MGI,173].[4] Then, some thirty years later, the gospel of Mark opens with: "The beginning of the gospel of Jesus Christ, the Son of God ..." After another thirty years or so, with John's gospel, continues Hick,

... this Christian language is attributed to Jesus himself and he is depicted as walking the earth as a consciously divine being [MGI,173].

More specifically, Hick focuses on the search for a title or titles for Jesus. He says that for the ordinary believer living in the tightly-knit Christian community, "it was sufficient to think and speak of him [Jesus] simply as the Lord" [MGI,174]. But soon there must have been pressures

> ... to use titles which would more explicitly present the challenge of Jesus' saving power, first within the Jewish community and then within the Gentile world of the Roman empire. And these could only be the highest titles available ... the most exalted terms which their culture offered [MGI,174].

These terms, argues Hick, began with the title "Messiah" and culminated in the Nicene definition of *homoousios*.[5]

Hick now asks, in stark fashion, how the deification of Jesus could have been possible:

> But how did the Jews come, with their Gentile fellow-Christians, to worship a human being, thus breaking their unitarian monotheism in a way which eventually required the sophisticated metaphysics of the Trinity? [MGI,173]

Hick offers three reasons: (a) cultural circumstances, (b) the nature of Christian religious experience, and (c) the tendency of the religious mind.

What cultural experiences conditioned the deification of Jesus? Hick first looks to the wider cultural environment of the Roman empire. He refers specifically to two other Chapters in *The Myth of God Incarnate*.[6] In these two chapters Michael Goulder and Frances Young respectively show, according to Hick,

> ... how widespread in the ancient world were ideas of divinity embodied in human life [MGI,174].

From their evidence, Hick concludes that

> ... there is nothing in the least surprising in the deification of Jesus in that cultural environment [MGI,174].

Next, Hick considers the more specific environment of Judaism.

Here he refers to the long tradition of the title "Son of God" being applied to a human being. For example, the Messiah was to be an earthly king of Davidic dynasty, which dynastic kings became Sons of God by adoption. Hick quotes Psalm 2:7 "He said to me: 'You are my son, today I have begotten you'", and 2 Sam 7:14 "I will be his father, and he shall be my son."

Hick's concluding point is that it was not the impact of Jesus that created a new language of divine sonship. Such language, he writes,

> ... was already present in the Jewish cultural tradition and was readily applied to Jesus by those who saw him as the Messiah [MGI,175].

The second reason Hick offers to explain why specifically Jesus was deified is based on the nature of Christian religious experience. Hick states:

> There can I think be no doubt that this deification of Jesus came about partly—perhaps mainly—as a result of the Christian experience of reconciliation with God [MGI,176].

The new life which Jesus brought "was pervaded by a glorious sense of the divine forgiveness and love" [MGI,176]. The followers of Jesus, influenced by the long tradition of priestly sacrifice in Judaism, were aware that "without the shedding of blood there is no forgiveness of sins" (Heb 9:22). Hence, there occurred "a natural transition in their minds." This transition involved three stages: (1) from the experience of reconciliation with God through Jesus, to (2) the thought of Jesus' death as atoning sacrifice,[7] to (3) the conclusion "that in order for Jesus' death to have a sufficient atonement for human sin he must himself have been divine" [MGI,176].

The third reason Hick offers to explain why the human Jesus became deified lies in the realm of human, specifically religious, psychology. Hick refers to the operative dynamic here as a "tendency of the religious mind" [MGI,170]. I shall consider first Hick's philosophical and psychological explanations of this tendency. Then I shall present the historical example Hick uses to illustrate this tendency at work.

In our account of the foundation of Hick's Christology, we referred to what Hick called his "impression of Jesus." We recorded Hick's own justification for using such impressions. He explained that what he was doing was the same thing that "everyone else does" in depicting a Jesus "who answers one's own spiritual needs" [MGI,172]. This kind of depiction Hick refers to as a "tendency of the religious mind" [MGI,170]. It is a form of psychological projection.[8] On this point, Hick makes specific reference to Feuerbach:

Clearly, Feuerbach's account of the idea of God as a projection of human ideals has a certain application here [MGI,168].

The "here" in the above text refers to the phenomenon that down through the centuries the Christian imagination, whether communal or individual,

... has projected its own ideal upon as much of the New Testament data as will sustain it, producing a Christ-figure who meets the spiritual needs of his devotees: while behind this gallery of ideal portraits lies the largely unknown man of Nazareth [MGI,168].[9]

Again, Hick writes that the "mental image" [MGI,168], or the "pictures" [MGI,167] of Jesus

... in different ages and in different parts of the church are so widely various that they must in part reflect the variety of temperaments and ideals, and above all the varying spiritual needs within the world of believers [MGI,168].

Hick lists ten such images or pictures of Jesus. These ten "pictures" are: (1) "a stern law-giver and implacable judge," (2) "a figure of inexhaustible gracious tenderness," (3) "a divine psychologist probing and healing the recesses of the individual spirit," (4) "a prophet demanding social righteousness and seeking justice for the poor and oppressed," (5) "a supernatural being, all-powerful and all-knowing, haloed in glorious light," (6) "an authentically human figure living within the cultural framework of his time," (7) "a pacifist," (8) "a Zealot" (9) "a figure of serene majesty," (10) "a 'man for others' who suffered human agonies, sharing the pains and sorrows of our mortal lot" [MGI,167].[10]

The list is not meant to be exhaustive. Each of these "pictures," continues Hick, is not an arbitrary projection. Each image can find some justification from one or other of the various New Testament traditions about Jesus. But Hick's point is that aspects of these New Testament traditions, by means of the "communal or individual imagination,"

> ... have fused with men's hopes and desires to form these different "pictures", so that like a great work of art the New Testament figure of Jesus has been able to become many things to many men [MGI,168].[11]

Rather than acting as a restraint on this tendency of the religious mind towards projection, the New Testament itself, claims Hick, has supported it. The New Testament has done so because the data which it provides the imagination is "fragmentary and ambiguous" [MGI,168]. One's spiritual needs for a saviour find here fertile ground for projection. Even from our critical, modern viewpoint, says Hick, given such "fragmentary and ambiguous" data, we can only begin to speak about "Jesus, the historical individual" amid much "confusion and uncertainty" [MGI,168]. The imagination under these conditions can be expected to make a significant contribution "to our 'pictures' of Jesus."

Hick's conclusion is that while in one sense it is true that Jesus has been worshipped by millions, in another sense,

> ... in terms of subjective 'intentionality', a number of different beings, describable in partly similar and partly different ways, have been worshipped under the name of Jesus or under the title of Christ [MGI,168].

We are in the process of presenting Hick's account of how Jesus came to be deified. We have been elaborating his explanation of the "tendency of the religious mind" to project its ideals and desires. Hick contends that such a tendency is both oriented towards and effects deification. To demonstrate his point, Hick employs an historical example, outside Christianity, of how this tendency toward deification has actually operated. Hick suggests we

... observe the exaltation of a human teacher into a divine figure of universal power in another religious tradition ... [MGI,168].

We now turn our attention to this historical example.

The example Hick chooses to consider is "the founder of Buddhism, Gautama (or Sakyamuni)" [MGI,168ff]. Here we are dealing with a "real historical individual" (ca.563-483 B.C.) who lived in north-east India. Renouncing riches, Gautama sought spiritual truth. After attaining Enlightenment, he travelled greatly teaching others. He founded communities of disciples, which continue to spread the Buddha's message and to influence a large section of mankind. Gautama, or the Buddha, made no divine claim. Hick writes:

He was a human being who attained to nirvana—the complete transcendence of egoism, and oneness with eternal trans-personal Reality [MGI,168].

Around the same time Christianity was being born, a branch of Buddhism, Mahayana Buddhism, was also emerging. In Mahayana Buddhism the Buddha came to be revered as much more than an outstanding human individual. Hick writes:

The human Gautama came to be thought of as the incarnation of a transcendent, pre-existent Buddha as the human Jesus came to be thought of as the incarnation of the pre-existent Logos or divine Son [MGI,169].

For this reason, Hick sees Buddhology and Christology as developing "in comparable ways" [MGI,169].[12] In Buddhology, Gautama became understood as the incarnation of a heavenly Buddha, which heavenly Buddha was one with the Absolute. Gautama was the *Dharma* (Truth) made flesh.[13] In Christology, says Hick, the analogy is clear. Jesus came to be thought of as the Incarnation of the pre-existent Logos or divine Son. The eternal Son is one with God the Father.

Hick's point is not to develop the analogy in depth. Rather, he wishes to draw attention to the fact that

> ... the human Gautama has been exalted into an eternal figure of universal significance, one with his human brethren through the incarnate life lived two and a half thousand years ago and one with Ultimate Reality in the *Dharmakaya* or Cosmic Buddha [MGI,169].

There were presumably two forces at work in the exaltation of Buddha, writes Hick. First, there was "the hunger of the human spirit for a personal Saviour," and secondly, the intellectual support of "the sophisticated metaphysical doctrine of the Three Bodies." Hick goes on to add that the Mahayana Buddhists

> ... of course claim that this entire development was implicit in the work of the historical Gautama and that later thought has only brought out the fuller meaning of his teaching [MGI,169].[14]

Hick says he is not making any statement about the rightness or wrongness of the mahayanist development. His point is merely to show how an historical occurrence of deification has occurred. He also acknowledges that the exaltation of Buddha and of Jesus has "of course taken characteristically different forms in the two religions" [MGI,170]. Hick's conclusion is that the process of deification or exaltation leads to speaking of the founder

> ... in terms which he himself did not use and to understand him by means of a complex of beliefs which was only gradually formed by later generations of his followers [MGI,170].

We have been presenting Hick's account of what deification means. We have recorded Hick's account that the process of deification is already at work in the New Testament. And we have elaborated Hick's example from Buddhism, which he employs to demonstrate that deification is not a theory. Deification has in fact occurred historically. It is now time to turn to the culmination of the historical process of the Christian deification of Jesus with the Council of Nicea's definition of faith.

Specifically in the case of Jesus, Hick says we can ask: what was the "complex of beliefs" which concluded the process of deification among Jesus' later followers? The answer, says Hick, is found in the Council of Nicea.[15]

We recall here that the foundation of Hick's Christology is the consciousness of the historical Jesus. Because of His intense consciousness of God, Jesus had a profound impact or effect on His disciples. We have also seen that, according to Hick, the process of Jesus' deification began with the disciples' search for an adequate language about Jesus that was commensurate with their powerful religious experience. This language-search, states Hick, began with their use of the title "Messiah," it developed with the title "Son of God", and concluded with the title "God the Son." Hick uses the title "God the Son" to refer to the Nicene definition. Thus, Nicea represents the culmination of the deification process. It is the high point in "the exaltation of a human being to divine status" [MGI,171]. The process of the deification of Jesus, which had its beginnings with the title "Messiah," reaches its culmination in Nicea with

> ... the exaltation in Christian faith of the man of Nazareth into the divine Christ, the only-begotten Son of God, Second Person of the Holy Trinity [MGI,168].

It must be understood that Hick does not see this process of deification as the product of ill will. On the contrary, writes Hick, it is "natural and intelligible" [MGI,176]. It was "natural and intelligible," as we have seen, given the cultural and religious environment of Jesus' time, the nature of Christian religious experience, and especially given the tendency of the religious mind to projection.

On the relationship between what Nicea defined about Jesus and the tendency of the religious mind, Hick asks the fundamental question: to what extent does Nicea represent

> ... a supreme example of this [Feuerbach-type] projection upon

86

Jesus of ideals to answer our spiritual needs [MGI,168]?

In asking this question Hick is aware he is asking the fundamental question of the identity of Jesus. He writes:

At first sight the very possibility [of the exaltation of Jesus being a Feuerbach-type projection] is alarming; for it questions the identification of the Galilean rabbi with the Christ-figure of developed Christian dogma [MGI,168].

Needless to say, for Hick, the Nicene definition does represent the supreme example of the Feuerbach-type projection in the Christian deification of Jesus. Hick's argument is that the traditional language of the Nicene definition, the language of "God-the-Son incarnate" is both optional and mythological. It is optional because it is the language of one particular culture and one particular time, namely the Greco-Roman world of the third and fourth centuries.[16] It is mythological because it has no literal meaning or content. Rather, the Nicene language simply represents a practical way of expressing the truth of Jesus' significance, His efficacy, and the total claim He made on His followers. The Nicene language describes the religious impact of Jesus on His disciples. It does not, contends Hick, say anything about who Jesus was. For Hick, then, the Nicene definition is easily "only one way of conceptualizing" the disciples' experience of the impact of Jesus [MGI,168]. We can say that for Hick, Nicea's Christology—despite what the Fathers may have thought they were doing—describes not who Jesus was nor His consciousness. Rather, it describes the consciousness of the later disciples.

This description of the consciousness of the disciples is not a Christological mistake. The mistake, contends Hick, was that the Fathers thought they were describing Jesus and His own self-understanding. But Christology, says Hick, must be based on the consciousness of the real, historical Jesus, and not on the supposed consciousness of a deified Jesus. The Nicene credal statement about

... the only-begotten Son of God, Begotten of the Father before all the ages, Light of Light, true God of true God, begotten not made, of one substance with the Father [MGI,171] ...

is quite remote from any self-understanding or teaching of the historical Jesus [GHMN,28; MGI,171]. The doctrine of the Incarnation "was not revealed by Jesus," says Hick, "but emerged in the mind of the early church" [GUF,169]. Thus, Hick wishes to distinguish between the consciousness or self-understanding of the historical Jesus and

... the understanding of Jesus which eventually became orthodox Christian dogma [which] sees him as God the Son incarnate, the Second Person of the Trinity living a human life [MGI,171].

The important point, he concludes, is that we must get behind the later centuries of Christological dogma to the historical Jesus. If the historical Jesus did not consider Himself God-Incarnate, then Christology cannot claim Him to be so—unless it recognizes that it is using metaphorical and not literal language. Whereas the Christ of Nicea poses many insoluble problems for interreligious dialogue, the Jesus of history does not. Since the former is in a serious way culturally bound, and the product of religious projection, the Christ of dogma need not be considered normative. It is true, writes Hick, that the Jesus of history is also culture-bound. But the Jesus of history is not, nor did He understand Himself to be, consubstantial with God the Father, nor to be God the Son Incarnate. The Jesus of history allows for fruitful interreligious dialogue, and for a global theology of religions to emerge. Since for Hick, the Jesus of history is the true or real Jesus, not only does it make sense to opt for that Jesus in interreligious dialogue, it is mandatory.

Hick says, as we noted above, that the language of Nicea refers to the disciples' experience of Jesus and not to Jesus Himself. By this Hick does not mean to say that that was what the Fathers of Nicea intended. He is aware they thought they were saying something about who Jesus was.

This leads Hick to ask the question: what kind of language is being used in the two-natures Christological definitions of Nicea and Chalcedon? Is the language, for example, factual, literal, metaphorical, symbolic, mythological, poetic? Does it express a commitment; make a value judgment? Hick uses the terms *metaphorical, poetic, symbolic* and *mythological* interchangeably. They are distinguished from *literal* statements. A *literal* statement for Hick can be either *empirical* or *metaphysical*. When empirical or metaphysical facts are combined, Hick refers to the result as a *factual* statement. The two-natures Christology of Nicea is such a factual statement, "undoubtedly intended to be understood literally" [MGI,177]. The two-natures definition is empirical in asserting Jesus was a human being. It is metaphysical in asserting He was God [MGI,177]. Nicea intended

> ... that Jesus was literally (not merely metaphorically) divine and also literally (and not metaphorically) human. As divine he was not analogous to God, or poetically-speaking God, or as-if God; he was, actually and literally, God-incarnate. And again, as human he was really, truly and literally a man [MGI,177].

For the modern mind, however, argues Hick, such a Christological statement cannot be accepted as having any literal meaning. These issues of language and meaning are treated in our next section.

The Language of Divine Sonship

We have just seen in Hick's understanding of Nicea, that for him the doctrine of consubstantiality represents the final act in the deification or the exaltation of the human Jesus to divine status. Jesus never thought Himself to be, nor taught that He was, "Son of God." Jesus never understood Himself to be the Second-Person-of-the-Trinity-become-man. Such ideas, argues Hick, were far from the consciousness of Jesus.

Hick wants to get behind the developed dogmas about Christ to the reality of the historical Jesus. What is most important and enduring in Christianity is the Jesus of history, which Hick refers to as "the Christ-event." The developed dogmas about Christ, Hick contends, represent a subsequent deification of Jesus. The deification of Jesus represents an action of the Church, and is not grounded in Jesus. As such, the Christological dogmas are distinct and separate from the Christ-event. Therefore, they are not to be considered as forming part of that "unchanging" and "permanent" quality of that Christ-event [GUF,114].

But once the step of deification was taken, Christian thought had opted for a path that would eventually lead down nineteen centuries. Hick writes:

> In time the belief that Jesus of Nazareth was God incarnate became entrenched within a comprehensive body of doctrine which both depends upon and reciprocally supports it. Indeed so central is the belief in the deity of Christ to the established system of christian theology that many people today would identify it as *the* essential christian belief [GUF,114].

Hick's project is to take theology back to the Christ-event, to get theology behind the developed deification process, and there to penetrate the use of language about Jesus' divine Sonship. It is to this latter point that I now turn.

The terminology "Son of God" raises the question of the divine Sonship of Jesus: was He literally or only metaphorically "the Son of God?" For Hick, this question is wrapped up in a complex but definable language problem. Hick asks: how are we to understand the ancient language of divine Sonship [MGI,175]? He does not confine the intent of his question to the title "Son of God" as applied only to Jesus. He is asking the broader question about the title's cultural and historical use before the time of Christ, both within and without Judaism.

"Son of God" as Metaphorical Title

The question of the language of divine Sonship is this: was the title "Son of God" understood to indicate that the person to whom it was applied was literally, or only metaphorically, "Son of God?" For example, asks Hick, was the Davidic king literally or only metaphorically the "Son of God?" Hick admits that the sharp distinction between literal and metaphorical is a modern one. Nevertheless, he says that the title "Son of God" seems to have been simply an honorific and metaphorical one [MGI,175]

We have already seen that within Judaism itself, there existed a long tradition of the notion of a man being called "Son of God." The tradition of the Messiah, writes Hick, was that he would be an earthly king in the Davidic line, and these Davidic kings "had been adopted as son of God in being anointed to their office" [MGI,174].[17]

Similarly, in turning to the New Testament, Hick speaks of the "splendid poetry" of Luke 1:32-33. Hick quotes R. H. Fuller's conclusion that these verses of Luke are not specifically Christian—apart from the context in which Luke has inserted them. They may well be a "pre-Christian Jewish fragment" [MGI,175]. Hick's point once again is that it was not the impact of any uniqueness of the Christ-event that necessitated or created a new language of divine Sonship. The language was already around and being used. The Christians simply applied it to Jesus.

Up to this point Hick has been speaking of the notion of divine adoptionism in Scripture. The implication is that Jesus is divine Son in the same manner as was the Davidic king. It is at this point Hick makes an important, explicit remark on this issue. He states, albeit parenthetically, his own *adoptionist* interpretation of the New Testament. He writes:

(Indeed it is probably only with the stories of the virgin birth of Jesus in Matthew's and Luke's gospels that the Lord's anointed is thought of within Israel as being physically God's son. However, this physical meaning of divine sonship is contradicted in the account of Jesus' baptism, at which one of the ancient adoption formulae used at the coronation of the king, 'Thou art my son' (Ps. 2:7), is spoken from the sky)" [MGI,175].[18]

Hick wishes to establish that the point of entry into the Hebrew tradition of the language of divine Sonship was the adoption of the human king as "Son of God." Since the king to whom this title was given was not considered to be literally or physically "Son of God," but only honorifically or poetically, Hick says the language of the title is *metaphorical* or *poetic*. The application to Jesus of this language of divine Sonship is equally metaphoric and poetic. The language of divine Sonship became applied to Jesus because (1) Jesus was believed to be of the house of David, and (2) he was understood to be the "Messiah." Hick sees these two reasons as accounting for the opening verse of divine Sonship in Mark's gospel: "Jesus, Messiah, Son of God" [MGI,175].

Transposition in Language

We have already seen in our presentation of Hick's account of the deification of Jesus, that a process is involved. This process begins with hailing Jesus as "Messiah" and culminates in defining Him "consubstantial" with God (the Father).[19] Hick now wishes to focus specifically on the kind or kinds of language involved in this process. I present here Hick's account of what this transposition in language entails.

Hick begins by noting that the early poetry of the metaphorical language about Jesus undergoes significant change. Hick writes:

And as Christian theology grew through the centuries it made the very significant transition from 'Son of God' to 'God the Son', the Second Person of the Trinity" [MGI,175].

By "Christian theology" Hick does not mean only what occurred after the writing of the New Testament. He also means what occurs within the writing of the New Testament, especially in John's gospel.[20] Hick describes John's gospel as

... a profound theological meditation in dramatic form, expressing a Christian interpretation of Jesus which had formed (probably in Ephesus) fairly late in the first century [MGI,171].

Specifically, in relation to the transition from a metaphorical to a literal interpretation of the title "Son of God," Hick writes that the

... transposition of the poetic image, son of God, into the trinitarian concept, God the Son is already present in the Fourth Gospel [MGI,175].

Ever since John's gospel first appeared, Hick reports, the Church has authorized such a notion of Jesus because the Church "pre-critically" accepted the Christological sayings in John's gospel as historical. Hick refers to such sayings as: (1) "I and the Father are one," [Jn 10:30] (2) "No one comes to the Father, but by me," [Jn 14:6], (3) "He that hath seen me hath seen the Father" [Jn 14:9]. (At this point Hick acknowledges that he must enter "unfortunately" the realm of New Testament criticism. He says "unfortunately" because of "the notorious uncertainties of this realm" [GHMN,72].)

Prior to modern biblical criticism, says Hick, these Christological sayings were understood to have been spoken by the historical Jesus, and therefore, proof that He both knew and taught himself to be God. If Jesus had spoken these things, then traditional Christology would have in its favour the strength of being grounded in the consciousness of Jesus. In fact, traditional Christology, although mistaken about what Jesus actually said, was on the right track in basing its reflections on the consciousness of Jesus. Hick explains:

> ... whereas until some three or four generations ago it was generally accepted among biblical scholars that Jesus claimed to be God the Son, with a unique consciousness of divinity, so that the doctrine of the incarnation was believed to be firmly based in the consciousness and teaching of Jesus himself, today this is no longer generally held and is indeed very widely thought not to be the case [GHMN,72-73].[21]

Hick later will say that if Jesus was God the Son Incarnate, He did not know this during His earthly life. For this reason, many theologians today are attracted to the theory that it was only in His resurrection that Jesus "either became, or became conscious of being, the Son of God or God the Son" [GHMN,125].

Hick cites Wolfhart Pannenberg in support of his position.[22] While Hick admits not everyone will agree with Pannenberg, he nevertheless is certain that no one today would hold that the New Testament proves that Jesus was God incarnate. Hick's point is that no Christology can be based on thinking that the historical Jesus uttered the Christological sayings of John's gospel. Hick attributes them to the "developmental theology of the church toward the end of the first century" [GHMN,73]. This developmental theology has already begun in the New Testament, most clearly in John's gospel.

On this basis one can trace in John's gospel the emergence of the traditional uniqueness of Jesus' divine Sonship. Hick writes:

For it is characteristic of the Fourth Gospel that in it Jesus' message centres upon himself as Son of God in a unique sense which is virtually equivalent to his being God incarnate [MGI,175-6].

For Hick, the author of John's gospel has re-written Jesus' teaching, and the Church in its theology has largely followed John. Hick writes:

It [John's gospel] *is* a re-writing, however, for it is striking that in the earlier, synoptic gospels Jesus' teaching centres, not upon himself, but upon the kingdom of God [MGI,176].

Hick's point is that John's gospel has already moved beyond the content of Jesus' historical consciousness and has entered the arena of theological doctrine. In this way, John's gospel functions much like Nicea. It is involved in the process of the "exaltation" or "deification" of the historical man Jesus.[23]

The point Hick is making in the discussion so far is that the language of divine Sonship has undergone a transposition. This transposition was already occurring within the New Testament. Just as the deification of Jesus was in process at the time of the writing of the New Testament, so too the language of the exaltation of Jesus to divine status was operative there. For this reason, the Christological statements are not to be understood as saying anything literal about who Jesus was. Hick writes:

What seems to have happened during the hundred years or so following Jesus' death was that the language of divine sonship floated loose from the original ground of Jewish thought and developed a new meaning as it took root again in Greco-Roman culture [GUF,116].

Hick provides a brief summary of the progression of this transposition of language. It occurs in stages. First, there is the poetic language of "Son of God." This poetry, becomes transposed into prose and then escalated from a metaphorical "Son of God" to the metaphysical "God the Son," "of the same substance as the Father within the triune Godhead" [MGI,176]. In *God Has Many Names* Hick makes the same point:

The proper conclusion seems to me to be that the notion of a special human being as a "son of God" is a metaphorical idea which belongs to the imaginative language of a number of ancient cultures. The Christian tradition, however, has turned this poetry into prose, so that a metaphorical son of God became a metaphysical God the son, second Person of a divine Trinity; ... [GHMN,8].

Like the deification of Jesus, says Hick, this transposition is "natural and intelligible" for two reasons: (1) through Jesus men and women had found a decisive encounter with God, and (2) through Jesus His disciples experienced a new and better life [MGI,176].

The purpose of the Incarnational language, then, is not to say something about Jesus so much as it is to articulate something that happened to the disciples. Hick explains:

As religious metaphor, however, the incarnational language provides a familiar way of expressing our discipleship to Jesus as Lord (the one whom we seek to follow) and Saviour (the one who has initiated our eventual transformation into perfected children of God) [GHMN,8].

The transposition in language, like the deification of Jesus, culminated in the Nicene creed. We might wonder why the end product of this transposition, the two-natures Christology of Nicea, became normative for expressing the significance of Jesus in subsequent centuries. The reason, says Hick, is "the inherent conservatism of religion" [MGI,176]. Hick's point is that *one* cultural way of expressing Jesus' significance, because of religious conservatism, has become normative for different cultures and for different periods of history. But, muses Hick, what if the gospel had originally moved east into India, instead of West into the Roman Empire? Probably, he continues, the impact of Jesus would have been expressed by speaking of Him, for example, within Hinduism, as "a divine Avatar" or

... within the Mahayana Buddhism which was then developing in

India as a Bodhisattva, one who has attained to oneness with Ultimate Reality but remains in the human world out of compassion for mankind and to show others they way of life [MGI,176].

Within these latter cultures, "Avatar" and "Bodhisattva" may have been the "appropriate expressions" of Jesus' significance.

By this example of cultural relativity, Hick intends to indicate that the Johannine, and later Nicene, language of the deification of Jesus is so culturally conditioned that it cannot reasonably be considered normative for other cultures and other times.

If religious conservatism maintained the Nicene definition as normative for so long, what accounts for the contemporary reinterpretation of the traditional Christological faith? The answer, says Hick, lies in the realm of philosophy.

It is only in the contemporary period and in Western culture that philosophy has examined the uses of language. Hence, it is only under these latter and limited conditions that questions have directly arisen concerning the kind of religious language involved when Jesus is spoken of as "God the Son incarnate" [MGI,177]. In the past Christians accepted the "established language" regarding who Jesus was, as part of their "devotional practice." They did not raise any questions about the "logical character" of such language. But today we must ask the serious questions about this "established language." Hick writes:

Is it [the statement: "Jesus was God the Son incarnate"] a factual statement (a combined statement, presumably, about empirical and metaphysical facts), or does it express a commitment, or make a value-judgment, and is its meaning literal, or metaphorical, or symbolic, or mythological, or poetic... [MGI,177]?[24]

We have seen that, according to Hick, the culmination of the process of Jesus' deification as well as that of the transposition in the language of divine Sonship, is the Nicene definition of Jesus as consubstantial with God the Father. At the end of the section on Jesus' deification, I indicated that, since the Nicene language had moved from metaphor to metaphysics, Hick contends that the two-natures Christology has no literal meaning. We are now in a position to take up Hick's arguments on this point.

The "big question" today, writes Hick, concerning the doctrine of the two-natures of Jesus as defined by Nicea, is whether such a doctrine "has any non-metaphorical meaning" [MGI,177]. Regarding Jesus' human nature, Hick says that one can speak of it in a "literally meaningful" way. That is, there is a literal content, a literal meaning to the statement: "Jesus was a man." By this we understand him to have been literally

> ... part of the generic stream of human life; finite in intelligence, information and energy; and conditioned by a particular cultural and geographical milieu [MGI,177].

But, asks Hick, what does it mean to say that this man, Jesus, was the Second Person of the Trinity? Hick's reply is straightforward:

> That Jesus was God the Son incarnate is not literally true, since it has no literal meaning ... [MGI,178].

On this point, Hick provides evidence aimed to demonstrate that all patristic attempts to give a literal meaning to the divinity of Jesus as found in the two-natures Christology of Nicea ultimately "proved unacceptable (i.e. heretical)."[25] Specifically, Hick refers to the attempts of the Arians, Eutychians, Nestorians and Appollinarians [GUF,171; MGI,177-8]. Every attempt to give a literal meaning to the doctrine ended up by denying or weakening either the full humanity or the full divinity of Jesus.

On the other hand, the orthodox definitions of Nicea and Chalcedon, says Hick, did not attempt to explain the mystery, they simply reaffirmed it. But this option meant that the Christological doctrine still went without any literal meaning [GUF,171]. Hick concludes:

> Indeed one may say that the fundamental heresy is precisely to treat the incarnation as a factual hypothesis [GHMN,74]!

Nevertheless, the orthodox dogma continued to insist on "two natures, human and divine, coinhering in the one historical Jesus Christ"

[MGI,178]. However, re-states Hick, the dogma has never acquired a content. "It remains a form of words without assignable meaning." In fact, for Hick the doctrine of the two-natures Christology is as contradictory as a square-circle. He writes:

For to say, without explanation, that the historical Jesus of Nazareth was also God is as devoid of meaning as to say that this circle drawn with a pencil on paper is also a square [MGI,178].

Hick adds that the two-natures Christology, based as it is on the notion of "substance" is positively misleading. He begins by noting that the use of "substance" in the doctrine of transubstantiation is misleading in a "logically similar" way as in the hypostatic union [GUF,150]. He says belief in transubstantiation of the bread and wine into the body and blood of Christ

... permits no kind of experiential confirmation or disconfirmation and is a sheer intellectual cul-de-sac [GUF,150].

Applying this critique of the doctrine of transubstantiation to the doctrine of the hypostatic union, Hick writes:

The incarnate Christ is two substances, divine and human, under one set of human accidents. Not only is such a doctrine open to the charge of meaninglessness, but any imaginative meaning that it may have is of a static kind which, in the light of the modern rediscovery of the bible, seems peculiarly inappropriate for the expansion of the biblical revelation. It is as though one were saying that Christ is made out of the same lump of divine substance as the Godhead and thus shares the divine nature, as two loaves of bread might be made from the same lump of dough and thus be composed of the same substance [GUF,150].[26]

Hick argues that the two-natures Christology needs some "semantic content." But all attempts to give it some content have been repudiated [MGI,178]. The result has been that, beginning even with the Council of Constantinople, 381, the Nicene dogma that Jesus was both God and man has merely been reiterated, and not interpreted. Hick concludes that the unsuccessful attempts to give the doctrine a content result primarily from the fact that the doctrine was never in fact literal, but only metaphorical. He concludes:

> ... the real point and value of the incarnational doctrine is not indicative but expressive, not to assert a metaphysical fact but to express a valuation and evoke an attitude [MGI,178].

The Nature of Myth

Why cannot the two-natures Christology be given any literal content? Why is the Nicene language only meant to "express a valuation" or "evoke an attitude?" We give Hick's reply at length:

> For the reason why it has never been possible to state a literal meaning for the idea of incarnation is simply that it has no literal meaning. It is a mythological idea, a figure of speech, a piece of poetic imagery. It is a way of saying that Jesus is our living contact with the transcendent God. In his presence we find that we are brought into the presence of God. We believe that he is so truly God's servant that in living as his disciples we are living according to the divine purpose. And as our sufficient and saving point of contact with God there is for us something absolute about him which justifies the absolute language which Christianity has developed. Thus reality is being expressed mythologically when we say that Jesus is the Son of God, God incarnate, the Logos made flesh [GHMN,74-75].[27]

Hick has already stated that the doctrine of the Incarnation is void of content. He now explains what kind of language is at work in expressing that doctrine. Because the doctrine of the Incarnation has no "literal" content, it cannot be "spelled out." This is why all patristic attempts failed to explain it. The Church Fathers, of course, according to Hick, did not realize this. It is now appropriate to ask: what does Hick mean by "mythological" or "myth."

Hick distinguishes between theory (or hypothesis)[28] and myth. A theory, he says, be it a theological or a scientific theory,

... starts with some puzzling phenomenon and offers a hypothetical description of a wider situation such that, seen within this wider context, the phenomenon is no longer puzzling [GUF,165-6].

As an example of a theological theory, Hick says that a theologian puzzled by the presence of evil in a world created by an all-good and all-powerful God, will develop a theory by which the presence of such evil "is no longer puzzling" [GUF,166].

A theory, continues Hick, is either true or false (or partially so), and is capable of verification or falsification within human experience.

Myths, like theories, "are also responses to problematic phenomena" [GUF,166]. However, a myth is a different kind of response. A myth does not pretend to explain the puzzling phenomenon; rather it enables one to relate appropriately to that phenomenon. Hence, Hick defines "myth" as

... a story which is told but which is not literally true, or an idea or image which is applied to something or someone but which does not literally apply, but which invites a particular attitude in its hearers. Thus the truth of a myth is a kind of practical truth consisting in the appropriateness of the attitude which it evokes—the appropriateness of the attitude of its object, which may be an event, a person, a situation, or a set of ideas [GUF,166-7].

While myths can be classified in many different ways, Hick wishes to focus on an important "formal distinction" between "narrative myths" and "mythic concepts or images" [GUF,167]. Hick explains:

A narrative myth evokes a particular attitude to a present situation by telling a story, which is not literally true—usually a story about how the situation came about. Or it may set a body of religious and moral teaching within a narrative framework which evokes a response of faith in the teaching [GUF,167].

An example of narrative myth, says Hick, is the story of the fall of Adam and Eve in the opening chapters of Genesis. At one time, the story of the fall was interpreted to be a hypothesis giving literal truth about what it described. Now it is understood to be a narrative myth, not literally true, but "a poetic, picturesque, parabolic way of saying something" [GUF,168]. In so far as the myth evokes the appropriate attitude towards the puzzling phenomenon, it can be considered a true myth [GUF,168-9].

A "mythic image or idea," however,

> ... is used to identify, and thus to indicate the significance of, a situation or a person and thereby to evoke a distinctive attitude towards it or him [GUF,167].

An example of mythic idea is the Son of God imagery applied by way of identification with Jesus of Nazareth.[29] Hick calls this kind of myth "an identifying myth," specifically, "the identifying myth of the Incarnation," i.e., "the application to Jesus of Nazareth of a family of roughly equivalent images, such as Son of God, God the Son, God incarnate, Logos made flesh, God-Man" [GUF,169].

Hick's point is that the doctrine of the Incarnation is not a theological hypothesis but a religious myth. He says that when we take both Jesus' Godhood and manhood seriously, we no longer have an explanation, but a mystery. But it is important to note that in this context, Hick uses "myth" and "mystery" interchangeably. Both do not have any explanatory value. He writes:

> The doctrine of the incarnation is not a theory which ought to be able to be spelled out but—in a term widely used throughout Christian history—a mystery. I suggest that its character is best expressed by saying that the idea of divine incarnation is a mythological idea [MGI,178].

Although Hick does not explicitly say so, he implies that what the traditional term "mystery" was really attempting to express was that the doctrine of the Incarnation was a "myth." However, the users of "mystery" did not understand that they were dealing not with a theory but with a myth. The traditional term "mystery" implied, says Hick, something affirmed in faith but never understood, nor discoverable by reason. The doctrine of the Incarnation affirmed the two natures in Christ, but never claimed to explain it. It was called a "mystery." But as we have seen, Hick claims the reason there were only failures in trying to explain it, i.e., give it literal content, is because it was not a theological hypothesis, but a religious myth. For Hick, "myth" expresses more accurately what "mystery" traditionally was meant to signify.[30]

The doctrine of the Incarnation, for Hick is "myth" or "mystery." The fundamental heresy which the Church continually rejected during the patristic era was that of treating the myth of the Incarnation as an hypothesis [GUF,171]. Hick writes at length:

The Church's rejection of the series of christological heresies expresses, then, its basic awareness that the idea of divine incarnation in Jesus of Nazareth is a mystery lying beyond human comprehension and not a concept that can be given a precise meaning ... I would say that the reason why no statable meaning or content has been discovered in it is simply that it has no such content. It is not an hypothesis still waiting to be adequately defined; rather it is not an hypothesis at all. It is a mythological idea. As such it cannot *literally* apply to Jesus. But as a poetic image—which is powerfully evocative even though it contains no literal meaning—it expresses the religious significance in a way that has proved effective for nearly two millennia. It thus fulfils its function, which is to evoke an appropriate response of faith in Jesus [GUF,172].

The doctrine of the Incarnation is not a theological hypothesis, then, but a myth. It is myth, according to Hick, because (1) it represents the "application to Jesus of a mythical concept whose function is analogous to that of the notion of divine sonship ascribed in the ancient world to a king" [MGI,178]. The reasons contributing to this process we have examined earlier. It is also myth, because (2) it has no literal meaning. It is a mystery with no explanatory power.

Hick adds a third reason for the doctrine's mythological character based on the use of "incarnation" in non-theological language. His argument is that the very concept itself of a "divine incarnation" is "metaphorical." Even in secular usage, he writes, the notion of "incarnation" functions as a "basic metaphor." In this secular sense, "incarnation" is understood to be "the embodiment of ideas, values, insights in human living" [GHMN,58]. As an example, Hick suggests that Winston Churchill could be said to be the embodiment or incarnation of the British spirit of defiance against Nazi Germany. Similarly, the same kind of application can be made to Jesus.

We began this section asking why Hick had concluded, in the previous section, that the purpose of the doctrine of the Incarnation was not to state a literal truth. Rather its purpose was to "express an evaluation" or "to evoke an attitude." We see now that the reason that that is the particular purpose of the doctrine results from the fact that the doctrine is a myth. The truth peculiar to myth is not that of being literally true or false, but of being practically true or false. And practical truth consists "in the appropriateness of the attitude [evoked] to its object" [MGI,178].

The Practical Truth of Nicea

Both the doctrine of the Incarnation and the Nicene Christological definition, according to Hick, are myths. They have no literal truth. Rather, they have only a practical truth. They give "vivid concrete expression" to the "religious significance of Jesus." They are intended to evoke an appropriate attitudinal response.

What precisely is the "appropriate" response in their case? The appropriate response is for the believer to adopt the "attitude to Jesus as saviour" [GUF,172,176]. Hick writes:

> For it is through Jesus that we have encountered God as our heavenly Father and have entered into a new life which has its ultimate centre in God. The absoluteness of the experience is the basis for the absoluteness of the language. For any amount of divine revelation or illumination has an 'absolute' character. Since it is God, the ultimate reality, that is being encountered, the experience cannot fail to have the accent of absoluteness and 'once for all' finality. That *God* has been encountered through Jesus is communicated mythologically by saying that he was God the Son incarnate. The myth is thus an appropriate and valid

expression of the experience. It is not the only way of expressing it; but amidst the conflict of religions in the early Roman empire this particular mythology was apt and effective ... Jesus, in following whom we have found our way of salvation, and in whose shared life we experience the life that is eternal, must be called divine, Son of God, God incarnate: this was an appropriate way of indicating his religious significance [GUF,172].

In his supporting arguments, Hick will say that (1) it is appropriate to respond to Jesus as saviour, even with the quality of "absoluteness" provided we do not conclude to exclusivity, and (2) we can worship Jesus, even though he is only mythologically Son of God, because he is an "image" of God.

First, let us consider Hick's reasoning about "absoluteness." From the above quotation we select the important reference to "absoluteness":

The absoluteness of the experience is the basis for the absoluteness of the language. For any amount of divine revelation or illumination has an 'absolute' character. Since it is God, the ultimate reality, that is being encountered, the experience cannot fail to have the accent of absoluteness and 'once for all' finality.

We have encountered this notion of "absoluteness" earlier in the opening pages of this Chapter as well as in the above section on myth.

Why is the issue of "absoluteness" an important one for Hick to examine? We recall that Hick is asking the question: is the attitude to Jesus as saviour an appropriate response to the myths of the doctrine of the Incarnation and the Nicene two-natures Christology? The practical truth of a myth depends on it evoking an appropriate attitude. Since the doctrine of the Incarnation and the Nicene definition cannot, according to Hick, be literally true, are they at least "practically" true? The Christian attitude to Jesus as saviour has traditionally disclosed the quality of absoluteness or finality about it. An objection to his Christology, which Hick now addresses, runs like this: it would seem rather inappropriate that a myth with only practical truth value should be able to evoke an attitude of absoluteness. Such an attitude could really only be evoked by something that was literally, and not merely mythologically true. Therefore, the doctrine of the Incarnation and Nicea are not merely practically true, but are literally true.

If Hick wishes to maintain the value of myth in religion (which he does), then he has to account for the appropriateness of "absoluteness" in the Christian response to the myth of the Incarnation of Jesus. But at the same time, he will wish to argue against the conclusion that Christianity is "absolutely" or "exclusively" the "*only* way to salvation" [GUF,172].

In order to confront these issues, Hick says we must get behind the myth itself and examine the religious experience that gives rise to the myth. Specifically, he says, we must look at the "quality of psychological absoluteness" of religious experience [GUF,173].

Hick states that salvation experiences are not the only experiences to have an "absolute" quality about them. He mentions other such experiences as falling in love, of being grasped by an important truth, and of utter loyalty to a monarch or country as all having a quality of being absolute and unqualified [GUF,173]. He writes:

> There is nothing tentative or provisional about them; each demands to be expressed in the language of ultimates—the perfect unity of two hearts in love; total illumination; absolute loyalty. Such language is ... inherently and unavoidably 'Ptolemaic'— one's own experience is normative and everyone else's is seen in relation to this as the centre [GUF,173].

Hick continues by noting that in experiences other than religious, a 'Copernican' point of view is not too difficult to achieve. One is not tempted in these cases "to translate the absoluteness of the experience into a doctrine of the validity of our own experience" [GUF,173]. One need not be exclusive, for example, and love no one but one's beloved, or contend that no one else loves his or her beloved.

Hick admits that in religious experience, the experience of finality is naturally expressed in language which, if taken literally, implies exclusive validity. But if in analogous situations, like being in love, the language of absoluteness does not imply exclusivity, then it need not do so in religious experience either. Hick writes:

That Jesus is my Lord and Saviour is language like that of the lover for whom his Helen is the sweetest girl in the world. Logically, there can only be one sweetest girl in the world; but if we treat the lover's words literally and infer from them the claim that every other girl in the world is less sweet than Helen, we shall not be doing justice to the kind of language he is using [COC,32].[31]

The conclusion regarding Christianity's exclusive claims about Jesus is obvious. Hick writes:

... if from the confession of Jesus as Lord and Saviour we infer that men cannot respond to God except through Jesus, we misuse the language of personal commitment and turn living religion into dogmatic exclusiveness [COC,32]

And if Jesus is not *the* saviour, but only *my* saviour, then even more so can the Christian not use the absoluteness of his religious language to imply any special uniqueness or exclusivity to Christianity. For Hick, the believer in each world faith experiences "divine revelation, divine activity, divine claim, divine grace, divine love with the same quality of absoluteness" [GUF,175]. The world religions contain a richness of myths that need not be set against each other. Hick sees these myths not as "rival scientific hypotheses" but "more like different art forms, each of which is at home in a different culture" [GUF,175-6].

With these distinctions on "absoluteness" established, Hick can directly address the key question: is it an appropriate response to relate to Jesus as saviour, if in fact He is not literally Son of God, but only mythologically so?

Hick's response is that since the idea of Incarnation has no literal meaning, the question has to be rephrased in this manner: in spite of the mythic character of the idea of Incarnation, can salvation through Christ be a reality and His God-Manhood an effective expression of that reality [GUF,176]?

Hick's initial remark is that Christians do not have to ask *whether* salvation through Jesus is real. They already start with that fact. Salvation comes through Jesus not because it is Jesus who saves, but because God saves and Jesus was "so fully God's agent ... that the divine reality was mediated through him to others" [GUF,177].

Hick now asks the central question about Jesus' uniqueness:

Did he [Jesus] mediate the presence and saving power of God in an unique sense, in which no other religious figure has ever mediated it or ever could mediate? [GUF,177].

Before he can answer the question, Hick says he must first clarify it. If the question is to be interpreted factually and answered on the basis of observation, it has a clear meaning. He writes:

The idea of the unique saviourhood of Christ would then entail that only those who have been saved through him are really saved. It would follow from this that the experience of salvation, of consciousness of God, of liberation from the bondage of sin, of new life in response to the divine call, reported from within other faiths is illusory [GUF,177].

But the only reason for taking such a position, claims Hick, is "sheer dogma." The position itself is impossible to support or refute. But should we not wish to make such a claim, then the "idea of the unique saviourhood of Christ ceases to have factual content" [GUF,177]. For Hick, while Jesus is *a* saviour, he is not *the* saviour in any unique fashion. He concludes:

What we then have is not an assertion of unique saving effectiveness in human life, but a particular redemption-myth attached to one great historical way of salvation [GUF,177].

We have been examining Hick's account of the sense in which it is appropriate to respond to Jesus as saviour. Hick accepted the appropriateness of "absoluteness" in language, but not the conclusion of "exclusivity" for Christianity or "uniqueness" for Jesus.

We now turn to another objection which Hick meets. The objection is this: how can it be appropriate for Christians to worship Jesus if he is not God? "Can we and should we worship a human being who is not literally God incarnate?" [GUF,177].

Hick begins his response by saying we must acknowledge the "elasticity of the concept of worship" [GUF,177]. He writes:

> In a sense only the ultimate—in Anselm's formula, that than which no greater can be conceived—is to be worshipped, and the worship of any lesser reality is idolatry. But in practice we are only able to worship the ultimate under some proximate, and indeed anthropomorphic, image ... Christ is the Christian's image of God. [GUF,177-8].

Hick says that in the history of religions, the images through which God has been worshipped have always been considered nearer to God than ourselves. But they have not been God Himself, merely servants of God. Hick explains:

> To worship such a mediator is not to regard him as the Infinite but to regard him as so vastly 'higher' than ourselves in the direction of God as to be for us an image through whom the ultimate divine reality can be worshipped [GUF,178].

Hick's final conclusion to this question about worship is given as follows:

> Thus I am suggesting that we have to distinguish between the distinctively christian faith-response to Jesus as Lord and Saviour, and the expression of this response in the mythological identification of him as God incarnate. Jesus is the concrete image of God through whom our worship is focused, and the idea of the Incarnation is an effective mythic expression of the appropriate attitude to him. In regarding the attitude as appropriate we are regarding the myth as true. But if we make the mistake (which lay at the root of all christological heresies) of trying to turn the myth into an hypothesis, we not only falsify its character but also generate implications that would make impossible any viable theology of religions [GUF,178-79].

Hick does not argue that, because the language of the doctrine of the Incarnation is mythological, it therefore should be dropped. Precisely because it does have a practical truth, it can be, it should be and it will continue to be used in the liturgical life of the Church. It will

... most naturally [be] at home in hymns and anthems and oratorios and other artistic expressions of the poetry of devotion [MGI,183].

However, the Church will gradually come to see the mythological character of this language, and then will consider it simply to be "the hyperbole of the heart" [MGI,183]. In doing so, Hick hopes that Christianity will "outgrow its theological fundamentalism, its literal interpretation of the idea of incarnation" [MGI,183], just as it outgrew its "biblical fundamentalism" [MGI,184]. The opening stories of Genesis are now seen to be "profound religious myths, illuminating our human situation" [MGI,184]. Similarly,

... the story of the Son of God coming down from heaven and being born as a human baby will be seen as a mythological expression of the immense significance of our encounter with one in whose presence we have found ourselves to be at the same time in the presence of God [MGI,184].

If the Church does not outgrow its theological fundamentalism in an easier and less divisive manner in which it outgrew its biblical fundamentalism, then, warns Hick:

... the future influence of Jesus may well lie more outside the church than within it, as a 'man of universal destiny' whose teaching and example will become the common property of the world, entering variously into all its major religious and also secular traditions [MGI,184].

Hick says that the symbols or titles of Jesus, e.g., Son of God, God the Son, God-Incarnate, served their purpose well for over a thousand years [MGI,179]. For countless people these symbols have been "effective expressions of devotion to Jesus as Lord" [MGI,179]. Hick says that it did not matter much that in the Christian mind these symbols had quickly come to be, no longer symbols, but "components in literal statements" [MGI,179]. This kind of literalism accompanied a simultaneous biblical literalism.

In neither case did the literalism do much harm. However, with the rise of modern scientific knowledge, the literalist approach was to come into serious conflict with the new discoveries. As a result, the biblical literalists

> ... were led into the false position of denying first what astronomy and then what palaeontology and evolutionary biology were revealing [MGI,179].

Something similar is occurring now with the theological literalists, with those who literally interpret the essentially poetic and symbolic language about Jesus [MGI,179].

For understood literally the Son of God, God the Son, God-incarnate language implies that God can be adequately known and responded to *only* through Jesus; and the whole religious life of mankind, beyond the stream of Judaic-Christian faith is thus by implication excluded as lying outside the sphere of salvation [MGI,179].

As long as "Christendom was a largely autonomous civilization," the literalist interpretation of the God-Incarnate language did little real harm [MGI,179]. But with more and more contact with other religions in the past few hundred years,

> ... the literal understanding of the mythological language of Christian discipleship has had a divisive effect upon the relations between the minority of human beings who live within the borders of the Christian tradition and that majority who live outside it and within other streams of religious life. [MGI,180]

Summary

In this Chapter we have presented Hick's reasons why the traditional understanding of the uniqueness of Jesus is no longer adequate. We can organize and summarize these reasons as follows.

1. *Consciousness of Jesus*: Christology must be exclusively grounded in the consciousness of the historical Jesus. Jesus did not understand himself to be, nor did He teach that, He was God in any sense.

2. *Scripture*: (a) In the Old Testament, the language of divine Sonship is poetic and adoptionist. There is no reason to think that language had any other meaning when applied to Jesus.

(b) In the New Testament, the Christological sayings of John's gospel were later constructions of the early Church already involved in a deification process. John's gospel goes beyond the consciousness of Jesus.

3. *Tradition*: (a) Nicea's "consubstantiality" represents the culmination of the deification process of projection. The language about Jesus has passed from metaphor to metaphysics. (b) Nicea's language is culture-bound and therefore optional.

(c) Nicea's language is mythological. It does not represent a theological hypothesis but a religious myth.

(d) Nicea's two-natures Christology has no literal meaning. It is as contradictory as is the notion of a square-circle.

4. *Theology*: (a) Jesus cannot be unique in the traditional sense, because that would violate God's universal salvific will. The problem of limited world communications up to now has prevented God from making a single self-revelation.

(b) It was mainly the Christian experience of reconciliation with God that contributed to the deification of Jesus.

5. *Language*: (a) The language of divine Incarnation is mythological language. The notion of Incarnation is itself a natural metaphor. The doctrine of the Incarnation is a myth adopted by the early Christians because of similar notions in their environment.

(b) The language about Jesus has an "absolute" or "total" quality because God is involved when one experiences Jesus. The resultant language is the language of love, the language of total commitment, but not necessarily of objective exclusivity.

With the conclusion of this Chapter I complete my analysis of Hick's reexamination of the traditional understanding of the uniqueness of Jesus. In the following Chapter, still on Hick's Christology, I present his major observations on the relationship between Jesus and

God, as well as his alternative to "divine incarnation," that is, his notion of "divine inhistorisation" and its advantages for the wider
ecumenism among world religions.

Endnotes

1. Hick gives another summary of his Christological position:
"Such a reconsideration [of Jesus' unique identity] is in any case required today by the realization that the historical Jesus almost certainly did not in fact teach he was in any sense God; and also by the fact
that Christian thought has not yet, despite centuries of learned attempts, been able to give any intelligible content to the idea that a
finite human being, genuinely a part of our human race, was also the
infinite, eternal, omnipotent, omniscient creator of everything other
than himself. The proper conclusion to draw, as it seems to me, is that
the idea of divine incarnation is a metaphorical (or, in technical language, a mythological) idea. When a truth or a value is lived out in
human life, it is a natural metaphor to speak of its being incarnated in
that life. Jesus lived in full openness to God, responsive to the divine
will, transparent to the divine purpose, so that he lived out the divine
agape within human history. This was not a matter of his being of the
same substance as God the Father, or of his having two complete natures, one human and the other divine. Agape is incarnated in human
life whenever someone acts in selfless love; and this occurred in the
life of Jesus to a startling and epoch-making degree. Whether he incarnated self-giving love more than anyone else who has ever lived, we
cannot know. But we do know that his actual historical influence has
been unique in its extent.

This kind of reinterpretation of the idea of divine incarnation ...
provides, as it seems to me, a basis for a form of Christianity which
can be part of the religiously plural world of today and tomorrow"
[GHMN,28].

2. In a letter to me, dated September 1, 1989, Professor Hick writes:
"I am, as it happens, in the midst of Christology again, and am to give
the Birks lectures at McGill, Montreal, in this area later this month ... I
hope to continue with writing in this area and eventually to produce a
smallish book."

3. See also: GUF, 93.

4. Unless otherwise indicated, when we quote Hick's use of Scripture, we use the translation he provides.

5. Hick notes that in the New Testament's effort to say who Jesus was for His followers, a variety of titles was attempted. He mentions three titles that "failed to catch on," namely: (1) the "Son of Man," (2) Paul's "second Adam," and (3) John's "Logos." The first, "Son of Man," explains Hick, was Jesus'self-affirmation in reference to the eschatological Son of Man who was to come on the clouds of heaven. This title was not used outside the reports of Jesus' own teaching. The second title, "second Adam," has persisted even down to today, but it has never been very widely used. The third title, "Logos," while it has remained important, is primarily a theologian's title [MGI,174].

6. Chapter 4, Michael Goulder, "The Two Roots of Christian Myth," 64-86, and Chapter 5, Frances Young, "Two Roots or a Tangled Mass," 87-121. Goulder argues that the idea that Jesus was a divine Incarnation was introduced into the early Church by the Samaritan, Simon Magus (Acts 8:9f). The Samaritans held, says Goulder, that God was a "binity." Simon Magus believed himself to be an incarnation of one member of this binity. Since the application of this myth to Jesus is clearly unbelievable today, concludes Goulder, the whole notion of Jesus' being a divine Incarnation is dispensable..

Young broadens the influences which introduced divine incarnation into Christianity. It was not only Samaritan influence, but also Greco-Roman influences. She refers to "redeemer myths" and "divine men." Young concludes: "Whether or not we can unearth the precise origins of incarnational belief, it is surely clear that it belongs naturally enough to a world in which supernatural ways of speaking seemed the highest and best expression of the significance and finality of the one they identified as God's awaited Messiah and envoy," 119.

7. For Hick's argument that Jesus' "atonement" is a mythological idea, see "Evil; and Incarnation," in *Incarnation and Myth: The Debate Continued*, Michael Goulder, ed., (London: S.C.M., 1979), 77-84.

8. We again recall Hick's epistemology of religion. But here we note that "projection" is applied specifically to Jesus' deification.

9. Here we see Hick's use of the Kantian distinction between noumenon and phenomenon applied to Jesus. Jesus is the historical noumenon, whereas the images of Jesus in later theology are

phenomena. In this sense, knowing Jesus is like trying to know the historical persons we mentioned in our Chapter 2.

10. This is an expansion of the list Hick provided earlier in Chapter 2.

11. We recall here that Hick argues that this same phenomenon is at work regarding God and His image in all world religions. Each religion has formed its own picture or image of God.

12. Hick draws out the comparison by referring to the mahayanist doctrine of the Three Bodies (Trikaya) of the Buddha. There is, first, the earthly or incarnate body (Nirmanakaya). This "body" is a human being who has become a Buddha and who teaches the way to others. Gautama was the most recent of these incarnate bodies, although there were others prior to him, and there will be others yet to come. The second body (Sambhogakaya), sometimes called the "Body of Bliss," is a "transcendent or heavenly Buddha, a divine being to whom prayer is addressed." The relation between the first and second bodies, is that the first Buddhas are incarnations of the second. Hick explains: "The earthly Buddhas are incarnations of the heavenly Buddhas, projections of their life into the stream of this world." Finally, all the transcendent Buddhas are ultimately one in the third, Dharma Body (Dharmakaya), which is Absolute Reality [MGI,169].

13. Hick notes that the Burmese translation of the New Testament treats Dharma as the equivalent of Logos, e.g., "In the beginning was the Dharma ..." [MGI,169].

14. Hick quotes from B. H. Streeter's *The Buddha and the Christ* (Macmillan, 1932),83: "... Mahayana stands to primitive Buddhism in a relation not unlike that of the gospel according to St. John to that according to St. Matthew" [MGI,169].

15. Sometimes Hick will speak of Nicea, at others of Chalcedon, at still others of Nicea-Chalcedon. The terms are interchangeable with him. He seems to use them as a shorthand reference to the traditional understanding of the uniqueness of Jesus. He also refers to Nicea or Chalcedon when he speaks of the "two natures Christology" as "substance" or "consubstantial" or "homoousios Christology," or as the "language of God-incarnate."

16. See GUF, 149-50.

17. On this point of adoption, Hick notes that the two Old Testament passages, Psalm 2:7 and 2 Sam 7:14 were originally said of an

earthly king or kings [MGI,174].

For a brief and popular presentation of Hick's argument on the title of "Son of God" as metaphoric, see "Changing Views of the Uniqueness of Christ," *The Times*, October 11, 1975, p. 14.

18. We may genuinely wonder why Hick inexplicably introduces the words "physically" and "physical" in the above text. Up to now he has been using such terms as *literal* or *metaphysical*, and *metaphorical* or *poetic*. Here he uses "physical" to mean "metaphysical" or "literal" or "real". This confusion is not at all helpful, especially when Hick is trying to clarify the language of divine Sonship.

19. Hick always speaks of simply "God" in this context, unless he is quoting the Nicene creed.

20. Hick rarely refers to Paul's letters. In one instance where he does, he seems to imply they too are theology, and that the process of the exaltation of Jesus in the language of faith is evidenced in them. Hick explains that the Christian use of the idea of incarnation "quickly developed a larger meaning in a process that was already far advanced in the writings of St. Paul and that was eventually to culminate in the doctrine of the incarnation of the Second Person of the Holy Trinity" [GUF,169].

21. See also: GHMN,124-25.

22. Wolfhart Pannenberg, *Jesus—God and Man* (London: Westminster Press, 1968),237. The quote from Pannenberg which Hick employs indicates that the titles of Jesus in John's gospel were applied to Him by the post-Easter community. Jesus' pre-Easter self-consciousness was not Messianic.

23. Hick makes only a few comments on the synoptic gospels. While John's gospel may have moved beyond the historical Jesus, Hick writes that the synoptic gospels on the other hand do give "an impression of a real person with a real message" [MGI,171-2]. The synoptics are "three sets of communal 'memories' of Jesus, variously influenced by the needs, interests and circumstances of the Christian circles within which they were produced". But even the synoptics, because they are "variously influenced," writes Hick, contain "conflicting indications [about Jesus]" [MGI,172].

24. See also: GHMN, 74.

25. See: GHMN,74; GUF,169.

26. Hick says that the doctrine of the hypostatic union is Hellenic and not Hebraic thought [GUF,150-1]. Hick wants a return to biblical categories which do not speak of God's "essence" or "substance," but of God's "purpose" and "action." Christ's Sonship, he argues, ought to be expressed in these biblical, rather than Greek philosophical, terms.

27. See also: GUF, 116, 149.

28. By "hypothesis" Hick says he does not intend to imply that something is affirmed merely hypothetically or doubtfully. An hypothesis, he says, can be affirmed as "indubitably true" [GUF,169].

29. Hick says his notion of myth applies not only to Christianity but to other religions as well. Hick mentions such non-Christian myths as: the verbal dictation of the Koran to Mohammed by God, the incarnation of Lord Krishna [GUF,175].

30. In stressing the mythological character of the doctrine of the Incarnation, Hick does not intend to suggest that in Christian consciousness the Incarnation was categorized as myth. He writes:"On the contrary, the doctrine of the Incarnation has generally been regarded as a literal truth—though one which, as a 'mystery', is opaque to human understanding" [GUF,170-71].

31. Hick also used this example in an earlier brief article "Christ's Uniqueness," *Reform*, October, 1974, p.19.

CHAPTER FOUR

Hick's Christology (Part Two)

In Part One of the presentation of Hick's Christology, I elaborated on the foundation of his Christology, the process of deification and the many aspects to the problem of the language of divine Sonship. Now I present in this Chapter, Hick's alternative to the idea of divine Incarnation. The first section lays the groundwork for Hick's position. It summarizes how Hick understands the relationship between Jesus and God, especially as it concerns salvation. I include two of Hick's responses to objections that relate to Jesus' death and resurrection.

In the second section I present Hick's alternate notion of the "divine inhistorisation" of God's *Agape.*

In the final section I present in brief some of the advantages Hick sees for the ecumenism among world religions should his Christology be adopted.

Jesus and God

Hick has claimed that Jesus cannot be God-Incarnate because such a notion is mythological and lacks any literal meaning. Nevertheless, Hick feels that he must say something of the relationship of Jesus to God.

He does not speak of "God-in-Himself" or the "immanent God." The reason is because such a notion constitutes the divine noumenon, and the noumenon is knowable only through its phenomenon. Therefore, Hick refers only to "God-acting-towards-mankind," or "God acting savingly towards mankind," or "God-in-relation-to-man"

117

[MGI,181]. Although Hick does not use the term explicitly, we can refer to his idea of God as the "economic God."[1]

Hick agrees that only God can save:

All salvation that is, all creating of human animals into children of God is the work of God [MGI,181].

It is to this "economic God," to the God who saves, that the different religions have given different names. Christianity, in fact, uses several overlapping names for God-in-relation-to-humankind. Hick lists them as: "the eternal Logos, the cosmic Christ, the Second Person of the Trinity, God the Son, the Spirit" [MGI,181].

Hick now relates Jesus to this economic God. He writes that if, for example, we refer to the economic God as the "Logos,"

... then we must say that *all* salvation, within all religions, is the work of the Logos ... [MGI,181].

Wherever God is doing his saving work, in whatever culture or religion, there is the Logos and salvation. While the various revelations of the Logos are particular, no one of them is superior to the others. They are different but equal. Hence, there is no traditional "scandal of particularity" in reference to Jesus being the one and only Saviour for all mankind. For in addition to the Logos being at work in human life through Jesus, the Logos has equally been at work through the Hebrew prophets, Buddha, the *Upanishads* and the *Bhagavad Gita*, the Koran, etc.

It is at this point that Hick makes an important statement for his Christology:

But what we cannot say is that all who are saved are saved by Jesus of Nazareth. The life of Jesus was one point at which the Logos that is, God-in-relation-to-man has acted; and it is the only point that savingly concerns the Christian; but we are not called upon nor are we entitled to make the negative assertion that the Logos has not acted and is not acting anywhere else in human life [MGI,181].

From the above statement, we see that Hick makes the decisive separation between the Logos and Jesus. The two are not to be identified as in traditional Christian faith and theology. The Logos has not "become flesh." It has simply "affected human consciousness for its liberation or salvation" [MGI,181]. It has done so by affecting Jesus' consciousness, and through Him by means of "spiritual contagion" transforming the consciousness of all who surrender to Him. But the Logos has similarly

... affected human consciousness ... in various ways within the Indian, the semitic, the Chinese, the African ... forms of life [MGI,181].

For Hick, then, the traditional Christian claim that Jesus was unique in God's salvation because He was the Second Person of the Trinity, true man and true God, plainly is not true. There is simply God who saves. He impinges on the consciousness of certain human beings and so effects the conversion of those who are open to God's ways. One such human being was Jesus.

Jesus enjoys no uniqueness as the only Saviour for the world. Because His disciples experienced the total claim of God through Him, they began to speak of Jesus in exalted ways. As we have seen, this process culminated by mistaking mythological language for metaphysical language. Jesus, for Hick, like other founders of the world's great religions, is true man. He is not true God. He is not the Logos. Hick does not accept the traditional Christian understanding of the unique identity of Jesus with the Logos.

Hick does, however, allow for a qualified uniqueness to be attributed to Jesus. Jesus was "intensely and overwhelmingly conscious of the reality of God," addressing God as *abba*. In the presence of Jesus, one felt oneself in the presence of God. Furthermore, Jesus was self-aware. He was aware of Himself as being related to God in this intense and overwhelming way. Therefore, argues Hick, Jesus would have been aware that He enjoyed a certain unique relationship with God that was lacking to His contemporaries. He would have been aware that "he was himself far more intensely conscious of God" and

... far more faithfully obedient to God, than could be said of any contemporaries" [MGI,173].

Whereas others would have had "only a faint and second-hand sense of the divine presence," Jesus was "directly and overwhelmingly conscious of the heavenly Father" [MGI,173]. This direct and overwhelming consciousness of God enabled Jesus (1) to speak about God with authority, (2) to summon men and women to live as God's children, (3) to declare God's judgment and forgiveness of sins, and (4) to heal the sick [MGI,173]. Most important of all, however, Jesus' self-awareness of this "unique" relationship He had with God, was at the basis of His attitude towards the two titles "Messiah" and "Son of Man". Hick writes:

Jesus must thus have been conscious of a unique position among his contemporaries, which he may have expressed by accepting the title Messiah or, alternatively, by applying to himself the image of the heavenly Son of Man two categories each connoting a human being called to be God's special servant and agent on earth [MGI,173].

It is clear, however, from this explanation, that Hick's understanding of the uniqueness of Jesus has nothing to do with the traditional understanding of who Jesus was. Hick's account of Jesus' uniqueness is simply that He was more aware of God's saving presence than was anyone else He happened to meet.

Hick Meets Objections

On this issue of Jesus and His relationship to God, Hick addresses two objectives. The first objection argues that Jesus' death was uniquely necessary for mankind's salvation. The second argues that Jesus was unique because of His resurrection.

In Hick's Chapter, "Jesus and the World Religions" in *The Myth of God Incarnate*, the issue of the death of Jesus arises at the end of a lengthy discussion on the language of divine Sonship and introduces Hick's position on a global vision of religions. The saving death of

Jesus as the only means by which men and women can be saved is presented as an objection to Hick's position, that neither Jesus' life nor His death is uniquely necessary for mankind's salvation. Hick puts the objection this way:

> If Jesus was literally God incarnate, and if it is by his death alone that men can be saved, and by their response to him alone that they can appropriate that salvation then the only door-way to eternal life is Christian faith [MGI,180].

Such a conclusion for Hick is not global but exclusivist. It excludes the majority of the human race from salvation. It is "excessively parochial" presenting God "as the tribal deity of the predominantly Christian West" [MGI,180]. Is it credible, asks Hick, that the loving God of all people would save "only those born within one particular thread of human history" [MGI,180]? It is in fact, so incredible, that even the theologians have developed

> ... a mass of small print to the old theology ... to square an inadequate theology with the facts of God's world [MGI,180].

This "mass of small print" is a reference to the epicycles to which we referred in our elaboration of Hick's Copernican revolution.

Hick's point is that the death of Jesus cannot be unique for salvation, because it excludes, by dint of the Christian faith in that death, most of humanity from the very salvation it was meant to effect. The saving death of Jesus, inasmuch as it requires belief as God's unique redemptive act, is for Hick, an exclusivist position. Since God's universal salvific will does not exclude anyone, Hick concludes that Jesus' death does not make Him the unique saviour for all men and women.[2]

We now turn to the objection based on the Christian faith in the resurrection of Jesus. In the same Chapter, "Jesus and the World Religions," the resurrection of Jesus appears as a brief digression within a wider context. This wider context elaborates on the comparable development of Christology and Buddhology regarding the exaltation of a human person to a divine status. We have already elaborated this wider context. The resurrection of Jesus is introduced into this context in the form of an objection. The objection, like that of the death of Jesus, is to Hick's claim that Jesus is no more unique to salvation than is Gautama. The objection means to establish, on the basis of his resurrection, that Jesus does enjoy a uniqueness which the Buddha does not. Hick writes:

> But, it will be said, there is at least one all-important difference between Jesus and Gautama which justifies the ascription of divine attributes to the one and not to the other namely that Jesus rose from the dead. Does not his resurrection set him apart from all other men and show him to be God incarnate [MGI,170]?

While admitting that such an argument "inevitably suggests itself," Hick contends that such an argument is "difficult to sustain." Because of the survival and growth of "the tiny original Jesus movement," Hick says the first disciples must have had

> ... some kind of experience of seeing Jesus after his death, an appearance or appearances which came to be known as his resurrection ... [MGI,170].

Hick's position is that today we simply do not know "in what this resurrection-event consisted." Hick mentions two extreme possibilities within which various interpretations of the resurrection fall: from (1) the resuscitation of Jesus' corpse, to (2) visions of the Lord in resplendent glory.

Hick's point, however, is that it does not really matter what the resurrection was, for it was never understood by the first disciples as proof of Jesus' divinity. Hick writes:

> But it must be doubted whether the resurrection-event whatever its nature was seen by Jesus' contemporaries as guaranteeing his divinity [MGI,170].

Hick then lists New Testament and patristic references to support his argument, that even a most literally understood resurrection at that time was not as astounding as it may be to the modern mind.[3] From this evidence, Hick concludes:

> Thus the claim that Jesus had been raised from the dead did not automatically put him in a quite unique category [MGI,171].

What the resurrection-event indicated, however, was that Jesus

> ... had a special place within God's providence; but this was not equivalent to seeing him as literally divine. For Jesus is not said to have risen in virtue of a divine nature which he himself possessed but to have been raised by God. Accordingly the first Christian preachers did not draw the conclusion that he was himself God but that he was a man chosen by God for a special role and declared by his resurrection to be Messiah and Lord (Acts 2.22 and 36) [MGI,171].

Hick's first point, then, in refuting the objection, is that the early disciples could easily accept a "physical resurrection," but such a resurrection, even if it occurred, did not prove divinity.

Hick's second point is that for the modern mind, it is difficult to accept "stories of a physical resurrection," especially (1) when they are 2,000 years old, and (2) "the written evidence is in detail so conflicting and so hard to interpret." But again argues Hick, even if such an event did occur, we would not conclude to the risen person being divine. On this point Hick quotes from George Caird.[4] Caird asks us to suppose that an acquaintance whom we had good reason to believe dead was, with irrefutable evidence, seen to be alive. We might revise our ideas about science, but not our ideas about God. We would not conclude that the "risen" acquaintance was God, or that God had approved of all this person ever said or did [MGI,171].

For Hick, then, the resurrection of Jesus does not make Him the unique Saviour of the world. Even if Jesus' resurrection occurred as traditionally understood, it would not prove the unique divinity of Jesus. Not even for the disciples did the resurrection prove Jesus' divinity. *A fortiori* for the contemporary mind, Jesus' resurrection does not prove His divinity. The scientifically-conditioned and critically-prepared person of today neither knows in what the resurrection-experience consisted, nor is he or she inclined to accept as literally true any stories about a "physical resurrection."

"Divine Inhistorisation"[5]

In this section we present Hick's alternative to "divine Incarnation." Borrowing a term from Herbert H. Farmer, Hick calls his alternate suggestion "divine inhistorisation." God's *Agape* is inhistorised as Jesus' *agape*.[8] Hick spends some time analyzing whether or not the identity between the two *agapes* is qualitative only, or also numerical. Hick concludes saying we should proclaim not *homoousios* but *homoagape*.

Hick says that we must return to the biblical categories of "action" and "purpose" to speak of Jesus' divine Sonship. He notes that Gregory of Nyssa provided a starting point for this kind of approach when he wrote that "the word 'Godhead' signifies an operation and not a nature (phusin)" [GUF,151].

Hick then proceeds to argue that we only know of God's nature from His deeds. These divine deeds are historical events received as revelation; they are "God's self-revealing activity in human history." Christian thought operates *ex post facto*, that is, after and upon these deeds which reveal God's purpose. Since these deeds are specific, we know God's purpose not simply in general, but specifically. And for the Christian, one knows specifically "the divine purpose of *Agape* which we see disclosing itself in the life of Jesus" [GUF,152]. Hick continues:

> For everything that Christianity knows concerning the divine attitude and activity towards mankind can be summarised in the assertion that God is *Agape*; and this assertion is a direct transcript of the faith that the *agape* which we see in Jesus in some sense *is* the eternal *Agape* of God [GUF,152].

According to Hick, since the Godhead is not a nature but an operation, then the *Agape* which is revealed in Jesus' life and death is a divine operation. It has nothing to do with Jesus having a divine nature. Quoting St. Paul (2Cor 5:19), Hick says we can say of this divine operation that "God was in Christ reconciling the world to himself." This means, interprets Hick, that "in Christ the divine *Agape* was at work dealing with sinful humanity" [GUF,152]. Hick goes on to say in what sense this operation is unique:

> And if we say, as twentieth century theologians, that in the life of Jesus christian faith finds, not divine substance injected into a human frame, but divine action taking place in and through a human life, we mean that in the that life is uniquely to be seen the divine *Agape* directly at work within our human sphere [GUF,152].

With these notions of divine operation and *agape*, Hick can now suggest an alternative to the term divine Incarnation. He suggests that, instead of "divine incarnation" we today should speak of the "divine inhistorisation" [GUF,152].[7] This term, says Hick, albeit inelegant, gets

> ... explicitly away from the picture of the eternal Logos descending into a temporary envelope of flesh and from there welding a sovereign power and rule. As against this we must ultimately affirm, ultimately on the authority of the New Testament witnesses themselves, that God in Christ has not merely acted *upon* or *into* human history, like a meteor falling from above, but has acted *within* and *through* man's life by influencing the course of our history from the inside. [GUF,152-53].

To have this kind of influence within history, the divine *Agape* would have to become "expressed in the actions and reactions of a human being or beings."

What does it mean to say that "the divine *Agape* has been inhistorised in the person of Jesus?" Hick says it means

> ... that the compassion and concern which were expressed in Jesus' dealings with the men and women whom he met were identical with God's *Agape* towards those particular individuals. For the idea which has sustained Christianity is that this *agape*

which we see reflected in the mirror of the gospel records at work in human time, in particular finite situations, is none other than the eternal and universal *Agape* of God ... [GUF,153].

Jesus' *agape* was God's *Agape*. And from this *agape* towards particular people in first century Palestine, one can perceive God's *Agape* towards all people of all time. Hick writes:

The gospels depict God's love inhistorised, operating self-revealingly in relation to certain individuals, but thereby in principle and in prolepsis taking the initiative to redeem human life in all its depths, dimensions and predicaments [GUF,154].

Hick adds that what the Chalcedonian formula of *homoousios* emphasized was that Jesus' *agape* was not *like* (the Arian homoi-ousios) God's *Agape*, but "literally *was* God's *Agape* acting towards them" [GUF,154].

At this point Hick says certain philosophical questions arise. For example: What does it mean to say the *agape* of Jesus *is* the *agape* of God? Hick asks: "Where in the *is-spectrum* are we to place the 'is' of the hypostatic union which occurs when we say that Jesus is divine, or that Jesus Christ is God incarnate?" [GUF,154-55].[8] Hick says it is only dodging the question to say that the "is" of Jesus' divine Sonship is "unique and that therefore nothing can be said about it" [GUF,155].[9] The theologian, argues Hick, does have some idea of what he means when he says "Jesus is God." Hick adds:

If we are going to use the christological 'is', we are under an inescapable obligation to say at least to some extent how its use is like and unlike other uses of 'is' [GUF,155].

Hick asks us to consider the two statements: "Jesus *is* both God and man," and "Jesus *is* both human and divine." The use of *is* in the statement "Jesus is *both human and divine*" is the *is* of predication. It predicates of Jesus two different characteristics of humanity and divinity. Philosophically, says Hick, this means that in Jesus we have the

... coingredience of two universals in one particular. ... Theologically, it treats divinity adjectivally, and suggests that the quality of divinity is something which may be present in varying degrees in different human beings, Jesus Christ being marked off from the rest of mankind in that he possessed this quality in a greater degree than other men [GUF,156].

However, the use of *is* in the statement "Jesus is *both God and man*" is to use the *is* of class membership regarding Jesus' humanity, but the *is* of identification as regards His deity.

With reference to Jesus' *agape* being identical with the *agape* of God, Hick says two possibilities present themselves. The identity can be qualitative or numerical. Qualitative identity, while difficult to measure, is not unclear in meaning. Two different mothers may love their respective children with a qualitatively identical love. However, one could not say that these mothers have a numerically identical love.

Regarding Jesus' *agape* as being identical to God's, there seems to be no trouble saying that it is qualitatively identical. But it does seem a misuse of the term to say it is numerically identical, argues Hick. Nevertheless, Hick says (in seeming contradiction to what he said above), that the issue of numerical identity will have to be modified "when we try to take account of the uniqueness of the divine nature and therefore of the divine *Agape*" [GUF,157].

The qualitative identity of Jesus' *agape* with God's is relatively clear in meaning and "by itself, leads to a Degree Christology." Hick writes:

If divine incarnation consists in the embodiment in a human life of a certain quality of *agape*, then incarnation is something that is capable of degrees and approximations. The divine quality of *agape* has been more fully incarnated in some lives than in others, and has doubtless been intermittently incarnated in a great number of lives, being predicable of some of an individual's actions and not of others [GUF,157].

But then Hick adds:

when we speak of degrees of incarnation we are speaking of the incarnation of divinity, adjectivally construed, and not of the incarnation of the numerically unique life of the Godhead [GUF,157].

Hick continues by noting that such Degree Christology, or qualitative identity of Jesus' *agape* with God's falls too short.

The little it does say is part of the traditional christian claim concerning Christ, and is indeed a very important part of it; but it is a part and not the whole. It does not encompass the central claim that Christ is uniquely the incarnation of God the Son; that, in a phrase of Irenaeus', 'the Father is the invisible of the Son, but the Son the visible of the Father' [GUF,157].[10]

The numerical identity of *agape* between two human beings, contends Hick, can only be said to be nonsense. Two human beings are numerically distinct and can never be numerically one. But says Hick, with the central Christian claim concerning Jesus being God, "we seem to meet precisely the paradoxical assertion that God and a man were numerically identical" [GUF, 158].

At this point Hick wishes the reader to note that by *agape* Hick means "not ... some kind of static substance" but "volitional attitudes and operations." Hence, we are to speak of the "activities of 'agapeing'" be they human or divine.

We are then concerned with the relation between the infinite Agapeing of God in relation to mankind and the finite agapeing of Jesus within a certain limited segment of man's history [GUF,158].

Hick says that whereas it is meaningless to say that two finite *agapes* are numerically identical, it is not necessarily meaningless to say that a finite and infinite *agape* are numerically identical. The reason is the infinite in some sense includes the finite [GUF,158-9].

Hick says such an interpretation of Jesus' agapeing agrees with what the New Testament says about Jesus. He adds that the Incarnation was "a temporal cross-section of God's Agapeing" [GUF,159]. As such, "the divine operation seen incarnate on earth was not the entirety of the divine operation." Hick's point is that while Jesus "was *totus deus*, 'wholly God,'" He was not "*totum dei*, 'the whole of God.'" Hence, Jesus' *agape* was "genuinely the *Agape* of God at work on earth." However, it was only a finite or limited expression of God's *Agape*. Hick writes:

> Jesus' *agape* is not a representation of God's *Agape*; it *is* that *Agape* operating in a finite mode; it is the eternal divine *Agape* made flesh, inhistorised. But 'made flesh' and 'inhistorised' signify a finite and hence a limited expression of the infinite love, a disclosure of that love at work, not in relation to every aspect of the created universe, nor in every possible situation, but in a set of specific human situations located in a specific stretch of the human story ... [GUF,159].

Hick now asks if this inhistorisation of the divine *Agape* in Jesus' *agape* can properly be said to be numerical identity? Hick says it depends on which of three understandings of numerical identity one uses. There is (1) self-identity, (2) identity through time, and (3) identity by continuity or inclusion (i.e., the relation of part to the whole). Hick's contention is that when we speak of the numerical identity of Jesus' agapeing with that of God's, it is some form of the third notion that is being employed [GUF,160].

Yet something further must be added in order to specify the "particular instance of continuity" that is referred to in Jesus' case. The continuity between Jesus' *agapeing* and that of God's is a "continuity of event rather than of entity." Hick explains:

> It is a continuity of agapeing considered as an activity, rather than of *agape* considered as some kind of substance or essence. Our question then is this: Can an instance be found of the continuous identity of actions, which might provide a conceptual model by which to interpret the statement that the agapeing of Jesus is continuous, and in that sense identical, with the divine Agapeing [GUF,160]?

Hick notes that in the Fathers of the Church, there was the analogy of continuity between "a source of illumination and the light which radiates from it."[11]

Hick picks up this analogy of light. He wishes to indicate that just as the Patristics used the example of light to illustrate their argument of continuity, so given the modern scientific understanding of light, Hick is able to illustrate his point. With the modern understanding of light as wave motion (rather than the rival theory of fast-moving particles), light is understood as a pattern of relations holding between certain events. The identity of a ray of light from the sun is now seen to consist in (1) an identity of pattern and structure, and (2) the identity of cause, i.e., the sun, and effect, i.e., the procession of light waves. Hick's conclusion is that the "set of light pulsations which affect ourselves is identical, numerically identical, with the radiating activity of the sun" [GUF,162].

Hick can now turn to his main point which is to apply this understanding of light to the numerical identity of the *agapeing* of Jesus with that of God. Hick writes that in this latter case, to assert numerical identity is

> ... to assert two things. First, there was an identity of structure or pattern, namely a moral pattern, between Jesus' agapeing and God's Agapeing in relation to mankind. Thus far this constitutes a qualitative identity between Jesus' *agape* and the divine *Agape*; and this is as far as an Arian type of christology is willing to go. But a Chalcedonian type of christology goes further, affirming, second, a direct causal connection between Jesus' attitudes to his fellow human beings and God's attitudes to them. This converts the qualitative identity of agapeing into a numerical identity. However, the causal connection postulated here is not, any more than is that between the successive events constituting the emissions of a ray of light from the sun, an external relation between distinct entities. To suppose otherwise is to create insoluble because false problems for physics and christology [GUF,162].

At this point Hick refers once again to his Kantian epistemology and states that the divine activity in this process is noumenal, and the life of Jesus is the phenomenal correlate. Hick concludes that Jesus had one nature which was "wholly and unqualifiedly human," and only one will, a human will. But Jesus' nature and will were directed by the *Agape* of God. Thus, Jesus' consciousness—and it is with Jesus' consciousness that we began our study of Hick's Christology—is that of having been given a special vocation at His baptism by God. This consciousness of God enabled Jesus to speak with authority about God's love and to act with power. However, according to Hick, Jesus was not conscious "of being God, or the Son of God, or the eternal Logos made flesh." What was Jesus conscious of? Hick writes:

He was consciously a human being, distinct from God ... But he was also conscious within himself of a love for all men and women in their plight of estrangement from God and from one another; and he was conscious that in this *agape* he was at one with God himself, so that in his actions God's *Agape* was enacting itself and God's Kingdom was being created. How, or why, did all this come about? We can only say that it was an act of grace, God's act of making his *Agape* towards mankind visible and tangible in the midst of human life for the saving of that human life [GUF,163].

Hick makes the interesting comment that "in the end ... christology must proclaim what it cannot explain." What in fact seemed to be Hick's explanation of the doctrine of the Incarnation for the modern mind, turns out not to be that at all. Hick says what he has been exploring

... is not a way of explaining Christianity's traditional claim about Jesus but only of indicating what that claim is. The assertion that Jesus' agapeing was continuous with the divine Agapeing is no more self-explanatory than the assertion that Christ was of one substance with the Father. Neither of these phrases, strictly speaking, explains anything. Each is an expression of faith; and each is an expression of the same faith. But nevertheless I wish tentatively to suggest that the continuity-of-agapeing formulation may today be more intelligible than the oneness-of-substance formulation [GUF,164].

131

Hick believes that what he has done is "to reformulate the doctrine of the Incarnation in its full traditional meaning" [GUF,ix]. He writes:

> ... we know, at least ostensibly (and what better way could there be?), what we mean by *agape*, but we do not know what we mean by substance or at least, whatever meanings of 'substance' we isolate we then have to disavow as failing to provide an interpretation of *homoousios* which would render that term acceptable to twentieth-century Christians let alone twentieth-century non-christians! [GUF,164].

And yet Hick states, rather strangely, that "whether it [the doctrine of the Incarnation] be expressed in terms of identity of substance or of identity of agape", it is mythological language. Hick concludes: "Let us proclaim the *homoagape* rather than the *homoousia*!".

Implications for World Religions

In the introduction to Hick's Christology, it was noted that his reflections on Jesus and the Church's traditional teaching about Him, were occasioned by his thinking on issues relating to world religions. It will complete this presentation of his Christology, if I explain, in brief, the advantages Hick sees for the relationships among the world religions should his own position be adopted.

These advantages can be listed as follows: (1) the mythological interpretation of the doctrine of the Incarnation exorcises that understanding of the uniqueness of Jesus which has "poisoned" interreligious dialogue; (2) since particular revelations of God have occurred among world religions, each religion can share its "unique" contribution and be enriched by the others; (3) Hick's Christology within the theocentric model makes possible a global theology of religions; his Christology allows new powerful images of Jesus to emerge, as well as encouraging a more effective and renewed understanding of Christianity's mission.

Particular Revelations Shared

One of the obstacles in interreligious dialogue is the Christian claim to a uniqueness among religions because of its foundational claim about the uniqueness of Christ. Hick writes that the doctrine of a unique divine Incarnation in Jesus

> ... has long poisoned the relationships both between Christians and Jews and between Christians and Muslims, as well as affecting the history of Christian imperialism in the far East, India, Africa, and elsewhere [GHMN,8].

Such an exclusivist position does not promote a harmonious and fruitful mutual exchange among religions. It is not a global view. Hick wishes to overcome all such exclusivist approaches to the relationships among the world religions. With his reinterpretation of the identity of Jesus through an analysis of the language of divine Sonship, Hick believes he has opened the door to a real solution. He writes:

> When we see the incarnation as a mythological idea applied to Jesus to express the experienced fact that he is our sufficient, effective, and saving point of contact with God, we no longer have to draw the negative conclusion that he is man's one and only one effective point of contact with God. We can revere Christ as the one through whom we have found salvation, without having to deny other points of reported saving contact between God and man. We can recommend the way of Christian faith without having to discommend other ways of faith. We can say that there is salvation in Christ without having to say that there is no salvation other than in Christ [GHMN,75].

While the Logos may reveal the divine in particular but equal revelations, these revelations, according to Hick, are not meant to be appropriated solely by the adherents of each faith. Rather, the Logos makes these particular revelations to enrich the whole religious life of mankind. God's gifts are to be mediated to all through each world faith sharing with the others what He has done for them. A particular world faith is not meant to displace another, but rather to deepen and enlarge the other's tradition. Each world religion has a specific gift to offer the world. In that sense, each world faith is unique. Christianity's specific gift to the world is Jesus. It offers Jesus to the other faiths[12] Similarly, from the other faiths, Christianity is invited to take into its own religious life the specific gifts of the other world faiths [MGI,181].

Global Religious Vision

With this particular Christology, Hick feels he can propose a global religious vision. The many particular saving actions of the Logos, and the resultant sharing among world religions of their experiences of the "economic God," form the basis of this global vision. This vision (1) affirms the unity of all mankind before God, and (2) seeks "to make sense of the diversity of God's ways within the various streams of human life" [MGI,180]. This is the pluralistic setting in which each religion and Hick refers specifically to Christianity must be understood [MGI,180].[13]

Writing in *God Has Many Names*, Hick elaborates at length on the nature and purpose of a global religious theology:

But while there cannot be a world religion, there can be approaches to a world theology. For if awareness of the transcendent reality that we call God is not confined to the Christian tradition, the possibility opens up of what might be called (for want of a better term) a global theology. Christian theology consists in a body of theories or hypotheses designed to interpret the data of Christian experience. Analogously, a global theology would consist of theories or hypotheses designed to interpret the religious experience of mankind as it occurs not only within Christianity but also within the other great streams of religious life, particularly the nontheistic traditions, including large sections of Hinduism, Buddhism, Confucianism, and Taoism, and also within the great nonreligious faiths of Marxism, Maoism, and Humanism. The project of a global theology is obviously vast, requiring the cooperative labors of many individuals and groups over a period of several generations. The increasing dialogue of world religions is basic to this work. Out of this there may be expected increasingly to come comparative and constructive studies both of particular areas of belief and of larger systems of belief. Thus my own discussion in *Death and Eternal Life* (Harper & Row, 1977) is intended as a Christian contribution to a global theology of death, exploring both the differences and the deeper convergences of insight on this subject between Christianity, Hinduism, and Buddhism. This kind of endeavor is both extremely demanding and extremely exciting, but is at present in its infancy and can only develop fully through collaboration between scholars possessing a wide range of expertise [GHMN,21-22].

Christianity

What effect does this "interpermeation" and "wider ecumenism" have on Christianity's teaching about Jesus and on its mission? Regarding Jesus, Hick is succinct:

The Jesus who is for the world is not the property of the human organization called the Christian church, nor is he to be confined within its theoretical constructions [MGI,182-83].

Just as Jesus has created "powerful images in men's minds" in the past, so within varying cultures and the changing circumstances of history He can continue to create fresh images and become Lord of men and women in yet further ways. There is no one single way to express a faith-response to Jesus. Faith in Jesus can be expressed in a variety of religious myths, writes Hick, and

... our own western mythology of the incarnation of the Son of God must not be allowed to function as an iron mask from within which alone Jesus is allowed to speak to mankind [MGI,182].

Regarding the Christian mission, in lands where Christianity is the minority, that mission must be founded on two important and related approaches: (1) to present Jesus in such a way that His person, His teaching, and a commitment of discipleship to Him are attractive; (2) to present Jesus and the Christian life in a way that recognize the other great world faiths as "ways of salvation." These two approaches constitute a new missionary policy, as opposed to an "older" policy. The older missionary policy held that Christianity had to convert the world to Jesus by converting the world to itself. Such a policy, accompanying as it did, Western military and economic imperialism, can now be seen to have failed, writes Hick. Nor can such a policy be renewed, given that imperialism has collapsed. In the new policy, the first approach of making Jesus and discipleship attractive aims at replacing Western political and cultural imperialism as a vehicle of Christian mission. The second approach of recognizing other faiths as ways of salvation aims at replacing Western insistence that Jesus can be presented only in its own "interpretive framework", a framework that has been built up around Jesus over centuries.

Interfaith Dialogue

Our final section in this part treats Hick's understanding of interfaith or interreligious dialogue. He gives a succinct account of this in the last Chapter, "Christian Belief and Interfaith Dialogue," of *God Has Many Names*.[14]

Hick begins by noting that interfaith dialogue can take place on three different levels. These levels are: (1) "discursive theological dialogue," (2) "interior dialogue," for example, that practiced by H.le Saux and Bede Griffiths, and (3) "practical dialogue," wherein the various faiths unite together to consider various human problems [GHMN,116]. Hick's main concern here is with the first level, that of discursive theological dialogue.

Hick states that there are a wide range of understandings about what constitutes discursive dialogue. The two ends of the spectrum are: (1) "purely confessional dialogue, in which each partner witnesses to his own faith convinced that this has absolute truth while his partner's has only relative truth," (2) "truth-seeking dialogue, in which each is conscious that the transcendent Being is infinitely greater than his own limited vision of it." Dialogue frequently moves back and forth along the scale.

In confessional discursive dialogue, the Christian proclaims his own faith

... that God has entered decisively into human history in the person of Jesus Christ, the second Person of the holy Trinity incarnate, who has revealed the divine nature and purpose for man in a unique and unsurpassable way in comparison with which all other revelations must necessarily be secondary, in the sense of being incomplete, or imperfect, or preliminary, or in some other way vitally inferior to the Christian revelation [GHMN,117].

In confessional dialogue the Christian sees his faith as "not one among many," but as "the only true revelation of God" [GHMN,118]. The problem, of course, is that in confessional dialogue, each faith sees itself that way. They are operating from a Ptolemaic point of view.

Confessional-type dialogue can only end in conversion of the other partners or in a "hardening of differences" [GHMN,121]. Since conversion is rare, Hick suggests that in order for dialogue to be mutually fruitful, "lesser changes than total conversion must be possible." Each partner to the dialogue must be open to learn and to change from the others.

It is at this point that Hick asks a crucial question of the Christian: "how serious and how radical can this possibility of change be in the Christian partner?" [GHMN,122].[15]

Hick begins his reflections by making a customary distinction, which he attributes to Karl Barth, between "the historical phenomenon called Christianity, which is one of the religions of the world," and "personal discipleship and devotion to Jesus Christ" [GHMN,123]. This "proper and helpful distinction" is between the historical Jesus and the "historical development of christianity ... a human, and often all-too-human, affair" [GHMN,122-3]. Hick had first presented the significance of this distinction in Chapter 7, "The Essence of Christianity," of *God and the Universe of Faiths*. There he distinguishes the Christ-event as "*that which is most important* to Christianity," from the Christian developed religion with its forms of worship and fixed system of beliefs as "*that which is uniquely christian* and not paralleled in any other faith" [GUF, 108,119]. Hick implies that what is "uniquely" Christian is not necessarily what is most important to it [GUF,108]. Hick writes:

I am suggesting, then, that in its essence Christianity is the way of life and salvation which has its origin in the Christ-event ... Christian belief consists in the beliefs of Christians, and the

Christians of one age cannot legislate for the Christians of another age, either past or future. Christianity, then, is an open-ended history ... [GUF,119].[23]

The point for interfaith dialogue is that the Christian should participate as a disciple of Jesus and not as an adherent of historical Christianity.

While Hick sees this distinction as "very fruitful," the extent of its fruitfulness will depend on the critical investigations of the historical Jesus on which it is grounded. How much of the man Jesus is to be understood in terms of the developed theology of the Church? Hick writes:

For the confessionalist it is usually an unquestioned assumption that belief in the doctrines of the incarnation and the Trinity are essentially involved in personal discipleship to Jesus. But it is precisely this assumption that has been directly questioned in many recent discussions of Christian origins and of the development of Christian thought, and that is today at the center of a considerable debate [GHMN,123].

Hick's view is that the doctrines of the Incarnation and the Trinity are part of the "intellectual construction" or "cultural packaging" in which Western Christianity has "wrapped the gospel" [GHMN,124]. The disciple of Jesus can therefore leave them aside and not simultaneously abandon the discipleship itself.[17]

With this kind of development it may be possible, then, for the Christian in dialogue no longer

... to insist, however gently, upon the uniqueness and superiority of Christianity; and it may be possible to recognize the separate validity of the other great world religions, and both to learn from them and enable them to learn from the Christian tradition [GHMN,126].

In any event, Hick says that Christians will have to move from the confessional to the truth-seeking pole of the spectrum of discursive dialogue.

Endnotes

1. We cannot say "economic Trinity" because Hick does not accept the doctrine of the Trinity, at least not as literally true.

2. For Hick's argument that Jesus' "atonement" is a mythological idea, see "Evil and Incarnation," in *Incarnation and Myth: The Debate Continued* (London: S.C.M., 1979): 77-84.

3. Hick refers to: (1) Jn 11:1-44: Jesus raises Lazarus, (2) Lk 7:11-17: Jesus raises widow's son, (3) Mk 5:35-43; Lk 8:49-56: Jesus raises Jairus' daughter, (4) Mt 11:5: Jesus has the report sent to John the Baptist which included the fact that the dead were being raised up, (5) Mt 27:52-3: Matthew records that at Jesus' crucifixion "... the tombs were opened, and many bodies of the saints who had fallen asleep were raised, and coming out of the tombs after his resurrection they went into the holy city and appeared to many," (6) Heb 11:35 [cf. 1K 17:17] The writer of this letter claims as a sign of faith in former times that "Women received their dead by resurrection," (7) Irenaeus, *Against Heresies*, bk.II, ch.31, par.2, refers to the raising of the dead both by the apostles and others within the early church [MGI,170-71].

4. G. B. Caird, "The Christological Basis of Christian Hope," *The Christian Hope*, SPCK 1970, 10.

5. Hick presents his account of the "divine inhistorisation" in Chapter 11, "Christ and Incarnation" in *God and the Universe of Faiths*, 148-64.

6. This point, already claimed by Hick to be a faithful alternate interpretation of *homoousios*, appeared very early in Hick's so-called "orthodox" period. It can be found fully elaborated in terms of divine inhistorisation as early as 1959 in Hick's "A Non-Substance Christology?" *The Colgate-Rochester Divinity School Bulletin* (May 1959): 41-54. This article retitled "Christology at the Cross Roads," reappears in F. G. Healey, ed., *Prospect for Theology* (London: James Nisbet & Co., 1967), 137-66. His argument appears the following year in *Christianity at the Centre* (London: S.C.M., 1968), 31-40. Hick also referred to this position in "A Philosopher Criticizes Theology." *The London Quarterly & Holborn Review*, 187, 6th Series 31 (April 1962): 103-10, esp. 108-10. Undeveloped references to this position of Hick's can be found at the beginning of his career in *Faith and*

Knowledge (Ithaca: Cornell University Press, 1957): 205, 206; and in the second edition, (1966): 190.

7. cf. Herbert M. Farmer, "The Bible: Its Significance and Authority," *Interpreter's Bible*, v.1, (Abbingdon: Cokesbury, 1952), 3-31, esp. 12.

8. Hick lists among the "is-spectrum" the following: (1) the *is* of predication, (2) the *is* of class membership, (3) the definitional or equivalence-of-symbols *is*, and (4) the *is* of identification [GUF,154].

9. Hick had made this argument earlier in his article "Christology at the Crossroads," in F. G. Healey, ed., *Prospect for Theology* (London: James Nisbet, 1967): 137-66, esp. 155-6.

10. See *Against Heresies*, bk.iv, ch.6, par.6.

11. Hick refers to Tertullian, *Apology*, ch.21; Athanasius, *Four discourses Against the Arians*, Discourse iii, par.4 (cf. *Defence of the Council of Nicea*, ch.3, par.12).

12. As an example of how Jesus can be Christianity's gift to other world religions, Hick refers to the impact Jesus and His teaching had on Gandhi. Gandhi remained a Hindu. Nevertheless he drew joy and comfort from the New Testament. Also, the suffering of Jesus was a factor in Gandhi's faith in non-violence. Notwithstanding the impact which the New Testament and the life of Jesus had on Gandhi, Gandhi never found it necessary or important to accept the traditional Christian doctrine of the Incarnation. Nor did Gandhi accept the more modified teaching that only Jesus was the gate to eternal life. This point is important for Hick. The significance and the impact of Jesus remain, and can be offered to others, without resorting to the later doctrines of the Incarnation or Consubstantiality. Hick quotes Gandhi:"He [Jesus] expressed as no other could, the spirit and will of God. It is in this sense that I see Him and recognise Him as the son of God".[MGI,183: quoting M. K. Gandhi, *What Jesus Means to Me*, compiled by R. K. Prabhu, Navajivan Publishing House, Ahmedabad, 1959, 9-10.]

13. This global religious vision is the first step in Hick's development of a theology of religions, which he undertakes in *God and the Universe of Faiths and continues in God Has Many Names*.

14. This Chapter was originally delivered as the second Younghusband Lecture at King's College, London, on May 3, 1977, and

published in *World Faiths* (Autumn 1977), and also delivered as a lecture at the quincentenary celebrations of Uppsala University in September 1977, and published as "Christian Theology and Inter-religious Dialogue," in *The Frontiers of Human Knowledge*, T. T. Segerstadt (Uppsala 1978): 1-14.

15. Hick seems to be suggesting something stronger is needed than what he implied earlier in *God and the Universe of Faiths*. There he wrote: "It is not, I would suggest, necessary to 'water down' the essential christian understanding of Christ in order to relate it realistically to the wider religious life of mankind" [GUF,106].

16. What is important about Christianity, says Hick, is that it, along with the other world religions, is a way of salvation [GUF,145]. What is unique about Christianity is the Christ-event and the subsequent cultural response known as Christianity. But this uniqueness, since it is simply one means taken by God and one cultural faith-response, is not nearly as important as being a way of salvation.

17. Hick had earlier suggested this distinction in *God and the Universe of Faiths* where he draws on Cantwell Smith's account of how a religion, every religion, has a "questionable relation" with its founding event [GUF,103].

PART TWO: Evaluation

CHAPTER FIVE

The Consciousness of Jesus

T he topic of this study is the uniqueness of Jesus Christ in the theocentric model of the Christian theology of world religions. Having completed the presentation of Hick's reassessment of the traditional understanding of Jesus' uniqueness, it is now appropriate to evaluate that understanding.

This evaluation, which covers the remaining chapters, is organized around the themes systematized in the Summary to Chapter 3: namely, (1) the Consciousness of Jesus, (2) Scripture, (3) Tradition, (4) Theology, and (5) Language. To these themes are added: based on Chapter 2, an evaluation of Hick's (6) Epistemology, and use of the idea of (7) Copernican Revolution; and based on Chapter 4, an evaluation of Hick's (8) Divine Inhistorisation and *Homoagape*, and (9) the Resurrection of Jesus.

The first three themes are the most significant and crucial to Hick's Christology. I refer to them as his primary arguments. Therefore, the evaluation of these arguments receives the most attention, three lengthy Chapters. Once this main critique is in place, we move to the remaining themes, or what I call his secondary arguments, which are addressed together in a fourth Chapter.

Consciousness of Jesus and Method

At the end of Chapter 3 we summarized Hick's position on Jesus' consciousness as follows:

Christology must be exclusively grounded in the consciousness of the historical Jesus. Jesus did not understand himself to be, nor did He teach that, He was God in any sense.

Based on the above summary, two questions need to be examined: (1) must Christology be exclusively grounded in the consciousness of the historical Jesus? (2) Is it true that the historical Jesus did not teach that He was in any sense God?

First, must Christology be grounded exclusively in Jesus' historical consciousness? I am not concerned here with the actual content of that consciousness. Rather, the question is a methodological one.

Hick claims that Christology must be *exclusively* grounded in the consciousness of Jesus. The operative word here is *exclusively*. It is true that Christology must be grounded—at least in part—in Jesus' historical consciousness. Christology cannot make Jesus out to be something or someone He was not. Otherwise, Christology would be fraudulent, mythological, proposing a lie or at least an unintentional error concerning the truth about Jesus.

Christology must be *partly* grounded in the consciousness of Jesus. For as James Dunn remarks, if it is not so grounded, it runs the "danger of losing touch with Jesus as he actually was."[1] Jacques Guillet also writes that "... the faith of the disciples rests on the consciousness of Jesus."[2] Thus, Jesus' consciousness must function as a corrective to faulty development in our coming to penetrate the full mystery of who He was/is.

But by transforming this valid principle of "*partly* grounded" into "*exclusively* grounded", Hick turns the principle into a reductionist norm, eliminating all development—not only invalid development. In fact, such a norm would practically eliminate all Christology for it would reduce Christology to nothing more than the reproduction of the contents of Jesus' self-articulated consciousness in the categories He himself would have used. This reproduction, of course, forms an important element in Christology, but need not be the sum and final aim of all Christological method.

But not only need it not be the sum of Christology, *can* it in fact be the whole of Christian reflection on Christ? Such a method would allow for no new questions to arise regarding Jesus, no new thinking about Him to occur, especially if that thinking involves categories that Jesus would not have employed. This would severly hamper the Church's mission to proclaim Christ in different cultures. In fact, it would so isolate Christ from all human understanding as to make Him something of an alien, if not completely unintelligible.

It would allow no penetration in faith into the mystery of Jesus under the guidance of the Holy Spirit. This would, and for Hick does, eliminate the gospels as expressing valid Christological development. That is, as we shall see, a serious limtation on the very process of the revelation-faith experience as it occurred historically. Consequently, if all went as Hick says it ought, there should be little or no Christology at all, not even in the New Testament.

Hick has argued that the Christological development which histori-cally occurred went beyond the consciousness of Jesus. This develop-ment took place not only in post-New Testament times, but also within the New Testament itself. Hick can only understand such a development as a deification process based on psychological projection and the spiritual needs of the disciples. He does not consider that the Christ-event could have been so astounding and full of mystery as to issue in new revelation of God that would give new meaning to old Judaic ideas. Nor can Hick envision that the Christ-event could have been so astound-ing or mysterious as to require time for the early disciples to grow in the understanding, under the guidance of the Holy Spirit, of what the Christ-event was all about. Nor does He allow that if the Christ-event is all that Christians claim it to be, that perhaps its riches will always be unfurling until the parousia—and perhaps beyond.

Hick assumes that the Christ-event was all more or less obvious. Anything that suggests otherwise for him could only be unwarranted and illegitimate, if understandable, development. Thus, Hick rules out of consideration that there might just be a valid revelation-faith dialogue that entails an implicit-to-explicit Christology.

I am not countering Hick by the *a priori* assumption that Jesus *was* someone significantly new. At this point I am drawing attention to the fact that Hick rules out from the beginning that Jesus *could possibly* represent anything radically new. The point I wish to make here is that Hick does not do a careful enough study, even of the synoptic gospels—which he accepts as providing data about the historical

Jesus. In fact, it can be said that he practically ignores most Scriptural evidence on this point.

For example, Hick would not ask what Matthew's idea of "fulfillment" is when the evangelist speaks frequently of Jesus "fulfilling" the Old Testament prophecies. Hick seems to assume that Matthew means that Jesus fulfills a prediction, that the meaning of the original prophecy retains its same meaning when Jesus fulfills it. But is this assumption warranted? Is it not possible that "fulfill" might mean something more than Hick's assumption allows for?

As scripture scholars point out, Matthew's notion of fulfillment cannot be accounted for by Hick's assumption. John L. McKenzie writes:

> The term [fulfillment] does not signify mere prediction and fulfillment ... The saving event of the Gospel gives the word of the Old Testament ... a new dimension of reality.[3]

Later in the same commentary, on Jesus as Messiah fulfilling the Law, McKenzie writes:

> In popular messianism the Messiah had a relation to the Law, but it was not a relation of bringing the Law to completeness. Jesus affirms the enduring, even eternal reality of the Law ... but it is the finished and perfect Law [finished and perfected in Jesus] that endures, not the Law of Moses ...[4]

This newness of Jesus in this context is reaffirmed in a footnote to "The Gospel According to Matthew" in *The New Jerusalem Bible*:

> ... by his [Jesus'] teaching and way of acting, [Jesus gave the Law] a new and definitive form, by which the goal of the Law is fully realised.[5]

W. F. Albright and C. S. Mann make the interesting observation that it is precisely because Jesus *does exceed* contemporary expectations about the Messiah that His opponents "were driven to find explanations of his exorcisms in a conspiracy with Satan" (Matt 12:22).[6] This example of "fulfillment" is simply one of the many Scriptural points that are significant to Hick's position, but about which he is silent.

Another example of Hick's failure to read the New Testament carefully, relative to Jesus constituting a new revelation, regards the issue of titles. Hick claims that the titles from the Old Testament, or from Judaism used of Jesus in the New Testament, indicate that Jesus was no more than a human being. There is nothing significantly new about Jesus. The point, which Hick does not refer to, is that *none of these titles as traditionally understood proved adequate to interpret Jesus.* The reason for their inadequacy was that Jesus transcended in a significantly new way the limited Jewish meanings for these titles. Both Aylward Shorter and Walter Kasper argue to this effect.[7] On the use of the title Messiah in this regard, I specifically refer to Kasper:

> If we want to talk about Jesus as the Messiah, we cannot take as a basis any of the ideas of the Messiah current in Jesus' time. Our premiss must be that, while the primitive community took over a Jewish title, it gave it a Christian interpretation. Even if it is admitted that the title was not used by the historical Jesus, what the primitive Christian preaching did was not to re-Judaize the message of Christ, but to give a legitimate answer to his claim to be the eschatological fulfilment of Israel. In its use of the title Messiah, the *primitive community was maintaining that Jesus was a fulfilment which went beyond all expectations* [emphasis added].[8]

If, for Hick, there can be no valid development in Christology, what could "Christology" possibly mean for him? Christology would amount to no more than the sum total of the Jewish meanings for the titles which Jesus may have applied to Himself or accepted. These were the only meanings available to Jesus for self-understanding. Equally, they were the only meanings his disciples had available to understand Him. For Hick there is no possibility of Jesus or others giving new meaning to these titles. What Hick in fact has done is to revert back to a closed, and eventually rejected, Christian view in the early Church. This view could not accept Jesus as transcending the then contemporary Jewish understanding. We recall here the first century roots of what later would become second and third century Ebionism.[9] These roots were already proving inadequate to the open and developing Christian faith. The first century Ebionites did not want the Christian faith to become distinct from Jewish faith. Ebionism, even in its roots, was considered to be a form of "undeveloped" Christianity and was rejected as being "rigid and unfitted to be the mouthpiece of the gospel in a new age."[10] If the Ebionites had represented the truth about Christian faith, it seems strange that the Jews would have had to expel the Christians from the synagogues, or that the Christians would have felt it necessary to develop outside the confines of the Old Law.

It is curious that Hick, in attempting to find a model for preaching the gospel to modern times, should return to the beliefs and attitudes of that group of early Christians whose contemporaries recognized it as being unwilling and incapable of meeting the demands of a new age. One would have thought Hick would have turned instead to those Christians who were developing a self-understanding in a changing context and who eventually proved successful at it.

There is a further and equally, if not more important, reason why Hick's *use* of the methodological principle of grounding Christology merely or exclusively in Jesus' consciousness is inadequate. On this point at least, he does not distinguish between faith and theology. He sees Nicea's definition, for example, as mere theological speculation.

It is true, of course, that Nicea depended on theology for its formulation. But the Council's definition moves beyond hypothesis to a doctrinal statement of faith, a judgment about what is true regarding Jesus. As a judgment it answers the question: Is Jesus consubstantial with the Father or not, yes or no? This type of question goes beyond theory, and wants to know what is in fact true.

Here one recalls Bernard Lonergan's important distinction between doctrines and systematics.[11] Doctrines are on the level of human consciousness that intends truth. Systematics represent hypothetical understanding. For example, Thomas Aquinas would admit that the psychological analogy of the Trinity is a hypothetical account. This admission would not mean, however, that he doubts the doctrine of the Trinity. Hick, on the other hand, questions not only the theological language about Jesus' equality with the Father, he doubts, in fact denies, any literal meaning to the doctrine itself.

The significant point for our evaluation of Hick is that, according to him, the Church, not only in its theological speculations but also in its very faith about Jesus, has made an important error. Apart from issues relative to the Holy Spirit leading the Church to the full truth about Jesus, and protecting her from error, Hick in confusing faith and theology has impoverished the nature and the role of faith itself.

Faith has been impoverished for theology in that it is no longer the ground and norm of Christology. Since it is faith that gives us access to the full truth about Jesus, such an impoverishment limts access to the full truth about Jesus' consciousness as well.

How has Hick altered the inter-relationship among (1) Christology, (2) the methodological principle we have been discussing, and (3) faith? First, we must state what their relationship is in order to detect what change Hick has made.

The methodological principle about which we have been concerned is a norm, but a norm *within* Christology itself. It forms part of the Christological inquiry. But Christology, including its method and principles, is grounded in the yet higher norm of the Church's faith. We have only to recall Anselm's definition of theology as "faith seeking understanding." We also recall Karl Rahner's statement that the "basis, norm and goal" of Christology is "the Christian faith."[12]

We can now clearly see how Hick has rearranged this relationship. The Church's faith for him is no longer the higher norm under which Christology operates. In fact, Hick has reversed the relationship so that now a methodological principle has become the norm of faith. Coupled with Hick's diminished understanding of the consciousness of Jesus, as well as other matters to be discussed, it is not surprising that Hick has significantly altered the meaning of the Church's faith about Jesus.

The only way Hick believes he can interpret Jesus for the contemporary person is to make optional all faith statements to date in the Church. Hence, he has elevated a methodological principle intended for speculation to the level of a norm for faith. But by proceeding in this way, Hick has cut himself off from the very norm which insures that it is *Jesus* he is interpreting to the world. Hick does not accept the development in Christology as legitimate since he cannot discover a notion of valid continuity. The reason he cannot discover such a notion is because he seems to have misunderstood the significant role of faith in its relation with theology.[13] With the notion of valid continuity done away with, all that remains is a series of isolated and unconnected articulations of the faith. Indeed, it may no longer be the one faith that is being articulated.

Consciousness of Jesus and Christ-Event

In this section we address the second question relative to this theme: namely, is it true that the historical Jesus did not teach that He was in any sense God?

It would be quite out of place and beyond the scope of this work to reproduce here the debate over the consciousness of Jesus. The issue of Jesus' consciousness forms only one component in Hick's Christology, and hence only one of the many arguments we must evaluate. Our task here is not to resolve the issue of Jesus' self-understanding. Rather, it is to evaluate the kind of approach Hick brings to bear on this issue.

What, succinctly, is Hick's position? Hick claims that Jesus did not think of Himself as God-Incarnate nor as consubstantial with the Father; that He certainly did not teach either of these things, and that therefore, He *was* neither of them.

My first response is to concede to Hick the obvious. It is true Jesus never taught explicitly that He was God-Incarnate nor consubstantial with the Father. I have no difficulty in agreeing with Hick that the Christological sayings about Jesus' being one with the Father, which occur in John's gospel on the lips of Jesus, were not likely uttered by the historical Jesus. I even agree that not only did Jesus not explicitly teach He was God-Incarnate nor consubstantial with the Father, but I also agree that Jesus would not have thought of Himself in those categories. They represent a later vocabulary.

Nevertheless, I find Hick's argument seriously deficient in two major ways. First, his position that there can be only explicit Christology involves implications which seriously distort the relationship between revelation and faith. Secondly, the scope of the assumptions behind his position is incomplete.

By way of introducing my response I wish to point out that Hick has phrased his argument in a loaded manner. By stating that Jesus did not teach that He was in any sense God, Hick is using the term "God" in an ambiguous way. We recall that Hick's overall argument is to deny the divinity of Christ as traditionally understood. The word "God," then, can mean simply "divinity." But given the context of the Old and New Testaments, the word "God" can also mean specifically "God the Father," that is the "God of Abraham, Isaac, and Jacob."[14] Hence, Hick's argument can mean either (1): that "Jesus did not teach that He was in any sense divine;" or (2) that "Jesus did not teach that He was in any sense God the Father." We have no quarrel with the latter interpretation. Jesus was not conscious of, nor did He teach, nor was He "God the Father." That concession, however, does not mean that the former statement is true, namely, that Jesus did not reveal His true divinity.

The whole struggle and itinerary of Christology from its earliest beginnings was precisely how to do justice to Christian faith in the divinity of Jesus, while at the same time acknowledging He is not God the Father. By phrasing the question the way Hick does, he confuses an already complex issue. In what follows, then, I am responding to Hick's claim that Jesus did not reveal in any sense that He was genuinely divine.

For Hick, Christology can only repeat back what Jesus has explicitly said about Himself. Most of what He says about Himself which affected later Christology occurs in John's gospel. But, as we have said, these Christological sayings most likely were not uttered by Jesus in the first place. They themselves, according to Hick, represent an invalid, if understandable, development.

In the synoptics, Jesus speaks very little directly about Himself. What He does say could not be interpreted as His explicitly proclaiming to be consubstantial with the Father. He does not even explicitly claim to be the Son of God or Lord. And it is doubtful that He explicitly claimed to be the Messiah. The main subject of His teaching is not Himself but the Kingdom of God. Since Jesus Himself has not said explicitly all or any of the things that later Christology claims for Him, Christology, claims Hick, can only say that Jesus was a man especially conscious of the presence of God.

If Jesus were consubstantial with the Father, Hick contends that He would have explicitly said so. But we might ask ourselves, what kind of revelation such a statement on Jesus' part would have been? What could it have meant for Jesus? How would it have been understood by his listeners?

153

If Hick's conditions were fulfilled, Jesus would have had to say to His disciples gathered about Him: "Repeat after me: I am consubstantial with the Father." That would be the revelation. Then, the act of faith would be the disciples' mouthed response: "You are consubstantial with the Father."

The first problem, of course, is that the word "consubstantial" would not have formed part of Jesus' vocabulary. Therefore, for Him to have used it would have been peculiar indeed. He would have had in some sense to violate His true humanity in order to have access to later cultural expressions.

The second problem is that His listeners would have had no idea what He was talking about. To have the disciples repeat an unintelligible formula is at best the lowest form of pedagogy. Even if Jesus explained what the term meant, one can hardly imagine his disciples ever catching the meaning or its significance or why He was even saying it all.

The third problem is that to reduce revelation and faith to the "Repeat after me" type of formula would no longer be revelation and faith as we know it. It would constitute a completely different order. Could we honestly say that Jesus was revealing *Himself* to the disciples if He employed such an explicit "Repeat after me" approach? On the disciples' part, is the repetition of a formula in rote fashion what faith is all about?

Even if we modify our proposed revelation on the part of Jesus, and make it more Biblical, would anything be accomplished? For example, suppose we had Jesus say explicitly: "Repeat after me: I am the Son of God." The phrase certainly would have been part of Jesus' vocabulary and that of His disciples. But He would still have had to explain in what new way it applied to Him, what interpretations were correct or faulty. But even in such a modified instance, would Jesus really be revealing Himself? He certainly, as Jacques Guillet remarks, would have opened up "boundless horizons to human thought and would [have left] us in conversation with just that—human thought, and no more."[15] Faith, as something which the Father grants, would have been reduced to the mere repetition of words. And revelation would have been the mere handing out of information *about* Jesus. The disciples' personal relationship with Him would have played a minor role, or perhaps would have been only a conclusion deduced from the information.

Guillet has examined this issue of the relation between implicit and explicit Christology and its significance for revelation and faith.[16] When the development from implicit to explicit Christology is denied as valid, the result is not just a change in method. The effects run far deeper. It would entail that we greatly alter our understanding of faith itself. And if that altered understanding were true, the nature of faith would be so seriously diminished as no longer to be faith at all.

The reason that there is a development from implicit to explicit Christology at all, is because there is a paradox at the heart of revelation and faith. Here we are speaking of Jesus' self-revelation. Guillet expresses the paradox this way:

On the one hand, Jesus alone can say what he is; and on the other, he cannot say anything concerning himself before men have spoken and said what they think about him.[17]

The first part of the paradox is required because if Jesus is the only-begotten Son of the Father, He is the only one who can both know it and reveal Himself as such.[18] The second part of the paradox is required, because in revealing Himself, what He says and does must be understood. His revelation must have meaning, and that meaning must be the same for the Revealer as for the believer. Guillet writes:

The words of revelation must be discovered by men, not dictated by Christ ... But at the same time, these words which men have found and formulated in their own language must denote what Jesus alone can say, since he alone knows who he is.[19]

For Guillet there is a visible growth in the disciples coming to find the right words of revelation. This growth is clearly traced in the synoptics. The right words of revelation then take us back to their source, Jesus Himself, who first initiated the revelation-faith dialogue. This focusing on the source is evident in John's gospel. Given the nature of the relationship between revelation and faith, and the paradox involved, the development from an implicit to an explicit Christology is not at all invalid. It is in fact demanded by the very nature of the

155

Christ-event itself. That is why, to revert to any earlier point, Christology *cannot* be grounded exclusively in the consciousness of the historical Jesus.

My point so far has been to demonstrate that Hick's position that only an explicit Christology be considered valid, ultimately distorts what Jesus' self-revelation and the disciples' faith are all about. The very relationship itself between revelation and faith requires a development that implicit/explicit Christology elaborates. If this is the case, then at least on the level of principle, Hick's claim does not hold. That is, the notion of a development from implicit to explicit Christology is in principle valid. (This conclusion does not answer the question of fact, i.e., whether in fact the development which did occur was valid or not. My point here is the more fundamental one that, contrary to Hick, development in Christology is in principle valid.)

The development from implicit to explicit Christology does not violate, therefore, the valid use of the methodological principle that Christology must be *partly* grounded in the consciousness of Jesus. To be grounded *partly* in the consciousness of Jesus and at the same time to undergo a development, are not only not mutually exclusive possibilities for Christology. They are required for fidelity to the very revelation-faith experience itself.

In evaluating Hick's position on the consciousness of Jesus, my first point has been to show that if Hick's account were true, that only an explicit Christology could be valid, then the very nature of revelation and faith would be different from what in fact it has been. I now turn to the second point: that Hick's assertion that "Jesus never taught He was God-Incarnate, and therefore was not," is over-simplified to the point of ignoring important data.

In the first place, Hick over-simplifies by unaccountably limiting Jesus' self-revelation to His words. Not only that, he builds his case on words which Jesus did *not* use. Because Jesus never said or taught that He was consubstantial with the Father or the Eternal Son of God, therefore He was not. Hick looks for certain words he thinks Jesus ought to have said (if traditional Christology were true). Since he does not find them, at least as uttered by the historical Jesus, he concludes that traditional Christology is false.

Hick does not even consider for the sake of argument the significance of words which scholars consider Jesus must have said. For example, such words include the teachings doubtlessly of the historical Jesus, which begin with the clause "But I say to you ..." Kasper writes:

> ... Jesus' 'but I say to you' makes a claim to say God's last word, a word which brings the word of God in the Old Testament to its transcendent fulfilment.[20]

Hick ignores this kind of data completely.

Nor does Hick take into account that even when Jesus came on the scene as a rabbi, a prophet, or a teacher, He was soon recognized to be something "more than" a rabbi, prophet or teacher. His teaching was experienced as something quite "new" (Mk 1:27); His authority exceeded that even of Moses (Mt 5:20-48); He spoke in such a unique way as a prophet that He made no distinction between His word and God's (Mk.1:22, 27; 2:10, par.). He was experienced as something "greater than" a prophet, even something "greater than" the wisdom of Solomon (Mt 12:41-2).

Not only does Hick overlook the data relative to Jesus' words, he also completely ignores any self-revelation that may have come from Jesus' deeds. When Hick says that Jesus did not "teach" that He was God in any sense, he means literally that Jesus did not "speak words" to that effect. Yet revelation in the Old Testament was never confined only to God's words. There were also His deeds. It is to the point here to refer to the well-known passage from *Dei Verbum*:

> This economy of Revelation is realized by deeds and words, which are intrinsically bound up with each other.[21]

Hick's notion of revelation, then, is unjustifiably narrow. We have already seen that Jesus' teaching and self-revelation in His words did reveal implicitly His true divinity. Now, again only to mention the most obvious of Jesus' deeds, we indicate that implicitly they too reveal His divinity.

Jesus is seen to be doing the things that only God could do in the Old Testament. He forgives sins as only the Father can do (Mk 2:10, par.); He feeds the people in a "desert place" (Mk 6:30-44, par.; Mk

8:1-10, par.); He rules the sea as the Lord does in the Psalms (Mk 4:35-41, par.); He raises the dead to life as only the Father can (Mk 5:21-43, par.; Lk 7:11-17,); He claims to be Lord of the Sabbath (Mk 2:28, par); He promulgates a New Law (Mt 5:20-48) and establishes a New Covenant (Lk 22:20).[22] None of these deeds or signs of Jesus strike Hick as being significant to Jesus' "teaching" who He was.

Perhaps even more important, Hick by-passes completely what modern scholars consider central to Jesus' self-understanding and self-revelation, namely, that Jesus understood Himself to be "the eschatological prophet." The significance here, as Edward Schillebeeckx points out, is that Jesus understood Himself to be not simply the last in a line, but to usher in the very end times themselves. He writes:

> Some critics think that the 'eschatological prophet' (which in no way means simply the 'last prophet') is too low a christological title ... In that case people are not thinking hard enough about the significance of 'eschatological.' Certainly in the New Testament, the term 'eschatological prophet' implies that this prophet is significant for the whole history of the world, ... Thus 'eschatological prophet' means a prophet who claims to bring a definitive message which applies to the whole of history. It is clear from texts from the Q tradition that Jesus himself was convinced of this, and even more that he attributed world-historical significance to his person: there is every guarantee here that we have a historical echo of Jesus' own self-understanding "Blessed is he who takes no offence in me" (Lk 7:23; Matt 11:6).[23]

By being the eschatological prophet, He enjoys a relationship to the Father of a different order than prophet. He is the "Beloved Son." This point is made clear in Jesus' self-revealing parable about the wicked tenants (Mk 12:1-12 par.).[24] This self-revelation is confirmed in Jesus' characteristic use of "abba" when addressing God,[25] as well as the eschatological nature of the Beatitudes.[26]

Further, the eschatological characteristic of Jesus' mission is evident at meals. It was especially at meals that Jesus accepted into His intimate company sinners and publicans. On this point Kasper writes:

Finally, every meal [of Jesus] is a sign of the coming eschatological meal and the eschatological fellowship with God ... They are an expression of the mission and message of Jesus (Mk 2.17), eschatological meals, anticipatory celebrations of feasts in the end-time (Mt 8.11 par.).[27]

Jesus' scandalous attitude towards sinners is completely overlooked by Hick as revealing something significantly new about Jesus. The fact that Jesus forgives sins, while noted by Hick, carries no Christological import. Yet Kasper writes:

Forgiving sins is something only God can do. Jesus' attitude to sinners implies an unprecedented Christological claim. Jesus acts here like someone who stands in the place of God.[28]

A further point, it is curious that Hick, who makes much of the disciples' experience of Jesus, fails to note significant implicit Christological aspects contained therein. Once again Hick omits relevant data. Jesus, like other rabbis, gathered disciples around Him. But unlike disciples of other rabbis, one could not ask to be taken into Jesus' company. Jesus did the choosing, freely calling to be with Him those whom He desired (Mk 3:13). In fact, His call is a command, "Follow Me!" (Mk 1:17). Kasper notes that it is even more than a command. He writes: "It is a creative word which makes disciples of those to whom it is spoken (Mk 1:17; 3:14).[29]

This way in which one becomes a disciple reveals something unique about Jesus' authority. The purpose of discipleship for Jesus was not the transmission of tradition, as with other rabbis. It was rather to share in the proclamation of the Kingdom of God. This meant sharing in Jesus' authority. This sharing in Jesus' authority involved a radical and inseparable discipleship that was not temporary, as with other rabbis, but permanent. The implied Christology in all this, writes Kasper, is "an unprecedented claim" regarding Jesus and his authority.

He [Jesus] is God's kingdom, God's word and God's love in person. That claim is greater and more exalted than any honorific titles can express.[30]

Up to now we have been noting the massive areas of relevant Scriptural data that Hick either omits or passes over lightly when He says that Jesus did not "teach" that He was God in any sense. Even with all the foregoing omissions noted, there remains yet a far greater omission on Hick's part. It relates to his understanding of the Christ-event. For Hick, the Christ-event is only the earthly life of Jesus, including His death, (but which death for Hick is not redemptive and certainly not an atonement). Hick has omitted from the Christ-event the resurrection of Jesus and His exaltation,[31] and the gift of the Holy Spirit. Not only has Hick massively limited the data he consults for his Christology, he does not even consider as foundational for Christian faith the crucial event itself of Jesus' resurrection and, integral to it, the imparting of the Holy Spirit. Kasper correctly states:

Nevertheless it is impossible to make the historical Jesus the entire and only valid content of faith in Christ. For Revelation occurs not only in the earthly Jesus, but just as much, *more indeed*, in the Resurrection and the imparting of the Spirit.[32] [emphasis added]

While Hick admits that after the death of Jesus, the disciples "experienced something," he disavows any central significance Jesus' resurrection has for faith.[33] The only Jesus known and experienced is the earthly Jesus. Christian faith is whatever faith the disciples had before the death of Jesus. By so diminishing the resurrection, Hick has once again reduced Christian faith. The faith that Hick claims to be interpreting for the modern world, is no longer the full Christian faith. For Christian faith was only fully inaugurated with the resurrection of Jesus. It was only after the resurrection and exaltation that Jesus could be proclaimed as "Lord." By dispensing with the importance of the resurrection, Hick has drastically shifted the basis of both faith and Christology. Neither faith nor Christology are now grounded in Jesus who died and who rose. The risen Jesus is no longer constitutive of what is being interpreted.

Not only has Hick drastically altered the nature of Christian faith. By giving no credence whatever to the gift of the Holy Spirit, he has diminished the significance of the Church as well. For Hick, there is no distinct Person of the Holy Spirit just as there is no distinct Person of the Son. The term "Spirit," like the term "Logos," simply indicates that God is experienced in relation to the world. Hick has no Pneumatology whatsoever. Hence, the Church is not enlivened by the Holy Spirit, nor is it a direct, if sacramental, mode of access to Jesus.[34]

The significant point for us is this: by so reducing the Christ-event to the earthly life of Jesus, and by reducing Christian faith to the kind of faith the disciples had before the resurrection, Hick can only account for the "newness" of Christian faith after the resurrection as the beginning of a deification process, a process that results merely from human needs. For Hick, the only valid faith for a Christian is that which the disciples had *before* the resurrection of Jesus. This faith is the model and norm for any future Christian faith. Hence, the faith of Christians of later generations can only validly be the same kind of faith as that of the first disciples *before* Jesus' resurrection. If there is a reductionism at work in Hick's thought, it reveals itself here.

The work and mission of Jesus were not complete until after His resurrection. Christian faith in Jesus, while already partly or initially grounded in the disciples' experience of the earthly Jesus, was substantially incomplete until after the resurrection. If there is anything clear from the New Testament, it is that even in primitive Christology prior to Paul, the resurrection of Jesus was at the heart of the Christian proclamation about Him.[35] And, of course, there is Paul's pointed remark that "if Christ has not been raised, then our preaching is in vain and your faith is in vain," 1 Cor 15:14.[36] All of this data, Hick silently passes over. His Christology is based on a truncated Christ and an impoverished faith.

Endnotes

1. James D. G. Dunn, *Christology in the Making: A New Testament Inquiry into the Origins of the Doctrine of the Incarnation* (London: S.C.M. Press, 1980), 33.

2. Jacques Guillet, S.J., *The Consciousness of Jesus* (New York: Newman Press, 1972), 3. Translated by Edmond Bonin from the French *Jésus devant sa vie et sa mort* (Paris: Editions Aubier Montaigne, 1971).

3. John L. McKenzie, "The Gospel According to Matthew," in *The*

Jerome Biblical Commentary, eds. Raymond S. Brown, S.S., Joseph A. Fitzmyer, S.J., and Roland E. Murphy, O. Carm., (Englewoord-Cliffs, NJ: Prentice-Hall, 1968), 67.

4. *Ibid*, 71.

5. Taken from *The New Jerusalem Bible*, p. 1617 fn. h, published and copyright 1985 by Darton, Longman and Todd Ltd. and Doubleday & Co. Inc., and used by permission of the publishers.

6. W. F. Albright and C. S. Mann. *Matthew*. The Anchor Bible (Garden City, NY: Doubleday, 1971), LVI.

7. Aylward Shorter, *Revelation and its interpretation* (London: Geoffrey Chapman, 1983), 102-4. Walter Kasper, *Jesus the Christ* (London: Burns & Oates, 1976), 103. Translated by V. Green from the original German *Jesus der Christus* (Mainz: Matthias-Grünewald-Verlag, 1974).

8. Kasper, *Jesus...*, 106-107.

9. James D. G. Dunn, *Unity and Diversity in the New Testament: An Inquiry into the Character of Earliest Christianity* (London: S.C.M. Press, 1977), 235-66.

10. Dunn, *Unity* ..., 245. On page 266 Dunn writes: "*One of the earliest heresies was conservatism!* [emphasis Dunn's] In short, the failure of heretical Jewish Christianity was that it neither held to the unity (the exaltation of Jesus showing Jesus to be the unique expression of God) nor allowed for the diversity (of developing Christianity)."

11. Bernard J. F. Lonergan, S.J. *Method in Theology* (New York: Seabury, 1972). Chapter 5 "Functional Specialties," 125-45. Chapter 12 "Doctrines," 295-333; Chapter 13 "Systematics," 335-53.

12. Karl Rahner, S.J. "Theology" in *Encyclopedia of Theology: The Concise 'Sacramentum Mundi*, ed. Karl Rahner, S.J. (London: Burns & Oates, 1975), 1686-1701, esp. 1688.

13. I do not wish at all to imply that the Church's faith is not itself grounded in the historical Jesus. Quite the opposite. Nor do I wish to suggest that theology is simply reflection on Church dogma. I am aware, as well, that one of the still unsolved problems in theology is the working out of the precise relationship among Jesus, the Church's faith, and Christology [cf. Kasper, *Jesus* ..., 28, 37-8]. My point is to demonstrate that the relationship among them which Hick has worked out is not adequate.

14. For a detailed analysis of the use of *ho theos* and *theos* in the New Testament, see Karl Rahner, "*Theos* in the New Testament," *Theological Investigations*, v.1, (New York: Seabury, 1974), 79-148, esp. 125-148.

15. Guillet, *Consciousness ...*, 11.

16. *Ibid.*, 3-14.

17. *Ibid.*, 12.

18. Although Guillet does not draw on Karl Rahner for support at this point, I wish to refer here to Rahner's reflections. Reasoning deductively, Rahner demonstrates that it would be strange indeed for Jesus to be the Second Person of the Trinity and not at the same time have this highest dimension of his being emerge into His consciousness. See Karl Rahner, "Dogmatic Reflections n the Knowledge and Self-Consciousness of Christ," *Theological Investigations*, v.5, (Baltimore: Helicon Press, 1966), 193-215.

Bernard Lonergan also, with many distinctions, makes the same kind of case from being to consciousness. He writes: "From all this we get some clarity as to how Christ as man can from his own self-consciousness make the affirmation, 'I am God.'" From an unpublished paper "The Consciousness of Christ," translated from the Latin by Michael J. Shields, S.J., p. 9. The Latin original is held by the Lonergan Research Institute, Toronto, Canada.

19. Guillet, *Consciousness ...*, 11.

20. Kasper, *Jesus...*, 102

21. "Dei Verbum," par.2. *Vatican Council II: The Counciliar and Post Counciliar Documents*, ed. Austin Flannery, O.P. (New York: Costello, 1981).

22. I have confined my Biblical references to the synoptics. I do this to indicate that even if one accepted Hick's argument that the synoptics (as opposed to John) are alone trustworthy regarding the historical Jesus, that even they provide abundant material which demonstrates that the deeds of Jesus reveal an implicit Christology which affirms His divinity.

For Michael Green's account of implicit Christology, in opposition to Hick, see "Jesus in the New Testament," in *The Truth of God Incarnate* (London: Hodder and Staughton, 1977), 42-57.

23. Edward Schillebeeckx. *Interim Report on the Books "Jesus"*

and "Christ". (New York: Crossroad, 1981), 66-67.

24. For an elaboration of the significance of this parable, see Rino Fisichella, *La rivelazione: evento e credibilità*, (Bologna: EDB, 1985), 297-9.

25. For a detailed account of Jesus' use of "abba," see Dunn, *Christology* ..., 26-28. For an insightful argument grounding a Christology of Jesus' consciousness in His faith, see Karl Rahner and Wilhelm Thusing, *A New Christology* (London: Burns & Oates, 1980), 143-54.

26. Schillebeeckx, *Jesus: An Experiment in Christology*. Trans. by Hubert Hoskins (New York: Seabury, 1979), 172. Later Schillebeeckx writes: "The eschatological prophet would come it was said, with glad tidings for the poor ... Jesus' beatitude signifies that is happening now ..." 177.

27. Kasper, *Jesus* ..., 101.

28. *Ibid.*, 102.

29. *Ibid.*, 103.

30. *Ibid.*

31. When Hick refers to the "exaltation" of Jesus, he means not the "ascension of Jesus to the right hand of the Father," nor Jesus being given "the name above every other name." By "exaltation" Hick means, as we have seen, that Jesus was "deified" in the minds of the disciples.

32. Kasper, *Jesus*, 35.

33. For Hick, the resurrection of Jesus is not something new in terms of life after death. Jesus simply follows the pattern that is available to every human creature. According to Hick, life beyond the grave is a spatial world or environment, although of a different kind of space than our present one. While it is spatial and a real environment, it is not material, but mind-dependent. There is no resurrection of the body in the usual sense of Christian faith. But there is continuity of memories, desires, etc. There are in fact many worlds beyond the grave. The particular world one enters depends on how one has lived in this life. Hick believes in reincarnation, not a reincarnation back into this world, but into higher worlds. Given enough time and enough worlds, everyone will come to his senses, and eventually acknowledge his dependence on God. Hick is unclear about what the final world is, but it will be that of an ideal community of everyone who has ever lived, only now living consciously in the divine presence. Although

Hick does not treat in any detail what happened to Jesus after He died, it seems He would have been reincarnated into one of the higher worlds, if not immediately into the highest. See Hick, *Death and Eternal Life* (San Francisco: Harper & Row, 1976), 171-93, 265-310, 450-464. For a summary of these views, see Hick, *The Second Christianity* (London: S.C.M. Press), 117-36. See also by Hick: (1) "Theology and Verification," *Theology Today*, XVII, 2 (April 1960): 12-31; this article was reprinted under same title in Basil Mitchell, ed., *The Philosophy of Religion* (London: Oxford University, 1971): 53-71; (2) "Mr. Clarke's Resurrection Also," *Sophia*, XI, 3 (October 1972): 1-3; (3) "Resurrection Worlds and Bodies," *Mind*, LXXXII, 327 (July 1973): 409-12; (4) "Present and Future Life," *Harvard Theological Review*, 71, 1/2 (January/April 1978): 1-15; this article appears as Chapter 9 in Hick, *Problems of Religious Pluralism* (London: Macmillan, 1985): 129-45; and (5) "Life After Death," *Epworth Review*, VII, 1 (January 1980): 58-63.

34. For Hick, there are only two ways of experiencing Jesus: to have been alive when He walked the earth and met Him then, or to experience God impinging on one's consciousness as one reads the New Testament [MGI,172]. Even in the latter case, while Hick would say the Bible was written by people of faith, he has no elaborated position on inspiration. See his *Philosophy of Religion*, (Englewoord-Cliffs, NJ: Prentice-Hall, 1983), 72-73.

35. See for example Dunn's exegesis of Rom 1:3f in *Christology* ..., 33-36. Other early texts that witness to the centrality of the resurrection for Christian faith: 1 Cor 15:3-8, Acts 8:37, Rm 10:9, 1 Cor 12:13, Eph 5:14, 1 Tim 3:16, Acts 2:24-8, 3:15,26, 4:10,33, 5:30f, 10:41f, 13:31-37, 17:3,31, 26:22f.

36. Translations of Scripture unless otherwise indicated are from *The New Oxford Annotated Bible with Apocrypha*. (Oxford: Oxford University Press, 1977), Revised Standard Version, expanded edition by Herbert G. May and Bruce M. Metzger.

CHAPTER SIX

Scripture

In the previous Chapter we evaluated the first of Hick's three primary cases against the traditional understanding of the uniqueness of Jesus: namely, the consciousness of Jesus. We now turn to the second of these themes, his Scriptural case.

Specifically, this Chapter evaluates Hick's position regarding the Scriptural understanding of Jesus' divine Sonship with special reference to John's gospel. At the end of Chapter 3 we summarized Hick's Scriptural arguments as follows:

(a) In the Old Testament, the language of divine Sonship is poetic and adoptionist. There is no reason to think that that language had any other meaning when applied to Jesus. (b) In the New Testament, the Christological sayings of John's gospel were later constructions of the early Church already involved in a deification process. John's gospel goes beyond the consciousness of Jesus.

Based on the above summary, we must address three questions: (1) Does the language of divine Sonship when applied to Jesus have a different meaning than Old Testament adoptionism? (2) Are the Christological sayings of John's gospel a deification? (3) Does John's gospel mistakenly go beyond the consciousness of Jesus?

The Language Regarding Jesus' Divine Sonship

The focus in this section is to evaluate Hick's interpretation that

Jesus was not truly divine because the Biblical language regarding divine Sonship is simply that of Old Testament adoptionism.

As already indicated in the previous Chapter, Hick assumes from the outset that Jesus did not represent something radically new in God's self-revelation. What Hick says about the prophets, their consciousness of God and God's presence to them, is what he says about Jesus and God's presence to Him. There is nothing else to be said about Jesus. Hence, the title "Son of God" when applied to Jesus can only mean what it meant in the Old Testament.

The evaluation of Hick's position will be two-fold. First, Hick has once again omitted important relevant Biblical data regarding Jesus' divine Sonship. That is, his conclusion deduced from the title "Son of God" assumes that the disciples' claim about Jesus' divinity and his personal and eternal pre-existence follows *solely* from this title. In fact, it does not. Secondly, Hick is unwilling to note the "newness" about Jesus who understood Himself to be *the* Son. The conclusion, then, is that the Old Testament language of divine Sonship does have a different meaning when applied to Jesus.

"Son of God"

Hick argues that Jesus is not truly divine, as traditionally understood, because the title "Son of God" in the Old Testament did not refer to any pre-existent divine person who became man. Rather, it referred to human beings who became spoken of as "Sons of God" because of a special relation with God they came to enjoy. Hick has in mind especially the Davidic kings who at their coronation and anointing as king were given the metaphoric title "Son of God." Yet traditional Christian faith has expressed Jesus' divinity by proclaiming Him "Son of God." Hick says the title does not support any claim about Jesus' literal divinity.

First, I acknowledge that the title "Son of God" in later Christological development became the crucial category in defining Christ's personal and eternal pre-existence along with His divinity. The title "Son" eventually replaced "Logos" as the most suitable langauge in formulating the relationships of the divine Persons within the Godhead: Father, Son and Holy Spirit.

It is clear as well within the New Testament that the title "Son of

God" was not used in the earliest Easter proclamations about Jesus.[1] Nevertheless, the title was used as the kerygma was being formulated in Palestinian Judaism, and certainly before the kerygma was taken into the Greco-Roman world.[2] Further still, even within the developing explicit Christology of the New Testament, the title "Son of God" emerged quickly as the one title to bear the unique Christian claim about Jesus. Dunn writes:

> ... *it is the title Son of God which regularly and repeatedly bears the primary weight of the claim made.* Whether the thought focuses on Jesus' resurrection and parousia, or on his anointing at Jordan, or on his birth, or embraces the whole of time, it is the language of divine sonship which appears again and again, sometimes without rival. The belief in Jesus as God's Son had the power to absorb and express all these different emphases, showing that ultimately they are not incompatible even if in the original contexts not wholly complementary. The emergence of 'Son of God' as the dominant title for Christ in the fourth century was well justified by its importance in earliest christology.[3]

I also acknowledge that the Old Testament use of "Son of God," while not simply confined to Davidic kings, did not contain any notion of a Son of God who descended from heaven to earth to redeem humankind. Thus, I concede that the title "Son of God," would not necessarily *of itself* have carried with it the designation, or even implication, of Jesus' divinity or personal and eternal pre-existence.

An important point I wish to make here is that the affirmation of Jesus' divinity and personal and eternal pre-existence *does not find its origin* in the title "Son of God." While the developing explicit Christology gravitated toward that title in an attempt to express the mystery of Christ, the affirmation of the divinity of Jesus was not some deduction based on the meaning of a title. Neither that title, nor any other, nor all of them together, would warrant any such deduction. There is more involved in the origin of the claim about Jesus' divinity than titles.

The titles reveal the more significant and dynamic underlying movement from implicit to explicit Christology. This movement, as we have already seen, is constitutive of the foundational revelatory experience of the full Christ-event. It is that experience seeking to be correctly articulated that is the prod relentlessly nudging the early Church towards its proclamation of Jesus' divinity and his personal and eternal pre-existence.

All this is not to say that a study of the Christological titles is unnecessary or unhelpful. In fact, such a study can be quite beneficial, as we shall see. But the proclamation of Christian faith of who Jesus is, cannot be reduced to a mere deduction.

Hick has mistakenly assumed that, since the title "Son of God" gradually became the title around which Christianity professed its faith in the uniqueness of Jesus, that therefore the claim had its origins in that title alone. Since the original title cannot support such a unique claim about Jesus, and Hick does not accept the historical development from an implicit to an explicit Christology, he concludes that any development around that title can only represent a deification of Jesus. The title says nothing literal about Jesus, only something mythological and honorific. It is now important to demonstrate in detail that Hick's position is seriously incomplete and therefore misleading.

In what follows I propse no new advance in the Scriptural data in this area. The immediate question becomes: then why spend so much time reproducing what is already known? Well, to whom is it "already known"? Since Hick does not meet this evidence in his own study, anyone without a background in Christology who studied his works would not "already know" of the following and other significant findings. Such data simply cannot be overlooked or gratuitously dismissed.

There are dozens of complex and as yet unsolved questions regarding Jesus and world religions. We are only just beginning to explore the territory. It is vital then that all the relevant data remain on the table. Otherwise, the quest for the truth in these issues can only be undermined from the very outset. One of my purposes in this work is to urge that we keep in mind all the important relevant findings, especially those discoveries which are presently "unknown" to many who are involved in interpreting Jesus in relation to world religions. That is why I believe it is crucial to include the following lengthy Scriptural elaboration. It indicates, at least, that the New Testament cannot simply be dismissed as a one-dimensional document of deification.

Since Hick focuses on a Christological title, our study will also take up the same object. Although, as said, the titles of Christ are not at the heart of our issue, such an approach also may be most accessible to those with backgrounds in the study of religion other than Christology. To that end, I draw mainly, but by no means exclusively, on Dunn's exhaustive and detailed study[4] of the origins of the doctrine of the Incarnation. In his conclusion to the Chapter on "The Son of God," Dunn writes:

> To put it another way, *the understanding of Jesus as Son of God apparently did not provide the starting point for a christology of pre-existence or incarnation* ... In short, the origins of the doctrine of the incarnation do not seem to lie in the assertion of Christ as Son of God. For the beginnings of a christology of incarnation we must look elsewhere [emphasis Dunn's].[5]

In this first section we shall see, by an all too brief study of the New Testament, that while there is development in the understanding of Jesus' Sonship, this development is not the origin of the thinking regarding Jesus' personal and eternal pre-existent divinity. Jesus' divinity did not simply follow from the affirmation of His Sonship. In the second section we will engage in a search of the New Testament to locate the origins of that divinity from the point of view of the Christological titles. This search is necessary because it is not enough to elaborate what data Hick has overlooked, we must also demonstrate a viable and acceptable alternative. We now begin our study of Jesus' Sonship.

The divine Sonship of Jesus in the earliest pre-Pauline texts shows it to be centrally linked with Jesus' resurrection. Rom 1:3f would certainly support this view, and there is no notion of personal and eternal pre-existent divinity here.[6] Other primitive texts, Acts 13:33 for example, with its inclusion of the Old Testament Psalm 2:7, only reinforce this view.

Paul, too, links Jesus' divine Sonship with His resurrection. But there is also the more distinctive Pauline association of Jesus' divine Sonship with His death on the cross (Rom 5:10; 8:32; Gal 2:20). Paul certainly thought of Jesus as being God's Son prior to His becoming "Son of God in power." But this is no clear indication that Paul thought of Jesus as pre-existing.[7] Even if we take into account Gal 4:4, where Paul speaks of Jesus as being "sent," we cannot conclude une-quivocally that he was teaching a doctrine of Incarnation. This passage is not even a clear Wisdom reference. But it may represent an allusion to Jesus' own self-understanding as the Son who was sent, in the parable of the dishonest tenants (Mk 12:1-12, par). The same observation could be made about Rom 8:3. This text suggests a Sonship of Jesus that is affirmed of His whole life. But again, this truth does not mean that Jesus' personal and eternal pre-existence or equality with the Father is being claimed.[8] These passages can be interpreted more accurately as part of Paul's "Adam Christology."

What of the relation of Jesus' pre-existent divinity and His Sonship in the synoptics?

No one disputes that the title "Son of God" is important to Mark's gospel. The title's prominence in the gospel is attested to, not in terms of its frequency, but by the fact that it occurs at key points. Whether or not the title occurs in the first sentence (the textual evidence is indecisive), Mark's gospel is clearly suspended between the heavenly intimation (1:11) and the centurion's confession (15:39). (It is to be noted that in Mark's version, the Petrine confession at Caesarea Philippi, 8:29, makes no reference to Jesus being Son of God). But in spite of this structure and significance, one cannot argue that Mark was teaching a pre-existent divinity of Jesus because He was Son of God.

Certainly regarding the baptism of Jesus, whether Mark intended it or not, he left his treatment of the event open to the interpretation that Jesus first *became* Son of God at the beginning of His ministry (Mk 1:9-11). His account of the transfiguration (9:2-8) is not meant as a statement about Jesus' pre-existent glory or incarnation. As a glorious manifestation of the hidden Messiah, it points in the direction of His glorification and exaltation after His death. More directly, the confession of the centurion beneath the cross (15:39) links Jesus divine Sonship with His death. This would seem to be supported by 14:33-36,61, as well as by the parable of the wicked tenants, where it is precisely because He is the *son* that the tenants put Him to death (Mk 12:1-12). Our point again is that Jesus' divinity is not directly arguable to from the Christology of Sonship as found in Mark. Dunn writes:

... Mark's chief emphasis is on the Son of God as one whose

172

anointing with the Spirit was with a view to his suffering and dying, as one who is to be recognized as Son of God precisely in his death and not simply in his subsequent resurrection and exaltation.[9] [emphasis Dunn's]

For Matthew, too, it can be argued that the title "Son of God" is his most important Christological affirmation. He reproduces nearly all of Mark's Son (of God) references, although with some modifications in some instances. Three other Matthean references come from Q, and another six are unique to Matthew. For example, there is Matthew's redactional additions of the title "Son of God" in 14:33 and 16:16. There is also Matthew's modification in 26:63 of Mark's 14:61. Matthew also strengthens Mark's association between Jesus' divine Sonship and His death by inserting extra material at 27:40 (echoing the temptation of 4:3,6) and 27:43, where he reinforces the allusion to Jesus' death in the parable of the wicked tenants (21:39). But again, none of these references can be said to be an affirmation of Jesus personal and eternal pre-existent divinity because of His Sonship.[10]

One of the striking aspects of Matthew's Son of God Christology is his clear identification of Jesus with Israel (Matt 2:15; 4:3,6). Jesus is the one who fulfills the destiny of God's Son, Israel. We have already seen that Matthew's notion of fulfillment indicates more than prediction come to pass. It is meant to indicate that in Jesus something beyond the expectations of the people has come to pass. In his Christology, Matthew is teaching that Jesus' descent from David is only part of the truth about Jesus. It is interesting that the title "Son of David" is most frequently found on the lips of those outside the immediate circle of Jesus' disciples (9:27; 12:23; 15:22; 20;30f; 21:9,15).[11]

What interests Matthew more than Jesus' human origin is His divine origin. To this effect, the narrative of the virginal conception of Jesus is probably the single most striking feature of Matthew's Christology. His contrast between Jesus' Davidic descent and His divine one, recalls Paul's earlier text Rom 1:3-4. For Matthew, Jesus' Davidic sonship is important, but not as important as His divine Sonship. This is true notwithstanding that there is no direct "Son of God" language in the conception story. The virginal conception account as a whole is intended to demonstrate Jesus' divine origins. As such, it can be considered to be one argument against adoptionism. But it is not an affirmation of Jesus' personal and eternal pre-existent divinity.[12]

But in two other places Matthew comes closer to attributing personal and eternal pre-existence to Jesus as Son of God than any Christian writer before him. These are: (1) Matthew's redactional addition of 11:28-30 to the Q passage 11:25-7; and (2) Matt 28:19, the Trinitarian formula. In the former, Matthew identifies Jesus with Wisdom (Si 51:23-30). Although it is not a strong reference to a text on the pre-existence of Wisdom, the idea of pre-existence is just a step away since Wisdom was familiarly thought of as pre-existent. In Matt. 28:19, while there is certainly not the Trinitarian doctrine of later Christology, the person of Jesus is linked, however, with the salvific work of the Father and the Holy Spirit. Again, the notion of pre-existence, while not directly intended, is certainly in the wings. Dunn concludes about Matthew's Christology:

> ... *Matthew has extended the understanding of Jesus' divine sonship by dating it from his conception and attributing that to the (creative) power of the Spirit* and by depicting Jesus' sonship in terms of his mission which fulfilled the destiny of God's son Israel.[13]

Although Matthew comes close to making Jesus' divinity depend on His Sonship, he does not directly make the affirmation.

We now turn to Luke's gospel. Development in the teaching about Jesus' Sonship is not one of the major concerns of Luke's gospel, nor of Acts. His gospel draws from Mark and Q regarding Jesus' Sonship, and makes no modifications of any significance. In the infancy narrative, however, Luke does make more explicit than Matthew the affirmation of Jesus' divine Sonship from conception. This is witnessed in the more significant role he gives to Mary. Brown writes regarding Lk 1:35:

[It, 1:35] takes us out of the realm of Jewish expectation of the Messiah into the realm of early Christianity. The action of the Holy Spirit and the power of the Most High come not upon the Davidic king but upon his mother. We are not dealing with the adoption of a Davidid by coronation as God's son or representative; we are dealing with the begetting of God's son in the womb of Mary through God's creative spirit.[14]

But even here, the stress on Jesus' divine origins is not a statement about Jesus' personal and eternal pre-existent divinity. Nor is there such a statement in Acts. Luke, like Matthew, has taken over the development of the "two sonships" of Jesus originally found in Rom 1:3-4. Again like Matthew, his interest is with Jesus' divine Sonship. There was never a time in Jesus' life when He was not Son of God. Such an affirmation, of course, does not deny the significance of the resurrection for Jesus' divine Sonship.[15]

Development regarding Jesus' divine Sonship does occur in the Letter to the Hebrews. The author talks of it regularly, particularly throughout the first seven chapters. In 4:14 he implies that "Jesus is the Son of God" was a basic confession common to the author and his readers.

In Hebrews there exists a curious tension on the issue of Jesus' pre-existence. The author describes Jesus as God's Son in language which seems to denote pre-existence more clearly than we have so far witnessed (1:2; 7:3). At the same time, there is far more adoptionist language here than in any other New Testament document. (We have not the space to unravel this tension.) Dunn suggests this juxtaposition of "seemingly contradictory themes" is due to the author's

... unique synthesis of Platonic and Hebraic world views, or more precisely Platonic cosmology and Judeo-Christian eschatology ... [16]

Myles Bourke would agree with Dunn on this point.[17]

The language of pre-existence is at least to some degree a reflection of the author's Platonic cosmology. Hebrews, then, ultimately has in mind an *ideal* (as opposed to a personal and eternal) pre-existence. That is, the Son pre-exists as an *idea* in the mind of God, as the divine intention for the last days. Perhaps this is why the author of Hebrews, unlike other New Testament writers, does not directly speak of God as the Father of the Son (except in quotations from the Old Testament).

The bulk of references to Jesus as Son revolve around the Melchizedek motif of the priest-king (7:2f).

Dunn's conclusion about Hebrews is that we do not find even here the clear notion of a personal pre-existence of Jesus as the eternal Son of God.[18]

When we come to the Johannine writings, however, especially the gospel, we do encounter for the first time in earliest Christianity, the explicit understanding of Jesus' divine Sonship in terms of the personal and eternal pre-existence of a divine being who was sent into the world. In John's gospel, Jesus is conscious of having personally pre-existed as the divine Son from eternity.

It is not to our purpose to investigate pre-existence itself in the fourth gospel. Our task in our search of Scripture is to look for the *origins* of what emerges explicitly in John's gospel. In the light of some of the comments we have made so far, we can and ought to make some observations.

John's gospel certainly echoes emphases which we have already seen in the synoptics. But the earlier understanding is now transposed to a higher plane. With Paul, for example, John understands the Son to be "sent." But unlike Paul, John's "sending" is more than a divine commissioning. The Son is explicitly thought of as having been "sent" from heaven into the world (John 3:17; 10:36; 17:18; 1John 4:9).

With the synoptics, John stresses the intimate relation Jesus had with the Father. But this intimacy is grounded in Jesus' personal and eternal pre-existence as Son (John 5:19,21,25f; 6:38,40; 8:16,23,38; 10:36; 16:28; 17:5,24; 5:11f; 5:23; 10:30; 14:7,10; 1John 5:11f).

Similarly, the Johannine writings maintain the earlier link between Jesus' divine Sonship and His death (John 3:16; 1John 4:10; 1:7), along with the whole motif of the glorification of the Son which includes His glorification on the cross (John 1:14; 17:1).

What is different in the Johannnine writings relative to what has gone on earlier, is that there is no thought of Jesus' status as Son being dependent on, or even influenced by, His resurrection. Dunn writes:

Whatever it means for Jesus that he is the Word become flesh it involves no diminution in his status or consciousness as Son.

And whatever it means for Jesus that he is glorified and lifted up on the cross, in resurrection and ascension, it involves no enhancement or alteration in his status as Son ... [They—death, resurrection, ascension—were] simply the continu-ation of an intimate relationship with the Father which neither incarnation nor crucifixion interrupted or disturbed.[19]

Conclusion

Why is this Scriptural review important for our study? In the New Testament data, up to John's gospel Dunn has demonstrated that there is no argument to Jesus' divinity from the fact of His divine Sonship. There certainly was a development in the understanding of that Sonship. But it never reached the point where there was a direct link made from Jesus' Sonship, even from the moment of His conception, to an affirmation of His personal and eternal pre-existent divinity. Even Hebrews, which has at least an ideal notion of pre-existence, does not make this link. Then, suddenly as it were, with John's gospel we have that link, not just hinted at, but clearly and intentionally affirmed. Jesus' divine Sonship flows from the fact that He was personally pre-existent Son from eternity.

Where did this Johannine affirmation come from? Hick has assumed that John has simply concluded to Jesus' personal and eternal pre-existent divinity from the developing notion of Jesus' Sonship. The reason we have included our review of Scripture on this issue is to demonstrate that Hick's assumption is unwarranted. It *is* true that the title "Son of God" in and of itself does not warrant a conclusion to Jesus' divinity. But it *is not* true that the affirmation of Jesus' divinity is simply a conclusion drawn from the developing notions of Jesus' Sonship. I do not say there is no mutual growth in the understanding both of Jesus' divinity and His Sonship. But it seems clear that the former is not simply a conclusion from the latter. There are other factors involved which account for the development in the understanding of the divinity of Jesus. The significance of this conclusion is that Hick's interpretation, that Jesus is not truly divine because the language of divine Sonship does not warrant such a statement, is over-simplified and deficient. It is over-simplified because it limits the discussion to the title "Son of God." It is deficient because it concludes that Jesus was not divine simply because the language of divine Sonship does not support such a notion of divinity. Hick's conclusion, therefore, is not sound in its claim that there is no literal truth to Jesus' divinity.

So far, I have been demonstrating that the idea of Jesus' personal and eternal pre-existent divinity does not flow simply or directly from developments regarding His Sonship. It is now necessary to address the question: from where, then, does this idea flow? What are its origins? These origins will also, of course, be the origins of the doctrine of the Incarnation.

Still following Dunn's lead, we will now search the main candidates, either titles or ideas about Christ, that occur within the New Testament, to see if they provide the grounds for the idea of His personal and eternal pre-existent divinity. If such a ground is located to meet Hick's claim the idea is myth, we must then assess whether or not that ground is mythological.

"Messiah"

Do the origins of the affirmation about Jesus' divinity stem from His being called "Messiah" [Christ]? I am thinking here of the *post-resurrection* understanding of "Messiah," for example, of the primitive pre-Pauline acclamation of Acts 2:36 "... that God has made him both Lord and Christ, this Jesus whom you crucified." The title "Messiah" of itself, of course, either in Old Testament usage or in Judaism contemporary with Jesus, would not imply divinity. In Judaism, the title was capable of many interpretations and misinterpretations.[20] Nevertheless, the *pre*-resurrection Petrine act of faith that Jesus was the Messiah (Mk 8:27-30, par), represents a breakthrough in the disciples' understanding of who Jesus was. This breakthrough was more than simply that Jesus fulfilled one of the then popular understandings of "Messiah." Kasper writes:

Peter's declaration does not therefore connect with political theories of the Messiah, but with the prophetic tradition of the anointed. In this strand of the tradition, the Messiah is the prophet of the last times who is anointed with the holy Spirit.[21]

But this breakthrough, occurring as it does before Jesus' resurrection, is still only inceptive. Jesus has to correct and develop Peter's understanding of even this prophetic tradition of the Messiah. The fuller understanding involves accepting the Messiah, the bringer of salvation, as one divinely ordained to suffer (Mk 8:31-33, par). This theme of suffering recalls Isaiah's suffering servant of God (Is 42:1-7; 49:1-9; 50:4-9; 52:13-53:12). The full implications of the Messiahship of Jesus could only be known after His death and resurrection.

Our specific interest here is to inquire if the primitive Christian community's post-resurrection affirmation of Jesus as Messiah constitutes the grounds for the later explicit affirmation of Jesus' personal and eternal pre-existent divinity.

There is no doubt that "Messiah" is the "supreme Christological title."[22] By the time that Paul wrote, it had become a kind of proper name for Jesus.[23] Although Jesus did not use the title of Himself, He was forced to declare Himself the Messiah before the Council of the Sanhedrin (Mk 14:61-2, par). At His trial Jesus could not simply deny messianic claims without giving up his eschatological mission. Given the state of Jesus' helplessness at that time, there was little need to correct any misunderstanding of the mission of the Messiah. He was already fulfilling it by entering into His passion. David Stanley writes:

> Whatever hesitations Jesus may have had about the title "Messiah" and whether or not during his ministry he ever used it or accepted it as a self-designation, he was crucified as a would-be Messiah-king.[24]

Kasper notes that the title "Christ" first appears within the Passion kerygma and Passion tradition (1 Cor 15:3-5).[25]

Yet after Jesus' resurrection, as we have seen, there is the fuller notion that He was made "Christ" (Acts 2:36; 17:3). At first, suggests Stanley, it was difficult for the early Christian community to maintain that Jesus, the suffering servant, was the Messiah of Jewish expectations. A very ancient way of overcoming this difficulty was to say that Jesus would be the Messiah in His parousia (Acts 3:20-22).[26] Still another explanation was to say that it was the exalted Christ who was Messiah (Acts 2:36; 5:31). This interpretation suggested that Jesus' Messiahship was in heaven and not on earth.[27]

However, none of these explanations proved adequate. The understanding of Jesus' Messiahship soon became that of one whose glory was hidden, and who delivered Israel not from political oppression but from the bondage of sin. With the acceptance of a suffering Messiah, the Christian community then could proclaim Jesus to be Messiah even during His earthly ministry. Eventually, He was understood as Messiah from His conception.

There is no doubt that the title "Messiah" was meant to affirm the significance and uniqueness of Jesus for salvation. Kasper summarizes:

> The confession of faith 'Jesus is the Christ' ... means first, that the person of Jesus is himself salvation; it therefore expresses the unique and irreplaceable character of the Christian gospel. Secondly, it contains Jesus' universal and public claim and thereby excludes any false idea that salvation is only interior and private. Finally, it says how Jesus is the salvation of the world; he is filled with the Holy Spirit and we share in this plenitude in the Spirit.[28]

It is clear from the above quote that Jesus, as Messiah, was considered to be "the divinely given answer to the messianic hopes of Israel."[29] It was God's creative fidelity to the crucified Messiah that subsequently constituted Him Messiah in the glory of His resurrection.[30]

Yet for all this, we cannot say, that this title of itself can account for the origin of what later would become the affirmation of Jesus' divine pre-existence and the doctrine of the Incarnation. There was certainly no notion of a personally and eternally pre-existent Messiah in pre-Christian Judaism to suggest such an idea to the early Christians.[31] Like the title "Son of God," the title "Messiah" underwent development in understanding. But that development does not account for the apparent leap from the synoptic tradition of Jesus' Sonship to John's explicit affirmation of the eternal, divine pre-existence of Jesus.

"Lord"

A good candidate to account for the rise of the affirmation of Jesus' pre-existent divinity is the title of "Lord." In addition to being made Messiah by God, upon His resurrection Jesus was also constituted "Lord" (Acts 2:36). This title does not result from Hellenization, but has its roots in Judaism.[32] The Septuagint used "Lord" ("kyrios") to render the Tetragrammaton *YHWH*. This title "Lord" also was used in the primitive preaching to refer to the risen and exalted Jesus.

It is clear that from the earliest days of the Christian community a theology of the Name ("Lord") developed.[33] One of the earliest formulations of Christian faith was the brief creed "Jesus is Lord" (Phil 2:11; Rom 10:9; 1Cor 12:3). Kasper writes that the title "Lord" was intended "to express the position and power in heaven of the Risen and Exalted Christ."[34] Paul unequivocally used "Lord" to describe the present resurrected Jesus: Jesus is risen, He is with God; but through his Spirit He is also present in the Church (2Cor 3:17).

The significance of being constituted "Lord" is that all things are made subject to the glorified Christ. All creation and even the Kingdom of God, are now handed over to Him. As "Lord," Jesus sits at the right hand of God. The early Christians used Psalm 110:1 to stress this point. It is no wonder that Stanley writes:

> It is this title, rather than "Son of God," which expressed for the primitive Christian community the reality of Jesus' divine sonship.[35]

Eventually, this notion of the kingdom of Christ, in John's gospel would be extended "to the whole cosmos and taken back to the beginning of creation."[36]

Yet, we must remain precise, and ask if the title "Lord" as applied to Christ is the root of the later understanding of His personal and eternal pre-existent divinity. Certainly, it is *open* to such an interpretation. It does bestow on Jesus, as Stanley writes, an "aura of divinity."[37] There is an allusion in certain deutero-Pauline writings (Eph 1:10; Col 1:15-20; Heb 1:2f) to the later protological extension of Jesus' "Lordship." But even here—although perhaps a starting-point—there is no direct link simply between the notion of "Lord" and Jesus' pre-existent divinity.[38]

"Son of Man"

The sayings about the "Son of Man" constitute one of the most difficult New Testament problems. If Kasper is correct, that "scholarship is still a long way from reaching anything like a clear and agreed interpretation of either their origin and their meaning,"[39] then this essay certainly cannot resolve the issue.

Nevertheless, the question must be asked: does the title "Son of Man" contain within itself the grounds for the later affirmation of the personal and eternal pre-existent divinity of Jesus? Oddly enough, if we had data only from second century Christology, we would not think this title were at all relevant to our inquiry. From that century onward, the title almost always denoted Jesus' humanity in contrast to His divinity as "Son of God."

But the gospels reveal that the term earlier had a much higher meaning than what later centuries gave to it. The title is used in the New Testament eighty times. With one exception (Acts 7:56), all the Son of Man sayings occur on the lips of Jesus. This alone makes it demand our attention. True, the New Testament tradition exhibits the strong tendency of putting this title as a secondary addition in the mouth of Jesus. Nevertheless, that Jesus used this title and used it of Himself remains certain.[40] Yet, even as used by Jesus, it "was more like a mysterious riddle which Jesus could use simultaneously to express and conceal his claim."[41]

There are two factors about this title, as used at the stage of New Testament writing, that are definitely clear: (1) the Son of Man sayings clearly refer to Jesus;[42] (2) these Son of Man sayings clearly allude to Daniel 7. Our concern with this title is specific: (1) is the affirmation of Jesus as Son of Man in the gospels an assertion of Jesus' personal and eternal pre-existent divinity? and (2) do the Son of Man sayings identify Jesus as a pre-existent heavenly being?

By way of introduction, we note that in Daniel, the Son of Man does not refer to the existence, let alone the pre-existence, of an individual. It is simply a reference to "Israel" in contrast to the enemies of Israel.[43] In the *Similtudes of Enoch* there is a pre-existent Son of Man. But as we have seen, the *Similtudes* were written much later in the first century, after the Christian interpretation of the Son of Man had been established. Similarly, *IV Ezra*, dated after 70 A.D., indicates only that the image of the Danielic vision could inspire hope after the catastrophe of 70 A.D. Although *IV Ezra* identifies the Messiah with the Son of Man, it seems that this identification is original with the author. It was not borrowed from contemporary Judaism. When later within Judaism, the Son of Man did become identified as a heavenly figure, a divine being, this interpretation was condemned by the rabbis as heretical, a threat to monotheism.[44]

The significance of these foregoing observations is that the interpretation of the Danielic Son of Man as an *individual* must have been an original interpretation by Jesus, and taken over by the early Christian Church.[45]

But in the synoptics, it is always a question of the Son of Man's eschatological role in judgment or his humility prior to exaltation. There is never a pre-existent role or status. The Christian interpretation of Jesus as pre-existent Son of Man only occurs at some late stage in the first century. John's gospel would seem to elaborate a pre-existence of the Son of Man. The Book of Revelation also appears to do the same.

Nevertheless, we are still left with the original question, of how personal and eternal pre-existence entered the picture. Certainly, the affirmation of Jesus as Son of Man was not an affirmation of His pre-existent divinity until quite late. The later references to a pre-existent, divine Son of Man indicate only that the notion of Jesus' pre-existent divinity was already around. But it did not originate with the title itself.[46]

"Last Adam"

In his attempt to show that the doctrine of Jesus' Incarnation is a myth, Hick draws on a general mythological notion among religions of a pre-existent divine being who comes from heaven and assumes human form. The History of Religions School saw the Christian idea of Jesus' Incarnation as simply a form of the general "Gnostic Redeemer Myth." The Pontifical Biblical Commission in 1983 argued that this understanding is oversimplified and inaccurate.[47] Dunn demonstrates that there is nothing during first century Christianity to indicate the existence of a general redeemer myth akin to Christian faith in the Incarnation.[48]

But in the non-Christian world there were ideas of a heavenly, pre-existent man in contrast to an earthly man. Certainly, Paul makes use of a similar distinction (1Cor 15:45-7). So we must ask ourselves if the notion of the personal and eternal pre-existent divinity of Jesus originates in this distinction of Paul's, which distinction may in turn originate in wider current religious thought. In the latter case, of course, although Hick may be wrong in the details of his argument, he would turn out to be right in terms of the kind of argument he employs.

This issue of a heavenly and an earthly man brings us to Paul's "Last Adam" Christology. His characterization of Jesus as "the Last Adam" is one of Paul's original contributions to New Testament Christology.[49] Although the title "Son of Man" does not appear anywhere in Paul's writings, the idea of "the Last Adam" would seem to include it.

Stanley detects three stages in the evolution of Paul's thought on "the Last Adam."[50] First, Paul conceives Jesus in His *risen* state as the new Adam (1Cor 15:20-22, 45, 49; 2Cor 3:18; 4:10-12). Then, at a later period, Paul perceives that the role of Christ as new Adam had begun with His redemptive death, accepted out of obedience to the Father (Rom 5:15-21). The third expression of Paul's theme of "the Last Adam" is found in the Captivity letters. Here, Christ is "all in all" (Col 3:9-11). Jesus' work reconciles Jew and Gentile into a new unity, creating a new man (Eph 2:15). The goal of the Christian's union with "the Last Adam" is to form the perfect Man, fully mature with the fullness of Christ himself (Eph 4:13).

In Paul's thought, the Adam motif is the means he uses to express the plight of man (Rom 1:18-25; 3:23; 5:12-19; 7:7-11; 8:19-22). Adam, who had been created in the image of God, damaged that image through his fall. All people share in that damaged image (1 Cor15:49). Salvation involves the reversal of Adam's fall. Precisely, salvation means the believer is reformed or reshaped into the image of God (2 Cor 3:18). It consists in a progressive renewal in knowledge according to the image of the Creator (Col 3:10; Eph 4:24). Adam soteriology, then, understands salvation as a restoration of man to that image in which Adam had been created. Indispensable to this process of being reformed, reshaped or renewed in the image of God, is Jesus. At this point it becomes clear that it is not simply into the image of the "unfallen Adam" that believers are to be transformed. No; God's purpose is to conform believers "to the image of his Son" (Rom 8:29; 1 Cor 15:49; 2Cor 4:4; Col 1:15). Here, Paul's theology diverges from that of his Jewish contemporaries. The latter, for the most part, would have accepted that all men were caught up in Adam's fall, and that salvation meant being renewed in the image of God. But for them that renewal would have been simply to the original image forfeited by Adam. Dunn writes:

> But in Paul's theology Adam is pushed aside at this point, and Christ alone fills the stage. Adam becomes merely the type of fallen man, and another Adam appears as alone the final man to whom believers must be conformed.[51]

The Adam motif, then, gives way to an Adam Christology. It is important to remember, therefore, that when Paul uses Adam-language of Christ, he is referring primarily to Christ risen and exalted. Christ, the last Adam, is the risen Adam. It is into the image of the risen and exalted Christ that the believer is to be transformed. For us, it is important to note that Christ's role as last Adam does not begin either in some pre-existent state, or at the Incarnation, but at His resurrection (1Cor 15:21, 45; Rom 8:29; Col 1:18).

If it is the exalted Christ who bears the image of God, is there not a discontinuity between Adam and Christ? No; because for Paul, Christ could not become the last Adam if He had not first been Adam, that is, if He had not in some way been one with fallen Adam. The connection between the two is made with the early Church's use of Psalm 8.6b "You have put all things under his feet." This verse was used in the early church to supplement the latter half of Psalm 110.1, "Sit at my right hand till I make your enemies your footstool," in the proclamation of Jesus' resurrection (1Cor 15:25-7; Eph 1:20-2, Heb 1:13-2:8).

Most likely, Paul did not originate this usage of Psalm 8. It represents an early Christian filling out of Psalm 110:1 as an apologetic for the exalted Lordship of Christ. But verse 8:6b cannot be considered isolated from the rest of the Psalm, which was a description of God's purpose and intention for Adam/Man. In this way Psalm 8 provided a ready vehicle for Adam Christology. If verses 5b, 6a and 6b refer to Christ after His resurrection, then 4a, 4b, and 5a most likely refers to Christ before His resurrection, argues Dunn.[52] Certainly, that is how Heb 2:6-9 interprets the passage. The same notion is behind Rom 5:12-19.

Our point is simply that the divine plan for man which broke down in Adam has been run through again, as it were, this time successfully in Christ. Christ had first to be Adam before He could become the Last Adam. Psalm 8:4-6 provides the scope for this larger Adam Christology, a Christology that embraced both the earthly as well as the exalted Jesus. If this be the case, then Rom 8:3 and Gal 4:4 refer to this Adam Christology, to Jesus who shared in the effects of man's fallen nature so that His death might be the means of creating a new man, a new humanity. These passages would not refer immediately to the notion of a pre-existent Jesus being sent into the world as later found in John's gospel. There is no discontinuity between Adam and Christ because the Last Adam follows the path taken by the first Adam, including the path of death. Christ begins His saving work by being one with Adam, not in sin, but in the effects of his fallenness.

Why is all this reflection on Paul's Adam Christology important for our study? The answer is that we have to ask ourselves if behind Paul's first Adam/ last Adam Christology there is a pre-existent Adam or pre-existent Man? If so, it would mean that perhaps the origins of later affirmations about Jesus' pre-existence are found here? And if these origins showed that the pre-existent Man of Paul was taken over from a general mythology, then Hick's argument would to some degree still stand.

While Phil 2:6-11 is open to and can be read as assuming the personal and eternal pre-existence of Christ, such an interpretation is not necessarily required. For if the pre-existence of Christ is assumed, it plays no significant part in Paul's over-all Christology. Besides this first observation, of course, there is the whole involved exegesis of this passage, which we cannot do here. The most informative and probable background to this hymn, however, seems to be the Adam Christology we have been discussing.[53] If this is the case, Adam cannot be construed as a copy of a pre-existent Christ, but rather as a type of Him who is to come (Rom 5:14). Although Phil 2:6-11 was later used by those who held to the Gnostic Redeemer myth, that is no argument that the passage itself envisioned such an idea. Similar observations can be made about 2 Cor 8:9. The context here is not necessarily a personal and eternal pre-existent Christ, but an Adam Christology.

Does 1 Cor 15:45-47 imply the beginnings of a redeemer myth? No. Any argument to the influence of Philo does not hold since Philo does not think of the heavenly man as a person.[54] Dunn writes:

Paul's use of Adam speculation was oriented not according to mythicizing preoccupation with the world's beginnings, but according to the eschatologically new that had happened in Jesus' resurrection, and the world's ending which that foreshadowed; and his Adam christology focused not on some original man who had descended from heaven but on the second man whom he expected to return from heavenly shortly, whose image as the resurrected one Christians would share.[55]

Paul's Adam Christology is not about the personal and eternal pre-existence of Christ, but about eschatological man. Since there is no notion of a pre-existent man akin to any redeemer myth behind Paul's Adam Christology, we can conclude that Hick's assumption that there is, has no foundation.

"Angel"

It may seem odd to introduce the idea that Jesus' divinity could have its origins in the Judaic understanding of angels. But in the Patristic period, there was some understanding of Jesus as angel.[56] And Paul at least alludes to Jesus as an "angel [messenger] of God" (Gal 4:14).

In the Old Testament, angels were ways of speaking about God in his active concern for men and women. In pre-Christian Judaism, there was a significant development of angels as intercessors and intermediaries. The notion of a divine intermediary, then, might have provided the beginning for some thought about Jesus' personal and eternal pre-existent divinity.

However, this is simply not the case. When it comes to Jesus, no New Testament writer thinks of Him as an angel, neither as a pre-existent angel who becomes man, nor as a man who after His death becomes an angel. Both Paul's Letter to the Colossians and the Letter to the Hebrews resist vigorously any attempt to place the exalted Christ on the level of the angels. In fact, it would seem that it is precisely this conception of a personally heavenly being, functioning as a mediator between human beings and God and independent of God, which the New Testament writers either ignore or reject as a model for their understanding of Christ.[57] Doubtless this rejection is because such a notion would render the mediator as neither true God nor true man.

"Spirit"

Our search now brings us to the three so-called, but misnamed "intermediary figures" of Judaism: Spirit, Wisdom and Logos.

If the Judaic understanding of angels did not provide the early Christians with the notion of Jesus' personal and eternal pre-existence, perhaps the Old Testament notion of "Spirit" might be the source. Paul does define the Last Adam as "the life-giving Spirit" (1Cor 14:45).

I cannot in this work explore Biblical Pneumatology. I aim only to see if there is grounds for thinking that these notions are the basis of later affirmations of Jesus' personal and eternal pre-existent divinity.

In the Old Testament "Spirit" denotes God's effective power. The Spirit of God is not distinct from God, it is simply the power of God. It denotes God acting powerfully in nature and upon humans (Jgs 14:19; 15:14; 6:34; 11:29; 1Sam 11:6).

In the intertestamental period, and in later Old Testament strata, it can be argued that the "Spirit of God" is represented as a distinct hypostasis. Psalms 104:30; 143:10 and Isa. 63:10 could certainly appear to suggest such an idea. What is noticeable, however, is that during this period it is not the Spirit that gets personified, so much as it is Wisdom and Logos.[58] Inspite of all this, however, there is no clear indication that the Spirit—nor Wisdom nor Logos for that matter—had become a divine hypostasis independent of God. There is certainly nothing to suggest the idea to Christians that Jesus could have been the personal pre-existent Spirit become flesh.

What, then, is Jesus' relation to the Spirit? Jesus Himself seemed to be conscious of the fact that He was a man of the Spirit. He was conscious of being inspired by and acting under the power by the Spirit (Matt 12:28; Lk 11:20). Aware of Himself as the eschatological prophet, He would have been aware of bearing the Spirit in a unique manner (Matt 11:3-6; 12:28; Lk 7:20-3; 11:32).

Similarly the first Christians saw the earthly Jesus as being inspired and empowered by the Spirit. The gospels present Jesus in the same way, as a man of the Spirit during his life and ministry.

What of the relation of the exalted Jesus to the Spirit? Two gospels depict Jesus after His resurrection as one who dispenses the Spirit. He who in His earthly life was inspired by the Spirit, in His glorified life now pours out the Spirit on others. This is the message of Luke-Acts and John. By virtue of His resurrection Jesus the man of the Spirit becomes Lord of the Spirit (John 14:17, 26). However, Jesus is not seen as pre-existent Spirit become flesh, nor as a prophet who became the Spirit. It would seem that prior to Jesus' exaltation, the Spirit was not thought of as an independent entity distinct from God. It is Jesus' exaltation and the His new relationship with the Spirit that requires Christians to rethink their concept of God. Once again, we see the resurrection at the heart of Spirit Christology.

But Paul's notion of the relation between Jesus and the Spirit is more complex than that found in the synoptics. Where Luke and John attribute the gift of the Spirit equally to God and to the exalted Christ, Paul retains the Judaic view in attributing the Spirit only to God. The Spirit is the dynamic power of God having an effect on men and women.

Yet Paul is very clear that the resurrection did bring about a new relation between the exalted Jesus and the Spirit (Rom 1:3f). But he does not say that Jesus is Lord of the Spirit. Interestingly enough, even though he has Jesus raised from the dead by the power of the Spirit, he does not present Jesus' exalted life as a creation of the Spirit. What results is a kind of mutual self-definition between the Spirit of God and the exalted Christ. Each defines and limits the other, but not in a way that subsumes the other.[59] God can now approach men through both the Spirit and through the exalted Christ. Hence, Paul can speak of the Last Adam as being "life-giving Spirit"(1 Cor 15:45). For the believer, according to Paul, there is no distinction between the experience of the Spirit of God, and the experience of the exalted Christ (2 Cor 3:6 when read with 1 Cor 15:45; Rom 8:9-11; 1 Cor 6:17). But that is only on the level of experience. Jesus has not become the Spirit (1 Cor 15:24-8). The point behind all this for Paul is that the exalted Jesus has assumed a unique status as mediator. Kasper would agree with Dunn's analysis.[60]

In conclusion to our study of "Spirit," it is clear that any understanding of the Spirit in Judaism or in early Christianity was not the source of the of the notion of Jesus' personal and eternal pre-existent divinity.

"Wisdom"

We come now to the second of what have been called the three "intermediary figures": Wisdom.

When compiling a list of passages that clearly express Jesus' personal and eternal pre-existence, most scholars would include John 1:1-18, 1 Cor 8:5-6; Col 1:15-17 and Heb. 1:1-3a. Within the synoptics, most agree that the highest Christology is found in Matt 11:27-30. What is at the same time both common and significant to all these passages is their dependence on Wisdom terminology. All express some form of a Wisdom Christology. By that we mean the language of these passages is the language used of the figure of Wisdom in the Old Testament and in the intertestamental period.

Dunn notes the influence of Sir 51 on Matt 11:25-30.[61] Raymond Brown re-expresses the dependence of John's prologue on Wisdom.[62] Similarly, 1Cor 8:6, where Paul speaks of Jesus "through whom are all things and through whom we exist,"[63] reflects pre-Christian Judaism's expressions about Wisdom. This parallel is also found in Col 1:15-20. Heb 1:3f shows dependence on Wisdom 7 as well as on Philo.[64] It is clear that the tradition of pre-existent Wisdom has been influential in the New Testament understanding of Christ.

Nor is the influence simply a matter of terminology; the very role of Wisdom is now being attributed to Christ. Jesus is even identified with Wisdom. Paul is very explicit, for example, proclaiming "Christ who is both the power of God and the Wisdom of God" (1 Cor 1:24; cf 1:30).

We must now ask ourselves what this identification of Jesus with Wisdom meant to the first Christians. Was it mere poetic hyperbole, as Hick would have us believe about this kind of language? Did it go as far to affirm a formulated doctrine of the Incarnation? What was its meaning?

First, something must be said about Wisdom in pre-Christian Judaism. Talk of Wisdom was deeply rooted in Palestinian soil and in Jewish faith. Yet, many images and words used to describe her were drawn from wider religious thought and worship. Does that mean that Judaism simply borrowed a myth from other religions? No; it is not as simple as that.

Jewish monotheistic faith had a uniqueness about it, (which I have not space to discuss here).[65] Because of this monotheism, when images or words were taken over by Judaism from a polytheistic faith, they were not simply "borrowed." Rather, they underwent a transformation of meaning. A polytheistic faith would have little difficulty understanding Wisdom as one god among the heavenly pantheon. But Jewish monotheism could make no such accommodation. We cannot understand the meaning of Wisdom in pre-Christian Judaism by elaborating an exegesis of an Isis hymn. This is the kind of mistaken assumption on which Hick's reasoning is constructed.

One of the first characteristics peculiar to Judaic Wisdom which we notice, is that Wisdom is not worshipped.[66] There is a vivid personification of Wisdom, but there is no worship offered her independent of God.

Secondly, in counterdistinction to the Isis cult, Wisdom within Judaism, besides its cosmic and universal role, also has a specific role. It is identified with the Torah (Sir 24:23,25). The universal Wisdom of God is also revealed, with no contradiction, as something specific and concrete.

Thirdly, we note that the affirmations of Wisdom by the Jewish writers do not in any sense threaten their monotheism. Wisdom refers to God's wise ordering of creation and of those who fear Him.[67] With Wisdom we are dealing with Hebraic personification and not with polytheism.

An important point to note here, is that during the development of Judaic Wisdom, Judaism was being "hellenized." Yet, the term "hellenized" is misleading. For here we have *a clear instance of the influence of a surrounding culture, while affecting the Jewish faith, not in fact altering its identity.* The Jewish faith adapted to itself what was helpful. It did not simply take over the surrounding cultural thought as it was.[68]

Now we turn to consider Christ as Wisdom in the writings of Paul. Dunn notes that Paul first speaks of Wisdom in 1Cor 1:20-5,30 as a corrective to Corinthian elitist gnosticism. In this passage Paul expresses God's Wisdom as essentially His plan to achieve salvation through the crucifixion of Jesus and through the proclamation of the crucified Christ. Jesus is the power that is God reaching out to men and women, and which power is now made visible. Although the identification of Jesus with Wisdom has cosmological implications (2:7f), there is no clear link here between God's Wisdom and the act of creation. Thus, there is no direct affirmation of Jesus as personally and eternally pre-existent. What is directly affirmed is that the pre-existence of God's hidden plan is now made visible in Jesus. (In 1Cor 1:30 there is the notion that Jesus was made Wisdom through His death and resurrection.)

In 1 Cor 8:6 Paul again is responding to special Corinthian problems regarding "knowledge." This response is so focused on the people of Corinth, that it suggests the arrangement within 8:6 is entirely Paul's. He starts with the basic affirmation of Jewish monotheism. Next, he affirms the traditional Christian faith that Jesus is Lord. But then he splits the *Shema* (Dt 6:4) between God the Father and Christ the Lord. Then he adds of Christ "through whom all things come."[69] Finally, he concludes with a reference to himself and his readers.

It seems in this passage Paul is stressing the unity of creation and salvation. But the observations are not about creation in the past, but creation in the present, as seen now by believers. For the Christian all things find their true being and meaning in Christ. If God's plan of salvation is continuous with His power in creation, then Jesus, who is now Lord, shares in God's rule over creation and believers. Jesus' Lordship, then, is the fullest continuation and expressionof God's creative power. Even more to the point, the splitting of God's creative power between God the Father and Christ is precisely what we find in the Wisdom writings of pre-Christian Judaism.[70] Presumably for Paul, Wisdom was not a being distinct from God. Therefore, in this passage there is not a break with Jewish monotheism, as might first be thought. What Paul is doing is asserting that Christ embodies the creative power and action of God. Again, it is not indisputable that Christ is being affirmed here as being personally and eternally pre-existent.

In a third crucial passage Col 1: 15-20 we have a pre-Pauline hymn interpolated and interpreted by Paul. The original form of the hymn was shaped by Wisdom language. That part of the hymn has been taken over by Paul without much modification.[71] Here Paul speaks of Jesus as the image of God. But in speaking of Jesus as God's image, it is only to the crucified and exalted Christ that Paul is referring. Whereas the Jews identified the Torah as the specific revelation of God's Wisdom, Paul now identifies such revelation as Jesus. Wisdom becomes "hypostasized" after this identification is made between it and the exalted Jesus.

Does this mean an immediate claim by Paul to Jesus' personal and eternal pre-existence? Not necessarily. While Christ is the fullest expression of God's creative power, it does not follow immediately in Paul, that Christ Himself was active in creation. The Wisdom of God is definitely now made visible and defined by Christ. But such a notion of itself, does not claim Christ's personal and eternal pre-existence.

In Col 1:19 Paul does seem to affirm that not only the exalted Jesus, but even the earthly Jesus, is the cosmic presence of God: that is, the universal creative power of God is now focused on this specific person, Jesus. In this case, Paul is not saying simply that creation and salvation or Christ are continuous, or that God's creative power and Christ are the same. He is saying that in Christ that creative power or Wisdom reaches a fullness of expression that surpasses the wonders of creation and even the Torah.

In the above three crucial passages (1 Cor 1:24,30; 8:6; Col 1:15-20), Paul identifies Christ with the Wisdom of God.[72] In the Wisdom language Paul found the tools to express the finality of Christ's role in God's purpose for man and creation. But it is, at least, not readily clear that by so doing Paul is affirming the eternal pre-existence of Jesus. Nevertheless, Paul is definitely saying that Wisdom is to be wholly identified with Jesus. This complete identification requires that the character of God's Wisdom is to be understood no longer from creation or the Torah or any gnosis, but from the cross. The very power by which God created and sustained the world is now made manifest in Christ's life, death and resurrection. Christ expresses without remainder the outreaching love of God. Jesus is the exhaustive embodiment of divine Wisdom: all the divine fullness dwelt in Him.

Among the synoptics, Matthew stands alone in maintaining a full Wisdom Christology, that is the identification of Jesus with Wisdom. What is important is that Matthew achieves this by his editing of Q. For example, over against Luke's use of the Q original (cf. Lk 7:35), Matthew introduces the thought of Wisdom's deeds (Mt 11:19). Where Q at most presents Jesus as the envoy of Wisdom, Matthew clearly took the step of identifying Jesus with Wisdom itself.[73]

We find the same kind of redaction occurring in Matthew 11:25-30 when compared with Luke 10:21-22. In Matt 11:25-27 and the Lucan parallel, we have a Q passage. It is widely accepted as a Wisdom saying spoken by Jesus. The exclusivity of the mutual knowledge between Father and Son reflects the exclusivity of the knowledge between God and Wisdom (Job 28:1-27; Sir 1:6,8; Bar 3:15-32) and between Wisdom and God (Prov 8:12; Wisd 7:25ff; 8:3f; 9:4,9,11).

Yet, it would seem, among other differences, that the reference to Wisdom is more to the "righteous man," the disciple of Wisdom, spoken of as the "Son of God," rather than to Wisdom herself (Wisd 2:13,16; cf. Sir 4:10; 51:10).

If this latter case be true, then the origin of the claim about exclusivity of mutual knowledge between Father and Son may not simply be traced back to the Wisdom parallels. Instead, *it may be traced back to the very claims which Jesus made of Himself.* Jesus understood Himself, as we have seen, as the climax of the prophetic tradition. But He was more than a prophet. As the eschatological prophet He was aware of a unique intimacy with His Father. Both in terms of Jesus' self-consciousness and the Matthean tradition of presenting Jesus as the fulfillment of Israel, this passage affirms a special uniqueness regarding Jesus. Yet, within the Q tradition, which Luke takes over simply, it is not an identification of Jesus with Wisdom itself.

But when we move from Q to Matthew, in the two verses immediately following, 11:28-30, which are his redaction, Jesus speaks *as Wisdom* and not merely as Wisdom's disciple or envoy. In Sir 51:23-26, on which this passage is moulded, the teacher of Wisdom invites her pupils to draw near and put their necks under the yoke of Wisdom, and he testifies to the rest he has found under Wisdom's yoke. In Matt 11:28-30 Jesus calls men to take *His* yoke upon them, and promises them rest under *His* yoke. Clearly Matthew has gone beyond Q. Jesus presents Himself as Wisdom. *This is a full-blown, explicit expression of Wisdom Christology.*[74]

We find the exact same phenomenon occurring in Matthew 23:34-39 (Lk 11:49; 13:34f). In the Q passages, recorded by Luke, Jesus speaks as an envoy of Wisdom. But in Matthew's redacted version, the saying of Wisdom becomes a saying of Jesus Himself. Matthew can do this because for him Jesus *is* Wisdom.[75]

What is the significance of Matthew's Wisdom Christology? Certainly we see in the earliest Christology a development from Q to Matthew.

Q was conscious of the implications and overtones of Wisdom in his material. But Matthew has gone beyond Q in his understanding of Jesus not simply as an envoy of Wisdom, but as Wisdom itself. Jesus as messenger of Wisdom is one thing; Jesus as Wisdom is another.

This Matthean development opens up new possibilities in developing New Testament Christology. It clearly opens up the possibility of understanding Jesus not just as different in degree from the prophets, but also different in kind. It opens up the possibility of moving from a Christology of Jesus' divinely given *function* to one which could speak of Jesus' metaphysical status. Certainly Matthew's Christology has to be considered a high Christology. While Jesus did not express Himself as identical with Wisdom, He did see Himself as God's final, eschatological and full revelation.

The link between Jesus' self-consciousness and the roots of what later would be the explicit affirmation of His personal and eternal pre-existent divinity are located here. Jesus is the final, eschatological, and full revelation of God because He is Wisdom itself. And all this is evident before the writing of John's gospel.[76] It is evident in the gospel of Matthew, a gospel Hick claims to be historically reliable, unlike John's.

What we have found, reproducing Dunn's line of thought, is that the earliest Christology to embrace the idea of Jesus' pre-existence is not the "Son of God" Christology or any of the other possibilities which we have examined. The roots for the later claim of the personal pre-existent divinity of Jesus from all eternity, and hence the Christian doctrine of the Incarnation, are found here in Wisdom Christology. The roots of Wisdom Christology are not the myths of other polytheistic religions, but the specific Wisdom theology of the Old Testament.

It is true, Jesus did not explicitly present Himself as the Incarnation of pre-existent Wisdom. But He did understand Himself to be the eschatological messenger of God in His Wisdom, an understanding which pointed to his uniqueness. This uniqueness is clearly affirmed in the full-blown Wisdom Christology of Matthew's gospel.

It is also clear this Wisdom Christology has roots at least in Paul, if not earlier. In Paul's first letter to the Corinthians, the crucified Jesus is presented as the Wisdom of God. In this understanding there is a link made between Christ and creation, a link intended to correct faulty Corinthian understanding of God's Wisdom and creation.

Paul presents Jesus as the full embodiment of God's Wisdom. Even if we acknowledge that some of the words about Wisdom are influenced by Hellenistic Judaism and Stoicism, it remains clear that the *meaning* of these words is determined by the new reality of the Christ-event itself. And this meaning makes evident that these passages, contrary to Hick's assertion, cannot be reduced to interpreting Jesus as a mere man inspired by God. It is true that Jesus, while He could not be identified with the Spirit, was presented as inspired by the Spirit. But it is equally clear that Jesus is not simply presented as inspired by Wisdom. He is identified as Wisdom itself. *It is with this identification, as Dunn points out, that we cross the boundary between humanity and divinity, between inspiration and incarnation.*

We can say that God's Wisdom became incarnate in Christ. But we must be clear that Wisdom was not thought of as a divine being. It was the identification of Wisdom with Jesus that moved the thinking about Wisdom in that direction. And in so doing, even in the ambiguous yet open passages of Paul, we see a Trinitarian direction being made possible. We conclude with Dunn's final observations about Wisdom:

> We can express this [Paul's understanding of Jesus as the full embodiment of Wisdom] as the *divinity* or even *deity* of Christ, so long as we understand what that means: the deity is the Wisdom of God, for the Wisdom of God is God reaching out to and active in his world. So the deity of Christ is the deity of Wisdom incarnate; that is, to recognize the deity of Christ is to recognize that in Christ God manifested himself, his power as Creator his love as Saviour, in a full and final way ... Herein we see the origin of the doctrine of the Incarnation.[77]

"Logos"

With our study of Wisdom we have reached the goal of our search, namely, to find the roots of the later explicit affirmation of Jesus' pre-existent divinity. For the sake of completeness, however, we ought to say something about the third "intermediary figure," the "Logos." It did not seem appropriate to treat of the Logos prior to Wisdom, since the former, being so central to John's prologue, comes into prominence *after* Wisdom has been in place. Again we depend on Dunn.

John's prologue 1:1-18, especially vv. 1-3,14, has been one of the most influential passages on subsequent theology. It was the claim that the Logos (Word) become flesh, and the identification of Jesus of Nazareth as this Incarnate Logos, which dominated second and third century Christology. It was in fact v.14, the central Christian affirmation of the prologue, which enabled patristic Christianity to maintain its distinctive testimony over against all other cults and religious systems. This uniqueness could hardly have been maintained if the whole notion of an Incarnate Logos were simply borrowed by the Christians from the surrounding religions.

It was Logos Christology that provided the bridge between Paul's early Wisdom Christology and the later Son Christology of the classic Christian creeds. It must be remembered, of course, that there was considerable overlap among all three. It was not a matter of a single linear development. Whereas in the West, Son Christology was popular prior to Nicea, in the East it was Logos Christology. Eastern Logos Christology gave way to Son Christology only during the conflict with Arius. This change resulted from Athanasius' distinction between "uncreated" *(agenetos) and "unbegotten" (agennetos)*. It was the expression "begotten not made" that determined that the prime Christological title should not be Logos, but Son. This title took root in both the East and the West.[78]

What, briefly, can we say about the Logos in pre-Christian thought? Most scholars agree that the principle background to John's prologue is the Old Testament itself and the thought of the intertestamental period, especially the Wisdom literature.[79] Important here for us to note is that there is no evidence of a pre-Christian myth to form the basis of John's incarnate Logos theology.[80]

In the Old Testament, over 90% of the more than 240 uses of "The Word of God (YHWH)" describe a word of prophecy. The phrase is a more or less technical one in which the prophet claims to express the authoritative will of God in a particular situation. Like Spirit and Wisdom, on some occasions the Word is given a quasi-independent existence (Ps 33:6; 107:20; 147:15,18; Is 9:8; 55:10f; Wisd 18:14-6). But as with the other two so-called intermediary figures, the Word of God is never understood as being independent of God. It was, in fact, precisely the Word of God, the utterance of God, God Himself speaking. All three figures are basically Old Testament variant ways of speaking of God's creative, revelatory or redemptive acts. Even for Philo with his Greek cosmological speculation about the Logos, there is no challenge to Jewish monotheism. The Word of God remains God in His self-revelation.

In early Christian thought, the Word is thought of as the word of preaching, the gospel. Although it is doubtful Jesus ever spoke of Himself or His message as the Word, in the New Testament the "good news" is both the word or message *about* Christ, and the message that *is* Christ.[81] But there is no immediate suggestion here of His personal and eternal pre-existence.

In the New Testament, however, there is an intermediate stage between the thought of Christ as the content of the word preached and the full identification of Christ as the Word Incarnate of John's gospel. This intermediate stage is the understanding of Christ as the one in whom God's pre-determined plan of salvation came to fulfillment (Acts 2:23; 1Cor 2:7; Eph 1:3-14).

We have already seen that in this understanding, that what was pre-existent in the will of God has come to historical actuality in Christ. From the beginning Christ had been pre-ordained for this role. Again, it was God's *intention* that "pre-existed," not the Christ. Paul speaks of the revelation in Christ (or the gospel) of God's hidden mystery (Eph 1:3-14; 3:4; 6:19; Col 1:25-7; 2:2). This mystery was God's plan to unite all things in Christ. Once again, it is the *mystery* that is pre-existent, not Christ. Neither Hebrews 9:23-26 not the Pastorals (1Tim 3:16; 6:14; 2Tim 1:10; 4:1,8; Titus 1:3; 2:13) alter this basic operative notion of what was in fact pre-existent and who was its fulfillment. Christ is the content of the word of preaching, the embodiment of the predetermined plan of salvation, the fulfillment of the divine purpose.

It is important to remember that it is not just that Jesus happened to do all the right things, and by so doing fulfilled the divine purpose. The risen Jesus was the one who from the beginning was predestined to be the fulfiller, the revealer, the redeemer. Thus, the divine purpose could be said to have been determined beforehand "in Christ." With this understanding we are between Jesus preached as the Christ and Jesus proclaimed as the Word Incarnate.

The full Word Christology is, of course, found in John's prologue (1:1-18). Here beyond dispute, the Word is pre-existent and Jesus is that Word in Incarnate. Jesus is identified with God's pre-existent intention; He is the pre-existent mystery. The prologue itself probably existed independently prior to the gospel.[82] Hence, the explicit statement regarding the identity of the Word with God—yet its distinction from God—along with the affirmation of the Incarnation, existed prior to John's writing. The prologue shows dependence on traditional Wisdom understanding. One is not forced to any conclusions regarding Gnostic cosmological dualism. Especially relevant would be the notion that Wisdom is revealed to God's own people in the Torah (Sir 24; Bar 3:9-4:4). As we have seen, the universal Word of God is revealed in the specificity not simply of the world, but in the Torah. This notion prepares the way for Wisdom's fullest specification in Jesus of Nazareth.

Yet, even with this preparation, Jn 1:14 is quite without parallel in pre-Christian Jewish thought. It was inconceivable for Philo, and for Greek thought generally, that the Word should become flesh. For John, the claim is not metaphoric but literal, as seen in the verb "became" (*egeneto*). God's word did not simply come to a man as with Old Testament prophets, nor did the Word enter into a man, or appear as a man (cf Gen 18), but *became* flesh.

It would seem, too, that only with v.14, can we speak of the *personal* Logos. As Dunn writes:

> In other words, the revolutionary significance of v.14 may well be that it marks *not only the transition in the thought of the poem from pre-existence to incarnation, but also the transition from impersonal personification to actual person.*[83] [emphasis Dunn's]

That is, it is not simply that an individual divine being became man, but that the *Word* became man. The language of personification is now identified with a particular person.

John's use of this prior hymn or poem conflates its Logos Christology with the Son Christology of his gospel. For John, the pre-existent Logos was a divine personal being. Hence, 1:18 acts as a link between the claim that Christ is the Incarnation of the Logos and the only Son of the Father (*monogenes theos*). It is no longer the Greek incorporeal Logos which is the link between God and man, but the man (incarnate Logos) Jesus Christ. What John has done is to unite Christ understood as the Wisdom of God with the Christ as the Son "sent" by the Father. The result is the understanding of Christ as the personally and eternally pre-existent Logos sent from heaven into the world.[84]

Conclusion to Search for Origins

Our lengthy, and yet still only schematic study of Scripture, was necessary to accomplish what Hick does not do: that is, search the New Testament for the origins of the doctrine of the Incarnation. Hick's claim, with only scanty evidence, is that the doctrine is a myth, and already evident as such in John's gospel. For Hick, the Fourth Gospel is just another expression of a general or common myth about divine beings coming to earth.

We, however, have seen that the language of divine Sonship, while of itself not affirming a personally and eternally pre-existent divine being, did take on a different meaning after the Christ-event, because of the very uniqueness of that event itself. But even here, we acknowledged that considered in isolation from other Christological developments, the language of divine Sonship could not account for the rise of the doctrine of the Incarnation. Therefore, it was not surprising that the title did not open directly on to a pre-existent divine Christ.

After sifting through many other Christological titles, it was only with the title Wisdom that we found what we were looking for. The origins of the claim regarding Jesus' pre-existence are found when the exalted Christ is spoken of in terms of pre-Christian Judaic Wisdom. The beginning of this development is found already in the letters of Paul, and perhaps earlier. In Matthew's gospel it reaches an important climax where Jesus is identified as Wisdom. John's gospel unites the Son Christology with the Wisdom and Logos Christologies—all expressing truth about Jesus the Christ.

Especially significant for our study is our conclusion that John's gospel was intended to do exactly what Hick says it could not possibly have done. It intended to prevent Christian thought from settling for a more accommodating faith. That is, it is John's gospel, more than any other New Testament document, that does not allow the Christian to see Jesus simply as an inspired prophet, or simply as some special revelation of God to man, or simply as God or a god appearing on earth in human guise. Hick has simply not read John's gospel carefully when he claims it to be a common myth.

Finally, John's gospel, while solving a certain tension between Logos and Son, in turn creates its own tension of how to understand the person of the Incarnate Logos and God the Father. For if Christ is indeed *theos* and not *ho theos*, the Son and not the Father, then modalism is ruled out. And if the Logos *became* Jesus Christ, and did not merely impinge on His consciousness, then the option of seeing Jesus simply as an inspired prophet is inadequate.

Hick, as we have seen opts for both these conclusions, which John's gospel forcefully argues against. Hick's view of God's relation to the world is modalistic. And his understanding of God's relation to Jesus constitutes Jesus no more than one among many people in the history of religion who were especially conscious of God's nearness. Any development in faith's understanding of Jesus is only deification.

It is John's gospel, guiding the development of later Trinitarian doctrine, that precisely in its original, explicit Christological affirmations, did not see itself as myth, and consciously argued against being understood as such. Myths could resolve themselves far more easily, as indeed they did.

It is inappropriate therefore to label the genuine development in understanding about Jesus as "myth." For one thing, in the beginnings of Christology we are not dealing with the general redeemer myth. That myth has its roots only in the second century. Nor can one call the Wisdom Christology "myth," since Jewish thought did not understand Wisdom as an independent divine being.

While the Christian faith in the hands of syncretists may lend itself to mythological language, as when the second-century Gnostics later took it over, it is misleading to describe the sophisticated thought of the New Testament writers as mythological. These writers are in fact attempting to keep myth at bay. Even John's gospel, which Hick over-simplifies, is wrestling with how to think of the one God, and Christ in relation to God, in the light of the newness of the Christ-event. Of course, if one, such as Hick, does not see the Christ-event as uniquely new, or chooses to reduces it to something less than it was, then the only alternative is to understand the Christological development as "going beyond" the original event. In such a case, development would be myth. If there were not the full truth to begin with, then development which purported to penetrate that truth could be interpreted only as imaginative and poetic. It is to the credit of John's genius that he was so successful, where Hick's "lowest common denominator" has falls short.

Christology must consider all the diversity that appears in the New Testament. To try to harmonize this diversity is to do the mystery an injustice. Equally, to ignore many aspects of the diversity in order to settle on one that seems acceptable today, is to do an injustice. The latter option is the direction Hick would have us follow. As Dunn writes:

> Again, a lowest common denominator approach which contented itself with some deliberately vague assertion about God acting through Christ, without committing itself on even the resurrection of Jesus let alone on any concept of incarnation, could only be advocated by deliberately ignoring the tensions and pressures within the earliest Christian assessment of the Christ-event which forced Christian thinking towards a modification of Jewish monotheism that would give adequate place to Christ, and could only be sustained by a somewhat arbitrary and blinkered resistance to the same tensions and pressures which are still there.[85]

Jesus "the Novum"

In our opening pages of this Chapter I indicated that the response to Hick's argument about the language of divine Sonship would be two-fold. We have just completed the first and by far the more lengthy of the two points. We now turn to our second point. The reply here has already been well-prepared both in the foregoing discussion in this Chapter, as well as in our previous Chapter where we had occasion to treat of the newness of Jesus. Here I wish to add to what I said earlier by bringing out aspects now possible only after the above Scriptural study.

The point to be made is that while the early language of divine Sonship when applied to Jesus does not of itself affirm Jesus' pre-existent divinity, the *meaning* when applied to Jesus exceeds Old Testament adoptionism. The reason for this development of meaning in the language of divine Sonship is due to the newness that is the Christ-event.[86]

That is why, as we have indicated, the Christological titles are not at the heart of the movement from implicit to explicit Christology.

Since Hick, as we have seen, reduces the Christ-event to the earthly life of Jesus, he is not in fact dealing with the full Christ-event which formed the foundation of subsequent faith and theology. The complete Christ-event was not revealed until after Jesus' death, resurrection and the gift of the Holy Spirit. *Jesus, therefore, could not simply say who He was before His work was brought to completion.* By then, He was no longer simply the earthly Jesus, but Jesus crucified for the world's salvation, and risen from the dead.

Christian faith is founded on the complete Christ-event, an event that includes not only His earthly life, but His atoning death and resurrection. Jesus' full Sonship is revealed only in His death and resurrection. And that Sonship went beyond any adoptionist meaning carried by the then contemporary language of divine Sonship. That is why the early Church had to find a fresh and new meaning for the titles at hand.[87] While there already is a newness about the historical Jesus, it is an inceptive newness which reaches full revelatory completion only after His resurrection.

In the first part of this Chapter we analyzed many kinds of Christologies according to the titles of Jesus. There we saw that as early as Paul's letters, Wisdom Christology was already opening on to the notion of Jesus' divine personal and eternal pre-existence. Yet, other Christologies, for example, Son of Man and the Last Adam, while certainly not closing the door to His pre-existence, did not explicitly affirm it either. Yet, the various Christologies regarding Jesus were not simply parcelled out among the faithful, one Christology per Christian community. There was much overlap. And, of course, Jesus of whom these titles spoke, was *one* person, crucified and risen.

The point here is that while the various Christologies need not be harmonized, they do not on the other hand compartmentalize Jesus. It is true, the analytic mind can proceed only by treating the Christologies discretely. But in their original instance, these various elements represented not an analysis of Jesus, but a movement towards a *synthetic* understanding of Him. These various Christologies and their development in the early Church were not carried on independent of each other. Rather, they constituted interlocking ways of coming to understand and express the newness and uniqueness of Jesus. As Martin Hengel writes:

> ... the development of christology was from the beginning concerned with synthesis: otherwise it was impossible to give satisfactory expression to the eschatological uniqueness of God's communication of himself in the man Jesus.[88]

This synthetic movement was required because of the "novum" which was Jesus. If Jesus did not constitute the uniqueness which later Christology explicated, it is hard to account for the particular Christological development—and so quick a one at that—which occurred within the New Testament. For if Jesus were simply a man especially conscious of God's presence, as Hick contends, why could the New Testament writers not simply have settled for the easily available and understood adoptionist interpretation? There would have been no need for any synthetic development. The available adoptionist meaning could even have expressed the "psychological absoluteness," to use Hick's term, of the disciples' religious experience. There would have been no need for any development beyond this notion.

Hick's argument that New Testament Christological development resulted simply from human spiritual needs for a Saviour does not in the end, even stand up even to common sense. Felipe Gomez, S.J., writes that such argumentation is "simply naive."[89] One of the basic human needs is for survival. By making the Christological claims that the early Christians did, they were *not*, humanly speaking, ensuring their survival, either within Judaism or within the wider Roman Empire. Some form of adoptionism would have proved far more fulfilling of that human need. Certainly the political and religious pressures at the time would have made it much easier for the Christian communities to choose this option. But, as the New Testament attests, that was not at all an adequate solution.

Our point is that it was impossible for the early Church to stop at a simple adoptionist Christology.[90] The life, death and resurrection of Jesus had been experienced as a "*unique, 'eschatological' saving event.*"[91] The goal of Christological development, even from the beginning, was to express God's self-communication in the quite unsurpassable and final Way that was Jesus. This Christological development already had begun during the earthly life of Jesus. But since the full revelation of Jesus was not complete during His earthly life, neither was Christian faith complete. Therefore, neither could Christology be complete. Only with the resurrection of Jesus and the sending of the Spirit, would the Christ-event and Christian faith reach its fullness. Therefore, Christianity's claims have never depended *solely* on Jesus' own earthly testimony regarding Himself. Constitutive to the Christ-event was not only the earthly mission of the Son, but also—and even more—His death and resurrection, as well as the mission of the Spirit. Hick by-passes these latter components totally.

Integral, as well, to the fullness of Christian faith was the realization that the richness of Christ could not be exhausted by any simple explanation. The Christ-event was not something simply to be looked at, or even understood, but to be shared in. And that sharing in the life of the Risen Jesus Christ was itself to constitute part of the foundational, revelational experience of the Church. That is, the development of Christology within the New Testament forms part of the revelation of the Christ-event. The gospels, then, are clearly more than what Hick calls "memoirs." The gospels reveal that the early Church could not naively settle on an adoptionist Christology as an adequate expression of the Risen Jesus in whose life they had come to share.

The marvel is not that the Christian communities took so long to reach an understanding of the pre-existent divinity of Jesus. The marvel is that they reached it so quickly. All the forces, political, social and religious, did not encourage such a quick development. Only the force of the Christ-event itself, both in its granting-side (revelation) and in its receiving side (faith) could have drawn Christology forward in so brief a time. We recall Hick's comparison of the deification of the Buddha with the development in Christology. By Hick's own acknowledgment, the deification of the Buddha began only *500* years after his death. One could hardly say, therefore, that "Buddhology," it impossible to live with an "adoptionist" interpretation of Gautama.

Martin Hengel points out that the movement of Christology in the direction of affirming Jesus' pre-existent divinity can at least be traced back to the 40's. Already by the year 50, gathering around the risen Jesus were notions of pre-existence, mediation at creation, and the sending of the Son into the world.[92] Certain passages in Paul, for example, Phil 2:6-11, while more plausibly read within the Adam Christology, certainly are *open* to the possibility of divine, personal and eternal pre-existence, and can support such an interpretation. Similarly, those passages which identify the risen Jesus with the pre-existent divine plan or "mystery" now revealed in Christ, are not simply neutral regarding the possibility of Jesus' divine, personal and eternal pre-existence and the subsequent idea of Incarnation.[93] And even Paul's early passages proclaiming Jesus the embodiment of God's Wisdom suggest Jesus was "more than" simply a man inspired by God.

Our point is that the explicit Christology of Jesus' divine, personal and eternal pre-existence and the identification of Him as the Word Incarnate *are truer affirmations about Jesus than their competitors, that is, truer to the implications found not only in the primitive proclamations about Jesus, but truer even to the consciousness of Jesus as uncoverable within the New Testament.*[94]

In conclusion to this section, the New Testament can be adequately accounted for only if Jesus is a *novum* that far exceeds any understanding of Him as simply a man intensely conscious of God. It is because Jesus constitutes a newness, a fullness, and a finality of God's self-revelation that exceeds anything that went before or to come, that none of the available titles proved adequate to express His uniqueness. And this newness of Jesus is not something that has its roots in the post-Easter faith. The roots of New Testament Christology are found in the earthly Jesus, even, as we have seen, in His consciousness. It is in fact only if Jesus is what later explicit Christology in the New Testament claims Him to be, that He can constitute a newness sufficient to explain New Testament development in the first place. Only if Jesus is the Word Incarnate can He be the "eschatological prophet" in the unique sense He understood Himself to be. And only such an identity is adequate to account for the development of Christology in the New Testament as it has historically occurred.

John's Gospel and Deification

At the beginning of this Chapter, it was stated that there were three questions about Hick's Scriptural theme which needed to be met. The first, regarding the language of divine Sonship, we have just completed. We now turn to the second and third questions. Both questions treat of John's gospel in particular. Given all that we have said in this chapter and in the previous one, the response to these questions can be brief. I address the first of these two questions in this section, and the second in the next.

The question to be answered in this section is: are the Christological sayings of John's gospel a deification? The three specific sayings Hick refers to are 10:30, 14:6, 14:9. For Hick, these sayings regarding the unity between Jesus and the Father, found on the lips of Jesus, represent the Christology of John's gospel. This Christology, we have seen Hick maintain, is a deification.

To answer this question, we need only draw on matter we have already raised. This question, and the next, are simply specifications of the foundational questions which we have already discussed.

First, the assumption behind Hick's argument claiming deification in John's gospel is that the Christ-event was only about the earthly life of the man Jesus. For someone to claim that a mere man is ontologically divine, and then to put such a claim in the mouth of that man, would indeed constitute deification.

The point here, however, is that this is not what John does. The Christ-event is more than simply the life of a mere man who was more than usually conscious of God. Therefore, the process at work is not that of deification, but of a development from an implicit Christology to an explicit one. This development is not a deification because the Christ-event which gives rise to it is "more than" that of the earthly life of Jesus, "more than" that of a man specially aware of God's presence. To elaborate further we would have to repeat everything we have said thus far. So we simply refer the reader to our presentation on Hick's limited view of the Christ-event in our above section *Jesus "the Novum."*

Secondly, Hick's understanding of Jesus' historical consciousness is impoverished. Jesus himself was aware of being "more than" especially conscious of God's presence. I acknowledge that Jesus' awareness of the union He shared with the Father was not that of later "representational conceptual knowledge."[95] Yet, His self-understanding as "eschatological prophet" indicated He was aware of being not only prophet, but "Beloved Son" (Mk 12:1-12, par). As the "Beloved Son" proclaiming that God's kingdom was at hand, Jesus was offering the

Father's eschatological and decisive summons to salvation. Not only that, Jesus has made acceptance of that offer dependent on acceptance of Himself.[96] In other words, even as eschatological prophet, Jesus was aware of his relation to the Father as being far more intimate than Hick allows.[97] These points, too, we have already made.

Thirdly, Hick's claim that John's gospel involves a deification argues that there is an alteration in language from that used in the synoptics. We will have more to say about this important linguistic issue later. But within the Scriptural context of this Chapter we wish simply to make a point regarding Christology and soteriology.

I readily admit that within the New Testament there is a development in Christology from what may be called a functional Christology to an ontological Christology. That is, there is development from the work of Jesus to the person of Jesus. We have already considered one aspect of this development in the previous Chapter where we discussed the relation between Jesus' self-revelation and the disciples' faith. Here we need to make another point on this issue.

In the early stages of "Son" Christology, it is true there are no ontological statements as such (cf. Rom 1:4; Mk 1:11). Then with the writing of John's gospel the intrinsic unity of functional and ontological Christology is both explicit and thematic. A first point, then, is that even this development has roots long before John wrote his gospel. Mark's transfiguration pericope (9:2-8) already speaks of a transformation of Jesus (*metamorphothe*). This certainly *implies* an ontological understanding not simply of Jesus' function, but of His Sonship. The narratives of Jesus' conception by the Holy Spirit (Matt 1:18-25; Lk 1:26-38) equally intend more than function; they speak of who Jesus is. The transition from function to ontology is not simply some need for mythology on John's part.

Secondly, even in John, of course, there is not the later kind of full metaphysical unity between Father and Son as occurs, for example, in the Nicene Creed. The unity between Jesus and the Father in John's gospel is a unity of willing and knowing, but a unity which is already operative within an ontological horizon. And yet, even with this development, functional Christology does not fade into the background. Rather, both functional and ontological Christology are found together.

Thirdly, Hick implies that this transition from functional to ontological Christology is simply the result of a human need for a Saviour. The assumption behind Hick's argument is that the risen Jesus was not the kind of Saviour He was experienced to be. In fact, however, the reason for the transition from functional to ontological Christology was *precisely* because Jesus was the Saviour He was experienced to be. If He were not, there would have been no need to penetrate the mystery of His person. It is only partly true that such an investigation in later centuries resorted to a "complicated metaphysics", as Hick refers to it.[98] Certainly no *myth* requires that kind of "complicated" explanation!

The first point, then is that the reason for the transition from functional to ontological language within the new Testament was due to the very uniqueness of the salvation wrought by Christ. The salvation brought about in Christ prompted the question about the person of Jesus. The reason His salvation prompted that question was because it exceeded any kind of salvation heretofore experienced. It went beyond what any ordinary prophet or wise man could bring. With the prompting of the question about Jesus' person, functional Christology, or soteriology, was moving into ontological Christology. Ontological Christology was necessary to safeguard its functional counterpart. That is, to safeguard the correct understanding of the salvation which Jesus brought, the early church had to ensure that the correct interpretation of who Jesus was, was attained. For if the salvation were new and unique, so must the Saviour be.

Hick's view of the salvation which Jesus brought is quite thin. While he uses expressions like "becoming children of God," and "overcoming sin," these phrases do not mean what they do in traditional Christianity. Salvation for Hick in this life is simply overcoming self-centeredness. While this aspect is part of Christian salvation, it is not what salvation is all about. Salvation for Hick is more like a mature adult emerging from a child, than it is a sharing in the very life of God Himself. For Hick, salvation is a kind of spiritual evolution on the level of nature, and not a supernatural gift.[99]

It is not surprising that since Hick's functional Christology is inadequate, that he is not going to see any need for an ontological Christology. After all, the salvation brought is not "new" enough to legitimately warrant the question of Jesus' person being raised or investigated. Hence, to make the transition from soteriology to ontological Christology can only be seen as the product of some myth-producing human need.

But in the New Testament, soteriology requires ontological Christology. The latter is at the service of the former, to safeguard the uniqueness of Christ's salvation by not allowing the Christ to be falsely interpreted. Christ's work and his person cannot be separated from each other. The inspired evangelists realized this. For only under this condition of their interdependence could God's nature as self-giving love be seen in the life, death, and resurrection of Jesus.

It is in fact because these two are so interconnected that the questions which eventually gave rise to the explicit doctrine of the Trinity are neither metaphysical musings nor mythological daydreams. These questions are grounded in the unity between the work and the person of the historical Jesus.[100] For the revelation regarding the Trinity, too, has to be grounded in Jesus. If there is a rupture between soteriology and ontological Christology, then, of course, Trinitarian reflections would be nothing more than a myth masquerading as complicated metaphysics. Hick's conclusion follows validly from his premise. Unfortunately, his premise which divorces Jesus' person from his work is unwarranted and erroneous.

It follows, therefore, that ontological Christology safeguards and does not go beyond, the consciousness of Jesus. By guaranteeing that the salvation brought by Jesus is what it is experienced to be, ontological Christology is preserving the very eschatological uniqueness of the personal work of Jesus. And as we have seen, He himself was aware of the eschatological uniqueness of His work. That eschatological work was grounded in God Himself. Therefore, Kasper is correct when he writes:

> Contrary however to a view sometimes maintained, these [New Testament] pre-existent statements are not merely the ultimate conclusion of a gradual process of extending backwards the divine sonship of Jesus from the Resurrection by way of his baptism and conception to his pre-existence ... [I]t is not a question of extending time into eternity, but of founding salvation history in God's eternity.[101]

210

Ontological Christology is expressing in a new and more profound way the eschatological character of the person and work of Jesus of Nazareth. It is because of this relation between soteriology and Christology that Christians claim that God has revealed Himself in Christ definitively, unreservedly and unsurpassably. It is, in turn, that relationship between soteriology and Christology that necessitated "a new, comprehensive interpretation of the term God."[102]

John's Gospel and the Consciousness of Jesus

The third question we put to ourselves in evaluating Hick's Scriptural argument is this: does John's gospel go beyond the consciousness of Jesus? With this question we have come full circle. Early in our previous Chapter 5, we evaluated Hick's position regarding the consciousness of Jesus. In our immediately preceding section we have evaluated Hick's argument that John's gospel represents a deification of Jesus because it has moved from functional to ontological Christology. Now these two evaluations come together in this section. We can be especially brief, therefore, because we have already been answering this question throughout these latter Chapters.

John's gospel goes beyond Jesus' consciousness in the sense that Jesus never said "I am the pre-existent Word Incarnate." But it does not go beyond Jesus' consciousness in a more foundational sense. As we have just seen, John's ontological Christology safeguards the very self-consciousness of Jesus as eschatological prophet and Beloved Son. In making this bond so explicit, John has put his finger on what would be recognized for centuries to come as the touchstone for Christian faith. Jesus was not just a divine being come down to earth; He was the Word made flesh.

We saw in our previous Chapter that the movement from implicit to explicit Christology is not only valid, but is demanded by the very nature and newness of the Christ-event itself. We now see another dimension of the importance and validity of an explicit Christology. It results from, and safeguards, the inseparable bond that exists between Jesus' work and who He is. Far from going beyond the consciousness of Jesus in the sense of creating for Him a deified consciousness, John's gospel ensures that the uniqueness of Jesus' consciousness is not lost to the pressures to reduce it to less than it was; to reduce it to something more manageable.

One final point needs to be made. We had cause earlier to refer to Matthew 11:27 (and its parallel Luke 10:22.) These sayings of Jesus speak of the exclusive mutual knowledge that exists between the Father and the Son. They are found in Q.[103] They are significant verses because they indicate that John's later explicit stress and elaboration on the exclusive, mutual self-knowledge between Father and Son, was not a theme that John himself created to justify his claims about Jesus and His self-consciousness. The fact that these verses are seen to be a root of Johannine Christology is evident in that these verses have been called "a meteor from the Johannine heaven."[104]

We saw that Dunn argued that these verses could be traced back to the very claims Jesus made about Himself:

> ... the claim that the mutual knowing of Yahweh and Israel had come to fullest expression in the eschatological immediacy of his [Jesus'] knowledge of God's will ('Amen', "But I say') as God's son ...; the claim that he came as the *climax* of the prophetic tradition ...; and the claim that through his ministry was already being realized the apocalyptic hope for the coming of the kingdom ..., the establishment of the new covenant ... wherein, according to Jer 31.31-4, all would 'know' Yahweh 'from the least to the greatest'.[105]

With these verses from Q, so representative of John's Sonship Christology, and so grounded in the consciousness of Jesus, it is difficult to see how Hick can argue that John's gospel is simply the expression of a mythologizing process that goes beyond anything that could have been in Jesus' consciousness.[106]

Endnotes

1. Joseph A. Fitzmyer, S.J. *A Christological Catechism: New Testament Answers* (Ramsey, NJ: Paulist Press, 1981), 90.

2. *Ibid.*, 87.

3. James D. G. Dunn, *Christology in the Making: A New Testament Inquiry into the Origins of the Doctrine of the Incarnation* (London: S.C.M., 1980), 64.

4. Dunn, *Christology* ... . I chose to organize my material around this work of Dunn's because: (1) he intends it to be an exhaustive Scriptural response to Hick's *The Myth of God Incarnate*, Dunn, 6; (2) his response accepts, as I do, that there is a valid development from an implicit to an explicit Christology; (3) he is cautious about concluding that Jesus' pre-existent divinity is obvious in such controverted passages as Phil 2:6-11. This caution serves our purpose better than, for example, the positions of Leopold Sabourin, S.J., *Christology: Basic Texts in Focus* (New York: Alba House, 1984) and Martin Hengel, "The Son of God" in his *The Cross of the Son of God* (London: S.C.M. 1976). Both conclude to the definite affirmation of the pre-existence of Jesus in such disputed passages. Dunn's caution better serves us because, should he eventually be proven wrong, and Sabourin and Hengel proven right, then our case is strengthened. If we opted to follow Sabourin and Hengel, and they eventually were proven incorrect, then our case could be weakened.

For a discussion of the titles of Jesus in the hastily-written response to *The Myth of God Incarnate*, see Michael Green, "Jesus in the New Testament," in Michael Green, ed., *The Truth of God Incarnate* (London: Hodder and Staughton, 1977), 29-33. A little later Green argues that more important than the titles of Jesus, are the implicit assumptions about Him in the New Testament, *ibid.*, 33-35.

5. Dunn, *Christology* ..., 64.

6. *Ibid.*, 35.

7. Aylward Shorter, *Revelation and Its Interpretation* (London: Geoffrey Chapman, 1983), 112.

8. Dunn, *Christology* ...., 33-46.

9. *Ibid.*, 48.

10. *Ibid.*, 48-49.

11. Raymond E. Brown, S.S. *The Birth of the Messiah: A Commentary of the Infancy Narratives in Matthew and Luke* (Garden City, NY: Doubleday & Company, 1979), 134.

12. *Ibid*, 141. Brown's complete account of Matthew's narrative on this point is found on 122-64.

13. Dunn, *Christology*, 50.

14. Brown, *Birth* ..., 312.

15. For Brown's commentary on Luke's account of the virginal

conception of Jesus, see *Birth* ..., 286-329.

16. Dunn, *Christology* ..., 52.

17. Myles M. Bourke, "The Epistle to the Hebrews," *The Jerome Biblical Commentary*, 382.

18. Dunn, *Christology* ..., 55-56.

19. *Ibid.*, 57, 59.

20. Walter Kasper, *Jesus the Christ* (London: Burns & Oates, 1976), 104.

21. *Ibid.*, 106. Later, Kasper indicates that it is in Isaiah 11:2, that we find evidence of the tradition that the Messiah was expected precisely to be the bearer of the Holy Spirit, 253.

22. *Ibid.*, 104.

23. Fitzmyer, *A Christological Catechism* ..., 86.

24. David M. Stanley, S.J. "Aspects of New Testament Thought," *The Jerome Biblical Commentary*, 770.

25. Kasper, *Jesus* ..., 106.

26. Stanley, *JBC*, 770. Fitzmyer notes that this Christology has been called "the oldest christology preserved in the New Testament," *A Christological Catechism*, 86.

27. Stanley, *JBC*, 771.

28. Kasper, *Jesus* ..., 253.

29. Stanley, *JBC*, 770.

30. Kasper, *Jesus* ..., 231.

31. Dunn writes: "The most obvious conclusion therefore is that *there was no conception of a pre-existent Messiah current in pre-Christian Judaism prior to the Similitudes of Enoch*," *Christology* ..., 72. Dunn dates the *Similtudes of Enoch* as not probable before 70 A.D., *ibid.*, 77.

32. Stanley, *JBC*, 770; Fitzmyer, *A Christological Catechism*, 87; Kasper, *Jesus* ..., 153.

33. Stanley, *JBC*, 770.

34. Kasper, *Jesus* ..., 153.

35. Stanley, *JBC*, 770.

36. Kasper, *Jesus* ..., 153.

37. Stanley, *JBC*, 770.

38. Eph.1:10 indicates that the divine choice or election of Jesus to be Lord was made "before the foundation of the world." It does not af-

firm Christ himself as pre-existent.

Heb 1:2f shows, within this earlier Christian hymn, the influence of Wisdom Christology. But the author of Hebrews has made it his own. In doing so, as we have seen earlier, he is not making an affirmation of the personal, divine, pre-existence of Jesus.

Col 1:15-20 would seem to be evidence against our argument at this point. But as we shall see later in this Chapter it is not the title "Lord" which makes this passage significant, for indeed the title does not appear. What makes this passage significant is the presence of a Wisdom Christology. The Wisdom Christology will prove to be the solution to our present search for the roots of Jesus' pre-existent divinity.

39. Kasper, *Jesus ...*, 107.

40. *Ibid.*

41. *Ibid.*

42. Fitzmyer lists the three ways the title is applied to Jesus in the synoptics:"(i) it is used of Jesus in his lowly, earthly condition (Matt 8:20; Luke 9:58); (ii) it is used of him in reference to his passion (lacking in "Q," but see Mark 8:31; 9:31; 10:33); and (iii) it is used of his coming in glory or judgment ("Q": Matt 24:27; Luke 17:24; and Mark 8:38; 13:26), *A Christological Catechism*, 89. For Kasper's elaboration on each of these three ways, see *Jesus ...*, 108.

43. Initially, of course, the phrase Son of Man was a typical Semitic universal or generalizing term for "human being." In this sense it appears ninety-three times in Ezekiel. But in Daniel 7 it represents the "saints of the Most High" (Dan 7:21-22,25), that is, the true Israel which will replace the world kingdoms. Kasper, *Jesus ...*, 107; Dunn, *Christology ...*, 68-75.

44. Dunn, *Christology*, 75-82.

45. *Ibid.*, 82-87.

46. *Ibid.*, 88-97.

47. Joseph A. Fitzmyer, S.J. *Scripture and Christology: A Statement of the Biblical Commission with a Commentary* (New York: Paulist Press, 1986), 7-8,22-23, and for Fitzmyer's commentary, 66-69, esp. 68.

48. Dunn, *Christology ...*, 99.

49. Stanley, *JBC*, 774.

50. *Ibid.*, 775.

51. Dunn, *Christology ...*, 106.

52. *Ibid*, 110.

53. *Ibid.*, 114-21.

54. *Ibid.*, 123.

55. *Ibid*, 124.

56. *Ibid.*, 132.

57. *Ibid.*, 162.

58. *Ibid.*, 135.

59. *Ibid*, 147.

60. Kasper, *Jesus* ..., 254-57.

61. Dunn, *Christology* ..., 164.

62. Raymond E.Brown, S.S. *The Gospel According to John.* 2 vols. The Anchor Bible (New York: Doubleday, 1966), 521-23.

63. Dunn's translation.

64. Dunn, *Christology* ..., 165-66.

65. See John L. McKenzie *The Two-Edged Sword: An Interpretation of the Old Testament.* (Garden City, NY: Bruce Publishing, 1966), 82, 316-25; R. A. F. Mackenzie, S.J. *Faith and History in the Old Testament* (Minneapolis: University of Minneapolis Press, 1963), 18-31.

66. Dunn, *Christology* ..., 170.

67. *Ibid*, 170-74.

68. This observation becomes important later when we discuss the relation of Nicea to Greek culture.

69. Dunn's translation.

70. Dunn, *Christology* ..., 182.

71. *Ibid.*, 188.

72. Two other passages need only be noted. In 1 Cor 10:1-4 it is not clear that Paul is making any link between Christ and Wisdom. Further, the passage is typological. It seems Paul intended his readers to see the "rock then" as equivalent to "Christ now." Paul's readers should compare themselves to the Israelites and understand the peril they now are in. Similarly, Rom 10:6-10 is not an argument to the pre-existence of Christ. It seems more a variation on the earlier Christian reflection on the death and resurrection of Jesus. Dunn, *Christology* ..., 183-87.

73. Dunn, *Christology*, 197-98.

74. It is on the basis of this pericope, Mt 11:25-30, that Lesslie Newbigin argues that one cannot drive a wedge between the Synoptics and John's Gospel, *The Open Secret*, 47-48.

75. Dunn, *Christology*, 201-204.

76. There is also an identification of Jesus with Wisdom in Hebrews 1:1-3. The hymn enclosed herein is definitely a Wisdom Christology with parallels to Col 1:15-7. But here the reference with Wisdom is to the exalted Christ. Since Hebrews nowhere else has any Wisdom Christology, we must assume that the author intends to mean that Jesus embodies God's Wisdom without remainder. What is pre-existent is the act and power of God, Christ is the eschatological embodiment of that act and power. It will ultimately be this "without remainder" that Hick in his own *homoagape* cannot accept.

77. Dunn, *Christology* ..., 212.

78. *Ibid.*, 213-15.

79. John Marsh, *The Gospel of Saint John* (Middlesex: Penguin Books, 1968), 96-7. David Stanley, *"I Encountered God!" The Spiritual Exercises with the Gospel of Saint John* (St. Louis: The Institute of Jesuit Sources, 1986), 46. Bruce Vawter, C.M. "The Gospel According to John," *JBC*, 422. Dunn, *Christology* ..., 215.

80. Dunn, *Christology*, 215-16.

81. Shorter, *Revelation* ..., 104-106.

82. Vawter, *JBC*, 421.

83. Dunn, *Christology* ..., 243.

84. Neither 1 John:1-3 nor Rev 19:11-13 develop these notions any further beyond the Incarnation in John's prologue.

85. Dunn, *Christology* ..., 266.

86. Kasper, *Jesus* ..., 259-68 gives an excellent summary of the newness, finality and uniqueness of Jesus, the eschatological prophet, as Truth, Life and Way.

87. Christopher Butler also makes this point in "Jesus and Later Orthodoxy," in Michael Green, ed., *The Truth of God Incarnate* (London: Hodder and Stoughton, 1977), 89.

88. Martin Hengel, "The Son of God," *The Cross of the Son of God* (London: S.C.M., 1976), 73.

89. Felipe Gomez, S.J., "The Uniqueness and Universality of Christ," *East Asian Pastoral Review*, 1 (1983): 12. Gomez argues against, among others, Gregory Baum's contention that it was survival needs that moved the early Church to speak of Jesus as the unique Saviour of the world. Gregory Baum, "Is there a missionary mes-

sage?" *Mission Trends* 1, (1974): 83-84.

90. Peter Hinchcliff argues similarly, when he writes: "And if one really wanted clear historical proof that Jesus of Nazareth was unique, it is here. For no one else has been both so clearly an historical figure and, at the same time, the catalyst for the crystallizing of such a persistent, complex, and accumulating set of beliefs. There *must* have been some original reality ... to have provoked it. Heroic figures may become the focus of myth and legend [e.g. Arthurian legends] ... But ... there was apparently no motivation sufficiently powerful and sustained to turn it [e.g., Arthurian legend] into a serious, intellectually systematized, metaphysical foundation for a faith," in *God Incarnate: Story and Belief* (London: SPCK, 1981), 88.

91. Hengel, "The Son of God," 87.

92. *Ibid.*, 64.

93. Shorter, *Revelation ...*, 130.

94. Brown, *The Community of the Beloved Disciple* (New York: Paulist Press, 1979), 104-105. Dunn, *Christology ...*, 254. Shorter, *Revelation ...*, 111, 124.

95. Kasper, *Jesus ...*, 248.

96. *Ibid.*, 75.

97. Edward Schillebeeckx writes in the *Interim Report on the books "Jesus" and "Christ"* (New York: Crossroad, 1981): "The [synoptic] affirmation of a real relationship between the decision which men make about Jesus and their ultimate destiny ... without doubt goes back historically, at least in germ, to Jesus' own self-understanding, which was presented in the whole of Jesus' career, in terms of the concept of the 'eschatological prophet': the intermediary in the coming kingdom of God. That in the coming of Jesus God himself touches us is a Christian conviction which therefore in the last resort goes back to Jesus' understanding of himself," 67. And a few pages later, he continues: "One can say that the continuity between Jesus before his death and Jesus after it is established by the recognition that Jesus is the eschatological prophet, an early Christian interpretation of Jesus' own understanding of himself," 70.

98. But the resort to complicated metaphysics was not an escape or a cover-up or even the Hellenization of the faith in the way Hick understands the term. It was occasioned by the questions raised in the

context of the culture at hand.

99. For Cardinal Ratzinger's critique of this contemporary way of thinking, see *The Ratzinger Report: an Exclusive Interview on the State of the Church* (Leominster: Fowler Wright Books, 1985), 80. Joseph Cardinal Ratzinger with Vittorio Messori. Translated from the authorized German manuscript by Salvator Attanasio and Graham Harrison.

100. Karl Rahner sees the link crucial when he writes that Jesus is not simply God in general but the Son, and therefore, the economic Trinity is the immanent Trinity and *vice versa*. *The Trinity* (New York: Seabury, 1974), esp. 21-33.

101. Kasper, *Jesus* ..., 172.

102. *Ibid.*, 175.

103. John L. McKenzie, "The Gospel According to Matthew," *JBC*, 83.

104. *Ibid.*

105. Dunn, *Christology* ..., 200.

106. Kasper writes: "A flat-footed theology can justify neither the uniqueness nor the universality of Christian faith." *Jesus* ..., 19. This is insightful on Kasper's part because Hick fails on both accounts.

CHAPTER SEVEN

Tradition

T his Chapter evaluates the third of Hick's three most important cases against the traditional understanding of Jesus' unique-ness. This third argument, or more properly, this group of arguments, focuses on the area I have called Tradition.

For our purposes I distinguish between Tradition and Theology. To some extent, this terminology is arbitrary. Tradition and Theology are part and parcel of each other. However, for the sake of this study, by *Tradition* I am referring to the doctrinal statements of the Councils, in particular Nicea (325) and Chalcedon (451). These are the two Councils to which Hick most frequently refers. By *Theology* I refer to theological analyses which Hick has put forward in addition to either his Scriptural case or to that relating to Tradition. This Chapter addresses Hick's important challenges to the Tradition.

At the end of Chapter 3 I summarize Hick's position on the Tradition as follows:

(a) Nicea's "consubstantiality" represents the culmination of the deification process of projection. The language about Jesus has passed from metaphor to metaphysics. (b) Nicea's language is culture-bound and therefore optional. (c) Nicea's language is mythological. It does not represent a theological hypothesis but a religious myth. (d) Nicea's two-natures Christology has no literal meaning. It is as contradictory as is the notion of a square-circle.[1]

There are four questions that must be faced in evaluating Hick's claims: (1) Is Nicea a culmination of the process of deifying Jesus? (2) In what sense is Nicea's language not culture-bound, and therefore not optional? (3) Does Nicea's language represent theological hypothesis or religious myth? (4) Is Nicea's two-natures Christology, as traditionally understood, a logical contradiction?

Nicea and Deification

The first question: is Nicea a culmination of the deification of Jesus?

In one sense, the simple answer is "no, it is not, because there has been no deification process in the first place." Chapters 5 and 6 have demonstrated that the process involved was one of development from an implicit to an explicit Christology. Given the nature of revelation and faith, we have shown that the roots of that process are valid. Accepting the complete Christ-event, I have argued that the Christological development is grounded in the Jesus who died and was raised. This development does not add on to Him anything that was not already there. It certainly is not the making of a god out of a man.

But we cannot leave our answer simply at that. As we move from Scripture to Tradition, there is a new, foundational challenge which enters the debate. Hick has put the issue in terms of "meaning," i.e., as the movement from metaphor to metaphysics. That is, with Nicea, the metaphoric title "Son of God" becomes the metaphysical claim "God the Son." Hick claims that Biblical language was abandoned for Greek philosophical concepts. The faith becomes Hellenized. Hellenization elevates the deification of Jesus to a new order of meaning. In so doing it alters that meaning. It mistakenly transposes mythical meaning into literal meaning.

Nicea represents for Hick, the culmination of this Hellenizing, deification process. A goal of Christology today is to disentangle itself from the results of deification and from the metaphysics that entrenched its conclusions. Christology must acknowledge the meaning of the Tradition to be metaphorical and mythological. Christology must, in brief, become de-Hellenized. It is to this new challenge that our attention is now directed.

As an initial, general response, I acknowledge with Hick that in the

Christological development from Scripture to Nicea there has been a shift, even a shift in meaning. But I disagree with Hick's understanding of the nature of that shift. I agree that Greek philosophical terms entered the debate. I disagree that the faith was Hellenized, in the sense that Hick understands the process. That is, I disagree that Christian faith and theology altered their own meaning so that they became a mere instance of Greek philosophy. I admit that Nicea was decisive in a normative way for Christological development. I disagree that Nicea was a culmination of that process. A careful reading of the history of the subsequent Councils shows that Christology continued to develop.

Before elaborating my response in detail, I wish to make a general observation. Hick is not especially precise when he discusses Nicea. As was noted in Chapter 3, Hick uses the terms Nicea and Chalcedon interchangeably to refer to the traditional teaching about Jesus' uniqueness. While this interchange can hardly be considered inappropriate, it is not a careful usage. Hick refers to Nicea when he speaks of the "two-natures" Christology. But the designation "two-natures" more precisely comes from Chalcedon than from Nicea. Since Hick focuses his case on the term *homoousios*, that is on Jesus being declared *homoousios* with the Father, as the culmination of the deification process, it would be more precise for him to refer only to Nicea, or even better to Nicea and Constantinople (381), to which latter Council Hick never refers. Finally, if at times Hick does intend Chalcedon with the term "two-natures" Christology, he reveals only a partial understanding of its definition. Hick never investigates the unity of Jesus, already defined at Ephesus (431), or the relation between *hypostasis* or *prosopon* and *physis*. In short, by focusing only on what is "two" in Jesus, Hick is unable adequately to treat what is "one."

At the heart of Hick's position is his contention that the shift in meaning, which culminates in Nicea, is a shift from metaphor to metaphysics. The poetic title "Son of God" becomes the philosophical "God the Son." Nicea, according to Hick, mistook mythological meaning and treated it as literal or metaphysical meaning.

But is this a true explanation of what has occurred? I do not think so.[2] In the discussion which immediately follows, I investigate the foundations of the shift in that meaning. Later, I address the specific issue of

Hellenization. While intimately related historically, the shift in meaning and Hellenization are not identical. The former is foundational in human consciousness, the latter an historical specification. The former is examined in this part of the Chapter, and the latter subsequently.

In order to demonstrate that Hick has misunderstood the "shift in meaning" which has occurred, I turn to Bernard Lonergan.[3] The key to what we are after is found in two sections in *Method in Theology* titled "Realms of Meaning" and "Stages of Meaning." In these sections Lonergan elaborates on the important notion of "differentiation of consciousness."[4] Western consciousness has been undergoing a developmental differentiation. Lonergan distinguishes three main stages of meaning in this on-going differentiation: (1) common sense, (2) theory, and (3) interiority.[5] He writes:

> In the first stage conscious and intentional operations follow the mode of common sense. In a second stage besides the mode of common sense, there is also the mode of theory, where theory is controlled by a logic. In a third stage the modes of common sense and theory remain, science asserts its autonomy from philosophy, and there occur philosophies that leave theory to science and take their stand on interiority.[6]

Two observations are important: (1) One must begin with the undifferentiated consciousness of common sense before one can experience the differentiation of theoretical consciousness. Only when the second stage has been reached, can the third stage of interiority occur. The differentiation builds on each preceding stage, but does not abandon what has gone before. (2) Not everyone in the West is at the third stage of interior differentiation. Though a culture may be in the third stage, large segments of the population may remain within an undifferentiated consciousness, or only at the second stage. Since the third stage in the differentiation of consciousness is occasioned by Kant and the "turn to the subject," it need not be elaborated on here. Our immediate concern is with the differentiation of consciousness that occurred in the West as it affected Christology during the first few centuries A.D. That is, we are interested in the differentiation of consciousness from common sense to theory.

To introduce this section on common sense and theory, it will be helpful to use a simple example which gets at the heart of the issue. Common sense is concerned with things as they relate to the knower; the theoretical differentiation of consciousness is concerned with things in their relation to each other. Thus, for example, to assert that the sun rises in the east and sets in the west, is a statement of common sense. To claim that the sun is stationary and the that earth revolves around it, is a statement of theoretical consciousness.[7] Common sense *describes*; theory *explains*.

Common sense is not a pejorative term for Lonergan.[8] It is not pejorative because, as a specification of intelligence, common sense knowing is a correct way of knowing. That is, it knows by experiencing, understanding and judging.[9] It does not know simply by taking a good look; that would reduce knowing to experiencing.

Common sense operates within the adult world mediated by meaning. It has moved beyond the infant's world of immediacy. Common sense is interested in knowing in order that it might respond, that it might do. Hence, common sense can be peculiar to particular times and places. For example, the common sense of medieval England is not the common sense of twentieth century Canada. The significance of common sense for human living is evidenced in the contemporary term "culture shock." The shock results from having to adapt, and quickly if one is to survive, to the common sense of a different culture.

The realm of common sense, then, is the visible realm of persons and things in their relation to us. We come to know it, not by applying some scientific method, but by the self- correcting process of knowing or learning. This is the process in which insights gradually accumulate, coalesce, qualify and correct one another.[10] Ultimately, a point is reached where we are able to meet situations as they arise, size them up by adding a few more insights to the acquired store, and so deal with them in an appropriate fashion.

Of the objects in the realm of common sense, we speak in everyday language, e.g., weight, heat. In common sense language, words do not have the function of naming the intrinsic properties of things, as for example, mass and temperature do in theoretical consciousness. Common sense meanings focus our conscious intentionality on things for us, of crystallizing our attitudes, expectations, intentions, of guiding all our actions.

But eventually certain questions arise that common sense cannot answer. The cognitional demand that these questions be answered constitutes what Lonergan calls a "systematic exigence." It is this systematic exigence that initiates the differentiation of consciousness from common sense to theory.[11] Lonergan writes:

> The systematic exigence not merely raises questions that common sense cannot answer but also demands a context for its answers, a context that common sense cannot supply or comprehend. This context is theory, and the objects to which it refers are in the realm of theory.[12]

It is important to note that the "objects ... in the realm of theory" do not refer to foreign relationships or meanings superimposed on what was under investigation in the realm of common sense. Rather, the differentiation of consciousness allows for new sets of relationships and meanings to be uncovered in whatever is being more fully understood. It is these new "objects" or relationships or meanings, which common sense cannot detect, which as heuristic goals call into action the systematic exigence. In turn, the dynamic of the systematic exigence can occasion the differentiation of consciousness. There is a shift, then, in the standpoint of meaning. This particular kind of shift in standpoint is possible only after a differentiation of consciousness. It is not a shift from a false form of knowing to a true form, nor *vice versa*.

Here with apologies to Eddington and Lonergan an example may be helpful. Common sense tells me my computer table is gray, solid and heavy. Theory tells me the very same object is colourless, mostly empty space, with here and there sub-microscopic protons and neutrons. It is the same object which is known in each case, known in one way by common sense and in another by theory. Both knowings constitute genuine knowing. The scientist continues to know the table in a common sense way, even after he has explained its constitution theoretically. Only for the person who does not recognize the differentiation of consciousness will such an observation pose troubling concerns about knowing itself.

Theoretical consciousness is a genuine knowing. It involves experiencing, understanding and judging; it is not just taking a better look than did common sense. But theory's concerns are not the concerns of common sense. Theory is concerned about explanation, not description. The reason both forms of knowing are valid is because each is a valid expression of the one foundational method of mind. That is, each represents the human cognitional structure of experiencing, understanding and judging in valid operation.

The difference between common sense and theory at this level of cognitional structure is that, in theoretical consciousness, the knower now makes specialties of the three cognitional operations.[13] The unity of consciousness now differentiated in two realms lies not in the undifferentiated homogeneity of common sense, but in the very method of the knowing mind itself. It is this method of mind that becomes differentiated in consciousness at the third stage of meaning, interiority. With the differentiation of interiority, the knower achieves self-appropriation of himself/ herself as knower. It is with the achievement of interiority, that the first two stages are critically grounded.[14] With self-appropriation accomplished, the knower can then relate his/ her different cognitional procedures to the various realms of meaning, he/ she can relate the various realms to each other, and can consciously shift from one realm to another by consciously changing his/ her procedures. Hence, the experience of the "two knowings" of my computer table is explained and grounded. Grounded in interiority, they represent the differentiation of consciousness into common sense and theory.

What is easy for differentiated consciousness appears very mysterious to undifferentiated consciousness. For a consciousness that is not fully differentiated, the assessment of common sense and theory, could be either: (a) if common sense is correct, then theory must be wrong, or at least complicated and abstract; or (2) if theory is correct, then common sense must be wrong, or at least a relic of a pre-scientific past.

There are then at least two realms of meaning, spoken about in different languages, the realms of common sense and theory. It is true that one can begin to ascend to the viewpoint of theoretical consciousness from the common sense viewpoint. But objects are only properly known in theoretical consciousness by knowing their internal relations, their congruences and differences, the functions they fulfill in their interactions. Similarly, just as one can begin from common sense, so too one can invoke common sense to correct theory. But, and here is a crucial point for us, and one we shall have cause to return to later,

> ... the correction will not be effected in common sense language but in theoretical language, and its implications will be the consequences, not of common sense facts that were invoked, but of the theoretical correction that was made.[15]

The differentiation from common sense to theory does not dispense with common sense meaning. Nor is the corrective to theory an abandonment of common sense. The knower alternates from one viewpoint to the other. The theoretical knower continues to operate through common sense in all his dealings with the particular and the concrete. But in addition to common sense, he also has developed another mode, the theoretical. Both common sense and theory are subject to the self-correcting process of knowing. However, that self-correcting process does not mean collapsing one into the other. The option to collapse, only arrests, distorts, and perhaps even denies, the valid differentiations of consciousness which do exist. The results can only be disastrous for human inquiry.

But what has this distinction between common sense and theory to do with our evaluation of Hick's case against the traditional understanding of Jesus' uniqueness?

It may be recalled that Hick's main point against the Tradition is that with Nicea there is a shift of meaning from metaphor to metaphysics. The shift for him represents a shift from poetic meaning meant to invoke an attitude, to a literal meaning intending a real relationship of consubstantiality between Father and Son. My point, however, is that while there has indeed been a shift in the realm of meaning, *it is a shift from common sense to theory, occasioned by a differentiation in consciousness*. Hick maintains the shift is from non-literal to literal meaning, and therefore invalid. *I maintain the shift is from common sense literal meaning to theoretical literal meaning*. That is, there is genuine literal meaning both before and after the shift. The shift lies in the standpoint of consciousness. Common sense is speaking about a literal meaning as it relates to the knower; theory is speaking about a literal meaning of the same objects in relation to each other.

Let me be specific. The language of the New Testament is the language of common sense.[16] That is, the consciousness in which revelation is received and faith expressed, is the undifferentiated consciousness of common sense. Thus, the New Testament makes statements about Jesus in his relation to the disciples and to creation: e.g., "Messiah," "Lord." It makes common sense statements about Him in relation to the Father: e.g., "Son." Because it is the realm of common sense, knowing involves the accumulation of insights. Hence, the deeper understanding of Jesus involves the accumulation of titles: "Son of Man," "Last Adam," "Wisdom." Whereas Hick sees this as a deification process, it is really more profound. It is the human mind in a common sense mode of consciousness, attempting to understand the full mystery of the Christ-event, a mystery which far exceeds the limited epistemological resources it can muster. Nevertheless, these resources of common sense consciousness are a valid form of knowing. That is, they intend and achieve literal meaning. Jesus is not just metaphorically Messiah, Lord, etc. He is all these things literally, as affirmed by common sense consciousness. The marvel is that the New Testament writers achieved so quickly such penetrating insights into the truth about Jesus and with such success.

The claim that the New Testament is written in the realm of common sense consciousness, is confirmed in the inspired writers' stress on functional Christology or soteriology. While soteriology can be spoken of in the language of theoretical consciousness, in the New Testament it is treated from the standpoint of common sense. That is, the saving work of Jesus is described as it relates to those who experienced it, and is intended to promote conversion or deeper faith in the reader. The New Testament has practical intent.[17] It is not a speculative treatise.

But the accumulation of common sense insights about Jesus soon reached a point where the context of common sense was no longer adequate to meet a new kind of question. The "systematic exigence" was initiating a move from functional Christology to ontological Christology. That is, the question was no longer "Who is Jesus for us and our salvation?" The question now became "If Jesus is who we claim He is for our salvation, what does this mean for who He is in relation to the Father?"

This move to ontological Christology, as we have seen, has its roots in the unity between Jesus's work and His person. To safeguard Jesus' work of salvation, a correct understanding of who Jesus was, became necessary. But this understanding could not be adequately answered in the context of common sense. Why not?

The question about Jesus' ontological relation to the Father is not just another question in the long series of common sense questions, which issued in the accumulation of insights of "Messiah," "Last Adam," etc. Rather, the question is occasioned by a shift in consciousness, a shift to theory. *It is a different kind of question.* Hence, it requires a different kind of answer. It required the context and language of theory. It required the language of *ousia, hypostasis* and *physis* to answer the question. These terms are not the concepts of common sense, but the concepts of a theoretically differentiated consciousness. They are not Biblical terms. *But to safeguard Biblical language, the correct language on the level of theoretical consciousness even though non-Biblical had to be discovered.* The question about Jesus' relation to the Father had moved beyond common sense, and was now in the realm of theory. Therefore, the only answer that could prove adequate would be one on the same level of consciousness as was the question. Lonergan states the case succinctly, when he writes that

... what corresponds to the gospels is undifferentiated consciousness, whereas what corresponds to dogma is differentiated consciousness.[18]

Hence, the shift from the title "Son of God" to "God the Son" does not represent the invalid shift of meaning from non-literal myth to literal metaphysics. Rather, *it represents the transposition of the literal meaning of Jesus' divine Sonship on the level of common sense, to the literal meaning of Jesus' divine Sonship on the level of theoretical consciousness.* The shift is valid because the differentiation in consciousness is valid. The meaning is literal in both cases because each instance is an expression of human knowing that issues in literal meaning. Lonergan writes:

Furthermore, no change from one pattern of consciousness to another can make what is true false, or what is false, true. Admittedly, different patterns of consciousness are bounded by different horizons; each has its own particular mode of feeling, thinking and speaking; within different patterns, therefore, there will be different expressions of the same truth.[19]

It is important to note as well, that the shift from Scripture to dogma is not the type of doctrinal development that moves from obscurity to clarity. It is, rather, a development that progresses from one kind of clarity to another. As Lonergan writes:

What Mark, Paul and John thought about Christ was neither confused nor obscure, but quite clear and distinct; yet their teaching acquired a new kind of clarity and distinctness through the definition of Nicea.[20]

The beginnings of the differentiation of consciousness already are evident in the New Testament. We have seen it with Matthew's identification of Jesus with Wisdom, and ultimately in John's identification of Jesus as the Word made flesh. But the shift to theoretical consciousness only really takes over during the Patristic period. It would eventually reach a full development with the medieval theological systems. Subsequently, there would come the third differentiation of consciousness, the shift or turn to the subject. But we need not investigate that shift in this work.[21]

My conclusion here is that the development from implicit to explicit Christology does not simply occur on one level of human inquiry or consciousness. At a certain point, which is more a phase than a point, the development undergoes a foundational shift which is nothing less than a differentiation of consciousness. Different kinds of questions are being asked; different kinds of answers are required. Explicit Christology is no longer explicit only in the realm of common sense, but has also become explicit in the realm of theoretical consciousness. Correct development of Christology on this level is necessary to protect the development on the level of common sense.[22]

I am inclined to conclude about Hick on this issue what Lonergan wrote about Leslie Dewart: "One begins to suspect that [Hick] is not a reformer but just a revolutionary."[23] It is not surprising, then, that Hick who is not enamored of Christology in the second differentiated realm, should not be able to safeguard Christology in the first, common sense realm. Hence, the literal meaning of common sense Christology for Hick, dissolves into mythology. The development of Christology collapses into deification. And in the end, Christology is reduced to anthropology.[24]

Some further observations can also be made now. In the light of our own account of the shift in meaning from common sense to theory, can we account for how Hick came to misinterpret this issue? I think it is possible. Hick was right to detect a "for us" quality about the language of the New Testament. Because of its "for us" quality, and because myth also is a "for us" language, Hick concluded that New Testament language about Jesus must be mythological. But he is mistaken in this conclusion. While myth and common sense are both "for us," the former is merely metaphoric, whereas the latter, as we have shown, issues in a literal meaning. Common sense is a "for us" language, but a "for us" language that has a literal content.

Hick is right to discern a process in Christology beginning in the New Testament. He is wrong to see it as a deification. The process at work there is the method of common sense coming to know through the accumulation of insights that are juxtaposed, but not theoretically harmonized. That is why, for example, to harmonize the accounts in the gospels is unnecessary. Theoretical harmonization is not the method of consciousness which was originally at work there.

The accumulation of insights about Jesus in the New Testament, as represented in the titles, is the synthetic movement of common sense knowing. The titles are not conclusions from a theoretical consciousness. The fact that they overlap, complement each other, and at times imply apparently opposite things, is both valid and to be expected. They need not be harmonized nor made to fit tidily in some over-all system. Unfortunately, the only option Hick has allowed himself to account for such a common sense Christology, is to view it as a deification resulting from spiritual and psychological needs.

Another example of what we are speaking about on the common

sense level is found in everyday proverbs. For example: consider "Strike while the iron is hot," and "Look before you leap." On the common sense level, inspite of their apparent opposition, there is no contradiction. Each represents an insight; both are true. But the two are not harmonized; nor need they be.

Hick is right when he observes a development in the New Testament from functional to ontological Christology. He is wrong to interpret it as a deification. It is, as we have pointed put, the initial stages of the differentiation in consciousness: a differentiation occasioned (1) by the matter at hand, namely the unity of Jesus' work and person, and (2) by a new kind of question being asked about Jesus. John's gospel is, therefore, not making mythological statements about Jesus, but valid literal ones. They are required, as even John knew, to safeguard the truth of functional Christology.

Hick is right to say that *homoousios* is not a Biblical term. He is right to say that the Nicene Fathers intended it to be understood literally. He is wrong to conclude that the shift to literal meaning is an invalid shift from metaphor to metaphysics. As we have indicated, the shift is not from non-literal meaning to literal, but from a common sense standpoint regarding literal meaning to a theoretical standpoint regarding the same meaning. By "theoretical" once again, we do not mean "hypothetical," but I mean Lonergan's technical notion of inquiring about things, not as they relate to the knower, but as they relate to each other.

We can now see how Hick has come to misinterpret Nicea. First, he fails to distinguish common sense from myth. By misunderstanding what common sense meaning is, he could not validly see the connection between it and the metaphysical language of Nicea. If his premise were correct, then his conclusion that there was an invalid shift from non-literal to literal meaning, would have some weight. But in fact, that is not the kind of shift that has occurred.

Secondly, it is understandable now why Hick has no use for metaphysical Christology. First, he does not see it as a safeguard for functional Christology. Secondly, he thinks only common sense consciousness is valid since that is the consciousness of Scripture. Metaphysics is too "complicated". This view of theoretical consciousness, as we have seen, results from a mind that wants to remain in an undifferentiated consciousness.[25] Although Lonergan was not thinking of Hick when he wrote these words, they are especially prophetic of the latter's position:

> Those who are afraid of intellectually developed consciousness, or who are all in favour of some other kind of truth, while branding propositional truth as mere nominalism or a product of a mythic mentality, or who see in dogmas the beginning of a metaphysics they abhor, will find in the Nicene dogma not a happy solution to difficult problems, reached with the assistance of the Holy Spirit, but an aberration or at best, a lamentable necessity arising out of a particular past situation.[26]

But the differentiation of consciousness is a valid development of the human mind. In fact, Hick would argue to its importance for modern science. He even wants to make Christianity more acceptable to the scientific mind. But he certainly cannot achieve that goal by remaining on the level of common sense. He is isolating Christology from a whole set of valid questions that cannot be answered by common sense.[27]

If God gave us minds and if He intends us to use them, there seems to be no reason why they cannot be used in thinking about Christ by means of a differentiated consciousness. Such thinking does not replace or dispense common sense thought. As we have repeatedly said, and as Athanasius saw, the non-Biblical language of theoretical consciousness is necessary to safeguard the Biblical language. Hick's exhortation, then, to leave aside the metaphysical "barnacles" [COC, Preface] of Nicea and accept only Biblical language is not a valid solution for contemporary Christology to take. It is true that the language of theory does not and cannot replace Biblical language. Scripture remains normative for all subsequent differentiations of consciousness. Biblical language can function as a corrective for theoretical language. But it will be a corrective that issues in *correct theoretical* language. It will not be a corrective by abandoning other differentiated levels of consciousness. Revelation was not meant for just one of the realms of human consciousness. In fact, Lonergan writes:

Differentiations of consciousness justify or lead to the discovery of previously unnoticed implications in the sources of revelation.[28]

With these conclusions in mind, we are able to make yet another point in our evaluation of Hick's earlier Scriptural argument. He claimed, we recall, that John's gospel "goes beyond" the consciousness of Jesus. It is, therefore, a deification.

We are able to see now, that in John's gospel, already there has begun the movement from common sense to theory. It is by no means complete, of course, just getting underway. Our point here is that John's gospel does not go beyond Jesus' consciousness. What it represents is the beginning of a differentiation in consciousness. It reflects a differentiation of consciousness that Jesus did not have. As we recall, a differentiation does not superimpose new objects or meanings, but uncovers those already present but heretofore undetected. Thinking about them in this way safeguards the common sense consciousness which Jesus did have. It adds nothing to, nor goes beyond, the original content. But it does ask a different kind of question that requires a different context for a correct answer.

If John's gospel indicates a coming differentiation in consciousness, then Nicea represents that differentiation achieved. Like John's gospel, Nicea does not "go beyond" Jesus' consciousness. It represents a differentiation of consciousness, and therefore, a need for a new language. Thus, when we said in Chapter 5 that Jesus did not have the vocabulary of Nicea for his self-understanding, it is clear now why that was so. Jesus did not have the differentiation of consciousness that issues in that vocabulary, because that differentiation was a later cultural achievement. It was not simply a vocabulary Jesus lacked, in the sense of a list of words. Nicea's vocabulary represented a whole new standpoint within human knowing. Even if Jesus had had this differentiation, it would have made no sense to express Himself through it, as those who heard Him would have had no idea what He was talking about. We have already treated aspects of this issue in a previous Chapter.

With John's gospel revealing a coming change in consciousness, and Nicea representing an advanced level of this consciousness, it is not surprising that John's gospel should figure so prominently in

Christological thought that developed for centuries at this level of consciousness. The prominence of John was not the result of an understandable mistake, as Hick suggests it was. It resulted from the fact that the kind of thinking about Jesus in the new level of human consciousness found its roots in John's New Testament Christology.

As a final point, ultimately what is at the root of Hick's confusion on this issue of the shift in meaning? It seems to come down to this: Hick has not correctly appropriated himself as a knower. That is, he does not know what it means to know; he is not properly cognitionally grounded. That does not mean that he does not know. It means he does not know what he is doing when he is knowing. He has not *correctly* made the third differentiation of consciousness to interiority.[29] That accounts for why he takes common sense consciousness to be only mythic consciousness, and why for him the shift from common sense to theory is a shift from non-literal to literal meaning. If he were properly grounded as a self-appropriated knower, he would be able to see that there is a literal meaning to common sense, as well as a valid shift in the standpoints of common sense and theory regarding that literal meaning. Hick certainly has made the Kantian turn to the subject. But, like Kant, he is mistaken about what goes on when we know. We will return to this in a later Chapter when we evaluate, in brief, Hick's epistemology.

Nicea: Optional or Normative?

We now turn to the second argument Hick brings to bear against the traditional understanding of Jesus' uniqueness. We recall his claim that Nicea's language is that of just one particular culture, the Hellenistic. Because it is bound to a certain place and time, the Nicene definition is optional. It is not normative for future generations of Christians. Just as Scripture needs to be demythologized, so writes Hick, dogma needs to be de-Hellenized. Hick does not like the Greeks.

Our present task is to evaluate this position. We do so in two parts: first, we address the issue of Hellenization, and then we consider the issue of whether or not Nicea is optional. Our concern here is not to present any kind of comprehensive or even summary analysis of the various Councils, their creeds or definitions. The focus is immediately on the issue at hand: namely, first, whether in fact the kind of Hel-

lenization which Hick claims took place did in fact occur, and secondly, whether the Conciliar definitions of the Church can be as optional
as Hick contends.

On the issue of Hellenization, Hick argues that with Nicea Christian
faith and theology became Hellenized. That is, both faith and theology
surrendered Biblical categories and adopted the categories of Greek
philosophy. Theology and faith interpreted their content as instances
of Greek philosophical concepts.

But is that in fact what occurred? I do not think so. It is true that the
intellectual environment of the first centuries of the Church was that of
Greek philosophy. The kind of questions being asked, the language
employed in the debates, and the ultimate formulations reflected the
philosophical culture. Of itself, this is not bad. Even Hick would argue
for the need of Christian faith to dialogue with the surrounding culture.
Can the Christian faith and message exist, we might ask, or even ought
they to exist, in a culture without coming to terms with it in some way?[30]

It would be off the point of our present work to launch into a discussion of inculturation. Nevertheless, the mere fact that theology con-
fronts itself with the ideas of the time hardly seems undesirable to the
mission of the Church. Hellenization, if it means that the Christian
message was translated to the culture of the time, certainly occurred.
However, this translation or inculturation was in no way an alteration,
let alone an abandonment, of Christian faith.

But the issue here is more specific than that. When Hick speaks of
Hellenization, he does not mean simply the articulation of the faith
within the Greek culture. Hick's claim is that the traditional understanding of Jesus' uniqueness itself results from ideas that stem from
Greek speculation. The language of the uniqueness of Jesus is Greek
philosophic language. Hick contends that Greek speculation has inter-
vened between Gospel and dogma. The implication is that without
Greek concepts the culmination of the deification process would never
have been achieved, or at least not achieved in that way. Without Greek
concepts, Jesus would not have been defined as consubstantial with the
Father. Hick supports this by saying that if the gospel went East and not
West, the term *homoousios* never would have entered Christian thought.
It was Greek philosophy, and not Christian faith itself, that made Jesus
unique. In this way, the Councils influenced by Greek speculation,

added something to who Jesus was; it went beyond Him.

In evaluating this argument of Hick's, we must ask ourselves whether the traditional understanding of Jesus' uniqueness is the result of the Church simply taking over ideas of Greek philosophy. Or, was the Church safeguarding the already-understood uniqueness of Jesus by ensuring that the right words continued to be spoken about Him?

Before elaborating a response in detail, it would be helpful to relate this section to the one immediately preceding. In the foregoing section it was shown that the shift in meaning that occurred with Nicea was the foundational one of a differentiation in consciousness. New kinds of questions were being asked which revealed that a common sense context was no longer adequate to furnish a reply. The new context of theory was needed. This new context was in fact being provided by the climate of Greek philosophical thought. Lonergan states that the shift in the West from common sense to theory began with the Greek discovery of mind.[31] Thus, when the questions about Jesus began to move beyond common sense consciousness, the thought patterns on the level of theory that were available were those of Greek philosophy.

But it would be a mistake to conclude that theology simply adopted without modification the meanings of Greek terms, or even worse, that it tied itself to Greek philosophy as a whole.[32] Our evaluation of Hick involves elaborating why such a conclusion is inaccurate.

Is the Nicene-Constantinople term *homoousios* simply the Christian adaptation of a Greek term that had the effect of bestowing a uniqueness on Jesus which He did not already enjoy? Do the terms *hypostasis* and *prosopon* of Ephesus and Chalcedon prove that the faith was Hellenized, as Hick understands the process?

No. In fact, instead of representing the Hellenization of the faith, the meanings of the Christological terms demonstrate that the Fathers were intent on preventing just that kind of Hellenization from occurring. *It was the heretical positions that Hellenized the faith by adapting the faith about Jesus to fit existing Greek categories.* Hence, the Fathers had to reject such a process.

Jean Daniélou notes that the concern of the Fathers not to allow the Hellenization of the faith, goes back even to the Apologists who were intent on presenting Christian faith both in terms of, but in opposition to, the philosophies of their day.[33]

Aloys Grillmeier, writing specifically of the Nicene use of *homoousios*, states:

> Above all, it should be stressed that the Fathers of Nicea did not want to 'Hellenize' the concept of God in revelation and the kerygma of the church by the word *homoousios*, that is, they did not want to superimpose a philosophical and technical concept of *ousia*. They were more concerned to clarify what the Scripture said about the Son.[34]

A very basic indication that the Nicene Fathers did not wish to Hellenize the faith or provide a philosophic, speculative account of the faith, is witnessed in the very genre of the definition itself. The Nicene definition is more than a definition; it is a liturgical creed, and remains so in the life of the Church to this day. It is seen to be a creed even from its opening words "We believe ..."[35]

As a creed, the Nicene profession is oriented towards salvation history.[36] So intent were the Fathers to remain within the framework of a creed, that they do not offer any philosophic explanation of the term *homoousios*. As Grillmeier points out, their understanding of the term must be worked out from other documents which were written after the Council.[37] The new ontological statements in Nicea are meant, once again, as Kasper states, "not to make void the salvation statements, but to help safeguard them."[38]

As for the term *homoousios* itself, it was not intended in the philosophic-technical sense from which its meaning was originally drawn. Its roots were Valentinian Gnosticism, a subordinationist position, which Nicea clearly intends to reject.[39] For this reason Kasper maintains that Nicea did not superimpose an already existing Greek meaning onto the Biblical idea of God. The term was intended to make clear that the Son is not on the side of creatures but on the side of God, that is, the Son is divine by nature and on the same plane as the Father "so that anyone who encounters him, encounters the Father himself."[40] What lay behind this usage, then, was not a speculative interest, but as Athanasius clearly saw, a soteriological one: if Christ is not true God, then we are not redeemed.

For Lonergan, while the term *homoousios* itself was a Hellenic term with an Hellenic meaning, that meaning was not sharply defined even in the context of Greek thought. The Fathers employed the term, but the meaning they gave it was not that of any of the existing Greek concepts. This new meaning, however, required by Christian revelation, was arrived at by Hellenic *technique.* Lonergan says this technique involved "reflecting on propositions." The Hellenization of the faith was, then, not the taking over of Greek meanings, but the use of Greek methods of thinking.

For example, Athanasius' *eadem de filio quae de Patre dicuntur, excepto Patris nomine* does not say what are the attributes of the Father. It does indicate the heuristic that whatever they are, they are also to be said of the Son, except the name "Father." Thus, the believer can conceive of the Father in Scriptural, Patristic, medieval, or modern terms, but whatever the mode of consciousness in which the thinking is done, or in whatever culture, the relation of the Son to the Father will always be *homoousios.*

This notion of consubstantiality, then, does not impede or prevent further investigation. But it does provide the norm under which future investigation in this area is to be carried out. The only way in which the notion of consubstantiality could be outworn, would be the rejection of the very notion itself.[41] This rejection is what Hick ultimately does in his attempt to explain Nicea to contemporary culture. But as Lonergan remarks, the Christological

> ... task is not helped, rather it is gravely impeded, by wild statements based on misconceptions or suggesting unbelief.[42]

Thus, while Athanasius' dictum requires the context of Hellenistic thought, the problem and the content are specifically Christian.[43]

The Nicene creed acquired the reputation of being, for subsequent Christological Councils, a fundamental statement of the Church's interpretation of the Incarnation. But, contrary to what Hick would have us believe, this reputation was not due to the introduction of a new Greek concept into the faith. The reason why the creed was fundamental was because it affirmed the unity of the subject of Jesus "as one and the same Son, of the same substance as the Father, who became flesh."[44]

Given Christianity's eschatological-universal claims about Jesus, it could not avoid entering into discussion with Greek philosophy about the *logos*, since this latter term too had a universal claim. The openness of the Church to such a dialogue, as John Baker states, "certainly did not imply the uncritical adoption of current ideas."[45] In fact, says Kasper, the Church's response to Greek philosophy was not that of self-surrender, but rather of self-assertion. Kasper writes:

> Essentially it [the Church's response] was a question of the *aggiornamento* of the day, of the hermeneutically necessary attempt to express the Christian message in the language of the time and in the light of the way in which the questions were then raised.[46]

The Church's response as self-assertion rather than self-surrender is evident at the Council of Constantinople. Its distinction between *ousia* and *hypostasis* even in principle

> ... meant breaking through Greek ontological thinking towards a personal way of thinking. Not nature, but person was now the final and supreme reality.[47]

This distinction and option was the result of the Church's reflection on the uniqueness of Jesus. Greek philosophy was not thinking in such terms. It was the special contribution of Christianity to introduce this newness. Such an introduction clearly could not result from self-surrender of the faith to Greek meaning. Rather, it re-interpreted Greek meanings to make them better explicate the truth about Jesus, and so safeguard the salvation He had brought. Baker writes that the use of Greek philosophic terms was undertaken

> ... not in order to establish equations which would make the Christian message no more than the Platonist philosophy in other dress, but to lead men beyond their philosophy to see how great might be the implications of the Gospel.[48]

Just as the uniqueness of the Christ-event required new meanings be given to Judaic titles when applied to Jesus, so too when the gospel encountered Greek philosophy, new meanings were required for terms when they too were applied to Jesus. Whereas self-surrender was the path of Hellenization, the Church in self-assertion was ensuring that Hellenization of the faith should not occur.[49]

This point is an important one. Hick has claimed that if the gospel went East to India, the Church would have simply adopted the cultural terms of the East to speak of Jesus, for example, "Avatar" or "Bodhisattva."[50]

His reasoning assumes that the Church simply adopted the terms of the Greek West, and therefore these terms are quite relative. We have been demonstrating that in fact the process was not so simple. The terms were used, but their content given a new meaning, a meaning that had to be forged within the unique Christian faith about Jesus. If we are to assume anything, and the argument Hick proposes is only hypothetical, we must assume that had the gospel gone to India, while the Church may have used the terms "avatar" and "bodhisattva," it may very well have given these terms a new meaning.[51]

There is also the important issue not to be overlooked, that these latter terms are not notions on the level of intellectual consciousness, but are common sense terms. Presumably, with the differentiation of consciousness in the East, the common sense terms would also have required a new meaning on that new level—whatever that might be for Eastern culture. Hick's case on this point, then, simply does not stand because it misses the original point.

If Nicea stressed the true divinity of Jesus, Chalcedon sought to discover the solution to only *one* question: *how* the confession of the "one Christ" might be reconciled with the belief that Jesus was both "true God and true man?" Although Chalcedon is more a "teaching" than a creed,[52] like Nicea there is no attempt at a philosophical definition or speculative analysis. As Grillmeier attests, the Chalcedonian Fathers "produce formulas as witnesses to the Word and not as scholars."[53] While their terminologies may seem formal to us, to the Christians of the time, "they were meant to express the *full reality* of the incarnation."[54]

Again, even though the concepts of *hypostasis* and *prosopon* are not defined in Chalcedon, the sense of the formula is quite clear. The Fathers teach that while there is a real distinction between divine and human nature, Christ is still to be described as "one," as one *hypos-*

tasis or person. As such, the dogma states only the bare essentials of what was needed to resolve the questions of the day. These questions and responses had been developing for a long time. Chalcedon, grounded in the tradition of the Church, did not add something new to Christian Christological faith. As Kasper notes, Chalcedon reaffirms Nicea.[55] The use of Greek terms did not "go beyond" *the truth* about Jesus. The purpose of Chalcedon, like the other Councils, was not to Hellenize the faith. It was not their task to produce a metaphysics, let alone reinterpret faith as an expression of a pre-determined philosophy.

But new questions had arisen since Nicea. Hence, after re-affirming Nicea, Chalcedon gives a more precise interpretation by means of one *hypostasis* or person in two natures. This distinction between nature and person safeguards the unity in duality, and the duality in unity of Jesus Christ. Like Nicea's definition, Chalcedon's is *not* a Hellenization of the faith. In fact, writes Kasper, it is a

> ... de-hellenization in face of Monophysitism. For it insists that God and man do not form any natural symbiosis ... Fundamentally, the council had to express in the language of Greek philosophy something that shattered all its perspectives, and for which the intellectual resources were still lacking ... The Council therefore does not express any metaphysical theory about Christ, but contents itself with a *christologia negativa* which safeguards the mystery.[56]

Once again, Kasper points out the originality of the distinction between nature and person. That originality resulted not from the inner logic of Greek philosophy, but from the Church's reflection on the uniqueness of Jesus. Kasper writes:

> The independence and originality of personal reality was only discovered and conceptually formulated in wrestling with the fundamental data of the history of revelation. This was one of the most important contributions of Christianity to human civilization, and meant the emergence of a new understanding of reality as a whole. The problem of traditional theology consisted to a

large extent in having to discuss and express this new element within the intellectual framework of a different kind of conception of reality.[57]

The purpose of the Conciliar definitions, then, was not to Hellenize the faith, but to serve the Church's proclamation of revelation. Thus, like Nicea, Chalcedon achieved a special place in the history of theology, not because it used Greek terms, but because of its interpretation of the person of Jesus Christ.

My point, then, is that the Councils in question did not intend as their goal, nor did they effect in their process, a Hellenization of the faith. The technical concepts and formulas which they used are not an end in themselves. They serve to explicate the traditional faith of the Church. Baker argues that while Christian revelation had to enter the debate with Greek philosophy, that revelation strained Greek categories to the bursting points.[58] Grillmeier, too, cautions us not to exaggerate the "technical" character of these terms. He then adds:

> In all the christological formulas of the ancient church there is a manifest concern not to allow the total demand made on men's faith by the person of Jesus to be weakened by pseudo-solutions ... The formulas of the church, whether they are the *homoousios* of Nicea or the Chalcedonian Definition, represent the *lectio difficilior* of the gospel, and maintain the demand for faith and the stumbling-block which Christ puts before men. This is a sign that they hand on the original message of Jesus.[59]

Kasper argues in similar fashion. He acknowledges that Christology can only properly be carried on against the widest possible horizon, more precisely, in confrontation with metaphysics. But this does not mean that Christology must follow or accept a particular or predetermined philosophic thought-form. In fact, genuine Christology will find it *cannot* do so. Kasper continues:

> On the contrary, faith in Jesus Christ is a radical questioning of all closed systems of thought ... It claims that the ultimate and most profound means of reality as a whole has been revealed

only in Jesus Christ, in a unique and at the same time finally valid way.[60]

From this it follows that to approach the issue of Hellenization and dehellenization of the faith from a fundamentally anti-metaphysical attitude, is inappropriate. This, however, is how Hick has proceeded. He has mistakenly claimed that the Church abandoned a functional Christology for an ontological one. Since for him the Councils represent the triumph of ontological Christology, the sole path open to him is to cast aside the latter as a false import from Greek speculation. This leaves him with only a functional Christology. He has divorced, once again, the person of Jesus from His work. Consequently, Hick has no means of safeguarding even his functional Christology. It is not surprising, then, that he succumbs to the extreme subjectivist position, that Christology is simply an elaboration of Christian self-consciousness. It is no longer the elaboration of the Christ. In the end, Jesus Christ for Hick is reduced to being simply a model, even if a first-class one, of the religious person.

We have seen in our presentation of Hick's Christology, that he groups together both the heretical and orthodox Christologies of the first few centuries. For him they are all equally Christian, equally Patristic, and therefore, no distinction can be made between orthodox and heretical. Patristic thought as a mode of theology represents the Hellenization of the faith. Each expression of Patristic thought, then, is undesirable in the sense that it moves, according to Hick, from metaphor to metaphysics. The whole lot is to be brushed aside. Therefore, Hick has no interest in distinguishing heretical from the orthodox.

The case so far being made is that in fact orthodox Patristic theology, as exemplified in the Councils, clearly shows the Church's concern that the faith *not* be Hellenized, that the faith not simply succumb to the easy adoption of Greek meanings.[61] The Church was not engaged in self-surrender, but self-assertion. There is a difference between what became the orthodox and what became the heterodox positions. The heterodox positions represent a Hellenization of the faith similar to the kind Hick is critical of. The orthodox reveal an attempt to keep the faith from being Hellenized in its debate with Greek intellectual culture.

245

This interpretation receives support from the various authorities we have been examining. Daniélou argues that "theology is not the Hellenization of Christianity."[62] For Grillmeier, it was the Arians who surrendered to Hellenization by undermining Christian monotheism.[63] On the point of the Christological heresies in general, Grillmeier writes:

On a closer inspection, the christological 'heresies' turn out to be a compromise between the original message of the Bible and the understanding of it in hellenism and paganism. It is here that we have the real Hellenization of Christianity.[64]

The heresies represent a movement to resolve the mystery of Christ, whereas the Conciliar statements prove that the Church was not seeking to resolve the mystery at all. Rather, the Fathers' aim was to preserve the mystery by ensuring that it was stated in its most accurate and true fashion. For they were very much aware, as Greek philosophy was not, that "in the end, human understanding will never be able to unveil the *mysterium Christi*."[65]

Kasper argues similarly when he writes that the so-called "new" statements in the Councils "represent not a Hellenization but a de-Hellenization of Christianity."[66] For Kasper too, Arianism was an "illegitimate Hellenization that dissolved Christianity into a cosmology and a morality."[67] As we have seen, Nicea's usage of *homoousios*, on the other hand, does not indicate a self-surrendering Hellenization was operative. In fact, Nicea's concern was "to maintain the teaching of the Bible against a philosophical falsification of it."[68] Not only Arianism, but Apollinarianism, Eutychianism, and Monophysitism are for Kasper, illegitimate Hellenizations of the faith.[69] In the end for Kasper, as for Grillmeier, the truth about Jesus is reached not through the intellect, but through faith. He writes: "What is believed can be known only in the exercise of belief."[70]

For Lonergan, those who claim that the Councils hellenized the faith make the fundamental assumption that there is a "disjunction between religious experience on the one hand and hellenistic ontology on the other."[71] This assumption is simply unwarranted, he says. Analyzing the issue at its roots, Lonergan concludes that the heresies, and he mentions Adoptionism, Sabellianism and Arianism, were Hellenizers because they dealt with essences, as Greek thought taught them. The Conciliar statements, on the other hand, were de-Hellenizers because their concern was only with what *is*.[72]

Lonergan states emphatically, as did Grillmeier and Kasper, that underlying the quest to articulate the mystery is the mystery itself. We do not grasp this mystery "by the power of our intellects, but believe [it] by faith,"[73] This is integral to the scandal of the mystery of Christ.[74]

The conclusion to this section, then, is this: if the definitions of the early Christological Councils are to be considered optional because they represent the Hellenization of the faith (as Hick understands it), then the conclusion does not stand. The uniqueness of Jesus Christ as true man and true God is not a conclusion drawn from Greek metaphysical thought. The Councils do not represent the Hellenization of the faith.

Up to this point we have been examining the first part of Hick's case that the Conciliar definitions are optional because they represent the Hellenization of the faith. Since, according to Hick, they do not represent the Biblical expression of the faith, especially not the synoptic view, then one is not bound to their statements.

We have shown, however, that the faith was *not* Hellenized in the way Hick thinks it was. Therefore, we can conclude, contrary to Hick, that neither are the Councils optional, but permanently normative. Such a conclusion, one might think, should draw to a close our discussion of these particular points. But it does not. The reason is that there is more to Hick's point about the Councils being optional than merely that they Hellenize Christian faith. What our conclusion claims is simply that if Nicea and Chalcedon are optional, it is *not* because of any illegitimate Hellenization of the faith. But Hick says the Councils are optional for a second, more fundamental reason than Hellenization.

His reasoning expands to claim that no Conciliar definition could be permanently normative because all of them are culturally bound, and no culture is normative. Hellenism is just one culture and one thought pattern among an immense number of possibilities. So even if the Councils did preserve the faith, they still are optional, because they apply only to the Hellenistic culture of the time. The Conciliar definitions have no permanent, normative value since Hellenistic culture is not a normative culture, indeed no culture enjoys such a privilege.

It is to this wider, more fundamental claim that our attention is now turned. This wider case opens on to such issues as: development of doctrine, pluralism, and cultural relativity. Needless to say, these issues are complex and vast, any one providing ample data for many books. My task is not to probe these issues here. My more modest endeavor is to attempt to discover if there are some grounds upon which a reasonable case can be built to the effect that the definitions of Nicea and Chalcedon (or any Council for that matter), do have a normative role to play in future generations of Christians. Does a cultural expression of the faith so tightly bind its meaning that outside that culture it has no place, except as an historical curiosity? Or to put the question as we directly asked it at the beginning of this Chapter: In what sense is Nicea's language not culture-bound, and therefore not optional?

I begin by accepting Hick's view that no one culture is normative for other cultures. As Lonergan writes:

> ... the contemporary notion of culture is empirical. A culture is a set of meanings and values informing a common way of life, and there are as many cultures as there are distinct sets of such meanings and values.[75]

Further, I accept too that theology "is the product not only of a faith but also of a culture."[76] If, then, there is to be a permanence of Conciliar statements as norms, such normative value cannot be grounded on the superiority or normative value of one culture over another.

This understanding of culture is, however, a contemporary one. Up to the turn of the twentieth century, culture was conceived not empirically but normatively. It was what Lonergan calls the "classicist" view of culture.[77] For the classicist, while there are differences among peoples, and while circumstances alter cases, such differences and circumstances are only accidental. Beneath these accidents there is some common substance that fits classicist assumptions and values. Things have their specific natures, over and above which there is only individuation by matter. The implication of this classicist view of culture for the permanence of doctrines as norms is obvious. Lonergan puts it clearly when he writes:

It follows that the diversities of peoples, cultures, social arrangements can involve only a difference in the dress in which church doctrine is expressed, but cannot involve any diversity in church doctrine itself. That is *semper idem.*[78]

But the empirical view of culture claims that when Church doctrines are articulated in different cultures, there is involved more than "only a difference in the dress." To change cultures is more than a change of clothes. It involves some change in meanings and values.

By accepting the contemporary, empirical view of culture over the classicist view, am I not opting for a diversity of meaning of church doctrine from one culture to another? Am I not agreeing with Hick that the Conciliar definitions are optional as we pass from one culture to the next?

I do not think so. The reason is that the permanence of Church doctrine ultimately does not derive from any supposed virtue of permanence in a culture or a particular viewpoint. The reason for the permanence of the Conciliar statements is far better grounded than that, even if theology does mediate between faith and culture.

We get our first clue to what this "far better grounded" character might be from Vatican I.[79] I refer to *Dei Filius*, specifically to the last paragraph of the fourth and final chapter of the decree, and to the appended canon.[80] In this passage and canon, which are responding to rationalist views of development of doctrine, the Council indicates what is permanent about Church doctrines.[81] There is affirmed, first, a permanence of meaning of Church dogmas, and secondly, that that permanent meaning is the meaning declared by the Church. Thirdly, it is stated that that meaning derives its permanence from the fact it conveys the doctrine of faith revealed by God. This revealed doctrine is not a philosophic invention to be perfected by human talent.

Fourthly, and here we come to an important point. It is true that the meaning of the dogma does not exist apart from a verbal formulation. This is evident if only because it is a meaning declared by the Church. However, as noted above, the permanence attaches to the *meaning* and *not* to the *formula.*[82] As the canon indicates, to retain the same formula and give it a new meaning is precisely what is excluded.

This is where Hick is mistaken. He has exhorted the Church to retain the language of the Nicene Creed and the Chalcedonian definition, but understand them as metaphoric and not literal. In other words, keep the formula, but change the meaning. Hick seems to think that the quality of permanence attaches to the formula, whereas, in fact, it refers to the *meaning*. The alternative, however, to maintain the meaning but to change the formula, for example, in articulating the faith in a different culture, is not at all ruled out by Vatican I.

Let us proceed even further. We still have to ask *why* the meaning of the dogmas is permanent. Vatican I gives two clues: (1) since what is true is permanent, the meaning that a dogma had in its own context can never be truthfully denied; and (2) what is known in faith are mysteries that lie beyond the range of human intelligence. That is, what is known is a revealed mystery and not some human substitute for the mystery. Whatever growth in understanding occurs, the dogmas retain the permanence of their meaning.

While Vatican I gives us a few clues, it does not resolve our difficulty. Because contemporary issues were only incipient at that time, Vatican I does not face the problem of the permanence of meaning given the historicity and cultural relativity of human meaning. We must delve a little deeper. However, we can begin with these clues from Vatican I.

These clues tell us that permanence attaches to the meaning of a dogma, not to the formula; that the original meaning can only be grasped by grasping its context; that the meaning is permanent because it is not a datum but a truth, and that that truth is not human but divine.

What we need to ask here is: what is a context? To say that a dogma or any statement can only be known by knowing its context, requires us to inquire: what do we mean by "context?" We mean quite simply "an interlocking set of questions and answers" such that when there are no more relevant questions to be asked and answered, we have a context.[83] That is, we have what we can call a "prior" context, "the context within which the original statement was made and through which the original meaning of the statement is determined."[84] The context of Nicea, then, was the two centuries of interlocking questions and answers in a dialectic encounter that gave rise to the meaning of the terms it was to employ.

But in addition to prior contexts, there are "subsequent" contexts.

Whereas Nicea was decisive, it was not immediately so. Even after the debate settled, the Christological context continued. Not only that, but Nicea itself laid the groundwork for and contributed to the rise of yet a new set of interlocking Christological questions and answers. As Kasper writes:

> In solving one problem while remaining faithful to scripture and tradition, Nicaea created another ... The dogma stated by the first ecumenical council thus makes it already clear that dogmatic formulations are never simply the concluding clarification of a dispute but are at the same time always the beginning of new questions and problems. Precisely because dogmas are true they are in constant need of new interpretation.[85]

Thus the Council of Constantinople (381) had to ask if the Holy Spirit too was consubstantial with the Father. Still later, Ephesus (431) had to clarify that it was "one and the same" who was born of the Father and born of the Virgin Mary. Chalcedon (451) had to clarify the distinction of natures in Christ yet maintain the unity of His person. Two centuries later the Christological context was still ongoing.[86] The Council of Lateran (649), later confirmed by Constantinople III (680), declared Christ to have two wills and two operations. Nor was that the end, as the Christological context was still to continue, asking about Jesus' sinlessness, His concupiscence, His knowledge, His consciousness.

My point is that a context is not an isolated thing. It is related to a prior context of meaning, and in turn gives rise to subsequent contexts of meaning. Subsequent contexts are not the same as prior ones, but nor are they completely divorced from them. Contexts of meaning are not islands of meaning unconnected to each other. Contexts exist in a wider on-going context, and they relate to each other, most commonly, be derivation and interaction. This is the kind of on-going context we have been accounting for in our Christological review. One question is, then, how is permanence of meaning brought about in on-going contexts of meaning?

But there is yet a further question: how is the permanence of meaning brought about in contexts of meaning that are not derivative of each other and have not interacted with each other? This question arises because on-going contexts of meaning do not account for all the changes that can occur in passing from one context to another. For example, there are changes of contexts that result from cultures foreign to each other encountering one another for the first time. The sets of meanings and values of the newly-encountered culture are not necessarily derivative of the sets of meanings and values of the culture from which one comes. Perhaps, the two cultural contexts of meaning have not, or have only marginally, interacted with each other.

If the character of permanence attaches to the meaning of a Church doctrine, how is that character maintained in both on-going contexts of meaning and in the encounter of unrelated contexts of meaning?[87]

The first point to be noted, recalling Vatican I, is that the permanence of meaning derives from the fact that Church doctrines are not data but truths, indeed truths which cannot be known by the human mind unaided by revelation. Secondly, the reason there is any development of doctrine at all, which Vatican I allows for within limits, is because doctrines as statements have meaning only in a context, and contexts are on-going and multiple. To re-phrase our question, then: how is the permanence of the meaning of a divinely revealed truth maintained when the context of meaning changes or a new one is encountered?

Permanence of meaning is maintained, as it always has been in the Church, by a dialectic carried out under the inspiration of the Holy Spirit. Grillmeier writes:

> The church must regard the *mysterium Christi* as a reality which is continually to be thought through afresh. It is Christ's promise that his Spirit will lead the church more and more profoundly into all truth (cf. John 16.13).[88]

The inspiration of the Holy Spirit guarantees that the truth will be maintained and thus be permanent. But the maintenance of the truth occurs within the dialectical context of meaning. The dialectic process is the developing context of meaning and accounts for the growth in understanding.

For example, there is the dialectical development that lead from

Scripture and early tradition through Patristic thought to Nicea.[89] The meaning of Christ's uniqueness within the context of late-Judaism and early Christian faith encounters the different, but not completely unrelated, context of Greek thought. Contributing to this change in context of meaning, in addition, was the incipient differentiation of consciousness from common sense to theory. The resulting encounter was a genuine dialectic which discerned the difference between positions and counter-positions and which sought to develop the positions and reverse the counter-positions.[90]

The truth about the uniqueness of Jesus, a truth held in faith, had to find the correct expression of its meaning in a new context. There was a development in understanding. But it was the fuller understanding of a truth, not the fuller understanding of data. On this important point, Lonergan writes:

> However, there is a notable difference between the fuller understanding of data and the fuller understanding of a truth. When data are more fully understood, there result the emergence of a new theory and the rejection of previous theories. Such is the on-going process in the empirical sciences. But when a truth is more fully understood, it is still the same truth that is being understood.[91]

What results, then, when one context of meaning encounters another, either in a wider on-going context or in a new cultural encounter, is dialectic. In the former, more easily than the latter, the dialectic can issue in a correct understanding or re-statement of the truth. This greater ease results from the fact, that in the on-going context there already exists a considerable history of interpretation and research. There is already present much common meaning.

But with a new cultural encounter the dialectic, always laborious and demanding, becomes even more so. For example, it took two centuries of dialectic to reach Nicea's *homoousios*. It may take much longer in the encounter of the contemporary West with the East, or among the world's religions.[92]

Before dialectic can occur in these encounters, there must first be massive amounts of research, interpretation and historical study. These initial three stages of the mediating phase of method will then issue in dialectic. Dialectic, in turn, which is concerned with conflict among horizons invites, not new data, but conversion: either intellectual, moral or religious.[93] Separating out horizons that are complementary or which are genetically related, dialectic focuses on those which are genuinely dialectically opposed. At Nicea, for example, this would have exposed the dialectical conflict between the Arian view of Jesus' Sonship and that of Athanasius. The term *homoousios* which affirms the truth by correct understanding, invites conversion to such correct understanding from those yet unconverted.

Once conversion has been attained, there can follow foundations. For example, the subsequent distinction between person and nature was the establishment of foundations. Later, there can emerge systematics. For example, in this case we mention medieval Scholasticism and Thomism.

If such developments took a long time in the on-going context of the West, one cannot expect a quick solution to the many Christological questions that arise from the contemporary encounter of world religions and cultures, each with different differentiations of consciousness and each with various unconversions operative. Even with all the recent advances in the study and dialogue among religions, there remains still much research, interpretation and history to be carried out.

One temptation, of course, is to want to reach for the quick solution: one that seems very plausible and makes life comfortable on the practical plane. But the issue at hand is not one of plausibility or comfort. Ultimately it is one of truth. Development in the understanding of the truth cannot be stunted or diverted away from the right understanding of that truth.[94]

The issue over the uniqueness of Christ focuses on the word of God precisely as true.[95] The Church has always been committed to the truth, even at great cost to herself. The reason is because the truth of her message and mission come from God. To be true to herself, she must be faithful in ensuring a correct development in the understanding of that truth to which she witnesses. The Conciliar definitions of Nicea and Chalcedon lie within the function of the Church's witness to the truth about the uniqueness of Jesus. It is the permanence of the meaning of that truth which must be maintained.

Some individuals and groups, perhaps scandalized by the uniqueness of Jesus, may surrender to an incorrect understanding of that truth. But the Church under the inspiration of the Holy Spirit, must, as she did in her encounter with Greek thought, assert her truth about Jesus as she engages in the dialectical encounter of religions and cultures.[96] As with Nicea, this assertion is not an abandonment of a search or the imposition of concepts. It is the assertion of truth which searches for and seeks the correct understanding of itself in a new culture. About Jesus' uniqueness, at least, it is not a search for a new truth, but a new understanding of the permanent meaning.

For this reason, the definitions of Nicea and Chalcedon are not optional, even given the relativity of cultures. For once a correct understanding of the truth is achieved in one cultural context of meaning, and declared to be such by the Church, that understanding becomes part of the faith itself.

Church doctrines, when they affirm an understanding to be correct, move from the second level of consciousness to the third. The definition is no longer simply an *understanding*, but an *affirmation or judgment about what is so*. It is now on the level of truth where faith properly occurs. It is this truth, now correctly understood and affirmed in a new way which becomes part of the Church as she encounters a new culture. She cannot abandon that truth about herself without betraying her witness.

Dialectic does not require the Church to engage in any betrayal or self-deception. Genuine dialectic in fact requires the Church, as it does all participants, to "come-as-they-are." Only in this way can genuine conversion be invited and correct understanding and truth be grasped and affirmed. The Church can enter the dialectic only with its whole truth.

This notion of the Church's "whole truth" refers to the *common* meaning of the Church, a meaning which constitutes her identity, her witness and her mission.[97] Doctrines are those judgments that actualize the common meaning of the Church.[98] If the meaning of doctrines can change, then the Church's identity, witness and mission can change. But for the Church to change in these fundamental aspects of herself, is for her to betray herself. And not only herself, but it is also to betray the Lord to whom she owes and from whom she receives her identity, witness and mission. The church cannot alter the truth about any of these foundational and constitutive meanings because they come to her from Jesus Christ, who is "the same yesterday and today and forever" (Heb 13:8).

The normative function of Church doctrines, then, first and foremost is grounded in the source of all the truth about the Church: namely, in the outer word of Jesus Christ received in faith through inner grace. We might call this a *normativeness from above*. Because the source is one, the doctrine is a common doctrine. To alter the meaning of the common doctrine, is to change the truth as it has been given to the Church by its Head. This alteration, as is abundantly clear by now, is what Hick has done regarding the uniqueness of Jesus. In Lonergan's terms, Hick has withdrawn from the actualized common meaning of the Church.[99] But these doctrines, while grounded in Jesus Christ and the fullness of revelation which He is, do not come to us from Him as a ready-made "Denziger." Church doctrines come into being, as we already noted, through a dialectical process. And it is the role of doctrines in relation to this process that provides them with a second normative quality. We might call this *normativeness from below*.

This second normative quality is grounded in the method of mind, that is, in the unrevisability of the operations of human consciousness. Specifically, Lonergan argues that it flows from the functional specialty, doctrines, in its methodological relation to the two previous functional specialties of dialectic and foundations.[100] This means that doctrines, as the true articulations of the Church's faith, are not foreign to human reason. Faith is conditioned by reason; otherwise, of course, one would not be able to give a reason for one's hope (cf. 1 Peter 3:15). As Juan Alfaro writes:

> ... l'indole intelligente dell' uomo è condizione previa e permanente della possibilità della fede ... la fede s'inserisce in questo dinamismo [il desiderio naturale di sapere] costitutivo della natura umana.[101]

Church doctrines, then, are normative for all generations of Christians in all cultural contexts because if they express the truth about the Church in one context, that meaning perdures in all other contexts.

This is so for two reasons: first, because the true meaning of the Church's identity, witness and mission come from Jesus Christ, the Word made flesh, and secondly, because doctrines are genuine judgments grounded in a dialectic which separates truth from error, and in foundations which establishes theological categories occasioned by conversion. For example, regarding Nicea's *homoousios*, it is the first reason that accounts for the fact that Nicea did not add anything to Jesus that was not there from the beginning. It is the second reason which accounts for the fact that the non-biblical term *homoousios* both entered the creed and in doing so had to acquire a new meaning within Christian faith.

For Hick to maintain that the Church's meaning should not perdure in on-going and changing contxts of meaning is to claim that there should be no perduring meaning to the Church's identity, witness, and mission. The Church, states Hick, should create a new identity, witness, and mission in every new context. This may entail declaring itself to have a meaning quite the opposite of what it had already declared itself to have in another context.

In fact, Hick's claims are meant to show not only that the Church's meaning should not perdure, but that in fact, it cannot. But the nature of his argument of cultural relativity also means that there can be no perduring identity of anything at all. Nothing constituted by meaning has any continuity or recognizability. Ultimately this undermines all meaning and implies in fact a kind of madness.

As on the individual level, so on the communal level, a loss of identity constitutes a breakdown. Under such conditions, there can be no re-articulation of one-self or of the community, because that which is to be articulated has been lost. A return to health is not to construct a new identity unconnected, and even at variance with the old. Rather, it is to rediscover the truth that was lost. There can be no new articulation in a new context if what is to be articulated no longer exists. Nor will the new articulation be a genuine articulation of what went before, if what went before does not perdure into the new context.

Hick wants the Church to restate its identity in new cultures and contexts without the ability to ensure that it is in fact the Church's identity that is being articulated. That would be mythology! Hick's argument on cultural relativity means the Church cannot carry its identity into new cultures. It has to be open to the possibility of having its identity completely altered. And this is to happen not once, but over and over again.

What makes for even further "madness," is that Hick says the Church can, and regarding Jesus' uniqueness, has already made a mistake about its identity. For, as we have seen, Hick does not even accept the Church' self-articulation as true even within the original Hellenistic context. It is not simply a matter today of finding a new cultural expression for *homoousios*; the original meaning of the term itself even within the original context was wrong. The meaning was not what the Fathers declared it to be. The Church thought it was saying something true, declared the meaning of what it said to be true, but in fact the Church made a mistake and was only being mythological.

Presumably, then, if we accept Hick's position, the Church could go the Parousia constantly proclaiming errors about itself, its Lord, its identity, its witness and its mission. Rather than being a witness to the truth, the Church could be a witness through its life to falsehood. This conclusion stems from the fundamental error Hick makes of mistaking the Church's articulation of itself as being hypotheses about data, rather than understanding of truth.

Conciliar definitions are not optional because they form part of the whole truth or the total common meaning of the Church. True, they may be required to be understood anew. But this re-understanding is aided, not hindered, by past Conciliar definitions. *For the definitions have already clarified in one context what the truth is that is being understood in a new context.*

An important analogy emerges, of the variety: as "a" is to "b," so "c" is to "d" such that "c" carries the same meaning as "a." That is, as Nicea's *homoousios* is to Greek thought, so a "new term" is to a "new cultural context of meaning" such that the "new term" carries the same meaning of *homoousios*.[102] In this way the new understanding, whatever it might be under the inspiration of Holy Spirit, is shown both to maintain the permanence of the true meaning while allowing for growth in understanding, both of which are affirmed in Vatican I.

Dialectic will invite conversion by correcting false horizons.For example, a horizon of thought may claim that because Christianity follows the sociological patterns of all religions, that Christian faith, therefore, is the same as other faiths. But dialectic may reveal that the Christian faith is not just religious faith in general, but that it is unique. That uniqueness may in turn reveal that it is so only because of the uniqueness of Jesus Christ. Thus, the invitation presents itself to the other to accept that truth.

One always remains free, of course, to reject it. And there will be many forces obstructing such a conversion. But here again, dialectic will uncover at least what those obstructions are. Dialectic cannot, of course, produce Christian faith. What it does is lay the groundwork which eventually issues in doctrines. This accounts for *normativeness from below*. The guarantee that *normativeness from below* can issue in a true expression of the Church's faith, is the guidance of the Holy Spirit. For the Spirit leads the Church to the full understanding of the truth that is normative because it comes "from above" (cf. John 16:13).

Hypothesis or Myth?

The third question this Chapter addresses, asks if Hick's claim is true that Nicea's definition represents religious myth and not theological hypothesis. We recall from our Chapter 3 that for Hick, a religious hypothesis, which may be affirmed as "indubitably true," seeks to explain some puzzling phenomenon such that the phenomenon is no longer puzzling. A myth on the other hand, which also responds to puzzling phenomenon, does not attempt to explain. Rather the function of myth is to enable a person to respond appropriately to that phenomenon. Hick's conclusion is that the doctrine of the Incarnation of Jesus, which he sees grounded in the definitions of Nicea and Chalcedon, is not a theological hypothesis or theory, but a religious myth.

It has been demonstrated, in this and the previous two Chapters, that the doctrine of the Incarnation is not a myth, nor do the Councils represent a culmination in any deification process to mythologize Jesus. So, at one level, we need only re-state here our disagreement with Hick on this issue.

But I wish to go even further. I disagree as well that the doctrine of the Incarnation and the Conciliar definitions are "theological hypotheses," even if proven to be "indubitably true."

My disagreement is based on what was said above about the difference between coming to understand and affirm the truth about data, and growing in the understanding of a truth already affirmed in faith. The notion of hypothesis belongs to the former. This is the kind of hypothesis, seeking verification in data, that is constitutive of scientific method. Truths change as new evidence is discovered. In fact, such hypotheses are never strictly speaking, indubitably true, although some can be of exceeding high probability. They are verified or falsified, says Hick, within human experience.

It is to this notion of hypothesis that Church doctrines belong, according to Hick. They are theological hypotheses, and as new evidence is found, these doctrines must be re-verified or falsified in the new empirical evidence. Thus, religious truths are capable of changing, and indeed must do so to maintain credibility. The doctrine of the Incarnation and the Nicene and Chalcedonian definitions are examples of such truths that can and must undergo change in meaning, even if the formulas are maintained.

The point is, of course, that the Church doctrines and definitions are *not* hypotheses about data. They are affirmations of what is true. Recalling Lonergan's distinctions of the levels of human consciousness, our point can be sustained. Data occur on the first level, the level of experience. Truths, however, occur on the third. In Lonergan's thought, for example, the functional specialty of doctrines is proper to the third level.[103]

Further, hypotheses are proper to the second level, which then seek affirmation on the third level. Hence, when new data appear, there are new hypotheses, and perhaps, newly proclaimed truths. But in Church doctrines, the truth has already been revealed by God, and affirmed by faith. There are attempts to grow in understanding of these truths. This growth in understanding occurs on the second level of human consciousness. But since the truths are truths and not data, the growth in understanding is not properly called an hypothesis. An hypothesis seeks verification in empirical data; attempts to understand revealed truths seek affirmation as expressions of Christian faith. Church doctrines are such affirmations. That is why their meaning has the character of permanence about them.

Just as we noted two chapters ago that Hick fails to distinguish between faith and theology, so here he fails to distinguish between doctrines and theology. The two admittedly are intimately connected.

The Nicene affirmation of *homoousios* is possible only because of theology. If theology is faith seeking understanding, then Church doctrines are affirmations of what is a correct understanding of what is already affirmed in faith. Lonergan writes:

> Now this distinction between understanding and judgment seems essential to an understanding of the Augustinian and Anselmian precept, *Crede ut intelligas*. It does not mean, Believe that you may judge, for belief already is a judgment. It does not mean, Believe that you may demonstrate, for the truths of faith do not admit human demonstration. But very luminously it does mean, Believe that you may understand, for the truths of faith make sense to a believer and they seem to be nonsense to an un-believer.[104]

Thus, Hick confuses theological understanding of revealed truths with the hypothetical understanding of data. Then he fails to distinguish theology from Church doctrines. This is not surprising since he has no ecclesiology and he does not distinguish faith from theology. Not only then are Church doctrines, e.g., the doctrine of the Incarnation and the definitions of Nicea and Chalcedon, not religious myths, they are not theological hypotheses either. They are affirmations and articulations of the correct understanding of revealed truths.

Logical Contradiction?

The fourth and final question we have to ask in evaluating Hick on the issue of Tradition is this: is the two-natures Christology, as traditionally understood, a logical contradiction? Hick usually refers to Nicea when he speaks of the two-natures Christology. Doubtless this is because he considers the affirmation of *homoousios* to be the culmination of the deification of Jesus. However, as we have pointed out above, such a reference to Nicea is imprecise. When speaking of the two-natures Christology, it would be more accurate to refer to Chalcedon.

In any event, we are still left with Hick's claim that the two-natures Christology constitutes a logical contradiction. Hick's position here echoes what he had to say about Church Christological doctrines being myths and not hypotheses. Basically, for Hick, the problem is that such doctrines cannot be verified in tangible data. For example, we recall Hick uses this argument against the Catholic doctrine of transubstantiation. For him, the doctrine of the two-natures of Jesus cannot be verified in data. It is not, however, that the doctrine is necessarily false, he would say. But rather, since it cannot be verified or falsified in the data, then it cannot be spoken of in any literally meaningful way. It is simply meaningless. Regarding transubstantiation, one cannot verify in the data of the bread and wine that they become the body and blood of Christ; therefore the doctrine has no meaning, at least no literal meaning.

Similarly regarding Jesus of Nazareth: to say that this man, Jesus, was also *homoousios* with the Father, simply cannot be verified in any data. Therefore, it is meaningless; it has no literal content.

Hick says we can give literal meaning to the statement "Jesus was a man." We understand him to be "part of the generic stream of human life." But, continues Hick, to say this same man is God the Son Incarnate, true God and true man, is as contradictory as claiming a circle to be a square.

My first point is to repeat again Hick's basic mistake in this area. He has confused truths with data.

The second point is that Hick seems to be involved in a bit of a contradiction himself. He first claims that the two-natures Christology is meaningless. But then goes on to say it is contradictory. But to be contradictory, as Brian Davies points out, does not entail being meaningless.[105] To be contradictory already requires the affirmation of some meaning. Hick is not consistent here.

Thirdly, the notion of a square-circle is contradictory. It ascribes mutually exclusive characteristics to one and the same thing. But is this what Chalcedon does regarding Christ? Is Chalcedon in affirming the two-natures of Christ ascribing mutually exclusive characteristics to Him? Hick provides no proof that that is what Chalcedon has done. He simply claims that since the definition looks contradictory, then it must be so.

Davies has responded to Hick's accusation by asking: why this assumption of contradictoriness in the two-natures Christology? First, the assumption of contradictoriness is unwarranted because circles and squares treat definable figures. But God is not definable, if we mean

His nature is something that is clear to us. Precisely because there is an infinite distance between God and man, we cannot put any limits on what God might choose to do. Why must we assume from the outset, asks Davies, that no subject could possibly have all characteristics of both God and man?

True, we may wonder how such a subject might come to be, or what it could mean. We may even conclude that a man could not become God. But why should we assume that God could not become man, and in such a way that while not ceasing to be God, He assumes a full human nature? We may not understand *how* or *why* this might come about, but that does not make it contradictory or even meaningless. It may even constitute a unique event, and therefore baffling; but again, not necessarily contradictory.

Here again, we come back to the very point of Christian faith: Jesus is unique. Hick assumes from the outset that there could be no uniqueness about Jesus, nothing radically new. Hence, Hick has to reduce Jesus and Christology to what he already knows about the world. But if Jesus is something so new that it has never been seen before in the world, Hick will miss that newness. This is what he has done. He is not open to God doing something quite new. He has decided what it is possible for God to do and what it is not. He has decided this, as Davies points out, by misapplying the principle of non-contradiction to Jesus.[106]

Chalcedon does not say Jesus is human in the same way He is God. In fact, Chalcedon is forceful in affirming the distinction of natures. But one can affirm of the same subject, the one Person, Jesus, that He acts through two natures, one human and one divine. This is not contradictory. This is not the same as claiming Jesus is both human and non-human in the same way, or God and non-God in the same way. That would be contradictory.

Hick's basic difficulty seems to be that he does not correctly understand the *communicatio idiomatum*. We have seen that the "is" formulas bother Hick. For him, to say "Jesus is both God and man" is to change the meaning of "is." For "is" in the first sense means "identification," and in the latter sense it means "class-membership." Hick also says that we cannot claim that Jesus is unique, and so argue that the "is" has a new meaning.

But again, why is such a possibility ruled out? Does this unwarranted assumption not reflect the kind of claims Hick made in the Hellenization of the faith? We recall there that he assumed that the Church simply used meanings about Christ in precisely the same way as they were used in Greek thought. But if Jesus is unique, does not *homoousios* take on a new meaning when applied to Him? If so, why can "is" when referring to the communication of idioms not take on a new meaning?

Rahner contends as much when he writes:

For when we say that Peter is a man, the statement expresses a real identification in the content of the subject and predicate nouns. But the meaning of "is" in statements involving an interchange of predicates in Christology is *not* based on such a real identification. It is based rather one a unique, otherwise unknown and deeply mysterious unity between realities which are really different and which are at an infinite distance from each other. For in and according to the humanity which we see when we say "Jesus," Jesus "is" not God, and in and according to his divinity God "is" not man in the sense of a real identification. The Chalcedonian *adiairetos* (unseparated) which this "is" intends to express (D.S. 302) expresses it in such a way that the *asynchtos* (unmixed) of the same formula does not come to expression. Consequently, the statement is always in danger of being understood in a "monophysitic" sense, this is, as a formula which simply identifies the subject and predicate.[107]

Because Hick does not accept the uniqueness of Jesus which Chalcedon was affirming, he can only assume that in fact the definition is monophysitic. But for him, such a meaning can only be mythological. As well it might be, which may account for why Chalcedon rejected such an interpretation. Thus, what Hick has done is reject a false interpretation of the "is" formula regarding Jesus.

The non-contradictoriness of the two-natures Christology rests in the fact of the unity of the one Jesus, a unity not based on nature but on Person. As Richard McBrien writes:

As a consequence of the union by which divinity and humanity are united in one person, we can predicate of the one person what is rooted in either nature.[108]

My fourth and final point: Hick's entire critique of the Tradition on this point of contradiction, whether about transubstantiation or the two-natures Christology, seems to be based on the neo-positivist principle of empirical verification. That is, Hick appears to accept that the only valid principle for all human knowledge, is the one that claims that a proposition has meaning only if it can be verified or falsified empirically. All other propositions are meaningless, that is, not capable of either verification or falsification. The Chalcedonian definition that Jesus is one Person in two natures is not empirically verifiable or falsifiable, therefore, it is simply meaningless. It is not even capable of being false.

Needless to say, we need not embark on this debate. I merely wish to indicate that the principle of empirical verification is itself not empirically verifiable. On this point Juan Alfaro writes:

> ... cioè, non c'è nessuna esperienza empirica capace di verificarlo o di falsificarlo (né direttamente né indirettamente), perché esso non esprime un fatto, un evento del mondo: non si può trovare nessun evento empirico, che in qualche modo lo confermi o lo contradica. Quindi il "principio" è un mero presupposto, né comprovato né comprovabile. Di conseguenza, stando alla divisione che lo stesso neopositivismo stabilisce fra le proposizioni analitiche, il "principio" deve essere catalogato fra le proposizioni analitiche, tautologiche.[109]

If this principle of empirical verification does in fact constitute Hick's basic approach to the meaning and possible truth of faith statements, and it would seem to be so, then we can only conclude that he is caught up in a series of meaningless statements himself. His own arguments within the limits he himself sets by his own method, amount to nothing more than tautologies.

Endnotes

1. For the moment we are going along with Hick's usual reference

to Nicea when he speaks of the two-natures Christology. This is imprecise.

2. I agree with Peter Hinchliff, although with a more critical foundation, when he writes: "Those who take the view that the development of the doctrine [of the Incarnation] was a series of radical and discontinuous stages are often inclined to suggest that each stage was a 'mistake' resulting from the transferring of an idea from one context to another ... It has to be said that there is no actual evidence that this is what happened," in A. E. Harvey, ed., *God Incarnate: Story and Belief* (London: SPCK, 1981), 85.

3. For a full appreciation of his thought it is necessary to work one's way through Bernard J. F. Lonergan, S.J. *Insight: A Study of Human Understanding* (London: Longmans, Green & Co., 1957), especially the first eleven chapters. His study of human understanding is not just another theory in epistemology. It represents a series of exercises that enable the reader to appropriate himself/ herself as a knower. For my purposes, however, here I draw on Lonergan's *Method in Theology* (London: Darton, Longman & Todd, 1973), especially Chapter 3 "Meaning," 57-99.

4. *Method...*, 85. See also, Lonergan's article "Unity and Plurality: The Coherence of Christian Truth," in *A Third Collection: Papers* by Bernard Lonergan, S.J., ed. Frederick E. Crowe, S.J. (New York: Paulist, 1985), 239-50, especially the first section "Differentiations of Consciousness," 239-43.

5. In "Unity and Plurality ...", Lonergan lists five differentiations of consciousness: common sense, science [theory], scholarship [history], intentionality analysis [interiority], and the life of prayer [religious differentiation], 247. In *Method ...*, he lists ten differentiations: (1) the infant world of immediacy; (2) common sense; (3) the religious; (4) the artistic; (5) theory and system; (6) post-systematic literary thought; (7) method; (8) scholarship; (9) post-scientific and post-scholarly thought; (10) interiority, 302-305.

6. Lonergan, *Method ...*, 85.

7. Obviously "theoretical" does not mean simply "hypothetical" or "possible." It means the verified hypothesis at least as scientifically probable. I use Lonergan's terms of theoretical consciousness and intellectual consciousness, as does he, interchangeably.

8. For Lonergan's complete treatment of common sense, see *Insight* ..., Chapters VI and VII.

9. In addition to the first eleven Chapters of *Insight* ..., one can find a summary of them, but not a substitute, in *Method* ..., Chapter 1 "Method," 3-25; in the last three articles of *Collection: Papers by Bernard Lonergan, S.J.*, ed. by F. E. Crowe, S.J. (Montreal: Palm Publishers, 1967), namely, "Cognitional Structure," 221-39; *Existenz* and *Aggiornamento*, 240-51; and "Dimensions of Meaning," 252-67.

10. For Lonergan's account of the self-correcting process of knowing, see *Insight* ..., 174-75, 286-91, 713-18.

11. Lonergan notes that in the West the intrusion of systematic exigence is beautifully illustrated in the early dialogues of Plato. To Socrates' request for a definition of a virtue, e.g., courage or fortitude or temperance, everyone admitted there was a common meaning, but no one, not even Socrates, could really say what that meaning was, *Method* ..., 82. With Aristotle, the shift to theory becomes evident, "Unity and Plurality ...," 240-41. Another example which Lonergan supplies to illustrate the systematic exigence at work, occurs when the mind moves from the common sense notion of "weight" and defines the theoretical notion of "mass," *Method* ..., 82.

12. Lonergan, *Method* ..., 82.

13. *Ibid.*, 93-94.

14. To understand what Lonergan means by "interiority" see *Method* ..., 83.

15. Lonergan, *Method* ..., 82.

16. Lonergan writes: "... it is not hard to see that what corresponds to the gospels is undifferentiated consciousness, whereas what corresponds to dogma is differentiated consciousness," *The Way to Nicea: The Dialectical Development of Trinitarian Theology* (London: Darton, Longman & Todd, 1976), 3. A translation by Conn O'-Donovan from the first part of *De Deo Trino* by Bernard Lonergan.

17. John L. McKenzie,"Salvation," *Dictionary of the Bible* (New York: Macmillan, 1965), 760-63.

18. Lonergan, *The Way to Nicea*, 3. He elaborates: "Dogmatic development, therefore, not only presents a subjective aspect, which is grasped by comparing earlier with later documents; it also demands a certain subjective change, involving a transition from undifferentiated

common sense, which is most widespread and most familiar, to the intellectual pattern of experience. And this transition does not occur spontaneously; it comes about only through a slow learning process, sustained by serious effort," 3.

19. *The Way...*, 10. Lonergan also writes, with Athanasius in mind: "Moreover, the Nicene concept of consubstantiality does not go beyond the dogmatic realism that is contained implicitly in the word of God. For it means no more than this, that what is said of the Father is to be said also of the Son, except that the Son is Son and not Father." 130.

20. *Ibid.*, 13. An example of a development from obscurity to clarity would be the very notion of dogma itself, grounded in the word of God as true. Lonergan also takes issue with those, like Hick, who claim that while the gospels are clear, dogmas are obscure. While claiming a clarity for both, Lonergan notes the far greater need for exegesis to be done on the Scriptures than on the dogmas; *ibid.*, 4-5.

21. Tad Dunne, S.J. gives an account of the development of the doctrine of the Trinity grounded in these differentiations of consciousness. *Trinity: God as Doubly-Processing*. 2nd ed. revised, unpublished lecture notes.

22. For a discussion of this issue, not in Lonerganian terms, see Karl Rahner and Wilhelm Thusing, *A New Christology* (London: Burns & Oates, 1980), 160-211.

23. Lonergan, "The Dehellenization of Dogma" in *A Second Collection: Papers by Bernard J. F. Lonergan*, S.J., eds. William F. J. Ryan, S.J. and Bernard J. Tyrrell, S.J. (London: Darton, Longman & Todd, 1974), 21. This article originally was a review in *Theological Studies*, 28 (1967), 336-51, of Leslie Dewart, *The Future of Belief: Theism in a World Come of Age* (New York: Herder & Herder, 1966).

24. Kasper, *Jesus ...*, 22-23.

25. Since Hick divorces ontological Christology from functional Christology, and misunderstands the distinction between intellectual consciousness and common sense consciousness, he has no alternative but to opt for and exaggerate the *pro me* principle and make it the centre and substance of all Christology. This option would seem to follow from Hick's acknowledged dependence on Schleiermacher's Christology, which in turn was grounded in Melanchthon's principle:

"Hoc est Christum cognoscere beneficia eius cognoscere, non, quod isti docent, eius naturas, modos incarnationis contueri," [This is what (true) knowledge of Christ is: to know his favours (to us), and not, as those people maintain, to speculate upon his natures and the modes of his incarnation], Kasper, *Jesus* ..., 22; my translation.

26. Lonergan, *The Way to Nicea*, 16-17, cf. p. 4. He also criticizes such people for misunderstanding metaphysics as "simply scientifically elaborated myth," *ibid.*, 130, fn. 60.

27. Lonergan states: "Further, the less differentiated one's consciousness and the fewer the patterns of experience in which one lives one's life, the less clearly, proportionately, does one grasp the diversity of human actions and the less capable, consequently, is one of drawing distinctions between one sphere of action and another," *Ibid.*, 5.

28. Lonergan, *A Third collection* ..., 250. Lonergan also concludes in *The Way to Nicea*: "There is little basis, then, for the romantic notion that undifferentiated consciousness is the religious consciousness *par excellence* ... It is plain therefore, that dogmas pertain to religion most of all because they render differentiated consciousness religious ... And so if one argues that there is nothing religious about intellect, one is not serving the cause of true religion, but rather that of secularism," 6-7. Lonergan also takes issue with the notion that dogmas have little to do with religious experience because they are not expressions of the Hebrew mind. This "glorification of the Hebrew mind, in its ancient simplicity [suggests] that it was some special gift to God to the Hebrews, sealed with the approval of the scriptures and offered to all future generations as a model to be imitated," *ibid.*, 5.

29. See Lonergan, *Insight* ..., Chapters, XI, XII, XIII.

30. Christopher Butler writes: "If the Church was to convert the Greco-Roman world, it had, sooner or later, to respond to the challenge of Greek philosophy. For this challenge, though Greek in its provenance, was really the challenge of the human intellect itself ...," *The Truth of God Incarnate*, 93.

31. Lonergan, *Method* ..., 90-93.

32. Lonergan writes: "This influence [of Hellenistic culture], however, has been recognized and affirmed since the Patristic age; far from supplying proof that the Church substituted for the Christian religion some other kind of religion, it merely assigns the cause,

prepared by divine providence, whereby the Christian religion itself was enabled to make explicit what from the beginning was contained implicitly in the word of God itself," *The Way to Nicea*, 131.

33. Jean Daniélou, *Gospel Message and Hellenistic Culture* Translated by John Austin Baker (London: Darton, Longman & Todd, 1973), 345. Daniélou writes that instead of simply re-presenting existing Greek thought, that the Apologists reveal "the emergence of a new thing, a Christian system of the universe," 346.

34. Aloys Grillmeier, S.J., *Christ in the Christian Tradition*, v.1 "From the Apostolic Age to Chalcedon (451)," 2nd rev. ed., translated by John Bowden (Atlanta: John Knox, 1965, 1975), 269. I simply note here in passing what I will return to in our conclusion to this work, namely the challenge to the concept of God that Christian faith required. This challenge stemmed from the uniqueness of Jesus Christ. It is interesting that in Buddhism, that challenge was not felt nor did it occur five centuries later even with the deification of Buddha. Hick's comparison of the two processes overlooks this fact, a fact which Grillmeier emphasizes in arguing that the heretical positions in Hellenizing the concept of God opted not to face the radical challenge, *ibid.*, 270.

35. Kasper, *Jesus* ..., 176. See also Kasper, *The God of Jesus Christ* (London: S.C.M., 1984), 182-4. First published as *Derr Gott Jesu Christi* (Mainz: Matthias Grünewald Verlag, 1982), translated by Matthew J. O'Connell. See as well Grillmeier, *Christ* ..., 266.

36. Kasper, *The God* ..., 183.

37. Grillmeier, *Christ* ..., 270.

38. Kasper, *Jesus* ..., 176.

39. Lonergan, "Dehellenization ...," 22. See also his *The Way to Nicea*, 31-2; as well as Kasper, *The God* ..., 183.

40. Kasper, *Jesus* ..., 176.

41. For Lonergan's application of these ideas to Augustine's notion of *persona* or *substantia*, see "Dehellenization ...," 25-26.

42. *Ibid.*, 27.

43. *Ibid.*, 23. We have already seen that Judaism followed an analogous pattern in taking over the idea of Wisdom from surrounding cultures. It did not simply adopt the non-Judaic meaning, but adapted it and remolded it to take on the meaning that was given it in the context of their faith.

44. Grillmeier, *Christ* ..., 272.

45. John Austin Baker, "Postscript: The Permanent Significance of the Fathers of the Second and Third Centuries," in Jean Daniélou, *Gospel Message* ..., 501.

46. Kasper, *Jesus* ..., 178. Kasper also writes "The supposed 'Hellenization' was in fact a sign of incarnational power and spiritual presence," *The God* ..., 182.

47. Kasper, *Jesus* ..., 178.

48. Baker, "Postscript ...," *op. cit.*, 502.

49. We ought to note here as well that Nicea's doctrine, as Kasper writes, was not only a metaphysical sedition, but also a political one as well. It subverted the very foundation of the Empire's political ideology, that is, it did not accept the identity of Christ's rule with the polity of Constantine's Christian Roman Empire with the latter's slogan "One God, One *Logos*, One Empire," *Jesus* ..., 265. For a detailed account of the relation between Nicea and the Empire, see Grillmeier, *Christ* ..., "Nicaea and the Rise of the Imperial Church," 250-64.

50. Lesslie Newbigin argues that it is an over-simplification to say that the Church "went West," *The Open Secret*, (Grand Rapids, Michigan: Eerdmans, 1978), 3-4.

51. Lesslie Newbigin picks up this point when he argues that the term *avatar* does not capture the true meaning of Jesus' Incarnation: "*Avatar* is usually translated "incarnation," but there have been many *avatars* and there will be many more. To announce a new *avatar* is not to announce any radical change in the nature of things ... Jesus is...not just *avatar*, but unique *avatar*," *The Open Secret*, 21.

52. Gerald O'Collins, S.J., *Interpreting Jesus* (London: Geoffrey Chapman, 1983), 172-73.

53. Grillmeier, *Christ* ..., 545.

54. *Ibid.*

55. Kasper, *Jesus* ..., 236.

56. *Ibid.*, 237, 238.

57. *Ibid.*, 240. Kasper elaborates on the unique Christian distinction between nature and person, 241. For his account of the unique Christian usage of *prosopon*, see also 241. By way of an aside, we note that this unique Christian contribution to the view of reality has an implication for another argument of Hick's, namely, that substance

philosophy is static. But as Kasper remarks, the point of this Christian contribution was quite the opposite. The Christian usage of *hypostasis* "... amounted in principle to an advance towards a dynamic conception of being and of God, for *hypostasis* meant not a state but an act, not being static in itself, but being as happening. Thus the term corresponded to the relational sense of the concept of person, and it was not long before the divine hypostases could be thought of as relations," *ibid.*, 241. Grillmeier agrees when he writes: "The Chalcedonian Definition may seem to have a static-ontic ring, but it is not meant to do away with the salvation-historical aspect of biblical christology, for which, in fact, it provides a foundation and deeper insights," *Christ ...*, 553-54.

58. Baker, "Postscript ...," *op. cit.*, 502. Christopher Butler makes the same point, "Jesus and Later Orthodoxy," in Michael Green, ed., *The Truth of God Incarnate*, 95-96.

59. Grillmeier, *Christ ...*, 555-56.

60. Kasper, *Jesus ...*, 21.

61. We are aware that terms like "heretical" and "orthodox" when applied to the early centuries of the Church, while clear to us, were not so to the participants. Orthodoxy only revealed itself in the dialectical process. Lonergan's *The Way to Nicea* provides an excellent account of that dialectical process. For a detailed account of what "dialectic" is for Lonergan , see *Method ...*, Chapter 10, "Dialectic," 235-66. This work is an example of doing dialectic theology, according to Lonergan's understanding of it.

62. Daniélou, *Gospel Message ...*, 303.

63. Grillmeier, *Christ ...*, 267-73.

64. *Ibid.*, 555.

65. *Ibid.*, 556.

66. Kasper, *The God ...*, 182.

67. *Ibid.*

68. *Ibid.*, 183. See also Kasper, *Jesus ...*, 178.

69. Kasper, *Jesus ...*, 211, 236, 237.

70. *Ibid.*, 23.

71. Lonergan, *The Way to Nicea*, 129.

72. *Ibid.*, 10-11. Lonergan writes: "Finally, it is this same failure to attend to the word as true that mars the thinking of those who reduce the

dogmas to hellenism; for hellenistic speculation was concerned with essences, whereas dogmas are affirmations of what *is*." See *ibid.*, 8-9.

The purpose of the Councils was not of course to make a contribution, no matter how original, to Greek philosophy. Their purpose was to preserve the truth about Jesus and the salvation He brought. In doing so, however, they did make an original and significant change in the view of ultimate reality and being.

73. *Ibid.*, 92.

74. Lonergan, "Dehellenization ...," 24.

75. Lonergan, *Method* ..., 301.

76. Bernard Lonergan, S.J. *Doctrinal Pluralism* (Milwaukee: Marquette University, 1971), The 1971 Père Marquette Theology Lecture, 32. The opening sentence of Lonergan's *Method* ... reads: "A theology mediates between a cultural matrix and the significance and role of a religion in that matrix," xi.

For a discussion of the theological and dogmatic issues involved in understanding theology as mediating faith and culture, see Jacques Dupuis, S.J., "Unity of Faith and Dogmatic Pluralism," *Jesus Christ and His Spirit: Theological Approaches* (Bangalore: Theological Publications in India, 1977): 59-82.

77. Lonergan, *Doctrinal* ..., 4-9. See also *Method* ..., 300-302.

78. Lonergan, *Doctrinal* ..., 6.

79. For a full account of this clue, see Lonergan's *Doctrinal* ..., 39-48; *Method* ..., 320-26.

80. Consult DS 3020, DS 3043, or *The Christian Faith in the Doctrinal Documents of the Catholic Church*, ed. by J. Neuner, S.J. and J. Dupuis, S.J., rev. ed (London: Collins, 1983) ND 136, ND 139.

81. Lonergan says "it seems better to speak of the permanence of the meaning of dogmas rather than of the immutability of that meaning." He refers to the Latin phrases of DS 3020, *Doctrinal* ..., 46.

82. Gerald O'Collins intends this distinction when he writes: "Nowhere does Chalcedon impose its 'two-natures' terminology as the *only* language to be used henceforth by all Christians of all times," *Interpreting Jesus* (London: Geoffrey Chapman, 1983), 173.

83. Lonergan, *Doctrinal* ..., 48.

84. *Ibid.*, 49.

85. Kasper, *The God* ..., 184.

86. Grillmeier writes: "... the Chalcedonian Definition already points to the future," *Christ* ..., 551.

87. On-going contexts of meaning and the encounter of unrelated contexts of meaning are not the only causes of pluralism. Pluralism results from the wide variety of differentiation of consciousness, and from the presence or absence of any one or all three kinds of conversion: namely, religious, moral or intellectual conversion. The presence or absence of conversion is frequently at the root of many problems that relate to pluralism. See Lonergan, *Method* ..., 237-44. We briefly note here that by "conversion" Lonergan means a complete about-face of one's horizon, that is, of the limits of one's vision, through the dialectical exercise of freedom, in which counter-positions and false values are reversed, either intellectually, morally or religiously.

88. Grillmeier, *Christ* ..., 556.

89. We refer the reader again to the insightful account of this dialectic in Lonergan's *The Way to Nicea: The Dialectical Development of Trinitarian Theology* (London: Darton, Longman & Todd), 1976.

90. Lonergan, *Method* ..., 333. For a detailed account of Lonergan's understanding of dialectic, see Chapter 10 "Dialectic," *Method*, 235-66.

91. *Ibid.*, 325. This difference is grounded in the method of mind uncovered by Lonergan. It involves levels of consciousness with their operations. The first level is experiencing ordered to data, the second is understanding ordered to the intelligible, the third is judging ordered to the true, the fourth is deciding ordered to the good. The method of mind in its four levels encounters the past, the mediating phase, and moves into the future, the mediated phase. To the four levels in the mediating phase, beginning with the first level and moving upward, relate the tasks of research, interpretation, history and dialectic. Dialectic invites conversion. With conversion the mediated phase moves downward from the fourth level, from foundations to doctrines to systematics to communications. Thus, data are on the first level, whereas truths are on the third. Doctrines as truths are affirmed prior to any development in understanding them, which occurs on the second level. Data, however, are only data, and the understanding of the truth about them leads only to probable truth, as in scientific method. Probable truth can and does change as development of under-

standing occurs. This, as we have said, does not occur in the development of understanding a revealed truth.

92. For a discussion of the theological importance of these two transitions in the life of the Church, see Karl Rahner, S.J., "Basic Theological Interpretation of the Second Vatican Council," *Theological Studies*, XX, (New York: Crossroad, 1981), 77-89. Translated by Edward Quinn.

93. For what Lonergan means by conversion, see *Method ...*, 237-44.

94. This is Grillmeier's *lectio difficilior*.

95. This is the point Peter Hinchcliff also makes when he writes: "Lonergan is right in maintaining that theology has to say what it believes to be the actual case, not what people *feel*," in *God Incarnate: Story and Belief* (London: SPCK, 1981), 94.

96. Lesslie Newbigin writes: "But his [the Christian's] commitment to Jesus Christ, so far from being something which he can leave behind him for the purpose of the study [of world religions], is precisely his point of entry into it," *The Finality of Christ* (London: S.C.M., 1969), 21.

97. Lonergan demonstrates that constitutive meaning is one of the four functions of meaning. Meaning is constitutive because it is the intrinsic component of language, social institutions and human cultures. Any change in these expressions of meaning involves a change in the constitutive meaning which gave them birth. Church doctrines are constitutive of the Church's meaning both on the individual level, as a set of meanings and values that inform one's living, knowing and doing; and on the common level, "for community exists inasmuch as there is a commonly accepted set of meanings and values shared by people in contact with one another" *Method ...*, 298. Three other functions of meaning are cognitive, efficient and communicative. For Lonergan's account of how these other functions relate to Church doctrines, see *ibid.*

98. See Charles C. Hefling, Jr., *Why Doctrines?* (USA: Cowley Publications, 1984), esp. 37-70; also Karl Rahner, S.J., "What is a Dogmatic Statement?" *Theological Investigations*, v.5, 42-66, esp. 51-58.

99. Lonergan argues that it is the achievement of common meaning that constitutes a community. He continues: "Common meaning is

potential when there is a common field of experience, and to withdraw from that common field is to get out of touch. Common meaning is formal when there is common understanding, and one withdraws from that common understanding by misunderstanding, by incomprehension, by mutual incomprehension. Common meaning is actual inasmuch as there are common judgments, areas in which all affirm and deny in the same manner; and one withdraws from that judgment when one disagrees, when one considers true what others hold false and false what they think true. Common meaning is realized by decisions and choices, especially in permanent dedication, in the love that makes families, in the loyalty that makes states, in the faith that makes religions," *Method* ..., 79.

100. Briefly, functional specialties are methodical distinctions or tasks based on the immanent directives of the method of mind, i.e., on the unrevisable operations of human consciousness. Lonergan uncovers eight functional specialties. Four which operate in the mediated phase are: research, interpretation, history and dialectic; the four which operate in the mediating phase are: foundations, dialectic, systematics and communications.

101. Juan Alfaro, S.J., *Dalla questione dell' uomo alla questione di Dio* (Rome: Gregorian University class *dispense*, 1985), Theme 1, p. 6. I translate: "... the intelligent nature of man is the prior and permanent condition of the possibility of faith ... faith inserts itself in this dynamism [the natural desire to know] constitutive of human nature."

102. I add, as well, that the new term need not necessarily be of the type that functions like *homoousios*. It may be the more simple type that simply fulfills the heuristic requirements of *homoousios*. Thus, in any culture, whatever is said of the Father, in whatever terms, must also be said of the Son, except the name "Father."

103. Lonergan, *Method* ..., 295-333.

104. *Ibid.*, 335-36.

105. Brian Davies, *Thinking About God* (London: Geoffrey Chapman, 1985), 284.

106. Christopher Butler makes a similar point when he argues that Christian faith is not about what God possibly might or might not do, but about what in fact God has done, "Jesus and Later Orthodoxy," in Michael Green, ed., *The Truth of God Incarnate*, 100. This point is

central also to Brian Hebblethwaite's argument in "Jesus, God Incarnate," *ibid.*, 101-6. The same point is made in Michael Green's article "Jesus and Historical Scepticism," *ibid.*, 113-14.

107. Karl Rahner, S.J. *Foundations of Christian Faith: An Introduction to the Idea of Christianity* (New York: Crossroad, 1978), 290. Originally published as *Grundkurs des Glaubens: Einführung in den Begriff des Christentums* (Freiburg im Breisgau: Verlag Herder, 1976).

108. Richard P. McBrien, *Catholicism*, 2 vols.(Minneapolis, MN: Winston Press, 1980), v.1, 445.

109. Alfaro, *Dalla questione* ..., Theme IV, p. 109. I translate: "that is, there is not any empirical experience capable of verifying it or falsifying it (neither directly or indirectly), because it does not express a fact, an event in the world: one can find no empirical event, that in any way confirms it or contradicts it, therefore the principle is a mere presupposition, neither proved nor provable. Consequently, basing ourselves on the division which the same neopositivism establishes between descriptive and analytic propositions, the "principle" has to be catalogued among the analytic propositions, the tautologies."

Alfaro continues by showing that in fact the principle of empirical verification is a real tautology. The principle says that "only propositions that are empirically verifiable are meaningful," but by "meaningful" is meant "empirically verifiable." So we are left with the principle that "only propositions that are empirically verifiable are empirically verifiable:" a tautology.

CHAPTER EIGHT

Secondary Claims

In the preceding three Chapters I have been responding to and evaluating the three main cases which Hick brings to bear against the traditional understanding of the uniqueness of Jesus Christ. The themes involved were: (1) The Consciousness of Jesus, (2) Scripture, and (3) Tradition.

In addition to these primary themes in his Christology, Hick also employs a series of secondary arguments. These latter claims are secondary, simply because Hick employs them in a subordinate manner. They may be considered supplementary or supporting reasons.

These supporting arguments I have organized according to the following categories: (1) Theology, (2) Language, (3) Epistemology, (4) Copernican Revolution, (5) Divine Inhistorisation and *Homoagape*, and (6) Resurrection of Jesus. Since these positions are subordinate, I do not repond to them with the same exhaustive detail as was done with Hick's primary claims.

Theology

We have already seen what is meant by Theology in this context. In Chapter 7 Theology is distinguished from Tradition. By *Tradition* is meant those arguments Hick brings against the Councils, especially Nicea and Chalcedon. By *Theology* is understood those theological claims other than those relating to Scripture or Tradition, which Hick brings to bear in elaborating his Christology.

What are these Theological claims? We summarized them at the end of Chapter 3 as:

(a) Jesus cannot be unique in the traditional sense, because that would violate God's universal salvific will. The problem of limited world communications up to now has prevented God from making a single self-revelation. (b) It was mainly the Christian experience of reconciliation with God that contributed to the deification of Jesus.

We hear in these theological claims of Hick's, an echo of his *a priori* assumption that God did not do anything radically new in Jesus. Jesus is not unique; He is not *the* Saviour of the world. He is merely a model religious person open to God—as have been other religious founders—and through whom God has been able to touch many other people. This secondary argument forms part of Hick's reduction of Christology to anthropology.

We have already discussed elsewhere the wider issues involved. But I wish to point out again that this methodological assumption of Hick's, that God can only do what present theory can explain, rules out of court any possible evidence that God may have done something far more astonishing than any hypothesis can imagine. I refer once again to Kasper, who writes:

However, when particulars receive their definition primarily from analogy and correlation with everything else, the sense of the incalculable, the unique, the once-for-all, disappears. Extraordinary events are no longer regarded with astonishment. They are reduced to the general level of what in theory can be explained.[1]

We see here a particular flaw in Hick's procedure. Christian faith holds that Jesus does not fit any formula; He is radically unique. But in arguing against this uniqueness, Hick sets up a method which by its very principles rules out the possible occurrence of any genuine uniqueness. Therefore, when such uniqueness does occur, it has to be reduced to something else, or explained in some other way. In other words, Hick already pre-determines in his method, what can possibly be said about

Jesus and God's universal salvific will, and what cannot be said.

What cannot be said is that Jesus is radically unique. He has to be made to fit what theory says is reasonable to expect of God in the exercise of His will. The ultimate mystery of God, in particular His freedom, is fundamentally limited by this approach of Hick's.

Hick arrives at this limitation in much the same way as he reached his limitation of the person of Jesus. He affirms only one side of the mystery, thus in effect, doing away with the mystery itself. With Jesus, Hick could only affirm His humanity but not His divinity. Thus, the mystery of Jesus is emptied. In this present case, Hick affirms God's universal salvific will, but not the uniqueness of Jesus as universal Saviour. Thus, the mystery of salvation is emptied. In Hick's account God's ways are not at all, nor can they be, above man's ways. Given Hick's view, there certainly is nothing scandalous in the way we might experience God at work in history. God works exactly as we would expect Him to.

It is possible now to address some specific issues within this theme.

Jesus as Representational

First, it is *because* of the uniqueness of Jesus that He can be and is universal.[2] This uniqueness of Jesus relates to both who He was and what He did. It is the uniqueness of Jesus as "representational," i.e., representational of the human race.[3]

In his argument, Hick empties Jesus of any "representational" role or function. Jesus can have no representational role because, logically enough for Hick, He is just another human being. This position goes against what has been basic and unique to Christian faith. What makes Jesus, unlike other religious founders, both unique and universal at the same time, is this very representational aspect of the Person and mission of Jesus. As Kasper writes:

> Jesus' unique yet universal position in history is founded in representation as the decisive centre of his existence. For it is through his representation that he has a universal significance as one and unique. Something occurred through him once and for all: the reconciliation of the world.[4]

But Jesus as uniquely and universally representational of the human race cannot be accounted for by His humanity alone.[5] It is true, Jesus must be truly human to represent humanity. As the Church Fathers saw clearly, what is not assumed is not healed. But if Jesus is *only* another member of the human race, there is no grounds for Him to be the unique and universal Saviour. To the question: Why Jesus exactly?, one could only answer, it must be the arbitrary will of God. God's intervention in Jesus would have been an accident.

But Christian faith claims that salvation in Jesus is neither arbitrary nor accidental. It was ordained from all eternity. Jesus, therefore, is not simply just another member of the human race. The claim about Jesus' uniqueness and universality is grounded in faith's affirmation of Jesus' divine Sonship. It is *who* Jesus is as divine Son that grounds and establishes Him as the unique expression of the universal salvific will of God. As Felipe Gomez succinctly says: "The ultimate ground of Jesus' absolutely unique universality is simply his Person."[6]

On this point Gomez makes the important distinction between Jesus's religious experience and Jesus Himself. Whereas Hick reduces Jesus to His experience of God, Gomez writes:

And yet, what constitutes the difference [between Jesus and any other religious person] is not *what* or *how* God was experienced, but *who* experienced Him ... What makes Jesus' experience of God unique is not its psychological impact or the knowledge derived from it or anything at all in that line, but the fact that the Son in His human consciousness met His Father.[7]

This point I feel is central to this whole discussion. The only reason there is no *real* conflict between the uniqueness of Jesus and His universality is because these affirmations about Him are grounded in the very nature of His "divine Sonship." It is because Jesus is both true man and true God, that He is not only "particular" but also representational and universal. This is the only valid reason that can account for the uniqueness of Jesus. Where the divine Sonship of Jesus is not acknowledged, as in Hick's case, then the inevitable question arises: "Why is Jesus *the* Saviour?" Since there is no adequate answer under those conditions, Hick logically opts for a non-representational and only relatively unique Jesus.

But where Christian faith proclaims the divine Sonship of the Person of Jesus, there is found the reason for His uniqueness and universality. As Gomez so clearly writes:

> All great men are God's special gifts to mankind; Christ is God's *self*-gift. And so our faith tells us that if Socrates is wise, Christ is Wisdom; if Krishna is Manifestation, Christ is the Manifested One; if Buddha is the Illumined, Christ is the Light; if Muhammed [sic] is the Prophet, Christ is the Word. Like Moses, these men served God as servants; Christ did it as the Son (Heb 3:5-6). Even as the historical figure of a founder of Religion Jesus appears unique ... [as] "the conscious self-reference" in claiming definitive authority for His words because they are His ("but I tell you ..."), and decisive value for the eternal fate of men for the attitude toward *Him* (e.g. Mt.25).[8]

In undermining, and indeed denying, the Christian faith in the divine Sonship of Jesus, it is not surprising that Hick cannot find adequate grounds for accounting for a uniqueness of Jesus that is not in conflict with the universal salvific will of God. How could Jesus have any universal significance when He is just a member of the human race? As Anselm has pointed out, Jesus could be representational only if He were true man, and universal only if He were true God.[9] But being representational and universal are the very definition of Jesus' uniqueness. And they are definitional of His uniqueness only because of the nature of Jesus' divine Sonship itself. There is no conflict between the specificity of Jesus and the universal salvific will of God because of who Jesus is, because He is uniquely who He is. Hence, the first specific point we have made brings us back to the central issue of the issue of Jesus' divine Sonship, an issue which has continually arisen and been addressed in our previous Chapters.

So far we have dealt with the "representational" aspect of Jesus only in terms of *who* He is, the God-man. But we mentioned above that the uniqueness and universality of Jesus also related to the "representational" character of His work. It was necessary to establish the first point, about *who* Jesus was, before proceeding to the present one, about *what* He did.

It is not enough simply to limit the discussion of Jesus as representational solely to the issue of His Person. That would imply that the salvation is *only* a matter of the Incarnation, that Jesus is the world's Saviour *only* because He is the Word made flesh. Such a limitation would imply that Jesus' ministry, passion, death and resurrection were really rather secondary to the business of salvation. I do not wish to leave the reader with such an impression.

The context of this essay does not require that one launch into any discussion of soteriology and its many aspects. And so I limit myself to a few remarks relative to Jesus' atoning death. The second specific point to be made is this: Jesus is uniquely and universally *the* Saviour because His death was one of universal atonement.

In a masterful essay, "The Atonement,"[10] Martin Hengel persuasively demonstrates that the affirmation of the universal, salvific atonement of Jesus' death was not something that occurred only in later New Testament times. It appears much earlier in Mark's gospel and in Paul's letters. Not only that, but such an interpretation of Jesus' death is evident even at the time of Paul's conversion. And if this were not enough, Hengel grounds the earliest Christian interpretation of Jesus' death in Jesus' own understanding of His approaching crucifixion.

The unique and universal character of Jesus' atoning death breaks through the "whole series of analogies" with atonement both in the Greco-Roman world and even in Judaism at the time of Jesus. Jesus' atoning death is both unique and universal because of its representational character. Hengel writes:

> It [Jesus' death] concerns not only the un-heard of scandal that here the Son of God died on the cross the most shameful death known to the Roman world, but also the universality of the atonement brought about by this Son, involving all men, which not only warded off the anger of God at particular misdeeds, but blotted out all human guilt and thus—as an eschatological act in the perspective of the dawning kingdom of God—reconciled the apostate creatures with their Creator.[11]

In this section and the preceding one, we have been making the point that Jesus' uniqueness and universality flow from Him as "representational." He is representational both because of *who* He is through His Incarnation, the God-man, and *what* He did through His death (and resurrection).

Regarding the former point, Hick has difficulty with Jesus' "particularity." In fact, because of the scandal of particularity, God could never become man, according to Hick. For to become man necessarily involves the taking of a concrete human nature. For Hick this is impossible for God to do. Yet this is the very affirmation of Christian faith (Phil 2:6-7). For Jesus to be "representational" of *all* mankind, He had to—or at least He did—assume the concrete nature of a servant.[12] Gomez notes: "... Jesus' universality was hidden in his *Kenotic* existence,"[13] and a little later he adds: "Christ's universality is nowhere else except in His "particularity" as a man, as a Jew, in this *concretum universale* of His unique personality."[14]

Not only is Jesus representational in the human nature He assumed. But because of universal sin and guilt, in order to be *the* Saviour of all, Jesus was humbler yet; He voluntarily submitted to the fate which enslaved all people (Phil 2: 7-8; 2 Cor 5:21). Therefore, Jesus is also uniquely and universally representational in the salvation He brought. And as Hengel has demonstrated, Jesus Himself understood His own death in this unique, universal and representational way.[15] This self-understanding by Jesus of His own death relates to His wider self-understanding as *the eschatological* prophet. Jesus' uniqueness and universality are grounded in the eschatological nature of His mission, a mission that reached its fulfillment not simply in spite of His atoning death, but because of it.[16]

By this voluntary obedience and vicarious service, Jesus gives all humanity a new beginning.[17] His death, as it were, swallows up death. Jesus' death, as we have seen, was for all people (Heb 2:9-11), and as such it established a new covenant with God.[18] Jesus is not simply a member of mankind, although He is that. He is the beginning of a new humanity (Rom 5:12-21; 1 Cor 15:45-7). It is Jesus' mission, grounded in who He is, that is at the heart of Jesus's uniqueness and universality.

It is because Jesus is unique in precisely the way He is claimed to be, that He can simultaneously be universal. Any reduced claim about

Jesus' uniqueness, would make universality only metaphoric. This is Hick's shortcoming. By claiming Jesus is not radically unique, Hick logically concludes there is a conflict regarding His universality. But our response is not simply that Jesus is some kind of "great exception," but that He is unique because He constitutes a new beginning for the entire human race. This "new beginning" was present in the initial stages of Christian faith, and grounded, as we have seen, in Jesus' own self-consciousness as *the eschatological* prophet. And this self-consciousness of Jesus understood that the kingdom of God was to come *through* His own death and vindication.[19]

There is still a further aspect implied in Hick's argument which must be met. Hick maintains that Jesus cannot be the world's unique Saviour because, if salvation comes only through Jesus, then people of other religions who do not know Him, or who do not accept Him as God's ultimate Saviour-Revealer, cannot be saved. Since God wills their salvation too, Hick concludes that Jesus cannot be *the* Saviour.

The problem here is that Hick allows for only one alternative: *either* Jesus is *the* Saviour and only Christians are saved, *or* non-Christians are saved as well as Christians and therefore Jesus cannot be *the* Saviour. But since the former violates God's universal salvific will, then the latter is the only possible option.

This limited dichotomy, which relates to Hick's Copernican Revolution, is unhelpful because it aims to resolve the difficulty by dispensing with one aspect of the truth. That is, Hick cannot see any alternative to either Jesus being *the* Saviour or non-Christians reaching salvation through their own religion. Either one or the other.

But is this dichotomy legitimate? True, it may be more difficult to find a solution to the problem by maintaining *both* Jesus as *the* Saviour *and* salvation of non-Christians even through, and not just in spite of, their religion. But that is no reason for declaring such a possibility inadmissible from the outset. There is no reason why there cannot be a third question or possibility: How is God's offer of universal salvation in Jesus Christ made available to people who do not acknowledge Christ's claims?[20]

Scripture itself affirms *both* the unique mediatorship of Jesus *and* the universal salvific will of God. In fact, both occur at one point in the same passage, 1 Timothy 2:1-6. Therefore, our theological thinking about any subsequent problems cannot let go of both these affirmations of faith. Because Hick finds unacceptable the problem which results from maintaining both affirmations, he concludes by dropping one of them. But such a solution is neither true to Christian faith nor to genuine theology. Ultimately, it is even arbitrary: if both God's universal salvific will and the uniqueness of Jesus as Saviour are maintained in Scripture, why drop the latter as opposed to the former?

The task before us does not involve exploring this third alternative.[21] My point is simply to indicate that Hick's dismissal of it as an unacceptable alternative, is itself unjustifiable.

Part of the reason why Hick comes up with his false dichotomy is because he has no Pneumatology.[22] For him, "Spirit" or "Holy Spirit," is just another way of talking about God's relation to the world. "Spirit" means the same kind of thing as does "Word." This terminology reveals Hick's fundamental modalism. In so doing, it also fails to distinguish the two but equal missions of the Word and Spirit in the economy of God's universal, salvific will.

My claim here regarding the uniqueness of Jesus and the salvific will of God is this: the mission of the Son is only one of the missions; there is also the mission of the Spirit. This point is important to this discussion since as Shorter writes:

The resurrection, freeing Christ's humanity from the limitations of a single lifetime, in a historical place and epoch, transformed it into a vehicle of universal salvation and released the Spirit to the whole world.[23]

God's universal salvific will involves both the mission of the Son and that of the Spirit.[24] Gomez notes that "Jesus' identity is *trinitarian*."[25] For this reason, both Gomez and Kasper opt for a "pneumatic Christology" in dealing with the uniqueness and universality of Jesus.[26] Jesus' work was unique and universal because of the uniqueness of who He was as the Word made flesh. But the mediation of the unique and universal salvation brought about by Jesus is through the power and presence of the Holy Spirit.

The mission of the Spirit did not begin with Jesus' life, death, and resurrection. It began at creation, was present in nature, civilization, jurisprudence and in all human wisdom.[27] It is the Spirit who will lead creation and history to fulfillment. He will do this by being the Spirit of the Messiah and of the Suffering Servant (Isaiah 11:2; 42:1). In the final days, the Spirit will be poured out on all peoples (Joel 2:28; Acts 2:17). The Spirit, then, is "the compendium of eschatological hope and eschatological salvation."[28] From the economic point of view, it is because the mission of the Spirit is eschatological, that that mission is so intimately connected with the eschatological mission of Jesus (Rom 8:18-30). Only in the Spirit can one proclaim "Jesus is Lord" (1 Cor 12:3).

Jesus "is different from any other bearers of the Spirit not only in degree but in kind," writes Kasper. "He [Jesus] is not simply moved by the Spirit but conceived and formed by the Spirit" (Mt 1:18, 20; Lk 1:35).[29] Jesus' mission comes under the aegis of the Spirit (Lk 4:14,18), who not only rests on Jesus, but compels Him (Mk 1:12). Jesus gives Himself on the cross to the Father "through the eternal Spirit" (Heb. 9:14) and is raised from the dead through the power of the Spirit (Rom 1:4; 8:11; 1 Tim 3:16). In as much as the Spirit brings creation and history to fulfillment, Jesus is the goal and culmination of the mission of the Spirit. In as much as the Spirit's mission is to universalize the reality of Jesus, that is, to integrate all reality into that of the risen and exalted Jesus, Jesus is the agent and starting-point of the mission of the Spirit. Kasper writes:

> Thus the Spirit is the medium and the force in which Jesus Christ as the new Lord of the world is accessible to us, and where we can know him. The Spirit is the active presence of the exalted Lord in the Church, in individual believers and in the world.[30]

The purpose of this brief elaboration on the mission of the Spirit and its relation to the mission of Jesus, is to indicate that reflection on the mission of the Spirit of Jesus Christ will be necessary in any theological thinking on the third alternative of maintaining both Jesus' uniqueness and the universal salvific will of God. Kasper writes:

> A Christology in a pneumatological perspective is therefore what best enables us to combine both the uniqueness and the universality of Jesus Christ. It can show how the spirit who is operative

in Christ in his fulness, is at work in varying degrees everywhere in the history of mankind, and also how Jesus Christ is the goal and head of all humanity.[31]

While both the missions of the Word and the Spirit are universal, it is because the mission of the Word involves becoming Incarnate that Jesus' particularity becomes a scandal. It is this historicity of the mission of the Word that Hick finds impossible to accept. And since Hick has no Pneumatology, the only solution to which he can conclude is that, to preserve God's universal salvific will, Jesus cannot be the unique Son and Saviour.

My point, however, is that salvation is Trinitarian. Kasper writes:

Salvation is participation in the life of God in the Holy Spirit through the mediation of Jesus Christ.[32]

There seems to be no scandal regarding God's universal salvific will and the mission of the Holy Spirit. Religions find it easy to speak of the presence of the Holy Spirit. It is, in fact, the mission of the Spirit that makes the Church "relatively" universal. That is, since the Spirit does not act only in the Church and in the sacraments, salvation is mediated by the Spirit outside the Church.[33] Wherever that mediation occurs, there is already, and can only be, the salvation brought in Jesus Christ.

But the mission of the Spirit is not the total economy of God's universal salvific will. It is not the total expression of God's will, simply because God chose to effect salvation also through the mission of the Word. And the Church, as the body of Christ, in its concrete historicity is the sacrament of the mission of the Word.[34] Just as Jesus in His historicity as the Word Incarnate is scandalous to those who cannot accept such a mission, so too is the mission of the Church scandalous. For by being a sacrament of the mission of the Word, the Church is also a sacrament of that scandal to the world.[35]

Kasper makes this same point. First, he notes it is the scandal of Jesus' particularity "alone which provides the assurance that God has entered into our human existence in a concrete way."[36] Then he immediately goes on to say that the "scandal of this actualness" has been imprinted on Christianity in its entirety. "That is why there is a concrete Church with concrete, binding statements and concrete, binding signs of salvation."[37]

Our point in raising this issue of the two missions is to suggest that when we speak of the "fragmentariness" of revelation/salvation in non-Christian religions, or of Christianity possessing the fullness of revelation/salvation, we are not speaking about Christianity as having more information than other religions. What we mean is that both the mission of the Word and the Spirit have reached their fulfillment—at least in terms of this world—in Christianity. The Word is fully ordered to the Spirit, and the Spirit fully ordered to the Word.

In non-Christian religions, while the mission of the Spirit is already at work, the mission of the Word in its *historicity* is to some extent still lacking.[38] That is why the mission of the Church is so crucial. Its function is to proclaim that Word to which the Spirit is ordered. Only the Church can proclaim that Word for it alone is witness to the Risen Christ who was crucified for the world's salvation. Just as the historical Jesus is a scandal to those who cannot accept Him as unique and universal Saviour, so the Church is a scandal to those who do not accept the (on-going) mission of the Word.

God's universal salvific will, then, involves both the mission of the Word and that of the Spirit. Because of the mission of the Word and Jesus' intention that that mission be continued in the Church, God's universal salvific will involves the Church as the sacrament of the world's salvation.[39] The Church is necessary for salvation[40] because she is the sacrament of the mission of the Word, which latter mission, by God's decree, is necessary for salvation. Faith and theology have to affirm both missions. Because a mystery is involved here, which should not surprise us, we must not try to "solve" the mystery by dispensing with one or other of the missions. Rather, we should allow ourselves to be drawn more deeply into the mystery, realizing that we live in the "last days" when the mission of both the Word and the Spirit are at work effecting the universal salvation willed by God. To proclaim Jesus as the unique and universal Saviour, then, is not a matter of Christian arrogance, but of humble submission to God's ways.[41]

Hick maintains that God could not have effected an historical, universal self-revelation and salvation, because communications on the globe would not have permitted its being transmitted to all peoples. Since all peoples could not have immediately known of such an event, therefore, God has not done it.

This claim is subsidiary to Hick's overall case that the historicity of the mission of the Word is unacceptable. It is unacceptable, because by being in history, the mission of the Word is subject to time in its unfolding. Of necessity, therefore, many people will be born and die without exposure to this mission. The only way Hick could accept such a mission of the Word, is if the world's telecommunications was such that as soon as God effected a complete and full self-revelation, it could be broadcast around the world at once.

As a first observation, it strikes me that presumably God knows that a mission of the Incarnate Word in its historicity will be subject to time and place. Presumably He knows, too, that the dependent mission of the Church is subject to time and place. One can hardly conclude that God is going to require the impossible from humankind for salvation. The mission of the Word, and by implication, that of the Church, is necessary for salvation. But they are not necessary is such a way that human persons could miss out on salvation precisely because of the exigencies of their creaturehood. But this is the very possibility Hick excludes from his false dichotomy.

Here Hick tries to rescue the possibility of an historic mission of the Word by suggesting that world communications would make such a mission legitimate. But if the mission has any legitimacy in its historicity at all, communications is not needed to rescue it. And if the mission of the Word has *no* legitimacy in its historicity, communications certainly cannot provide it.

Secondly, given even a universal communication system, what guarantee is there that everyone would hear the first broadcast? Perhaps someone might die before hearing it. How is Hick to account for such a person being saved? Would Hick not have to construct some "epicycles" of his own to bring such a person under the salvific will of God?

Thirdly, even without world communications, in Hick's own Christology this problem of historicity and God's universal salvific will is clearly present, and Hick does not notice it.

I refer to the fact that Hick has opted for the axial period of Karl Jaspers. During the six axial centuries, God impinged on the consciousness of certain people and groups of people in an effort to reveal Himself, if not completely, at least more fully than heretofore. Yet, even during this period of self-revelation God did not impinge Himself in this fuller way on everyone. Jaspers leaves out Africa completely in his understanding of the axial period. Hick, too, considers African religions to be among the "pre-revelation" religions.

Given Hick's constant claim that God's will is universally salvific to the point of denying the specific mission of the Son, how does Hick account for this selectivity of God's universal salvific will in his own theory? The fact is, he does not account for it. He overlooks the issue completely. There are whole groups of people, indeed whole continents, that did not benefit from the axial period. In addition the axial period involves at least six centuries—no small time period for the unfolding of revelation if one's salvation depends on it. Hick has conveniently not accounted for the salvation of those who, during that time, did not experience God impinging on their consciousness. I say "conveniently," because it would seem that to have to account for such people's salvation, Hick himself would have to resort to "epicycles."

Fourthly, although Hick talks of a self-revelation of God in the axial period, it would seem there is not really a *self*-revelation at all, not in Jesus, not in any of the founders of the world religions.[42]

Hick has claimed that Jesus, like other holy men, is simply an image or symbol of God. As such, Jesus is like a finger pointing to God. But since every culture has its own images and symbols pointing to God, all are equally relative. More important, none, including Jesus, are God. This is so for Hick, as we have seen, for two reasons: (1) from Kant, God is the noumenon, unknowable in Himself, known only through the phenomenon or symbols and images; (2) from Hinduism and certain Christian mystics, the Absolute God is simply beyond being addressed and named.

If none of the images or symbols are God, then only these *images* are the "Thou" of man's address. In the dialogue between God and man, it is in fact not God at all who is dialoguing. It is only the images or symbols of God that are in dialogue with man. Gomez points out, with reference to Joseph Ratzinger, that such a position is really the basis of polytheism.[43] Gomez writes:

By making Christ a finger pointing to God who alone is the absolute mystery beyond the symbol, we empty the *reality* of Jesus Christ. We can accept a "symbolic distance" of Jesus from God, but not a *real* one.[44]

Reconciliation and Deification

The second of Hick's two subsidiary theological arguments relates to the Christian experience of reconciliation. He maintains that it was mainly the Christian experience of reconciliation with God that contributed to the deification of Jesus. We recall from Chapter 3 that Hick claimed that in the Christian experience of God's forgiveness through Jesus, the early Church began to think of Jesus' death as an atonement. From there it was just a matter of concluding that in order for His death to be sufficient for human sin, Jesus Himself must have been divine.

We have already addressed throughout our preceding evaluative Chapters, the wider and more basic issue of the deification of Jesus, and so we do not need to repeat ourselves here. The assumption behind this present argument, as always with Hick, is that Jesus is not who He is claimed to be, nor who He Himself implicitly revealed Himself to be.

It is true that the Christian community experienced reconciliation with God through Jesus' forgiveness of sins during His earthly life. It is true that it interpreted His death as universal atonement, as Hick suggests. But that interpretation was not an inflated one, but a genuine interpretation about what really happened. Christians experienced Jesus as the agent of the divine power to forgive sins. Jesus, too, understood Himself as such an agent of that divine power (Mt 9:2ff; Mk 2:5ff; Lk 5:20ff.) There was no inflated interpretation going beyond what the experience involved. Rather, it was the only accurate interpretation that accounted for the full fact of what was experienced. John L. McKenzie writes:

The essential difference between the OT and the NT conceptions lies in the fact that in the NT forgiveness of sins comes through Christ (AA 13:38; Eph 1:7; Col 1:14; 1 Jn 2:12). The forgiveness of sins comes through Christ not only by his own personal forgiveness ... but is also gained through his redeeming death.[45]

In addition, Hick gives the impression that the interpretation of Jesus' death as universal atonement occurred to the Christian community only some time after the event. That is, the original experience did not carry such a meaning.

But as we have already seen in this Chapter[58], that understanding of Hick's is simply incorrect. Hengel has pointed out with care and caution, that in fact the interpretation of Jesus' death as universal atonement was already part of the original experience. He writes:

> It was not primarily their own theological reflections, but above all the interpretive sayings of Jesus at the Last Supper which showed them how to understand his death properly. As a saying of Jesus, Mark 10:45 probably also belongs in the context of that last night; ...[46]

Finally, if Hick's position were true that the early Church deified Jesus, the Christian community would have been guilty of idolatry. With the strong Jewish roots of the early disciples, it is hard to accept they could engage in such a process without being aware that that was what they were doing, and without some of their number objecting. It is, therefore, difficult to believe that given the disciples' monotheism regarding God's holiness, that the early Christian community would have opted to deify a man. Such a movement would have been so foreign to them, and so dangerous socially, one cannot imagine it really happening. And for the deification process to have happened so quickly and so easily within the community, makes Hick's position look all the more untenable. There is needed a religious experience of a far more significant and unique variety than Hick allows for in order to account for the faith of the early Christians.

The disciples and the early Church did not experience God forgiving sins simply *through* Jesus. Rather they experienced Jesus freely and of His own authority exercising the divine power of forgiveness, even universally so in His atoning death.

Language

The second of Hick's subordinate themes which we examine in this

Chapter is multiple, but this multiplicity can be grouped under the heading of Language. At first it may appear to be a whole new set of claims. In fact, however, it is simply a re-statement of positions we have already treated.

At the end of Chapter 3 we summarized Hick's points on the issue of language as follows:

(a) The language of divine Incarnation is mythological language. The notion of Incarnation is itself a natural metaphor. The doctrine of the Incarnation is a myth adopted by the early Christians because of similar notions in their environment. (b) The language about Jesus has an "absolute" or "total" quality because God is involved when one experiences Jesus. The resultant language is the language of love, the language of total commitment, but not necessarily of objective exclusivity.

Based on the above summary, there are three questions we must address: (1) Why is the language about Jesus' Incarnation not mythological language? (2) Did Christianity adopt the language of divine Incarnation from its environment? (3) Is the language of Jesus' Incarnation simply a subjective statement of commitment? Questions 1 and 3 are closely related, and so we shall treat them together. It may be beneficial, therefore, to deal with the second question first.

We have already encountered this question earlier in Chapter 4 where we evaluated Hick's arguments on the Scriptural langauge of divine Sonship. We saw that, for Hick, the origins of the Christian doctrine of the Incarnation were simply that of general mythological language, in particular, the General Redeemer Myth. The Christians simply picked up the language from their environment, says Hick.

My response claimed, among other things, that the Gnostic Redeemer Myth could only be traced back to the second century. It was in fact the Christian doctrine of the Incarnation, misunderstood and misapplied, which was one of the factors in giving rise to the Gnostic myth. We saw, too, that Jesus was in fact not the Incarnation of a divine being.

I need only re-state my position again: there is simply no good evidence that the early Christian Church reached its affirmation of the

Incarnation of Jesus because of similar ideas in its environment. The notion of a god descending from heaven to earth to become a human being to bring mankind salvation—especially by dying on a cross—was quite outside the religious thinking of the times.[47]

We now turn to what were our questions 1 and 3.

The answer to both questions is the same. The language of Jesus' Incarnation is not mythological, and therefore not simply a subjective statement about the significance of one's religious commitment. Christian faith claims that the events it affirms did happen literally and objectively. The meaning of faith's language is not metaphorical or non-literal as Hick would have us believe. It is this particular point that Shorter picks up in responding to Hick on this issue. He writes:

Quite apart from the fact that the doctrine of the incarnation is logically and chronologically secondary to the experience of Jesus of Nazareth as God in the evolution of Christology, Hick's view bristles with unacceptable assumptions. The most basic one concerns the relationship between poetic or metaphorical meaning and 'literal' or non-metaphorical meaning.[48]

Shorter's critique is that Hick has separated interpretation from experience. Hick claims the Christian interpretation cannot be literal because the experience could not be what it is claimed to be. Therefore, the language about that experience can only be non-literal or mythological. Shorter replies that in fact the Christian interpretation is an interpretation of what was experienced. The original objective experience already contained its objective interpretation. Shorter writes:

... interpretation is dovetailed with experience. Poetic meaning may not be palpable to our material senses, nor need it be scientifically demonstrable, but to limit it to a mere interest, a 'devotion' or a 'commitment' is to deny to artists, writers and musicians any capacity to convey true meaning through the exercise of the creative imagination.[49]

Shorter's point is that the language of faith and hope and love may very well be a language of symbol. But, as we have already seen, Hick has an impoverished notion of symbol. For Hick, symbol simply points to something that it is not. For Shorter, and others, there is a "symbolic meaning" which displays truth more clearly in all its richness.[50] Even if Revelation makes use of secular metaphor, it gives these metaphors whole new meaning. This is what happened with Revelation in Jesus Christ.[51] Because there is a noetic characteristic to this kind of symbol, the language of faith is not simply the language of subjective commitment. It is also a truth-claim. This type of symbol conveys, therefore, literal meaning.[52]

It is true that the language of faith is the language of love. It is the language of response to God's self-revelation. It may even be the language of symbol. But faith statements also make a claim about what is objectively true independent of the knower. They make a claim about who God is and what He has done.[53]

For this reason, Hick's comparison of faith statements with the statement "My Helen is the most beautiful girl in the world," simply is not a valid one. The latter is *not* a faith statement.[54] Thus, it may very well not be able to make any objectively unique claims about Helen, except in a non-literal, "mythological" way. Faith-statements, on the other hand, are a different kind of affirmation.[71] They not only express confidence and commitment, but they also constitute an objective confession of truth.[55]

Hick has made the fundamental error of opposing the Jesus of history with the Christ of faith. He sees an unbridgeable rupture between the historical Jesus and the Christ of Christian faith. He can find no continuity between the disciples' relationship with Jesus and their faith in Him before His death and resurrection, and their relationship and faith after those events. This is especially interesting, if somewhat odd, since Hick does not accept the traditional faith in Jesus' resurrection. What should provide the basis of such a "rupture" is in fact so evacuated of radical content, that one wonders how Hick could maintain the gap to be so wide. Nevertheless, he does.

Hick seems to be unaware of the work of such scholars as Joachim Jeremias,[56] Ernst Käsemann,[57] Günther Bornkamm,[58] Heinz Schürmann,[59] Birgery Gerhardsson[60] to mention only a few.[61] This may be why Hick still lingers in "the mists of critical uncertainty."[62] As René Latourelle has persuasively demonstrated, contemporary scholarship, without denigrating the uniqueness of the resurrection, has established the continuity between Jesus and the pre-paschal community, the post-paschal oral tradition and the tradition of the evangelists.[63] This continuity is not just a sociological continuity, but a continuity of meaning and faith. This continuity is grounded in the continuity of the Jesus of history and the Christ of faith. As Shorter writes: "The Jesus of history is already an object of faith."[64]

The Christian faith rests on a revelation that took place in and through the historical life, death and resurrection of Jesus of Nazareth. This full Christ-event already contained the truth of its meaning, a meaning that would be affirmed in faith and developed in theology. It is for this reason that the language of Jesus' Incarnation is not mythological, and that it does affirm the objective truth about the uniqueness of Jesus as the world's Saviour.

Epistemology

Since this essay is in the field of theology, it would be out of place to engage in a lengthy critique of Hick's epistemology. But Chapter 2, did present as part of the context of Hick's Christology, an account of his epistemology of religion. I wish to make only one observation on that issue here. Hick's epistemology is grounded in Kant. God-in-Himself is unknowable, the divine noumenon. God as experienced by human beings is knowable, but only through phenomena. One of these phenomena is Jesus. Another would be the Buddha. We have already considered the theological implications of this epistemology. In this section I wish to make only one point regarding the Kantian basis of Hick's epistemology.

I focus on the distinction between the thing-in-itself and the thing-as-it-appears as understood in the Kantian system.

This distinction arises in Kant from his confusion of two types of knowing: (1) the complex dynamic process of human knowing which experiences, understands and judges, and (2) the extroverted, biological or animal "knowing" which simply experiences something as "already out there now real"[65] Both types of knowing occur in man, although only the first type is genuine human knowing.

Kant is aware that the second type is not genuine human knowing; but he ends up defending some qualified version of it as though it were such.[66] This unfortunate compromise results from Kant's failure to correctly isolate that component in the dynamism of human knowing called "judging." Judgment does not occur on the level of extroverted knowing. Rather, it is part, indeed a crucially constitutive part of the dynamic process of genuine human knowing.[67] That dynamism goes beyond the question for intelligence, i.e., beyond "What is it?" to the question for judgment, "Is it true: yes or no?"[68]

Judgment has its own set of conditions to be fulfilled before it can decide positively or negatively. It aims not at description, that is, not at things as they appear to the knower. It aims at things in themselves. Judgment intends what is true, what is real. Its object is not phenomena but being. Or, to put it another way, judgment intends things-in-themselves and has its own criteria for deciding when things-in-themselves, and not just things-as-appearances, have been reached.

The object of judgment is a "thing;" the object of extroverted, animal knowing is a "body."[69] Bodies can be related to as real. For example, the cat recognizes the dish of milk as real and drinks it. But the cat does not *know* the milk as real, as something intelligently grasped and reasonably affirmed. For the cat, the milk is a body and not a thing.

But in human knowing, the body becomes a thing. That is, it can not only be related to as real, it can be *known* as real: it can be intelligently grasped and reasonably affirmed.

For Kant, the unknowable thing-in-itself (i.e., "body") is claimed to exist because of our extroverted stance to the real. But since the "body" in extroverted knowing is not known by intelligent grasp and reasonable affirmation, Kant assumes it is not known by such a process even in genuine human knowing. That is why the thing-in-itself is a noumenon.

If the thing-in-itself is not knowable, we must ask: what, for Kant, is knowable? What is knowable is merely the effect of the stimulation which the "body" produces on the mind, namely the appearances. Judgment for Kant simply regulates concepts as they operate under the governance of the categories.

What Kant has done in declaring that only appearances are knowable, is to switch from one way of knowing to the other. He has switched from knowing as taking a good look, to knowing as experiencing, understanding and judging. In the former, extroverted

299

knowing, Kant affirms that the thing-in-itself exists but it is unknowable. Then, unaware, he switches to the latter, to genuine human knowing, where he maintains that the thing-in-itself is still unknowable; only the appearances are knowable. But in genuine human knowing the thing-in-itself *is* knowable.

Kant has made his switch without knowing that in fact that is what he has done. This switch is evidence that Kant is not correctly cognitionally grounded. If he were, he would recognize that in the operations of cognition there is no evidence for assuming that the operation of judging intends only appearances.

More to the point, Kant would claim that his description of human cognition is in fact true. That is, Kant intends his description of human cognition not to be just an account of how cognition *appears.* Rather, he intends it as an account of *human-cognition-in-itself.* As such, he is claiming to have reached at least one thing-in-itself, namely, human cognition.

But Kant can reach a knowledge of human cognition only by an exercise of human cognition. Thus, by claiming that he is giving a true account of human cognition, he is in effect saying that what human cognition intends and achieves is the thing-in-itself—and not just its appearance. Then, having reached human-cognition-in-itself by an exercise of human cognition, Kant declares, quite irrationally, that human cognition cannot reach things-in-themselves, only the appearances of things. Thus, Kant's account does not square with his practice. He says he is doing one thing when he knows, when in fact he is doing something different.

What accounts for human cognition being able to reach the thing-in-itself is the role of judgment on the third level of human consciousness. Judgment decides if the insight into the original appearance is in fact true. Thus, it yields up the thing-in-itself. The phenomena are only that, phenomena or data. By means of insight into the phantasm which is into the phenomenon, a tentative explanation of the thing-in-itself—not just of the phenomenon—is proposed. Then judgment is called into play to decide whether this particular insight is in fact true. The distinction between thing-in-itself and its appearance is not the unbridgeable gap that Kant claims it is.

Therefore, for Hick to apply this particular epistemology to Christology is already misleading and indeed erroneous. But that is what he has done. Hick's epistemological claim is that we cannot know God-in-Himself because we cannot know anything in-itself. His position is that God is the noumenon, unknowable in Himself, and Jesus is the—or more accurately—*one* phenomenon of God.[70]

True, God is unknowable in Himself unless He chooses to make Himself known. True, too, Jesus makes the Father visible (Jn 14:9; He is the image of the unseen God (cf. Col 1:15; 2 Cor 4:4). But if God chooses to reveal Himself fully, God can be known in-Himself, even if only as ultimate Triune mystery. Our point is simply the epistemological one that human cognition is not prevented from reaching the mystery of God-in-Himself on the grounds it can reach nothing at all in-itself.[71]

What the judgment of faith proclaims is an "in-itself" regarding God: namely, Jesus is the full self-revelation of God. My point, again, is simply epistemological: that the affirmation of faith can (and does) give us truth about God, and not just about images of God. One cannot argue against the uniqueness of Jesus on the grounds of Kant's epistemology.

Copernican Revolution

As with the foregoing issue of epistemology, the present topic, the Copernican revolution in theology, formed part of our elaboration of the context of Hick's Christology. As context, it belongs to what we have called "secondary claims." But the idea of a Copernican revolution is something of a hallmark of Hick's theology of religions. Because it is the Copernican revolution which grounds the theocentric model, and thus raises "the Christological question," something needs to be said about it.

The use of this particular model, Copernican revolution, is somewhat seductive in its attraction. Drawn from the realm of science, it carries the authority of having represented a major breakthrough in the understanding of the motion of planetary bodies. It reveals the triumph of a new insight over weighted, archaic thinking. Those who found themselves arguing against the scientific Copernican revolution found themselves arguing against the truth.

The implication behind Hick's call for a Copernican revolution in theology is that if one does not accept it, one might end up in a similar position. Further, the use of the paradigm shift of a Copernican revolution in theology seems to bear some important relevance to the situation of world religions, especially to the Christian claim that Jesus is at the centre of all salvation. Religions appear to think out of Ptolemaic models. Attempts to account for salvation outside the Church, may seem at first blush to constitute the kind of epicycles Hick claims they are. A Copernican Revolution in theology presents itself as the breakthrough required.

My response is that Hick's particular understanding and use of the Copernican revolution, and the resultant theocentric model, does not constitute in theology the same kind of breakthrough which it did in science. The reason is because Jesus is precisely what Christian faith claims He is.

It goes without saying, of course, God is at the centre of all salvation. To speak of salvation is already, and can only be, to speak of a theocentric model of world religions. In that sense, Hick is simply affirming the truth. But to say God is at the centre of salvation does not say anything about *how* God has effected or is effecting that salvation. Here is where Hick misses the point. While he could accept the mission of the Spirit, although not in a Trinitarian sense, he finds the mission of the Incarnate Son too much of a stumbling block. He cannot accept that God has made Himself the centre of salvation through the historically specific mission of the Incarnate Son.[72]

But the significance of the Christian claim is that Jesus is at the centre of salvation because God has put Him there.[73] And God has put Him there, because Jesus is in fact, the Word of God made flesh. It is precisely because of Jesus' uniqueness that He is the centre of salvation. Being at the centre of salvation does not displace God and push Him off to the side or relegate Him to some remote area. God has chosen to be at the centre of salvation through two missions, the mission of the Word and the mission of the Spirit. Since the mission of the Word involved entering human history, God has made Himself the centre of salvation within human history through the mission of the Incarnate Word.

When Christians believe and proclaim such a mystery, it is not out of group pride, but out of humble acknowledgment and praise of what God in fact has done. The mission of the Church, as we have already seen, is to be the historical on-going mission of the Son. The Church's mission is to bear witness to, and so to continue, the mission of the Word in the world under the same conditions the Son Himself carried out that mission during His earthly life. To accept the mission of the Church is to accept the Son (Lk 10:16). And to accept the Son is to accept the One who sent Him (Mk 9:37; Lk 10:16; Jn 5:19-47; 6:28-40; 12:44-50; 13:19-20; 14:7 etc). It is to accept that human salvation is not effected only by the mission of the Spirit, but also by the completely unexpected mission of the Son. Just as the mission of the Son was misunderstood, resisted and even rejected, the Church should not be surprised that its own mission is met with a similar response (Mt 10:22,24-5; Jn 15:18-16:4).

In as much as Hick uses the Copernican revolution to argue against the divinity of Jesus and His uniqueness in salvation, then that model, unlike its scientific original, is not the helpful breakthrough that is required.[74] It fails to do justice to the whole truth of God's salvific work.

The most important criticism to be brought against the use of the Copernican revolution in theology is that it grounds methodologically Hick's false dichotomy of *either/or*. It reduces the possible alternatives in a Christian theology of world religions to *either* an exaggerated exclusivist position *or* Hick's own extreme relativism. Duncan Forrester says the either/or method of Hick's Copernican revolution allows him

... to reject out of hand and without discussion the varying attempts to formulate a christocentric theology of religions.[75]

This either/or method of Hick's, which pervades all his Christological thought, is simply unfaithful to the full Christian tradition. This tradition is far more nuanced in holding in a balanced tension the two faith-affirmations: Jesus is the unique Saviour of the world, and God's will is universally salvific. The Christian tradition constitutes a *both/and* approach. This tradition may make thinking about the divine mystery more difficult, and indeed may mean that no ultimately neat construct can be wrought where everything fits tidily. Nevertheless, it is far better to acknowledge the truth that God's foolishness is wiser than human wisdom (1 Cor 1:25), than to assume that a finite intelligence can come up with a scheme that explains away the unfathomable mystery.[76]

This criticism of Hick's Copernican revolution in theology is picked up by J. Lipner who writes:

> Further, it does not follow from the affirmation of the uniqueness of Christ that all non-Christians are either damned or rejected by an omnipotent and loving God, as Professor Hick seems to think.[77]

In another article Lipner argues that this false dichotomy of Hick's is "basically incoherent and misleading," and that the project of constructing a Christian theology of world religions does not resolve itself into "a simple either/or issue."[78]

Similarly, Gavin D'Costa asks:

> ... what justification is there, in the first place, for Hick's either/or choice between the Ptolemaic and the Copernican views? Has he demonstrated the necessity of a Copernican revolution?[79]

D'Costa notes that Hick reduces the possible solutions to only two: (1) an obviously unacceptable alternative, and (2) his [Hick's] own reasonable one. All other positions are mere "epicycles" to the unacceptable alternative. While this reduction is a convenient way of dismissing the opposition, it is simply not faithful to all the data at hand. Further, Hick's account that the Christian "Ptolemaic" view consigned all non-Christians to damnation, is certainly not an accurate statement of the mainline traditional Christian viewpoint.

D'Costa points out that Hick has nowhere made any attempt to investigate the context of meaning of the "fixed point," as Hick calls it, of Christian Ptolemaic theology: namely, of the Christian axiom: *extra ecclesiam nulla salus*. D'Costa writes that Hick:

> ... neglects both its [the axiom's] development and context and thereby unintentionally distorts its meaning.[80]

Hick's error lies in assuming that the exaggerated exclusivist view is and had has always been the true Christian position. Forrester writes:

... it is not only surprising but sad that he [Hick] can produce a stereotype of 'Ptolemaic theology' which is as much a travesty of the Christian tradition as was J.A.T. Robinson's assertion that most people think of God as 'an old man in the sky.[81]

Hick unnecessarily links the definitive status of Christ with the erroneous restriction of grace and salvation exclusively to Christians. This inaccurate linkage allows Hick, of course, to view any attempts to modify the "Ptolemaic" position only as artificial additions or "epicycles."

While it is true that *extra ecclesiam nulla salus* has been affirmed at times in an exaggerated form, such an interpretation is never the whole story and has been rejected for precisely that reason.[82] It is simply not the case that the Christian tradition has taught that God's saving grace can be experienced only within the borders of the visible Church. As one argument to this effect, D'Costa points to the Patristic notion that the community of the elect dates back to the beginning of the human race. He refers to Augustine, Justin, Ireneus, Origen, Eusebius, Jerome and Ambrosiaster. The subsequent, so-called "epicycles," therefore, are not attempts to cover up an embarrassing error, but represent continuing efforts to keep in tact the whole mystery which is "ever ancient, ever new." The contemporary theological thinking about the religious and salvific value of non-Christian religions is "not so much a Copernican revolution as a recovery of fundamental Christian insights."[83]

By his label "epicycle," Hick has mistakenly simplified an important middle ground in the theology of religions. He has failed to appreciate the "via media" between what he calls a Ptolemaic theology and his own Copernican position. Lipner writes:

It is quite unjustified then for Professor Hick to criticize current attempts as the reworking of new epicycles into tired dogmas. What has changed is not the basic understanding of the traditional dictum ... but the implications of its scope and range.[84]

The notion of "epicycle" prejudices Hick's basic arguments because it assumes the current theological context resembles accurately enough the original scientific context so that the same fundamental dynamic is at stake. But, in fact, as we have just seen, Hick has to distort the full Christian tradition in order to make the notion of "epicycle" appear to fit.[85]

Hick's either/or ultimatum is meant to eliminate any middle ground as a valid alternate position.[86] But as Peter Schineller has demonstrated, this false dichotomy is simply not the case. In a helpful article "Christ and Church: a Spectrum of Views," Schineller uncovers "four exclusive, noncomplementary positions on the extent to which Jesus Christ is Saviour for all mankind."[87] The first position corresponds to Hick's false portrayal of the mainline Christian tradition. Schineller calls it the "Ecclesiocentric universe, exclusive Christology" position. The fourth position reflects Hick's own extreme relativism: "Theocentric universe, nonnormative Christology."

In between these two extreme positions, Schineller discerns *two* other moderate positions: (1) "Christocentric universe, inclusive Christology," and (2) "Theocentric universe, Normative Christology." For the first of these two positions, Christ is "constitutive" of salvation; for the second, Christ is "normative."[88] For the first, the Church is seen: (1) by some, as also constitutive for salvation, although non-Christians do not have to explicitly join the Church to be saved; (2) by others, as a "privileged mediator of salvation." For the second position, the Church is less important as a mediator of salvation.

My task has not been to enter into an analysis of Schineller's four positions. I wish only to indicate once again, that Hick's call for a Copernican revolution in theology is not the only alternative to a "Ptolemaic" theology. Indeed, given the Church's full affirmation of the mystery of salvation, there may very well be *two* reputable alternatives to the dichotomy which Hick has set up.

To claim that these two alternatives are only epicycles of Schineller's first position is to miss the major distinction between the first position and that of the second and third. The first eliminates from the mystery the affirmation that God's grace is operative outside the visible Church. The second and third positions, however, consider that affirmation, along with the uniqueness of Jesus, to be constitutive to any theology of salvation and of world religions.

These latter two positions are not epicycles since the first position does not reflect the basic fullness of the mystery to begin with. Rather, it *eliminates* part of the mystery and only then proceeds to build its conclusions. The second and third positions start with the whole mystery. They do not ground themselves in the first position at all and only then try to doctor it up. They reject its starting point as being seriously incomplete. Hence, they are not "epicycles." Rather, they are independent positions based on a different, since complete, foundation.

Thus, Hick's own position, which has misread the second and third positions, reacts to the first extreme position thinking it is the Church's "real" position. Finding that first position unacceptable, Hick creates his own. But he goes to the other extreme and rejects the uniqueness of Jesus. Thus, Hick's conclusions are analogously as one-sided and distorted as are those of the first position. He, too, is only dealing with part of the mystery. The call for a Copernican revolution, therefore, is invalid since the very basis on which it is constructed is not the whole mystery to be considered. Whatever the contemporary solution is to a deeper understanding of the mystery, it is not the Copernican revolution or the theocentric model as understood by Hick.

Divine Inhistorisation and *Homoagape*

In place of "divine Incarnation" and "homoousios," Hick suggests that Christians should proclaim "divine inhistorisation" and "*homoagape*." It is to this alternative that we now turn our attention.

Before responding, it may be helpful to recall the basic position Hick is recommending we adopt. Because, according to Hick, the notion of "divine Incarnation" is mythological, and because "homoousios" is meaningless to the contemporary mind, Hick proposes we speak of "divine inhistorisation," and of Jesus as being "*homoagape*" with God.

"Divine inhistorisation" overcomes the image of Jesus as being "a meteor falling from above." "*Homoagape*" indicates Jesus' attitude towards people was numerically identical with God's.

Hick believes his alternative overcomes the mythological notions of Nicea's affirmation while maintaining the significance of its intent.

The point behind Hick's use of the term *inhistorisation* is to indicate that God's action in human history through Christ, was not *external* to that history but from *within* that history. Hick contends that "Incarnation" does not carry such a notion.

Certainly a *mythological* understanding of "divine Incarnation" does not carry such a meaning. But this mythical understanding is *not* the meaning of the Christian doctrine of the Incarnation of the Word. Nevertheless, this mythological meaning is the one Hick attributes to the Christian doctrine, and against which he proposes his alternative. In other words, Hick has set up a straw meaning. What he subsequently knocks down is not the *Christian* doctrine of the Incarnation.

For example, the Christian doctrine has never proclaimed nor understood the doctrine of the Incarnation as "the eternal Logos descending into a temporary envelope of flesh," or that Jesus was a "divine substance injected into a human frame," or that the Word being made flesh was "like a meteor falling from above." These are Hick's mistaken notions. If Hick's understanding of the Christian mystery were accurate, he would see that the true doctrine proclaims that God has acted *within* human history in a far deeper and more radical way than ever Hick's "inhistorized homoagape" could ever permit.[89]

If we ask Hick what precisely Jesus inhistorises, he would answer: it is not really "He," i.e., the person of Jesus, who inhistorises anything. It is Jesus' *attitude* towards people which inhistorises God's *attitude*. It is God's *Agape*, i.e., "compassion and concern," inhistorising itself as Jesus' *agape*, i.e., "compassion and concern." The person of Jesus is merely the vehicle to provide the possibility of God's *Agape* being inhistorised as a human *agape*.

At times Hick's language can almost sound orthodox.[90] In some cases *as far as it goes* and out of context, it might not immediately appear as unsound.[91] Yet, one does not have to probe deeply to discover that, in fact, his meaning is not faithful.

First, I do not agree with Hick's notion that God is an operation not a nature.[92] To some extent this distinction reflects Hick's Kantian epistemology. God-in-Himself, His nature, is unknowable. What is knowable is God as He appears in relation to men, that is, God as operation. But at this point Hick goes even further, as he claims there is no "nature" to God at all; He is only operation. Does this mean that God-in-Himself is operation? If so, how does Hick claim to know that, since God-in-Himself is unknowable? Alternately, if there is a God-in-Himself beyond God-as-operation, how does Hick know that God-in-Himself is not a nature?

It is difficult to know in Hick's thought whether God's *Agape is* God, or is to be considered a quality or attribute of God in such way that it is not to be identified with God Himself. It seems that Hick does opt for the latter since *Agape*, as he defines it, is an external relation. If this is so, Hick violates the simplicity of God. There is no self-revelation of God, only a revelation of aspects or attributes of God, and one can never be certain that these aspects, including *Agape* reflect God-in-Himself.

Further, Hick's choice of God as operation mistakenly thinks of God's nature or substance as static. Hick occasionally refers to substance as "a lump." In order to have a dynamic God, Hick believes God as operation and love must *replace* notions of substance and nature. But this only indicates Hick's failure to understand the notion of God as "pure act," as well as his failure to understand that in the Christian tradition to say "God is love" is an affirmation of the unfathomable mystery of God's freedom.

Secondly, I find objectionable the lack of human integrity Hick's *homoagape* introduces into Jesus. Hick says that Jesus' *agape* is numerically identical with God's *Agape*. That is, there is a "continuous event" of God's *Agape* as it inhistorises itself as Jesus' *agape*. Jesus' *agape* is not *like* God's *Agape*; it *is* God's *Agape*. Hick is very clear about this [GUF,159]. Therefore, Jesus' "compassion and concern" were not a human compassion and concern, but a divine one. Thus, and very important, Jesus is not fully human because He does not have *human* compassion and concern.

Hick states clearly that Jesus had only one nature, and that was wholly human. Hick also writes that Jesus had only one will, and that was wholly human. And, says Hick, Jesus had only one *agape*—but that was "wholly God" [GUF,159]! It seems that Hick has tried to maintain the divine operation in Jesus by having it replace a human operation. This is not unlike early Christological heresies maintaining Jesus did not have a human soul because the Logos took over its operations (Apollinarianism).[93] Or that Jesus did not have a human will because it was taken over by the divine will (Monothelitism).[94] None of this is surprising, of course, given Hick's monophysitism.[95]

Now Hick argues that Jesus did not have a human *agape* because the divine *Agape* takes it over in Jesus' human nature. Jesus has become an *altertium quid*. Most of the human Jesus is human, but a part of Him is not human because it is numerically identical with God as *Agape*. On the other hand, one could say Hick is a neo-Nestorian claiming there is a fundamental division of two subjects in Jesus, rather than a unity. The human subject performs all operations except those which fall under "compassion and concern." These latter are the operations of the God as *Agape*. It is odd indeed, that Hick who wishes to affirm only the humanity of Jesus, ends up, in his efforts to maintain some divine action in Jesus, claiming that Jesus was not fully human. This is hardly an improvement over traditional Christology.

Thirdly, I disagree with Hick's claim that the "is" formula regarding Jesus' humanity and divinity cannot have any unique meaning. We have already given our response to this in our Chapter 7, under the section "Logical Contradiction?"

Fourthly, I find confusing Hick's argument that Jesus' *agape* while truly and numerically identical with God's *Agape* is only a part, a cross-section of that *Agape*. This position reflects Hick's difficulty in viewing the infinite in juxtaposition with the finite. It also stems from Hick's misunderstanding of the Christian notion of the Incarnation.

The Word is not a *part* of God, nor did the Word cease being infinite God when He took to Himself a human nature. It is this notion that Jesus expresses "without remainder" the self-revelation of God, that Hick cannot accept. Ironically what follows for Hick in formulating his own position, is that he ends up trying to make sense of a mythological way of thinking of which he thought he had rid himself. He in fact is more mythological than he realizes.

Fifthly, I find odd Hick's final inconsistency. He began by claiming that divine Incarnation is mythological, that it explains nothing because it has no literal content. His own divine inhisorisation of God's *Agape* was meant to make sense for a contemporary mind what the doctrine is really all about. Then Hick concludes by saying that *homoagape* does not explain anything either. In fact, he states that the claim that Jesus is *homoagape* with God is just as mythological as that of *homoousios* [GUF,165]. Presumably, this means that Hick's position has no literal content either. If that is so, it can only be arbitrary to say it is preferable over *homoousios*.

Finally, what I find unacceptable is Hick's contention that his alternative of *homoagape* "reformulates the doctrine of the Incarnation in its full traditional meaning" [GUF,ix]. The traditional doctrine affirmed the mystery of Jesus' full humanity and full divinity in the unity of a single subject. Hick has not done this. Rather, he has denied both the full divinity of Jesus, and as we have just seen, he has also denied in effect His full humanity. There could be nothing *further* from the traditional meaning of the doctrine of the Incarnation than Hick's proposal.[96]

Resurrection of Jesus

Hick's treatment of the resurrection of Jesus is subordinate to his main claims. He sees it simply as a brief digression within his general discussion of deification. Hick's point is that Jesus' resurrection does not prove His divinity. It did not do so for the disciples, and certainly does not do so for the modern mind.

First, it is true that the resurrection does not *prove* the divinity of Jesus. But here we again come up against one of Hick's fundamental mistaken assumptions. He assumes that the Christ-event is only the historical life and (non-atoning) death of Jesus. He fails to see that the resurrection forms part of the revelation of Jesus. The Christ-event includes the resurrection of Jesus, and it is in the *whole* event that one is invited to believe. The resurrection of Jesus is not a datum outside the Christ-event meant to prove the content of Christian faith prior to the resurrection. The resurrection, however, does vindicate Jesus in His claims as "eschatological prophet" and "beloved Son," the uniqueness of which claims were already present in His earthly ministry and even more deeply revealed in His death.

Secondly, Hick too much underplays what can be said about the resurrection.[98] Christian tradition has never claimed, as Hick mistakenly writes, that the limits of the interpretation of Jesus' resurrection lie between (1) the resuscitation of Jesus' corpse, and (2) visions of the Lord in resplendent glory [MGI,170].

Traditional Christian faith has never held that Jesus' resurrection was the resuscitation of His corpse. Hick frequently speaks of Jesus' "physical" resurrection. The proper term is "bodily." Whereas the former term leans towards the notion of "resuscitation;" the latter more accurately implies that while the body is involved, the event is not a resuscitation.

As for the "visions of the Lord in resplendent glory," one can only wonder what Hick is referring to. First, there is the minor point that "visions" is a more loaded term than the proper one, "appearances." Gerald O'Collins writes:

> In fact nowhere in the New Testament are the Easter encounters described as 'visions.'[98]

Secondly, and more important, one wonders what Hick means by "resplendent glory." If He means "resplendent light," the only appearance of the Risen Lord where such light is connected is found in the three accounts of the *one* appearance to Paul at Damascus (9:1-9; 22:5-16; 26:10-18). And even in this instance, there is no "vision" of the Lord, only His voice is heard. *None* of the gospel accounts of the appearances of the Risen Lord portray Him in resplendent light.[99]

Thirdly, Hick argues that Jesus' resurrection was not at all that surprising since in those days resurrection was not completely uncommon. But once again Hick identifies Jesus' resurrection with the resuscitation of a corpse. All the examples which he provides are of resuscitation: Lazarus, the widow's son, Jairus' daughter, and similar events in apostolic and patristic times. The passage in Hebrews 11:35, to which Hick refers is also usually interpreted as referring to old Testament resuscitations (cf. 1 K 17:23; 2 K 4:36). As Stephen Neill writes:

> ... not one of these occurrences [examples of resuscitation given by Hick] bears the smallest resemblance to the resurrection of Jesus.[100]

What Hick does not advert to regarding Jesus' resurrection is that it ushers in the eschatological resurrection from the dead. It is unique, and vindicates His own claims to have been the eschatological prophet. None of the resuscitations are ever given that importance. It is with this meaning in mind that the passage of Mt 27:52-3, again referred to by Hick, is to be read. This passage reflects the Old Testament belief in the resurrection of the upright, "a sign of the eschatological era."[101]

Fourthly, Hick claims that the modern mind cannot accept the notion of Jesus' resurrection as easily as the disciples did. Hick still seems to be referring to some kind of resuscitation. And since an event of that type that happened 2,000 years ago cannot be scientifically verified, it is beyond human belief. Here we notice again Hick's "principle of empirical verification" at work. We have already critiqued this elsewhere. What we need only say here, is that Hick clearly on this point reduces faith to science. That is, if the content of faith cannot be verified by scientific method, then it should not be believed in.

Similarly, Hick claims that historical method cannot verify Jesus' resurrection. The question underlying this claim is: to what extent is Jesus' resurrection an historical event like other historical events? It would be out of place here to enter into a discussion of the relation between history and faith. Yet, we can say the resurrection of Jesus has roots in history, lies on the fringes of history, and left traces within history.[102]

Nevertheless, Jesus' resurrection lies more outside than inside, the realm of historical objects or events investigated by historians. This is so for two reasons, writes O'Collins:

> The New Testament both (1) expounds this event as the transit of the dead Jesus *out of history* to a glorified life in the 'other' world of God, and (2) attributes it to divine causality *alone*.[103]

By being made *"Lord" of history* upon His resurrection, *it is no longer history which contains Jesus, but it is the Risen Jesus who contains history.*

Fifthly, Hick claims that if today we should be told a relative who died was now seen alive, that such a "resurrection" would not prove our relative's divinity. True enough. But Hick is missing the point. My reply relates back to three earlier points. First, The resurrection forms part of the Christ-event, even for the first disciples. It was not added by them as independent datum to prove a pre-paschal faith. Nor is it so today. Hick has misunderstood the role of Jesus' resurrection in faith, both then and now. Secondly, the resurrection of Jesus relates directly

313

back to His claims. The example which Hick gives of one's dead relative has nothing of this crucial aspect about it. The rising of the dead relative seems to be an independent oddity, as Hick himself suggests. Thirdly, the rising of the dead relative in Hick's account seems to be the resuscitation of a corpse.

Endnotes

1. Walter Kasper, *Jesus the Christ*, (London: Burns & Oates, 1976), 89.

2. For an excellent survey of the literature on the uniqueness and universality of Jesus, see Felipe Gomez, S.J., "The Uniqueness and Universality of Christ," *East Asian Pastoral Review* 1 (1983): 4-30.

3. For a discussion of Jesus as representational, see Gerald O'-Collins, S.J., *The Calvary Christ* (London: S.C.M., 1977), 106-14.

4. Kasper, *Jesus* ..., 217.

5. Gomez, "The Uniqueness ...," 22.

6. *ibid.*, 25.

7. *ibid.*, 22.

8. *ibid.*

9. For an analysis of Anselm's *Cur Deus Homo?*, see Kasper, *Jesus* ..., 219-21.

10. Martin Hengel, *The Cross of the Son of God*, "The Atonement," (London: S.C.M., 1986), 189-284. "The Atonement" was first published by S.C.M. as "Der stellvertretende Sühnetod Jesu. Ein Beitrag zur Entstehung des urchristlichen Kerygmas," *Internationale katolische Zeitschrift* 9, 1980, 1-25, 135-47.

11. *ibid.*, 262.

12. There are many passages in the New Testament that affirm this concrete assumption in relation to its universality, but we mention only these: Jesus is not only incorporated into the history of His own people (Matthew's genealogy, 1:1-16), but into the history of mankind as a whole (Luke's genealogy, 3:23-38). Paul expresses this universal notion in Gal 4:4 when he speaks of Jesus as "born of woman, born under the Law."

13. Gomez, "The Uniqueness ...," 14.

14. *ibid.*, 15. We recall that Hick as a philosopher finds unacceptable the juxtaposition of such notions as infinite-finite, eternal-histori-

cal, fullness-emptiness, absolute-relative. To be startled and skeptical of such juxtapositions is of itself not an unwarranted reaction. Such a response can lead to a child-like wonder which asks further questions, as in Nicodemus' case, and so it can open onto the possibility of faith. But such a reaction can also declare that any such juxtaposition is absolutely impossible, and so it can blind a person to the *magnalia* of God. It is true that hybrid concepts breed uneasiness for both philosophy and mysticism. How can the Unspeakable be spoken about? How can the God beyond all names in unutterable Silence, be named? But as Gomez writes: "And yet the threatening fact is that Silence contains a Word, and it has been spoken, summoning all mind and will to the obedience of faith, questioning all answers and 'christening' all ideas of God," 28-29. On the juxtaposition of opposites which is an obstacle to reason, Kasper writes that their only legitimate ground can be God's "completely underivable event of freedom which cannot be made speculatively intelligible," *Jesus* ..., 183.

15. For a discussion of Jesus' intentions regarding the crucifixion, see also O'Collins, *The Calvary Christ*, 56-63.

16. For a discussion of the death of Jesus (and the resurrection) as the finality of revelation, see Karl Rahner and Wilhelm Thusing, *A New Christology* (London: Burns & Oates, 1980), 32-41.

17. For a discussion on Jesus' knowledge and acceptance of His death, see Gerald O'Collins, S.J., *Interpreting Jesus*, (London: Geoffrey Chapman, 1983), 79-92.

18. For a discussion of the evidence of this statement, see O'Collins, *ibid.*, 89-92, 94.

19. Writing against a mythological interpretation of Jesus' death and resurrection, Michael Green states: "He [Jesus] endured no mythical labours of Hercules but a literal and agonizing cross. He was not deified by decree of the Senate but raised by God to the place of power in the universe," in "Jesus and Historical Scepticism," *The Truth of God Incarnate*, 116.

20. This is Aylward Shorter's question in *Revelation and Its Interpretation* (London: Geoffrey Chapman, 1983), 171. Vatican II took initial steps in dealing with this third alternative in such celebrated passages as: *Lumen gentium* 16, *Gaudium et spes* 22, *Nostra aetate* 2. We

might mention as well the Apostolic Exhortation on "Evangelization in the Modern World" which concluded the 1974 Synod of Bishops, *Evangelii nuntiandi* 53.

21. For such an exploration of this third alternative, see Shorter, *Revelation* ..., 190-204.

22. Hick also does not have a theology of the Word. This is not surprising since for him the Word is just a way of speaking about God's impingement on human consciousness, and since the Word has not become flesh. Hick, therefore, can find no grounds for seeking salvation in non-Christian religions through such notions as *logos speratikos, vestigia Christi, semina verbi.* For the importance of these notions, see Shorter, *Revelation* ..., 176-77. See also Chrys Saldanha, *Divine Pedagogy: A Patristic View of Non-Christian Religions* (Roma: Libreria Ateneo Salesiano, 1984); and James Dupuis, S.J., "The Salvific Value of non-Christian Religions," *Jesus Christ and His Spirit* (Bangalore: Theological Publications in India, 1976), 141-66.

23. Shorter, *Revelation* ..., 175.

24. For an elaboration of the significance of these two missions for ecumenism among religions, see Frederick E. Crowe, S.J., *Son of God, Holy Spirit, and World Religions: The Contribution of Bernard Lonergan to the Wider Ecumenism* (Toronto: Regis College Press, 1984). This originally was a lecture, Chancellor's Address II, delivered at Regis College, November 26, 1984. See also Yves Congar, O.P., *The Word and the Spirit* (London: Geoffrey Chapman, 1986). Originally published as *La parole et le souffle* (Paris: Desclee, 1984).

25. Gomez, "The Uniqueness ...," 25.

26. *ibid.*, 24-5; Kasper, *Jesus* ..., 254-68.

27. Kasper, *Jesus* ..., 255.

28. *ibid.*

29. *ibid.*, 256.

30. *ibid.*

31. *ibid.*, 267-8.

32. *ibid.*, 253.

33. This point was made once again by Pope John-Paul II in his encyclical *Redemptor hominis* 6.

34. I do not wish to imply the one-sided notion that the Church is the continuation of the Incarnation. Although there is a truth to that

idea, I also intend, however, to include the notion that the Church is the locus of the encounter of the Risen Christ who was crucified for the world's salvation. For an elaboration of this issue, see Karl Rahner and Wilhelm Thusing, *A New Christology* (London: Burns & Oates, 1980), 18-31.

35. It is for this reason that it can be said, as does Lesslie Newbigin, that Christianity, while a religion, is "not merely a religion," *The Finality of Christ* (London: S.C.M., 1969), 31, and later, *ibid.*, 46-7, "... not even the culminating religion." The point that Christianity is more than religion is one that Hick would not accept, as evidenced in the fact that while Hick will accept a history of Christianity, he has no theology of the Church.

36. Kasper, *Jesus* ..., 198.

37. *ibid.*

38. That is *not* to say, of course, that the mission of the Word is entirely absent in non-Christian religions. Pope John-Paul II has written in his encyclical *Redemptor hominis* 13, quoting Vatican II's Pastoral Constitution on the Church in the Modern World, *Gaudium et spes* 22: "by his Incarnation, he, the Son of God, in a certain way *united himself with each man*" [emphasis mine],(cf. also *RH*, 14). In the document "The Attitude of the Church towards the Followers of Other Religions: Reflections and Orientations on Dialogue and Mission" (Vatican: Polyglot, 1984), 16-17, the then Secretariat for non-Christians writes: "This vision induced the Fathers of the Second Vatican Council to affirm that in the religious traditions of non-Christians there exist 'elements which are true and good' (*OT* 16), 'precious things both religious and human' (*GS* 92), 'seeds of contemplation' (*AG* 18), 'elements of truth and grace' (*AG* 9), 'seeds of the Word' (*AG* 11, 15), and 'rays of the truth which illumines all mankind' (*NA* 2)."

I would add as well, that whereas prior to the Incarnation of Word, the *vestigia* or *semina* of the Word were *preparatio evangelica*, after the resurrection of Jesus, they become specifically *vestigia Christi* and so are transformed into *preparatio eschatologica*. The point of the *preparatio eschatologica* is grounded in the fact that Jesus is the eschatological prophet. On this point Newbigin writes: "... the finality of Christ is to be understood in terms of his finality for the meaning and direction of history," *The Finality of Christ*, 8, see also 46-87. Later, in *The Open Secret*, 95, Newbigin continues this point that the end or goal of world history —which can only occur at the end—has been "revealed" to us *before* the end, in Christ. That is why the search for the truth among *all* world religions is done in the light of Christ. There is not another end to be looked for. No amount of searching or researching can enable one to see the end before it comes—unless the end is somehow revealed. With the end revealed in Jesus, it is possible "to have a universal history, a way of understanding the whole story which is not determined by a starting point in the particular culture, time and place where each of us stands."

39. *Lumen gentium* 1; 48.

40. *Lumen gentium*, 8.

41. Lesslie Newbigin writes: "... discussion about the finality of Jesus is often confused by emotional arguments about the arrogance of western Christians," *The Finality of Christ* (London: S.C.M., 1969), 11-12.

42. For Peter Byrne's argument against Hick on this issue, see Peter Byrne, "John Hick's Philosophy of World Religions," *Scottish Journal of Theology* 35, 4 (1982), 297-98.

43. Gomez, "The Uniqueness ...," 16. The reference is to "J. Ratzinger, 'The problem of the absolute in Christianity,' *Dialogue* (La Salle Manila) 15 (1980), 45-53." We recall here that Hick said that Christians could worship Jesus because, although He was not God, He was more "in the direction" of God than we are. This is playing quite loose with the meaning of worship. "Worship" is the adoration due to God alone; it cannot be given to any image or symbol of God which is not God, no matter how close "in the direction" of God it might be. "For philosophy, the 'scandal' of Christianity," writes Christopher Butler, is "the Church's worship—in the full sense of that term—of the man Jesus," *The Truth of God Incarnate*, 94. Either Hick does not take Christian worship seriously, or he is countenancing idolatry.

44. *ibid.*, 15. For the Catholic notion of Jesus as symbol, or sacrament, see Edward Schillebeeckx, *Christ the Sacrament of Encounter with God* (New York: Sheed and Ward, 1963). See also Karl Rahner, S.J., "The Theology of the Symbol," *Theological Investigations*, IV, 221-52.

45. John L. McKenzie, *Dictionary of the Bible* (New York: Macmillan, 1965), 285.

46. Hengel, "The Atonement," 261.

47. James G. D. Dunn, *Christology in the Making: A New Testament Inquiry into the Origins of the Doctrine of the Incarnation* (London: S.C.M., 1980), 13-22, 98-100.

John Macquarrie writes that Michael Goulder's argument [MGI, 64-85]—that the Christian doctrine of the Incarnation was taken over from the religious thinking of the Samaritans—is an example of the "genetic fallacy," in "Christianity without Incarnation? Some Critical Comments," *The Truth of God Incarnate*, 141. This point is also made by Peter Hinchliff, "Christology and Tradition," in A. E. Harvey, ed., *God Incarnate: Story and Belief* (London: SPCK, 1981), 86, who defines genetic fallacy as "... the opinion that the existence of broadly similar ideas in the context within which a belief is born wholly accounts for that belief and proves it to be false."

48. Shorter, *Revelation* ..., 106-107.

49. *ibid.*, 107.

50. Shorter writes: "Symbolism, as we have pointed out several times, is of the essence of human experience. Everything that exists conveys meaning because it is a symbol, or manifestation of further or deeper reality. It follows that symbolism is *par excellence* the language of divine revelation," *Revelation* ..., 107.

51. Shorter writes: "It is then that new significations appear and that the 'revelation' of divine reality receives tangible expression. The process is altogether different from the process of comparison (poetic or otherwise) which John Hick equates with religious language and which he opposes to 'literal' propositions ... It is in a very real sense an 'unveiling' or *revelatio* of certain aspects of divine reality. Taken literally, there is nothing in common between, say, a shepherd or a fortress on the one hand, and God on the other. Yet it is a fact that the meaning of the metaphorical words is enhanced when they are spontaneously applied to the experience of God. New meaning is present and new information is received," *Revelation* ..., 10-11.

52. See: (1) Avery Dulles, S.J. *Models of Revelation* (Dublin: Gill and Macmillan, 1983), 131-54. On the truth of symbolic representation; (2) Hans-Georg Gadamer, *Truth and Method* (New York:

Seabury, 1975), "FIRST PART: The question of truth as it emerges in the experience of art," 5-150, esp. 73-90. Originally published as *Wahrheit und Methode* (Tubingen: J.C.B. Mohr, 1960). See also Karl Rahner, "What is a Dogmatic Statement?" *Theological Investigations*, V, 42-66, esp. 46-8; (3) Janet Martin Soskice, *Metaphor and Religious Language* (Oxford: Clarendon Press, 1985).

53. For a further development of these notions, see Gerald O'-Collins, S.J. *Fundamental Theology* (London: Darton, Longman & Todd, 1981), 130-91, esp. 178-80.

54. On this "language of love" argument of Hick's, Stanley H. Russell, "The Finality of Christ and other Religions," *Epworth Review*, 4, 1 (January 1977): 80, writes: "So 'Jesus is Lord' is to be paralleled with the lover's maudlin affirmation that 'Kate is the sweetest girl in the world'—to my mind a singularly implausible interpretation of what Christians have been saying from the earliest times."

55. Russell, "The Finality ...," 137-38.

56. Joachim Jeremias, *The Problem of the Historical Jesus* (Philadelphia: Fortress, 1960, 1964); *The Central Message of the New Testament* (New York: Charles Scribner, 1965); *New Testament Theology* (London: S.C.M., 1971).

57. Ernst Käsemann, "Das Problem des historischen Jesus," *Zeitschrift für Theologie und Kirche*, LI (1954): 125-53, appeared in English as "The Problem of the Historical Jesus," *Essays on New Testament Themes* (London: S.C.M., 1964), 15-47.

58. Günther Bornkamm, *Jesus of Nazareth* (New York: Harper & Brothers, 1956, 1960).

59. Heinz Schürmann, "Die vorosterlichen Anfänge der Logientradition: Versuch eines formgeschichtlichen Zugangs zum Leben Jesu," in H. Ristow und K. Matthiae, eds., *Der historishche Jesus und der kerygmatische Christus: Beiträge zum Christusverständnis in Forschung und Verkündigung* (Berlin: Evangelische Verlagsanstalt, 1962), 342-70.

60. Birger Gerhardsson, *Memory and Manuscript. Oral Tradition and Written Transmission in Rabbinic and Early Christianity* (Uppsala: G.W.K. Gleerup, 1961); *The Origins of the Gospel Traditions* (Philadelphia: Fortress, 1979).

61. John Macquarrie in his list of scholars Hick is unaware of or

passes over, lists: Pannenberg, Rahner, Schoonenberg, Kasper, and von Balthasar, in "Christianity without Incarnation? Some Critical Comments," *The Truth of God Incarnate*, 141.

62. Stephen Neill, "Jesus and History," in Michael Green, ed., *The Truth of God Incarnate* (London: Hodder and Stoughton, 1977), 76, writes: "One of the most notable phenomenon in critical research today is the re-emergence of the historical Jesus from the mists of critical uncertainty." It is Neill's contention that the secular historians have more quickly and effectively emancipated themselves from the Enlightenment than have contemporary theologians, *ibid.*, 77.

Michael Green, too, argues that Hick's reductionist, historical skepticism is unwarranted, in "Jesus and Historical Scepticism," *ibid.*, 107-39, esp. 122-23.

Lesslie Newbigin makes the same point that theologians, like Hick, who find the New Testament data too fragmentary and ambiguous a source for reliable knowledge about the historical Jesus, have uncritically accepted the assumptions of the Enlightenment, *The Open Secret*, 177-78. See also, *Newbigin The Finality of Jesus*, 120-21.

63. René Latourelle, S.J. *Finding Jesus Through the Gospels: History and Hermeneutics* (New York: Alba House, 1979). This is a translation by Aloysius Owen of *L' accéss à Jésus par les évangiles*.

64. Shorter, *Revelation ...*, 108.

65. Bernard J. F. Lonergan, S.J., *Insight: A Study of Human Understanding* (London: Longmans, Green & Co., 1958), 251-54.

66. Lonergan, *Insight*, 414.

67. For Lonergan's account of judgment see Chapters IX and X of *Insight*. For a comparison of Kant's and Lonergan's account of judgment, see: (1) Giovanni Sala, S.J., "The *A Priori* in Human Knowledge: Kant's *Critique of Pure Reason* and Lonergan's *Insight*," *The Thomist*, XL, 2 (April 1976): 179-221; (2) Giovanni Sala, S.J., "Il Bicentenario della 'Critica della Ragion Pura' di Kant," *La Civiltà Cattolica* 1981, IV: 343-60; (3) Otto Muck, S.J., *The Transcendental Method* (New York: Herder and Herder, 1968): 274-5. Translated by William D. Seidensticker.

68. In A. E. Harvey, ed., *God Incarnate: Story and Belief* (London: SPCK, 1981), the various authors argue that while the intelligibility which gives rise to the question of judgment can take the form of a

proposition, there is also a sense in which that intelligibility can take the form of a story or narrative, to which the question of judgment can also be put. At times, however, the authors seem confused about the difference between intelligibility and judgment.

69. See Joseph Flanagan, S.J., "From Body to Thing," in Matthew L. Lamb, ed., *Creativity and Method: Essays in Honor of Bernard Lonergan, S.J.* (Milwaukee, Wisconsin: Marquette University, 1981), 495-507.

70. Peter Byrne, "John Hick's Philosophy of World Religions," *Scottish Journal of Theology* 35 (1982): 292, argues that to overcome skepticism about the cognitive value of religious truth-claims, Hick has introduced a skepticism regarding the object of faith. Byrne goes on to say that one cannot separate knowing God from responding to Him, as Hick does, since responding correctly to God requires some knowledge of Him (p.293). For this reason, Byrne sees Hick's epistemology leading to "tolerant agnosticism" (p.296). Gavin D'Costa, "John Hick's Copernican Revolution: Ten Years After," *New Black-friars* July/August (1984), 329 is aware of the same difficulty in Hick's philosophic foundations. He describes Hick's position of trying to maintain cognitive religious truth-claims within a broader Kantian epistemology to be an "irresolvable dilemma" which "tends towards agnosticism." Lesslie Newbigin in *The Finality of Christ*, 16, argues that Hick's basic theory of religions understands religions as an "illusion" because of his foundation in Feuerbach, and the theory itself is a form of "scepticism" because of his use of Kant. Critiquing Hick's use of the elephant analogy in this regard, Newbigin claims that "this tale implies a stupendous claim on the part of the teller [i.e., that he sees where everyone else and every religion is blind], or [implies] a confession of total agnosticism."

71. It should be clear that I am not saying that human cognition can know God-in-Himself of its own accord. Nor are we even claiming that with faith, we can know God as another datum clearly figured out. We see through a glass darkly, and not face to face (cf. 1 Cor 13:12). [This quote can hardly be used to affirm Kant's epistemology as true, which is how Hick uses it].

But what we see through the glass darkly is what God has freely granted us to see, namely the mystery of Himself. Revelation is not the removal of God's mystery, but that mystery revealed precisely as mystery in Jesus Christ. Lesslie Newbigin says of the mystery of the Christ-event [death and resurrection of Jesus] that it "... can never be fully grasped by our intellectual powers and translated into a theory or doctrine. We are in the presence of a reality full of mystery which challenges but exceeds our grasp," *The Open Secret*, 55.

72. Stephen Neill states: "... the fundamental error in the study of Christology is the assumption that it is a doctrine about Jesus Christ, when it is, of course, a doctrine about God," in Michael Green, ed., *The Truth of God Incarnate* (London: Hodder and Stoughton, 1977), 69. While agreeing with Neill, Brian Hebblethwaite adds: "... nevertheless the doctrine [of the Incarnation] also asserts the real humanity of Jesus," *ibid.*, 102. The point of both writers is that "theocentric" is "Christocentric" because of the uniqueness of Jesus.

73. For an elaboration of the theocentricity of Christocentricity, see Karl Rahner and Wilhelm Thusing, *A New Christology* (London: Burns & Oates, 1980), 73, 93-97, 119, 123-24.

74. Lesslie Newbigin writes that Hick's attempt to apply the model of the Copernican revolution in science in theology involves a "logical fallacy," namely that he overlooks the fact that God is a different reality from sense objects of scientific investigation, *The Open Secret*, 184-85.

75. Rev. Duncan B. Forrester, "Professor Hick and the Universe of Faiths," *Scottish Journal of Theology*, 29 (1976): 68.

76. This is not to say that one ought not to set one's mind to the task of trying to understand what can be understood of God's ways with us. After all, God gave us minds, and so presumably, He intends us to use them. But understanding the mystery involves accepting the whole mystery as mystery, and not trying to reduce it to simply another controllable datum.

77. Rev. J. Lipner, "Christians and the Uniqueness of Christ," *Scottish Journal of Theology* 28 (1975): 364.

78. J.J. Lipner, "Does Copernicus Help? Reflections for a Christian Theology of Religions," *Religious Studies* 13, 2 (June, 1977): 252. Forrester, "Professor Hick ...," 70, states that Hick's own alternative, the Copernican map of the universe, may in fact be completely inaccurate. He writes: "And it would by no means be absurd to suggest that there are today more similarities and a more significant relation-

ship between Christianity and Marxism [which latter Hick excludes as a religion] than between, say, Christianity and Sikhism, and that many Christians share more of their concerns with the marxist than with the non-theistic Hindu. Which might suggest that Professor Hick has produced a map which, unlike that of Copernicus, totally disregards known heavenly bodies."

79. Gavin, D'Costa, "John Hick's Copernican Revolution: Ten Years After," *New Blackfriars* July/ August (1984): 324. See also his (1) *Theology and Religious Pluralism: The challenge of Other Religions* (Oxford: Basil Blackwell, 1986), and (2) *John Hick's Theology of Religions: A Critical Evaluation* (Lanham, MD: University Press of America, 1987).

80. D'Costa, "John Hick ...," 325. D'Costa himself provides a brief account of the context and development. He notes the axiom was formulated in the third century by Origen (c. 185-254) in Alexandria, and by Cyprian (c. 206-258) in Carthage, primarily with reference to Christians who separate themselves from the Church and not with reference to non-Christian religions. The axiom was taken up by Augustine (354-430) and by his disciple Fulgentius of Ruspe (467-533), from whom it entered into medieval theology. It was Fulgentius' formulation of the axiom—to the effect that pagans, Jews, heretics and schismatics who die outside the Catholic Church are damned—that was quoted by the Council of Florence, and to which Hick refers. D'-Costa says two important considerations must be stressed regarding Florence's usage: (1) it is meant more to affirm that salvation comes only through Christ, than as a reference to world religions, and (2) it applies to those in bad faith who separate themselves from the Church. And since Fulgentius thought the gospel had in fact somehow already been offered to everyone, he concluded that by not joining the Catholic Church they must be acting in bad faith.

81. Forrester, "Professor Hick ...," 66.

82. Letter of the Holy Office to the Archbishop of Boston, dated August 8, 1949. *The Christian Faith in the Doctrinal Documents of the Catholic Church*, eds. J. Neuner, S.J. and J. Dupuis, S.J., rev. ed. (London: Collins Liturgical Publications, 1983), 240-2.

83. Forrester, "Professor Hick ...," 67.

84. Lipner, "Does Copernicus ...," 257.

85. D'Costa "John Hick ...," 324, and Forrester, "Professor Hick ...," 70, note that Hick over the years has had to add a few epicycles of his own.

86. One reason for this elimination Michael Green points out is that Hick makes the "inexplicable blunder" of assuming that to say that "all salvation is through Christ" means the same that "to be saved one must have explicit faith in Christ," in "Jesus and Historical Scepticism," *The Truth of God Incarnate*, 118.

87. J. Peter Schineller, S.J., "Christ and Church: A Spectrum of Views," *Theological Studies* 37, 4 (Dec. 1976), 545-66.

88. In *No Other Name?: A Critical Survey of Christian Attitudes Toward the World Religions* (London: S.C.M., 1985), Paul F. Knitter calls for a "theocentric nonnormative" Christology. This would seem to place him in Schineller's fourth category along with Hick. The problem is to understand what exactly is meant by "normative" and "nonnormative." See Paul F. Knitter, "Author's Response," to *Review Symposium*, in *Horizons*, 13, 1 (Spring 1986): 130-35, esp. 133.

89. See Karl Rahner, S.J., *Foundations of Christian Faith: An Introduction to the Idea of Christian Faith* (New York: Crossroads, 1984), 176-228. First published as *Grundkurs des Glaubens: Einführung in den Begriff des Christentums* (Freiburg im Breisgau: Verlag Herder, 1976).

90. For example: "God is *Agape*; and the assertion is a direct transcript of the faith that the *agape* which we see in Jesus in some sense *is* the eternal *Agape* of God" [GUF,152].

91. For example: "The gospels depict God's love inhistorised, operating self-revealingly in relation to certain individuals but thereby in principle and in prolepsis taking the initiative to redeem human life in all its depths, dimensions and predicaments" [GUF,154].

92. Hick mistakenly claims support from Gregory of Nyssa. For a well-founded critique of Hick's misuse of Gregory, see: Noel K. Jason, "A Critical Examination of the Christology of John Hick, with Special Reference to the Continuing Significance of the *Definitio Fidei* of the Council of Chalcedon, A.D. 451," Unpublished Ph.D. dissertation, University of Sheffield, 1978, 40-1. The philosophical issues involved in the discussion of God's nature, operations, attributes, etc., lie beyond the scope of our work.

93. See *The Christian Faith in the Doctrinal Documents of the Catholic Church*, eds. J. Neuner, S.J. and J. Dupuis, S.J. (London: Collins, 1983), 146, no. 602.

94. *ibid.*, 143-44, 165-66, 172-73, nos. 635-37.

95. *ibid.*, 151-55. We are aware, as is John Macquarrie, *Truth of God Incarnate*, 144, that "It would be an anachronism to describe the positions in this book [*Myth of God Incarnate*] as Arian, deist or Unitarian ..." but we also agree with Macquarrie that "unquestionably there are affinities, and it is hardly likely that an updated Christianity without incarnation will prove any more successful than these dead ends of the past."

96. This is not to say the Christian notion of *agape* as revealed in Jesus cannot play a significant role in a theology of religions. See Peggy Starkey, "Agape: A Christian Criterion for Truth in the Other World Religions," *International Review of Mission*, LXXIV, 296 (October 1985): 425-63. Among the responses, one that makes our point is Jacques Dupuis, S.J., "The Practice of Agape is the Reality of Salvation," *ibid.*, 472-7, esp. 477. It is not enough to say that Jesus' *agape* is God's *Agape*, but that Jesus Himself is God's *Agape*.

Also on this issue, see the Editorial Symposium, *Horizons*, 16, (Spring, 1989): (1) William M. Thompson, "Jesus' Unsurpassable Uniqueness: A Theological Note", 101-15; (2) Leonard Swidler, "Jesus' Unsurpassable Uniqueness: Two Responses", 116-20; (3) John Hick, "Comment on Jesus' Unsurpassable Uniqueness", 121-24; and (4) William M. Thompson, "The Hermeneutics of Friendship and suspicion: A Response to Professors Swidler and Hick", 125-30.

97. Michael Green writes: "It is an astonishing fact that most of the writers in *The Myth of God Incarnate* have little to say about the resurrection, ... None of them have begun to come to terms with the evidence afforded by the New Testament itself ..." *The Truth of God Incarnate*, (London: Hodder and Stoughton, 1977), 53.

98. Gerald O'Collins, S.J., *The Easter Jesus* (London: Darton, Longman & Todd, 1973, rev. ed 1980), 21.

99. The angels at the tomb, described as being in bright light, are not the Risen Lord (Mt 28:2-3; Lk 24:2-3). And the transfiguration of Jesus is not properly an Easter appearance (Mt 171-2; Mk 9:2-3; Lk 9:29-30).

100. Stephen Neill, "Jesus and Myth," in Michael Green, ed., *The Truth of God Incarnate* (London: Hodder and Stoughton, 1977), 69.

101. See fn. "x," *The New Jerusalem Bible* (London: Darton, Longman & Todd, 1985), 1659. This point is also made by Lesslie Newbigin, *The Open Secret*, 39.

102. For a discussion of the issues involved here, see O'Collins, *The Easter Jesus*, 57-62.

103. *ibid.*, 59.

CHAPTER NINE

Conclusion

The conclusion involves: (1) two critical objections of a foundational nature relative to Hick's work as a theologian; (2) some reflections on the implication of my own position for world religions.

On Hick the Theologian

Chapter 1 provided a section on Hick the theologian. Now that we have witnessed Hick doing theology, I can make some final evaluative observations, no longer about his evidence or conclusions, but about his general theological perspective.

The first serious critical observation that I raise regarding Hick the theologian is that his Christology is dated. His theology is uncritically grounded in principles and attitudes of the late nineteenth century. He seems unaware that significant progress has been achieved in such areas as the quest for the historical Jesus, Scripture and Tradition. Hick believes he is presenting us new ideas for consideration. But in fact he is re-iterating, with not much new formulation, ideas that have seen a hundred years of discussion. As Stephen Neill notes, these ideas "have long been before the Churches."[1]

By his own admission, Hick acknowledges his roots in Friedrich Schleiermacher. Hick's reduction of Christology to the *pro me* principle, his collapsing of faith into religious experience, and his fundamental explanation of the doctrine of the Incarnation as nothing but a way of saying something about Jesus' consciousness of God, all originate from the influence of Schleiermacher. It is clear from James Dunn's history of the development of thought regarding Jesus' consciousness, that Hick has completely ignored the fourth stage of that development.[2]

Although Hick accepts the religious interpretation of religion, ultimately that which dominates religious experience for Hick is psychological projection. For this view, Hick acknowledges his reliance on Ludwig Feuerbach.[3]

For his critique of Nicea and his account of the origin of the doctrine of the Incarnation, Hick merely restates the turn-of-the-century thought of Adolf Harnack. Harnack, as James Dunn notes, had

... already defined the development of dogma as the progressive hellenization of the gospel, as the transplanting of the gospel of Jesus 'into Greek modes of thought'.[4]

Similarly, Hick is reliant on nineteenth century history of religions for his mistaken view that the doctrine of the Incarnation was an alien intrusion into Christianity from the environment.

This reliance on the history of religions encompasses for Hick not just its conclusions, but expands to include its method. This brings me to my second critical observation regarding to Hick the theologian. He has not successfully integrated the method of the history of religions with that of theology. This lack of integration results from Hick's more radical inability to integrate reason and faith. Although he does not seem to realize the split, if not the contradiction within his epistemology, Hick at times grants that the cognitional power of reason can reach the truth of things-in-themselves, whereas the cognitional element of faith can reach only the truth of appearances. That is why whenever reason, in particular science (natural and social), seems to come into conflict with faith, it is the truths of faith that must surrender. After all, appearances must always yield to facts. This radical disjunction between cognition in reason and cognition in faith betrays that in Hick there is a foundational split between how Hick knows and how he thinks he knows. Hick does not seem to realize there is only one method of mind. That is, the human cognitional processes operate according to a self-constituting, dynamic pattern that is always the same and yields, by the structure of its very dynamism, the objectivity of things-in-themselves.[5] This is true for both reason and faith.

Hick's significant error is thinking that objectivity applies only to reason, and not to faith. He does not only not know what it means to know, he does not know what it means to believe. Thus, the truths of reason end up, as he sees it, being more solidly based than the truths of faith. From there it is a short step for Hick to conclude that the exercise of reason, e.g., the social scientific method of the history of religions, is more to be trusted in yielding objective truth than is theology. The result is that theology for Hick has no real independence, and in the end must yield to the more "scientific" study of God and religions. The pivotal import of all this means that for Hick, the very content of faith itself is not the result of revelation, but is in fact determined by the results of scientific method. Theology is no longer faith seeking understanding, but the history of religions seeking understanding. This basic methodological confusion on Hick's part undermines any ultimately helpful contribution Hick might be able to make to the serious and admittedly complex Christological issues which he addresses and which face us all today.[6]

One of the fundamentally erroneous results of this confusion on Hick's part is that knowledge of what God has done and is doing in the world is to be arrived at through reason and not by faith. That is, access to or recognition of God's activity is the result of an exercise of reason and not of faith. For Hick, the correlative of revelation is not faith but reason.

But it is only by faith that one can come to know if God has done anything unique, and what that unique thing might be. God's self-revelation is inaccessible to unaided reason. But Hick's theological method, since it originates from the data of reason and not from the truths of faith, does not permit even the possibility of a positive response to the question: has God in fact done anything unique in human history? Since his method cannot answer the question and if it could, it could only reach a negative reply since it reduces faith to reason, Hick assumes that God not only has not, but in fact could not do anything unique. Therefore, if faith claims otherwise, faith is mistaken, or at least is speaking only metaphorically.

We have been using the word "faith" throughout this discussion. By it we refer to Christian faith. And we contend that Christian faith is a unique human act. That is, the act of religious faith is not simply the same kind of thing no matter where it is found. The assumption that all acts of faith are the same is a mistake of the history of religions school and certainly of John Hick.[7] By going beyond reducing faith to reason, to the further reduction of all acts of faith to the same kind of thing, Hick has in fact ruled out of court the very access to any possible recognition of any unique self-revelation on God's part. The results, as we have seen, are disastrous not only for theology but also for faith, and ultimately for any discernment of the mystery of Jesus in the meeting of world religions.

It is not that the historical, comparative, or the phenomenological study of religions is invalid. Not at all. The point is that their methodologies frequently go beyond simply bracketing the question of uniqueness, to the point of declaring that the question itself is invalid.

The history of religions, like any social science, can study only, and aims to study only, what is repeated, what is common and predictable. Such phenomenon do occur and ought to be studied. Further, comparative religion is satisfied with description. Even when it compares, it is only for the sake of description, not evaluation.[8] All of this is not in itself invalid or undesirable. What is objected to is the further conclusion that because history of religions does not ask evaluative questions, that therefore evaluative questions are invalid and merely "subjective." Because comparative religion does not have the capacity to resolve multiplicity, but only describe it, does not mean that it is invalid for theology to go beyond analysis to integration. Indeed, that is theology's proper aim. Because Hick does not allow an aim to theology different from that of the history of religions, he can only conclude that for theology not to do what the history of religions does must be wrong.

Christian theology grounded in Christian faith has proper to its method the very question that comparative religion brackets: namely the question of uniqueness. Theology does not reduce uniqueness, but wrestles with its facticity. Theology aims not at the repeated or the predictable. Rather, because Christian faith is rooted in history, theology aims to ask the question of history, the valid question of uniqueness. That is, theology is not interested in cycles, but in what is going forward, in the unrepeated, the breakthrough, what is unique, what makes a difference, what was not and could not have been predicted, what needs therefore to be related to all else.

The mistake of comparative religion is that it claims because its method cannot ask the question of uniqueness , that therefore the question is not a valid one. This is obscurantist. All the relevant questions can and must be asked. Phenomena that are repeated do not account for all that occurs. Because comparative religion cannot handle what is unique, unpredictable, unrepeatable, unalterable and irreversible is no argument that such phenomenon do not occur and should not be asked about. It is not in the competence of social sciences, including comparative religion, to uncover and evaluate such phenomena.[9]

It is, however, the very purpose of history, to explain not the repeated patterns, but to examine what was "going forward," the new, the departures from the common and the routine.[10] That is why it was said above that the question about the possibility of the occurrence of the unique is an historically valid question.[11] The historical question leads into dialectic which paves the way for conversion. By repressing the historical question Hick short-circuits dialectic and so can only opt for an ultimately agnostic, "relativistic," position regarding the uniqueness of Jesus Christ.

Implications for World Religions

Chapter 4 included a section on the advantages Hick saw that his position on divine inhistorisation had over the traditional one of divine Incarnation, for a theology of and dialogue among world religions. Since I believe that Hick's Christology is ultimately unhelpful, I feel some obligation to address the issue of the implications of my own position for a theology and a dialogue of world religions.[12]

I maintain the traditional affirmation of Christian faith that Jesus is the unique and universal saviour, because He is in fact, God become man, the Second Person of the Trinity, Incarnate. I wish now to offer a few observations this position has for (1) theology of world religions, and (2) interreligious dialogue. I am aware of course these two areas overlap, and so I employ this division simply as a helpful way of organizing the following reflections.

Theology of World Religions

Hick has said that the mission of Christianity is to share God's revelation in Jesus with the other religions. In return, Christianity is to receive from these other religions what God has revealed to them. A theology of world religions must be based on and can only be the result of considering the data from all religions.

On the surface of it, I have no objection to this statement. I agree that the mission of the Church is to make known to the whole world what God has done in Jesus Christ. I agree as well, that the Church is to welcome and indeed search out God's revelation, presence and saving activity in other religions. And thirdly, I agree that a theology of world religions must encompass the evidence and testimony of those religions.

The central difficulty I have with Hick's position is the interpretation he gives to "God's revelation in Jesus" or to "what God has done in Jesus." In sharing Jesus with other religions, who is it precisely that the Church is sharing? Hick says the Church is sharing simply one human person's intense consciousness of God. The Church claims it is sharing the unique and unrepeatable God-man through whom the fullness of God's self-revelation and salvation is manifested and achieved. This entire work has been a systematic and detailed response to Hick's position on this point.

But if the Church's mission is as we claim it to be, what are some implications for a theology of world religions? That is, how do other world religions figure in the Church's theology about its mission?[13]

First, I am in agreement with Tibor Horvath, that religious pluralism in the divine plan is not a chastisement of the Christian's position on the uniqueness of Jesus! I believe pluralism is meant to contribute to the fuller understanding of the whole truth about Jesus Christ, and so to enrich faith in that mystery.[14] The implication for theology is that non-Christian religions must take their rightful place, along with Scripture, Tradition, etc., as a proper *locus theologicus*. The inexhaustible riches of Jesus Christ have not yet been fathomed. Jesus as "recapitulation" will not be fully known until all the world religions have been known "known" not just in the sense of "getting information about," but entered into by means off faith, hope and love seeking understanding.

Secondly, if one maintains the Christian affirmation of the uniqueness of Jesus Christ, and simultaneously contends that non-Christian religions are to be a *locus theologicus*, the result is a set of problems far more complex than simply writing off either the uniqueness of Jesus or the value of non-Christian religions. The point here is that *faith does not solve problems for theology, it creates them.* It is faith that introduces the paradoxes, the affirmations of both/and that so boggle the mind.

Hick's unfortunate, and I think, most fundamental misinterpretation of all, is to think that Christian faith in the uniqueness of Jesus is meant to solve problems. In fact, it creates problems on many levels, not the least of which is human understanding. But Hick, like every good theologian, wants to solve problems. However, Hick solves his problems by dispensing with the very faith itself. Hick rightly recognizes that Christian faith is the source of the problem. But he is so scandalized by this fact that he cannot accept it. The higher good for Hick is to have all problems solved at the bar of reason. If faith gets in the way of what appears to be an immediately reasonable solution, then there must be something wrong with that faith, and so it must surrender. To solve the problems that result from the uniqueness of Jesus Christ in the meeting of world religions, Hick opts to change the faith. Thus, when the uniqueness of Jesus becomes the problem for a neat theology of world religions, Hick resolves the issues by dispensing with that troublesome affirmation of Christian faith.

The implication of my point here for theology is that we are presently engaged in a complex of problems, the solutions of which are not easily reached. But the certainly erroneous path to take towards a solution is to dispense with Christian faith itself. The Christian would then no longer be authentic, and would not be able to share the true Jesus with the world. The world then would be without the unique and full revelation which has in fact come through Him.

It is far better to live with the at-present unsolved problems, to endure the uncomfortableness, the ambiguity, yes the scandal, on the difficult and long road to some rightful and true understanding, than it is to grasp quickly at a tidy, attractive but false resolution. We are only beginning to plumb the issues involved regarding the uniqueness of Jesus and world religions. If it took the Church four centuries to penetrate the early Christological problems, we must expect a similarly lengthy time in sorting out our present ones. Just as the early Church did not try to escape its theological problems by opting for an incorrect faith affirmation, or by prematurely and too hastily grabbing at what happened to be lying about, so must we proceed with what Horvath calls "creativity in patience."[15] The strength of the theologian is not immediate success but Christian hope. As Horvath writes:

> The mystery of in-hominization [of Jesus] continues the incarnation of the Word of God; it is the revelation of Jesus Christ, in his relation to the world, which is not yet finished. We do know that Jesus is with us but we do not know yet what it means that he is the saviour of the world, and how is going to bring to completion his saving and redeeming work.[16]

By implication, we do not yet know (theology) what it means for Jesus to be the unique and universal saviour (faith) in the meeting (problems) of Christianity and world religions.

Thirdly, from our first point about Jesus as "recapitulation," now linked with the preceding one that we do not know yet what that recapitulation means in relation to world religions, we must be open to the possibility that world religions may prove to be a mediation between Christ and His Church. What do I mean?

My meaning is a specification of a point made by Pope John-Paul II. During his 1980 visit to Africa, he proclaimed: "Christ, in the members of his Body, is himself African."[17] This is an enrichment, an advance over the traditional notion that Jesus is truly human. The traditional argument as repeated in *Gaudium et spes* is that by His Incarnation "Christ united himself with each man."[18] Having assumed a human nature, Jesus' divinity was now mediated through that human nature to all human persons. Or, coming at it from the other side, human nature becomes the medium of God's revelation. Not only does Christ reveal man, as *Redemptor hominis* affirms,[19] but man reveals Christ (*RH*, 13).

Even more important, however, as Horvath argues, quoting from *Redemptor hominis*, this "man" is not simply human nature, nor is it just existential man, but

... man in the full truth of his existence, of his personal being and also of his community and social being in the sphere of his own family, in the sphere of society and very diverse contexts, in the sphere of his own nation or people ... *this* man is the primary route that the Church must travel in fulfilling her mission: *he is the primary and fundamental way for the Church*, the way traced out by Christ himself ... [*RH*, 14].[20]

That is, man in his historical, social and cultural entirety is the way for the Church traced out by Christ Himself. This is new. This is more than saying that the Church is the mediator between Christ and human nature, more than saying the Church is the mediator between Christ and culture. This is even more than saying that human nature is the mediator between Christ and His Church. It *is* saying that the mediator between Christ and His Church is human culture, even specifically, human cultures. As Horvath writes:

It was John Paul II again who emphasized that we will not develop a better and deeper understanding of Jesus Christ until we come closer to the magnificent heritage of the human spirit and approach all cultures, all ideological concepts of all people ([*RH*], no.12).[21]

Christ in His members is not simply human, but African, and not only African but Chinese, Indian, Canadian, etc., as well. John Paul II in the same encyclical writes that it is "by means of the continually and rapidly increasing experience of the human family" that "we penetrate ... into the mystery of Jesus Christ" [*RH*, 13]. Once again we see the notion that human cultures, not just human nature, are the mediators between Christ and His Church.

Neither John-Paul II nor Horvath make special reference to world religions in this regard. My own development of their approach is simply to make that specification now.

At the heart of a culture is its religion. Thus, if a specific culture is a mediator between Christ and His Church, it follows that its religion is at the heart of that mediation. If the Church penetrates the mystery of

337

Christ by means of cultures, it must do so by means of religions as well. This is what we meant by our above statements that "we must be open to the possibility that world religions may prove to be a mediation between Christ and His Church," and that "Jesus as 'recapitulation' will not be fully known until all the world religions have been known— 'known' not just in the sense of 'getting information about,' but entered into by means off faith, hope and love seeking understanding."

Fourthly, it was stated above that faith is not a problem-solver but a problem-creator. I wish now to make a modification to that position. Faith is a problem-creator in the *first instance* only. This is because Jesus Himself does not fit any category, and to encounter Him can throw one into sudden confusion. But that is not the goal of the encounter. The confusion yields to conversion, and conversion issues on to a higher integration which may not, and in fact, will not be the final state of affairs.

The implication here for theology is that while in the first instance we may have to live with the ambiguity and scandal of unresolved problems, the theologian in hope, faith and love waits to see how Christ will emerge as redeemer again and again. In this sense, or *second instance*, Christ does emerge as the answer, and faith as a problem solver. On this point, Horvath writes:

> The task of theology of the future is to analyze the manifold problems of different peoples and individuals [and we would add, different world religions] in each particular case and explain faith which affirms that Christ as Saviour has the power of raising questions [first instance] and of solving problems [second instance] as well as of creating contexts in which the insufficiency of other problem-solving paradigms becomes manifest [our paper's task regarding Hick's paradigm].[22]

Fifthly, and finally, considering all the above points, the implication of my position for theology is that we must be open to a whole new concept of God which may emerge. Hick believes he is in fact introducing a whole new concept of God, and that it is Christians (among others) who are holding out, being uncritically attached to older, fixed concepts. But in fact, Hick is reverting to a pre-Christian concept of

God. His faith, like that of the Ebionites, has failed him in this regard. They could not make the switch from the God of Judaism to the genuinely Christian God. That is, they could not move from a monotheism without an explication of Trinity, to a monotheism which included Father, Son and Holy Spirit. They opted for the old understanding. They could not adjust to their concept of God undergoing any change.

Hick, too, cannot accept his concept of God undergoing any genuinely developed change. The only alternative he allows himself is to choose between an undeveloped concept of the Christian God, or to drop that concept altogether. Hick chooses the latter, and ends up reverting to a prior notion of God that does not include Father, Son and Holy Spirit, nor a Jesus who is the Second Person of the Trinity, Incarnate.

But the New Testament reveals the struggle of the Jewish Christians to change their concept of God under their experience of Jesus. That is what we must be open to today. Under the experience of Jesus, we must be open to a fuller understanding of who He is in relation to world religions, to emerge. To drop the experience of Jesus will not solve the problem, but only render a genuine and true solution impossible. The first century Ebionites were not able to reach a true understanding of God. Nor, apparently, has Hick. My hope is that the theology of the future will be able to reach the new integration.

Given the uniqueness of Jesus Christ and non-Christian religions as mediating Christ to the Church (as well as the Church mediating Christ to non-Christian religions), we may find we must undergo a similar change in our concept of God. By that I do not mean a change in the reality of the Trinity or its doctrine, nor in the uniqueness of Jesus Christ and its affirmation. Rather I mean the Church may genuinely have to adjust its understanding in some as yet unknown manner.

Interreligious Dialogue

Hick maintains that the traditional Christian claim of the uniqueness of Jesus has poisoned interreligious dialogue. As we have seen, Hick concludes by pitting "confessional" dialogue against "truth-seeking" dialogue. "Confessional" dialogue is Ptolemaic; "truth-seeking" dialogue is Copernican. Hick grounds the Copernican-style dialogue in the parable of the blind men and the elephant. My question here is this:

is it true that "confessional" dialogue poisons interreligious dialogue?

It can do so, of course, but not because it is confessional. Confession can be poisonous if its adherents are not willing to acknowledge that confession is only one perspective on the truth, and that even that perspective is capable of, and indeed requires, valid development.

I refer here to a Scriptural example: Acts 10. This Chapter recounts the conversion of Cornelius. But it could just as easily have been titled: "The Conversion of Peter." Peter's concept of God underwent a radical change. It was a conversion not away from the uniqueness and universality of Jesus as Saviour. In fact, it is precisely *because* Peter affirms that mystery of Jesus, that he is able to make the required adjustment in his understanding of God and the Church's relation to the pagans (Acts 10:36). Further, it took illumination from on high, to both Peter and Cornelius, to effect the conversion of each. The Church did change as a result; it did learn from the pagans even while confessing its faith.

Similarly, within interreligious dialogue, the Church has to put its faith at risk. In order for it to genuinely learn from other religions, and to seek the full truth with them, the Church must be open to the possibility of some real change. As with Peter in his encounter with Cornelius, the Church will undergo significant change in its encounter and dialogue with world religions. But this change will not be away from Jesus. It will be but another step towards the fullness of Him who fills all creation. As Newbigin writes:

> He [the Christian] must be ready to face the possibility of radical reconsideration of long-accepted formulations. But he does so within his ultimate commitment to Jesus Christ as finally determinative of his way of understanding and responding to all experience.[23]

My point is that truth-seeking dialogue is not in opposition to confessional affirmations, but in fact it can only be genuinely reached by maintaining the latter. And, of course, there must always be the help of the Holy Spirit to guide all partners to the whole truth. In this sense, I agree with Hick, that dialogue involves a genuine search for truth by all participants and not just by some. This dialogue, properly understood, is what in the body of our work we called "dialectic."[24]

Hick makes a sharp distinction between the mission of the Church, which he sees as confessional, and interreligious dialogue which he sees as seeking the truth together. The implication of our own position is once again significantly different from that of Hick's.

Here I accept Jacques Dupuis' modification of #13 of the document from the *Secretariatus pro non christianis*, "The Attitude of the Church Towards the Followers of Other Religions," 1984. The Church's mission, according to Dupuis quoting the Secretariat, is "a single, but complex articulated reality," constituted by the following elements: (1) the simple *presence* and living witness of Christian life; (2) the promotion of *justice*, (3) interreligious *dialogue* in which all partners "walk together towards truth," (4) *proclamation* or confessional affirmations, i.e., announcement and catechesis, and (5) *liturgy*, prayer, sacraments.[25]

In turn, interreligious dialogue has its own dimensions: (1) dialogue of life, carried on by everyone; (2) dialogue of works, carried on by people working together for common cause; (3) dialogue of religious experience, carried on by committed adherents for the purpose of sharing, and (4) dialogue of specialists, carried on by theologians for mutual understanding.[26]

Our more nuanced position overcomes the false implications in Hick's simplistic dichotomy of "confessional" versus "truth-seeking" dialogue. Lesslie Newbigin well points out these false implications, when he writes:

> The implication is that those who take the confessional stance are not seekers after truth. This is surely a very serious matter. One cannot enter into real dialogue if one begins by denying the intellectual integrity of one's partner. Under the guise of openness and teachability, Hick is in fact asserting that his own presuppositions are the way to arrive at truth and are acceptable as such, whereas those of the Christian are not. It is in line with this that Hick regularly uses the word "dogma" to describe the basic presuppositions of Christians, while his own basic presuppositions are simply a transcript of reality as it is. Among many examples I [Newbigin] will cite only the key phrase ... [GUF,

131]: 'A shift from the dogma that Christianity is at the centre to the *realisation* that it is God who is at the centre.'[27]

Newbigin goes on to argue that a further implication of Hick's position is that there can be no real encounter among religions in dialogue. Encounter is eliminated from the outset by proclaiming that only one set of presuppositions can provide the conditions of truth-seeking. This is not what genuine dialogue and dialectic is all about.

Newbigin continues to a third point: Hick adopts a "Ptolemaic" outlook of his own: "modern science." Hick is even "confessional" about it; modern science is at the centre, and all other world views and faiths are in its periphery. Newbigin argues that for Hick, modern science, which awakened Christianity from its Greek-laden "dogmatic slumbers," is the basis now of Christianity and of all religions. Newbigin concludes once again that with Hick's position there is no real encounter or dialogue:

> There is therefore no dialogue, no encounter. There is only the monologue of the one who is awake addressed to those who are presumed to be asleep.[28]

My approach, however, to the issue of the Church's mission and dialogue is genuinely dialectic and dialogic. It allows for the conversion of both Peter and Cornelius. The confessional elements are maintained but a full range of possibilities are also preserved, which possibilities enable all partners to seek the truth together under the guidance of the Holy Spirit. This position, of course, requires living with the unknown for a while longer, and accepting the fact that an easy solution is not likely to be quickly attained.

The position maintained in this work also reveals the inadequacy of basing the search for the truth on the parable of the blind men and the elephant. While at first blush, that parable may seem to express equality among the partners in dialogue, it is in fact loaded against any fruitful outcome of a dialogue which "seeks the truth together."

Newbigin sees the parable as undermining both "seeking the truth" and seeking it "together." Regarding the first point, he writes:

What is often not noticed is that this tale [elephant parable] implies either a stupendous claim on the part of the teller or a confession of total agnosticism. Either it implies that the teller is in the position of the king among the blind men: he knows the reality after which the religions of the world blindly grope. In that case we must ask him to share this knowledge with us, and allow us to test its claims. Or else it implies a total agnosticism: the reality after which religions grope is unknowable. In that case one must observe his conduct and see whether it reveals commitments which he is not willing explicitly to acknowledge.[29]

Regarding the second point, Newbigin believes the parable undermines the "together" element of dialogue. He writes:

The whole point of the story is that the blind men represent the religions, but the king, who is not blind, represents the one who has attained to this realization and who therefore "sees." Once again, there is no encounter. There is no possibility that one of the religions might call into question the interpretation of the mystical experience on which the whole philosophy of the Vedanta rests" [i.e., that the ultimate reality is not a matter of knowledge]. "The story implies simply that the philosophy of the Vedanta is that which corresponds to reality and that all else is blindness.[30]

By far the best critique of Hick's use of the elephant parable comes from Gavin d'Costa.[31] D'Costa first critically evaluates Hick's position on Wittgenstein. He agrees with Hick that adopting a "form of life" approach to religious language could in some circles undermine the cognitive character of that language. However, D'Costa demonstrates that for a proper translation of religious texts, some "form of life" hermeneutic is required by the very cognitive operations themselves.

Next D'Costa traces the influence of T. S. Kuhn's work on "paradigm."[32] Kuhn's conclusions complement and correct the weaknesses in Wittgenstein. The point is that Hick's use of the elephant parable *falsely* assumes that different religions (paradigms) necessarily solve the same problems, that they point to a common solution. In fact, there is no evidence that such an assumption is at all warranted.

D'Costa concludes:

> We cannot simply assert that the varying phenomenal images are referring to the one noumenal divine reality. Without paying detailed attention to the 'form of life' within which those images are used and the basic paradigm which infuses them with meaning, the blind-men elephant theorist [and D'costa refers specifically to Hick] is likely to be misled.[33]

I come now to my final remark. The most significant implication of my position for interreligious dialogue is that the *scandal* of the historical mission of the Incarnate Word cannot be mitigated. Quite the contrary, that scandal is at the centre. It is at the centre of revelation and salvation, of faith and theology. It is at the centre because God is at the centre—and not just God as Hick or myself, think He ought to act, but God as He has in fact acted. The scandal of Jesus Christ is the sacrament of the unfathomable mystery that God's ways are not our ways (Is. 55:8-9). For this reason I maintain that it is my position, and not Hick's, which is genuinely theocentric.

It is true that such a scandal makes theology and dialogue difficult. I recall here what was quoted from Grillmeier in our Chapter 7:

> In all the christological formulas of the ancient church there is a manifest concern not to allow the total demand made on men's faith by the person of Jesus to be weakened by pseudo-solutions ... The formulas of the church, whether they are the *homoousios* of Nicea or the Chalcedonian Definition, represent the *lectio difficilior* of the gospel, and maintain the demand for faith and the stumbling-block which Christ puts before men. This is a sign that they hand on the original message of Jesus.[34]

But surely the response to the gospel's *lectio difficilior* is not to agree with Hick and to say: because the situation at hand is difficult we ought to pretend we are really working with a different set of facts, a set that will allow us the false consolation of coming up with an easy solution, and then pretend again that this solution is really to the original set of facts. This latter is Hick's option.

I agree with Hick wholeheartedly that the role of Christianity in religious dialogue is to present Jesus. But unlike Hick, I maintain that the role is to present the *true* Jesus, the One sent by the Father, the unique Son and universal Saviour.

This *true* Jesus is a scandal (1 Cor 1:22-3). Michael Green writes that

> ... the scandal of particularity lies at the heart of the religion of Jesus ... The particularity of Christ, the absolute claims made for him, have always constituted a major stumbling block to those who seek salvation through ideas.[35]

Lesslie Newbigin addresses the issue of the scandal of particularity in Chapter 7 of *The Open Secret*.[36] He argues that revelation presents us with God's universal purpose being carried out not by universal revelation, but by certain people selected to be bearers of revelation that *all* may be beneficiaries. The "inner logic" of this is found in the doctrine of election. To say God could not have or should not have carried out His salvific will in this particular way is not to allow oneself to be challenged by the strangeness of God's ways. Rather it is to decide that there should be no "scandal" at all.

If the doctrine of election in general is a scandal, the doctrine of Jesus' Incarnation, as the pinnacle of election, is the ultimate scandal. Yet the scandal of election and the universality of God's will are maintained in Scripture as a single vision (cf. Eph 1:3-14).

If the example of Hick is at all representative, it would seem that Jesus' uniqueness is a scandal not only for the non-Christian, but also for the Christian in dialogue. The temptation is to escape the uncomfortableness of that scandal and of being an ambassador of that scandal. But in so doing the Christian is abandoning what s/he alone can contribute to the quest for full truth. And not only does s/he fail to contribute her/his part to interreligious dialogue, but in so doing fails also to contribute to the salvation of the world.

For the witness to Jesus Christ to be scandalized by Him is not something new. The greatest prophet of the Old Testament, the precursor of the Incarnate Word, had his own questions and asked if Jesus were the One, or whether he should expect another. Jesus' reply to John the Baptist is addressed with equal intent to us today: "Blessed is he who is not scandalized in me" (Mt 11:6 [my translation]).

Endnotes

1. Stephen Neill, "Jesus and History," in Michael Green, ed., *The Truth of God Incarnate* (London: Hodder and Stoughton, 1977), 86.

2. James D. G. Dunn, *Christology in the Making* (London: S.C.M., 1980), 23-24.

3. For an interesting comparison of Hick and Feuerbach, see Peter Byrne "John Hick's Philosophy of World Religions," *Scottish Journal of Theology* 35, 4 (1982): 300.

4. Dunn, *op. cit.*, 2.

5. Bernard Lonergan, S.J., "Cognitional Structure," *Collection: Papers by Bernard Lonergan*, S.J., edited by F. E. Crowe, S.J. (Montreal: Palm Publishers, 1967), 221-39.

6. For a clarifying discussion on a correct integration of the history of religions and theology, see Vernon Gregson, "The Historian of Religions and the Theologian: Dialectics and Dialogue," in Michael L. Lamb, ed., *Creativity and Method: Essays in Honor of Bernard Lonergan* (Milwaukee: Marquette University, 1981): 141-51. See also Denise Lardner Carmody and John Tully Carmody, "Lonergan and the Comparative Study of Religions," *Religious Studies and Theology*, 5, 2 (May 1985): 24-41.

7. By the act of faith we mean the *fides qua* and not simply *fides quae*. The practitioners of comparative religion will admit that the object of different faiths is not identical. But they contend that the act of faith, of all religious faith, is the same. For a critique of this error, as maintained by Wilfred Cantwell Smith, see Tibor Horvath, S.J., "Three Responses to *Faith and Belief: A Review Article*," *Sciences religieuses / Studies in Religion*, 10, 1 (1981): part 3, 122-26.

8. See Mariasusai Dhavamony, *Phenomenology of Religion*, in series *Documenta Missionalia 7* (Rome: Gregorian University Press, 1973): 9-10; Vernon Gregson, S.J., *op. cit.*, 142-43.

9. Such methods claim to be "objective" in their study of religion. But as Lesslie Newbigin in *The Finality of Christ* (London: S.C.M., 1969): 120-1, notes, quoting from Gerard van der Leeuw, *Religion in Essence and Manifestation* (London: ET, 1938), Chapter 100, par. 1: "For 'unprejudiced' investigators are usually accustomed to beginning

without further ado, with an interpretation of religion borrowed either from some liberal western European Christianity, or from the deism of the Enlightenment or from the so-called monism of the natural sciences."

Hick does address the question of the possibility of uniqueness, not from a theological or a comparative religion point of view, but from an epistemological base. But he resolves the issue by a Kantian-type agnosticism, thus in effect reverting to his methodological viewpoint (comparative religion) that it cannot be known if God has acted in a unique way within history. The assumption, then, is that He has not.

10. See Stephen Neill, "Jesus and History," in *op. cit.*, 72; Bernard Lonergan, S.J., *Method in Theology* (New York: Seabury, 1979, first published Herder & Herder 1972), 178, 180; Vernon Gregson, S.J., *op. cit.*, 142-46.

11. I do not imply, however, that the correct answer regarding God's acting in a unique manner can be attained simply by historical method. But the historian can accept that a community of believers do claim God has acted in a unique way. Should he then ask; is their claim true?, he is opening himself to dialectic and the possibility of conversion. In other words the historical question of uniqueness can occasion faith. But until the question is asked, the occasion does not present itself. Hick undermines the very question that provides a context for the faith response.

12. Since this is the conclusion to the work, I am not about to launch a detailed analysis of theology of religion or of world religions, nor of the many problems and issues involved in a dialogue among world religions.

13. My aim is not to treat all implications, and certainly not to work out a theology of world religions. Rather, given my Christian faith in the uniqueness of Jesus, what is my personal opinion about a few of the theological problems involved?

14. Tibor Horvath, S.J., "Theologies of Non-Christian Religions," *Science et Esprit*, XXXIII, 3 (1981): 229-322, esp. 315. Horvath has uncovered thirty varieties of theology of non-Christian religions, which he then classifies systematically.

15. Horvath, *ibid.*, 321.

16. Horvath, *ibid.*, 315-16.

17. *L'Osservatore Romano*, June 2, 1980, Weekly edition, English translation, p. 4. The statement was made in the Pope's address to the bishops of Kenya, at Nairobi, on May 7, 1980. The complete statement, which appears within a discussion of catechesis and inculturation reads: "Thus, not only is Christianity relevant to Africa, but Christ, in the members of his Body, is himself African."

18. *GS*, 22.

19. *RH*, 8.

20. Horvath, "After Rahner What? a Tribute to his Memory and Achievement," *The Thomist*, 49, 2 (April 1985): 157-67, esp. 164.

21. Horvath, *ibid.*, 165.

22. Horvath, *ibid.*, 166.

23. Newbigin, *The Open Secret* (New York: Wm. B. Eerdmans, 1978), 200. Newbigin later writes that to seek the whole truth under guidance of the Holy Spirit (Jn 16: 12-15) "does not mean, however, that they [early Christians] will be led beyond or away from Jesus," *ibid.*, 202.

24. See also Vernon Gregson, S.J., "The Historian of Religions and the Theologian," in Matthew L. Lamb, *Creativity and Method* (Milwaukee, Wisconsin: Marquette University, 1981): 141-51, esp. 146-51.

It should be obvious that I am not suggesting as does Paul Knitter in the final chapter of his *No Other Name? A Critical Survey of Christian Attitudes Toward the World Religions* (New York: Maryknoll, 1985), that the specific truth-claims of Christian faith regarding the uniqueness of Jesus ought now to be dependent on and the result of inter-religious dialogue. Christian faith is no more the simple result of dialogue than it is simply (1) of reason or (2) method.

25. The Secretariat's document, however, has (5) as number (3).

26. The document has (3) and (4) in reverse order from ours.

27. Lesslie Newbigin, *The Open Secret* (New York: Wm. B. Eerdmans, 1978): 188-89.

28. *ibid.*, 189.

29. Lesslie Newbigin, *The Finality of Christ* (London: S.C.M., 1969): 16-17.

30. Newbigin, *The Open Secret* (New York: Wm. B. Eerdmans, 1978): 183-84.

31. Gavin d'Costa, "Elephants, Ropes and a Christian Theology of

Religions," *Theology*, LXXXVIII, 721 (July 1985): 259-68.

32. Kuhn, *The Structure of Scientific Revolutions* (Chicago, 1962).

33. D'Costa, *op. cit.*, 267.

34. Grillmeier, *Christ ...*, 555-56.

35. Michael Green, "Jesus and Historical Scepticism," in Michael Green, ed., *The Truth of God Incarnate* (London: Hodder & Stoughton, 1977), 115.

36. Newbigin, 73-101.

Bibliography

Almond, Philip. "John Hick's Copernican Theology." *Theology*, LXXXVI, 709 (January 1983): 36-41. For Hick's reply, see "The Theology of Religious Pluralism." *Theology*, LXXXVI, 713 (September 1983): 335-40.

The Attitude of the Church Towards the Followers of Other Religions: Reflections and Orientations on Dialogue and Mission. Vatican: Polyglot, Pentecost 1984.

Brown, Raymond E., S.S. *New Testament Essays* Milwaukee: Bruce, 1965.

_____. *Jesus God and Man: Modern Biblical Reflections.* London: Geoffrey Chapman, 1968.

Callahan, Daniel, ed. *God, Jesus, and Spirit.* New York: Herder & Herder, 1969.

Carmody, Denise Lardner and John Tully Carmody. "Lonergan and the Comparative Study of Religions," *Religious Studies and Theology*, 5, 2 (May 1985): 24-41.

Crowe, Frederick E., S.J. "Son and Spirit: Tension in the Divine Missions?." *Lonergan Workshop* V. Edited by Fred Lawrence. Chico, California: Scholars, (1985): 1-21. Delivered at the Lonergan Workshop, Boston, June, 1983.

_____. *"Son of God, Holy Spirit, and World Religions: The Contribution of Bernard Lonergan to the Wider Ecumenism."* Chancellor's Address II. Delivered at Regis College, Toronto, November 26, 1984. Toronto: Regis College, 1985.

_____. "The Church as Learner: Two Crises, One Kairos," in Michael Vertin, ed., *Appropriating the Lonergan Idea* (Washington, D.C.: The Catholic University of America Press, 1989): 370-84. Originally a lecture given at Boston College, 23 October 1986, and in revised form, at the fifth annual Lonergan Colloquium, Regis College, Toronto, 4 December 1986. First published (in earlier form) as "'The Role of a Catholic University in the Modern World'—An Update," in *Communicating a Dangerous Memory: Soundings in Political Theology*, ed. F. Lawrence. Supplementary issue of *Lonergan Workshop* 6 (Atlanta: Scholars Press, 1987): 1-16.

Daniélou, Jean, S.J. *Gospel Message and Hellenistic Culture.* Ed. and translated by John Austin Baker. London: Darton, Longman & Todd, 1973.

_____. *The Origins of Latin Christianity.* Translated by David Smith and John Austin Baker. Edited and with postscript by John Austin Baker. London: Darton, Longman & Todd, 1977.

Davies, Brian. *Thinking About God.* London: Geoffrey Chapman, 1985.

D'Costa, Gavin. *Theology and Religious Pluralism.* Oxford: Basil Blackwell, 1986.

_____. *John Hick's Theology of Religions: A Critical Evaluation.* Lanham, MD: University Press of America, 1987.

_____. "Elephants, Ropes and a Christian Theology of Religions." *Theology*, LXXXVIII, 724 (July 1985): 259-68.

Dunn, James D. G. *Christology in the Making: A New Testament Inquiry into the Origins of the Doctrine of the Incarnation.* London: S.C.M., 1980.

_____. *Unity and Diversity in the New Testament: An Inquiry into the Character of Earliest Christianity.* London: S.C.M., 1977.

Dupuis, James, S.J. *Jesus Christ and His Spirit: Theological Approaches.* Bangalore, India: Theological Publications, 1977.

_____. "The Practice of Agape is the Reality of Salvation." *International Review of Mission*, LXXXIV, 296 (October 1985): 472-77.

_____. "Forms of Interreligious Dialogue." *Bulletin*, 59, XX/2

(1985): 164-71. Secretariatus pronon christianis. *Città del Vaticano.*

Fitzmyer, Joseph A., S.J. *Scripture and Christology: A Statement of the Biblical Commission with a Commentary* New York: Paulist, 1986.

————. "The Biblical Commission's Instruction on the Historical Truth of the Gospels," *Theological Studies*, 25, 3 (September 1964): 386-408.

Gomez, Felipe, S.J. "The Uniqueness and Universality of Christ." *East Asian Pastoral Review*, 1 (1983): 4-30.

Goulder, Michael, ed. *Incarnation and Myth: The Debate Continued.* London: S. C. M. 1979.

Green, Michael, ed. *The Truth of God Incarnate.* London: Hodder & Stoughton, 1977.

Gregson, Vernon, S.J. "The Historian of Religions and the Theologian," in Matthew L. Lamb, ed., *Creativity and Method: Essays in Honor of Bernard Lonergan*, S.J. Milwaukee, Wisconsin: Marquette University, (1981): 141-51.

Grillmeier, Aloys, S.J. *Christ in Christian Tradition.* v.1 *From the Apostolic Age to Chalcedon.* 2nd. rev. ed. translated by John Bowden. Atlanta: John Knox, 1965,1975.

Guillet, Jacques, S.J. *The Consciousness of Jesus.* Translated by Edmond Bonin. New York: Newman, 1972.

Hefling, Charles C. *Why Doctrines?* USA: Cowley, 1984.

Hengel, Martin *The Cross of the Son of God.* London: S.C.M., 1986. The three articles "The Son of God," "Crucifixion," and "Atonement" first translated from the original German by S.C.M., 1976, 1977, 1981.

Hill, Edmund. *The Mystery of the Trinity.* London: Geoffrey Chapman, 1985.

Hick, John. *Faith and Knowledge: A Modern Introduction to the Problem of Religious Knowledge.* Ithaca: Cornell University, 1957. 2nd ed., 1966. Collins-Fontana edition, 1974. Presented in *Masterpieces of Christian Literature in Summary Form.* Edited by Frank N. McGill. New York: Harper & Row, 1963, 1156-61.

————. *Evil and the God of Love.* London: Macmillan, New York:

Harper & Row, and London: Collins-Fontana, 1966. 2nd ed., 1977.

_____. *God and the Universe of Faiths: Essays in the Philosophy of Religion*. London: Macmillan, and New York: St. Martin's, 1973. Collins-Fontana edition, 1977.

_____. *Death and Eternal Life*. London: Collins, and New York: Harper & Row, 1976. Translated into Dutch, 1978.

_____, ed. *The Myth of God Incarnate*. London: S.C.M., and Philadelphia: Westminster, 1977. Translated into German, 1979.

_____. God Has Many Names. Philadelphia: Westminster, 1982. Translated into German, 1985.

_____. *Problems of Religious Pluralism*. London: Macmillan, 1985.

_____, and Paul Knitter, eds. *The Myth of Christian Uniqueness*. London: S.C.M., 1987.

_____. *An Interpretation of Religion*. London: Macmillan, 1989.

Horvath, Tibor, S.J. "Theologies of Non-Christian Religions." *Science et Esprit*, XXXIII, 3 (1981): 299-322.

_____. "Part 3: Three Responses to *Faith and Belief*: A Review Article." *Sciences religieuses/Studies in Religion*, 10, 1 (1981): 122-26.

Pope John-Paul II, *Redemptor Hominis*. Milano: Ancora. 1979.

Kasper, Walter. *Jesus the Christ*. London: Burns & Oates, 1976. Translated by V. Green from the original German *Jesus der Christus*. Mainz: Matthias-Grunewald-Verlag, 1974.

_____. *The God of Jesus Christ*. London: S.C.M., 1983. Translated by Matthew J. O'Connell from the original German *Der Gott Jesu Christi*. Mainz: Grüneweld Verlag, 1982.

Lipner, J. "Christians and the Uniqueness of Christ." *Scottish Journal of Theology*, 28, 4 (August 1975): 359-68.

_____. "Does Copernicus Help? Reflections for a Christian Theology of Religions." *Religious Studies*, 13, 2, (June 1977): 243-58.

Lonergan, Bernard, J.F., S.J. *Insight: A Study of Human Understanding*. New York: Longmans, Green & Co., 1957.

_____. *Method in Theology*. London: Darton, Longman & Todd,

1973.

_____. *Doctrinal Pluralism*. Milwaukee: Marquette University, 1971.

_____. *The Way to Nicea: The Dialectical Development of Trinitarian Theology*. Translated by Conn O'Donovan from *De Deo Trino, Pars dogmatica*, 1964. London: Darton, Longman & Todd, 1976.

_____. *Collection: Papers by Bernard Lonergan, S.J.* Ed. F. E. Crowe, S.J. Montreal: Palm Publishers, 1967.

_____. *A Second Collection: Papers by Bernard J. F. Lonergan, S.J.* Eds. Wiiliam F. J. Ryan, S.J. and Bernard J. Tyrrell, S.J. London: Darton, Longman & Todd, 1974.

_____. *A Third Collection: Papers by Bernard J. F. Lonergan, S.J.* Ed. Frederick E. Crowe, S.J. New York: Paulist, 1985.

Neuner, Joseph, S.J., ed. *Christian Revelation and World Religions*. London: Burns & Oates, 1967.

Newbigin, Lesslie. *The Finality of Christ*. London: S.C.M., 1969.

_____. *The Open Secret: Sketches for a Missionary Theology*. New York: Wm. B. Eerdmans Co., 1978.

O'Collins, Gerald, S.J. *The Easter Jesus*. ed. rev. London: Darton, Longman & Todd, 1973, 1980.

_____. *The Calvary Christ*. London: S.C.M., 1977.

_____. *What are they saying about the resurrection?* New York: Paulist, 1978.

_____. *Fundamental Theology*. London: Darton, Longman & Todd, 1981.

_____. *Interpreting Jesus*. London: Geoffrey Chapman, 1983.

Rahner, Karl, S.J. *The Trinity*. Translated by Joseph Donceel. New York: Seabury, 1974.

_____. *Foundations of Christian Faith: An Introduction to the Idea of Christianity*. Translated by William V. Dych. New York: Crossroad, 1984. First published as *Grundkurs des Glaubens: Einführung in den Begriff des Christentums*. Freiburg im Breisgau: Verlag Herder, 1976.

_____, and Wilhelm Thüsing. *A New Christology*. Translated by David Smith and Verdant Green. London: Burns & Oates, 1980. First published as *Christologie— Systematisch und Ex-*

egetisch. Freiburg im Breisgau: Verlag Herder, 1972.

_____. *"Theos* in the New Testament." 79-148. In *Theological Investigations*, I. Translated by Cornelius Ernst, O.P. London: Darton, Longman & Todd, and New York: Seabury, 1961, 1965, 1974.

_____. "What is a dogmatic statement?." 42-66, "Christianity and the Non-Christian Religions." 115-34, and "Dogmatic Reflections on the Knowledge and Self-consciousness of Christ." 193-215. In *Theological Investigations*, V. Translated by Karl-H. Kruger. Baltimore: Helicon, and London: Darton, Longman & Todd, 1966.

_____. "A Small Question Regarding the Contemporary Pluralism in the Intellectual Situation of Catholics and the Church." 21-30, "Reflections on Dialogue within a Pluralistic Society." 31-42, and "Anonymous Christians." 390-98. In *Theological Investigations*, VI. Translated by Karl-H. and Boniface Kruger. Baltimore: Helicon, and London: Darton, Longman & Todd, 1969.

_____. "The Second Vatican Council's Challenge to Theology." 3-27, "Atheism and Implicit Christianity." 145-64, and "One Mediator and Many Mediations." 169-84. In *Theological Investigations*, IX. Translated by Graham Harrison. New York: Herder & Herder, 1972.

_____. "Church, Churches and Religions." In *Theological Investigations*, X. Translated by David Bourke. New York: Seabury, 1973, 30-49.

_____. "Anonymous Christianity and the Missionary Task of the Church." 161-78. In *Theological Investigations*, XII. Translated by David Bourke. New York: Seabury, 1974.

_____. "Observations on the Problem of the 'Anonymous Christian'." 280-94, and "The Church's Commission to Bring Salvation and the Humanization of the World." 295-313. In *Theological Investigations*, XIV. Translated by David Bourke. New York: Seabury, 1976.

_____. "Anonymous and Explicit Faith." 52-59, "Reflections on a New Task for Fundamental Theology." 156-66, and "The One Christ and the Universality of Salvation." 199-224. In

Theological Investigations, XVI. Translated by David Morland, O.S.B. New York: Seabury, 1979.

_____. "Jesus Christ in the Non-Christian Religions." 39-50, In *Theological Investigations*, XVII. Translated by Margaret Kohl. New York: Crossroad, 1981.

_____. "A Basic Theological Interpretation of the Second Vatican Council." In *Theological Investigations* XX. Translated by Edward Quinn. New York: Crossroad, 1981, 77-89.

Rossano, Piero. "Lordship of Christ and Religious Pluralism." *Bulletin*, 43, XV/1 (1980): 17-30. Secretariatus pro non christianis. Città del Vaticano.

_____. "Gospel and culture at Ephesus and in the Province of Asia at the time of St. Paul and St. John." Bulletin, 45, XV/3 (1980): 282-96. Secretariatus pro non christianis. *Città del Vaticano.*

_____. "Relationship between Religion and Culture in the different Religious traditions of the World." Bulletin, 47, XVI/2 (1981): 102-13. Secretariatus pro non christianis. *Città del Vaticano.*

Russell, Stanley. "The Finality of Christ and Other Religions." *Epworth Review*, 4, 1 (January 1977): 77-84.

Saldanha, Chrys. *Divine Pedagogy: A Patristic View of non- Christian Religions.* Roma: Libreria Ateneo Salesiano, 1984.

Sala, Giovanni, S.J. "The *A Priori* in Human Knowledge: Kant's *Critique of Pure Reason* and Lonergan's *Insight*," *The Thomist*, XL, 2 (April 1976): 179-221.

_____. "Il Bicentenario della 'Critica della Ragion Pura' di Kant," *La Civiltà cattolica*, IV, (1981): 343-60.

Schillebeeckx, Edward. *Christ the Sacrament of Encounter with God.* New York: Sheed and Ward, 1963.

_____. *Interim Report on the Books "Jesus" and "Christ".* New York: Crossroad, 1981.

Schineller, J. Peter, S.J. "Christ and Church: A Spectrum of Views." *Theological Studies*, 37, 4 (December 1976): 545-66.

Schlette, Heinz Robert. *Towards a Theology of Religions.* New York: Herder & Herder, 1966.

Shorter, Aylward. *Revelation and Its Interpretation.* London: Geoffrey

Chapman, 1983.

Smulders, P., S.J. *The Fathers on Christology: The Development of Christological Dogma From the Bible to the Great Councils.* Translated by Lucien Roy, S.J. De Pere, Wisconsin: St. Norbert Abbey, 1968.

Soskice, Janet Martin. *Metaphor and Religious Language.* Oxford: Clarendon Press, 1985.

Swidler, Leonard. "Jesus' Unsurpassable Uniqueness: Two Responses." *Horizons*, 16 (Spring, 1989): 116-20.

Thompson, William M. "Jesus' Unsurpassable Uniqueness: A Theological Note." *Horizons*, 16 (Spring, 1989): 101-15.

_____. "The Hermeneutics of Friendship and Suspicion: A Response to Professors Swidler and Hick." *Horizons*, 16 (Spring, 1989): 125-30.

Towards the Meeting of Religions: Suggestions for Dialogue. Vatican: Polyglot, 1967. Secretariatus Pro Non Christianis.

INDEX

- deification of: 78-89; Chs. 5, 6, 7
- and divine inhistorisation: 124-32; 307-11
- and God's universal salvific will: 279-94
- and homoagape: (*See* Homoagape)
- impact of: 77-78
- and John's gospel: 206-212
- and language of divine Sonship: 89-112; 167-206
- relative uniqueness of in Hick: 119-20
- resurrection of: 121-24; 311-14
- as Angel: 187
- as Eschatological Prophet: 149; 158-59; 178; 183; 186-87; 188; 194; 195; 204; 206; 207; 211-12; 284-86; 288; 311-12
- as Last Adam: 183-87
- as Logos: 117-20; 196-200
- as Lord: 180-81
- as Messiah: 178-80
- as the Novum: 202-206
- as scandal: 344-46
- as Son of God: 168-77
- as Son of Man: 181-83
- as Spirit: 187-89
- as Wisdom: 189-96

LANGUAGE
- and Jesus' Incarnation 294-98
- of divine Sonship: 89-112; 167-206; Pre-Pauline 171; Paul 171-72; Synoptics 172-75; Hebrews 175-76; Johanine Writings 176-77
- myth and environment: 295-96

LONERGAN, Bernard J.F.
- contexts of meaning: 248-52
- differentiation of consciousness: 223-31
- epistemology: 321,nn.65,66,67; 346,n.5
- functional specialties (esp. dialectic): 10-12; 150; 252-59

About the Author

Fr. Carruthers was born in 1945 in Halifax, Nova Scotia. After receiving his B.A., political science (St. Mary's, Halifax) and an M.A., Canadian Studies (Carleton, Ottawa), he taught in the political science department at Loyola College (now Concordia University), Montréal. In 1972 he entered the Society of Jesus (Jesuits). He received an M.A., philosophy (Gonzaga, Spokane) and an M.Div. and Th.M. (Regis College/University of Toronto). In 1988 he was awarded a doctorate in Sacred Theology, (Pontifical Gregorian University, Rome). Since June, 1988, he has been a Fellow at the Lonergan Research Institute, Toronto.